BALLIOL COLLEGE

The College Arms, as used since about 1900

BALLIOL COLLEGE

A History

SECOND EDITION

JOHN JONES

Dean and Archivist

OXFORD UNIVERSITY PRESS

1997

Oxford University Press, Great Clarendon Street, Oxford OX2 6DP

Oxford New York
Athens Auckland Bangkok Bogota Bombay
Buenos Aires Calcutta Cape Town Dar es Salaam
Delhi Florence Hong Kong Istanbul Karachi
Kuala Lumpur Madras Madrid Melbourne
Mexico City Nairobi Paris Singapore
Taipei Tokyo Toronto
and associated companies in
Berlin Ibadan

Oxford is a trade mark of Oxford University Press

Published in the United States by
Oxford University Press Inc., New York

British Library Cataloguing in Publication Data
Data available

Library of Congress Cataloging in Publication Data

ISBN 0–19–920181–1

1 3 5 7 9 10 8 6 4 2

Typeset by Selwood Systems, Midsomer Norton
Printed in Great Britain
on acid-free paper by
Butler & Tanner Ltd
Frome and London

FOREWORD TO THE
SECOND EDITION

By the Master, Colin Lucas

WRITING the foreword to this second edition, even with its new and enlarged Epilogue, is somewhat akin to revisiting a great garden. Despite a few new plantings, the vistas and general plan are familiar and of course a general introduction already exists to guide the visitor. Indeed, Sir Anthony Kenny's foreword to the first edition touches on the major themes to which one would most wish to refer when guiding visitors to Balliol and its past.

Naturally, each of us captures a slightly different perspective when looking across the long centuries of Balliol's history. I myself am struck by Balliol's recurrent capacity for being out of tune with the prevailing orthodoxy of the times. If the legend has any substance, even in its foundation the College was the product of a conformity imposed upon a fractious man. Whatever the truth there, we can point with more certainty to the College's association with Wyclif in the fourteenth century and then, by contrast, to the apparent persistence of Roman Catholicism for at least five decades after Balliol was the only college to qualify its submission to the Act of Supremacy in 1534.

In the 1640s, Balliol Fellows were probably not unusual in Oxford for mostly refusing to submit to Parliament and Puritanism, but that fact does fit the general pattern. Again, from the late seventeenth century to nearly the middle of the eighteenth, Balliol seems to have been a principal centre in Oxford for Tory and Jacobite sentiment, which was out of sympathy with the dynastic shifts of the period.

In an important sense, one can also read Balliol's nineteenth-century rise to pre-eminence in these same terms. Under Jenkyns and Jowett, Balliol moved to open itself to those outside the dominant social group to which Oxford in general was devoted. It placed emphasis on ability over connections in the recruitment of undergraduates. It began to teach them in a regular tutorial system and to incorporate them into a new kind of academic society. It made space available to significant numbers of students from overseas. Finally, it was one of the major sources of energy for the general reform of the University. In each of these initiatives, Balliol essentially stood against prevailing habits and accepted practices.

In the twentieth century too, the pattern holds. So much is clear from the Masterships of Lindsay and Hill, with their personal attachment to politics of the Left, their passionate concern for democracy and their desire for Balliol to be, in the words of Lindsay, a 'classless society'. Certainly, in this century Balliol students have often shown a robust scepticism of prevailing orthodoxies.

Perhaps, however, one should not refine this theme too far. It has been an episodic rather than a consistent phenomenon, interspersed with periods of conformity, not to say ordinariness. Moreover, one could certainly argue that there is a great difference between the examples cited from before Jenkyns and subsequent events. What we see in the sixteenth, seventeenth, and eighteenth centuries is really evidence of a reluctance to change, an adherence to defeated orthodoxies. In the nineteenth century, by contrast, Balliol's unwillingness to conform placed it in the vanguard of progressive change. Furthermore, for most of the College's existence (and at no time more than during the last 150 years) former members have occupied significant positions of influence and governance in society at the same time as the College itself appeared critical or oppositional.

In truth, of course, the College has always been a complicated society. Whilst we naturally and rightly represent it as having a particular stance or character at particular times, it has always contained people of widely diverse attitudes and interests. Moreover, not all of them have been concerned with matters of public debate. That is as true of Balliol's recent history as of its more distant past.

Nonetheless, reading this history, one cannot help feeling that there is an underlying consistency here. Perhaps I have misrepresented it as a capacity for being out of tune with prevailing orthodoxy. It might be truer to say that one can see in Balliol's history a perennial corporate spirit of independence, a predisposition to difference, and a concern for principle rather than convenience. These three traits run through the history of Balliol rather like a river runs through limestone country, disappearing out of sight for periods and suddenly welling up again for no very obvious reason. Of course, one must also acknowledge that these characteristics can lend themselves sometimes to bloody-mindedness and sometimes to a high-mindedness which, in periods of collegiate success, may well be seen by others as preachy smugness. However, inasmuch as such institutions do have enduring temperaments, then these three traits do specify the historic character of Balliol.

So, it seems somehow emblematic that in 1793 Balliol should have admitted Robert Southey, a rebellious youth rejected elsewhere in the University as a potential troublemaker. Visiting Oxford in later life, the poet was to write in jaundiced mood that the place has 'an enduring sameness ... like that of the sea and mountains'. Returning old members are more usually comforted by the familiarity of the College, even though in reality Balliol's buildings are a physical record of change. To read John Jones's history, however, is to realize that, despite the enduring sameness of temperament, this is a chronicle of change.

The new Epilogue can only emphasize that point. In many respects, Balliol in the 1990s is as different from the 1890s as Balliol then was from the 1790s, even though the 1890s are more clearly the direct ancestor of Balliol today than the 1790s were of Balliol a century ago. The Epilogue brings up-to-date the account of this century's changes whose first phase was described in the last chapter of the first edition. These changes have to do, first, with the size and composition of the body—the rising numbers of junior and senior members, the strong presence of graduate students, the diversity of social backgrounds among undergraduates, and the inclusion of women at all levels of the College. Second, they are to be found in the academic enterprise—the multiplication of degrees and disciplines (notably, but not only, in the sciences), the effect upon teaching of the increasing complexity of knowledge, and the appearance of research as a major activity of Fellows. Since the Second World War, these changes have been very much an accelerating effect of the wider context of social change and of modifications in higher education generally.

I conclude my foreword where my predecessor concluded his. The College is indeed fortunate to have in its Dean a Fellow so scrupulous in conserving the evidence of its past and so precise in interpreting that evidence for us. I am glad to adopt Sir Anthony Kenny's description of the book as sober scholarship and a brisk, economical narrative. I would add another quality: impartiality that rises above a perfectly natural affection for the author's College. Only once, I think, is there a partisan note (and even that somewhat ambiguous): it is when we are told that a young man was rusticated for 'the absurd offence' of making the Dean of Trinity dance round a bonfire.

FOREWORD TO THE FIRST EDITION

By the then Master, Anthony Kenny

ONE of the duties of a head of house in Oxford is to guide visitors through his college and recount its history. Every Master of Balliol in his time must have devised his own concise version of the College's past, skimming over the humdrum and highlighting the picturesque. Since neither I nor most of my guests can claim professional expertise in history, I find it more comfortable to tell the story in the style of *1066 and All That* than to follow unswervingly the track of Salter's *Oxford Balliol Deeds*.

To give perspective to the story, it helps to take items century by century, perhaps comparing the year or decade in which one is speaking to the corresponding period in each of the College's previous centuries. Speaking in 1988, for example, one can look back to see what was happening in Balliol in the eighties, and particularly the '88s, in each century since the College's foundation.

If one accepts the traditional date for that foundation, then in 1288 the College was celebrating the silver jubilee of John de Balliol's act of penance for kidnapping the Bishop of Durham. Only six years had passed, however, since the Lady Dervorguilla had amplified her husband's parsimonious endowment and set up the College as a corporate body with its Statutes. The first Scholars on the Foundation will just have been completing their course in Arts.

A hundred years later, in the 1380s, Oxford rang with the disputes surrounding Balliol's most famous Master, John Wyclif: long the leading theologian in the University, he was expelled from Oxford for Eucharistic heresy in 1381 and died in 1384. Wyclif was long revered as the author of the first Bible in English; historians nowadays seem to believe that probably—like other Balliol Tutors from time to time—he has been given credit for an achievement which really belongs to his pupils. But if he has been deprived of his claim to be the author of one great contribution to English civilization, he has, in compensation, been allowed another. Scholars tell me that he is the first Englishman on record to have had his own locked privy—though that was at Queen's rather than at Balliol.

The 1480s saw the completion of the College's surviving medieval buildings: Master Abdy, who died in 1483, completed the Library started early in the century under Master Chace, and made room in it for the magnificent collection of books presented by Bishop Gray of Ely. In 1488 John Morton, the first of Balliol's three Cardinals, and one of the first of its many ministers of state, was beginning his career in the service of King Henry VII.

In the next century, the Reformation of Henry's son was not welcomed in Balliol: the Fellows of the College refused to swear to the Royal Supremacy without adding a damaging qualification. The Spanish Armada of 1588 was the outcome of a policy urged on the Pope and King of Spain by the best-known and best-hated Balliol man of his generation, the Jesuit Robert Persons. Throughout the eighties of the sixteenth century Balliol was regarded as a hotbed of papistry.

Yet anyone standing in the Master's Lodgings at Balliol is within fifty yards of monuments to the two decisive events of the English Reformation. Outside to the south is the cross in the pavement which marks the site of the burning of Latimer, Ridley, and Cranmer after proceedings presided over by a Catholic Master of Balliol. Across the quadrangle to the north-west is the site of the Catherine Wheel Inn, where the Oxford conspirators met to plan the Gunpowder Plot. These two events branded on to the consciousness of Protestant Englishmen an image of Papist perfidy: henceforth propagandists could argue that if they were in power the Catholics burnt Bishops, if they were out of power they tried to blow up King, Lords, and Commons.

The Protestant Reformation was finally consummated by the Glorious Revolution of 1688. Balliol's modest contribution to this was to provide hospitality for the Whig peers who came to Oxford to vote against the future King James II in the debate on the Exclusion Bill of 1681. Soon after I became a Fellow I was excited by being given my half-pint of lunch-time beer in a silver tankard presented by the Duke of Monmouth, the Earl of Shaftesbury, and half a dozen other peers. Though awed by confrontation with this relic, I could not help thinking that such a wealthy clutch of magnates might have given more than a half-pint mug. Only later did I discover that this was one of a set made from the melting down of an enormous silver gilt bowl.

Balliol's greatest contribution to posterity in the seventeenth century, however, was nothing to do with either politics or religion. For we learn from John Evelyn that it was a Balliol man, the Cretan Nathaniel Konopius, who introduced the drinking of coffee into this country.

A century after the Glorious Revolution, the 1780s saw the end of the fifty-nine-year mastership of Theophilus Leigh. Not only was Leigh the longest ruling Master the College has ever had, he was also the one whose election was the most bitterly contested. For those who enjoy scandal it is sad that recent research has shown that it was not quite the corrupt affair of College legend. I like to fancy that in Leigh's last years he may have been visited by his niece Jane Austen—she was ten when he died—and that she may have admired the handsome Chippendale chairs dating from his Mastership which are still in the Master's Lodgings.

By 1888 Balliol was very much the College we know today. Benjamin Jowett was seventy, and had five more years to live; he had presided over the erection of the new Hall, had completed a reforming Vice-Chancellorship, and had seen his Balliol pupils carry his ideals to the most distant parts of the Empire. He devoted the year to an edition of Plato's *Republic* and the compilation of a new hymn-book for the College Chapel. The illustrations in Jowett's Life by Abbott and Campbell show that the dining-room of the Lodgings has changed hardly at all since his time. On each side of the fireplace, however, there are now portraits of him: to the left, a young, serene, almost debonair face in the drawing by Richmond; to the right, a copy of Watts's portrait showing the worn features and hooded glance of the old Master. I like to point out the contrast to visitors as an illustration of the toll taken by service as Master of Balliol.

The scholars, poets, novelists, churchmen, and statesmen who have made the name of Balliol famous receive only a brief mention in my idiosyncratic history of the College. This is partly because it is woven round the physical memorials to be seen in the course of a guided tour, rather than round great events of national life or great works of academic or literary culture. But I find it also oddly comforting that of all the Balliol men of the past the ones who have left the most enduring mark on our lives have not been the writers or politicians, but the men whose innovations we perpetuate whenever we lock the lavatory door or drink our breakfast cup of coffee. And even if we concentrate on the writings of Balliol graduates, what volumes of learning or *belles-lettres* have ever achieved the immortality of Southey's fairy tale of *The Three Bears*, or Oakeley's translation from the Latin *O Come All Ye Faithful*?

So much, then, for 1263 and all that. Leaving legend behind, the reader can learn, in the pages that follow, the true history of the College as revealed by John Jones's patient scholarship. Members of Balliol owe a lot to the history of the College first written by H. W. C. Davis in 1899, and revised by his son in 1963, aided by Sir Harold Hartley and Richard Hunt. But much that is in that history has now been superseded by more recent research, and some of it is written from a perspective which it is no longer natural to adopt. The time is ripe for a new College history, building on the achievements of the College's historians in the past.

The College is most fortunate in having a Fellow who was willing to undertake the task and who has carried it out so magnificently. This history makes the third of a trilogy in which John Jones has set out for our perusal the elements of Balliol past and present. In 1983 he published the current *Balliol Register*, in 1984 a *Guide to the Balliol Archives*, and now in 1988 this complete *History*. In a preface to the *Register* I wrote: 'John Jones has been a Tutor of the College since 1968 and Dean since 1972. Many Fellows would have thought that the devoted performance of these two offices was a sufficient service to the College. Not so John, who for the last five years has been active in reorganizing, restoring and repairing the College Archives.' By now John has completed six further years of service as College Archivist, and once again he has placed all members of the College in his debt. They will long be grateful for such a full account of the past of their society. But others beside Balliol men and women will admire and enjoy a narrative so briskly and economically distilled from such a variety of primary and secondary sources. Even within the sober scholarship of these pages there are to be found many vignettes which are no less vivid than many a College legend.

PREFACE TO THE SECOND EDITION

THE first edition was received with a warmth which surprised me, and it generated a lot of interesting correspondence, from which many of the additional points now made are derived. There has been some gentle pressure to bring my coverage nearer to the present. I have yielded only to the extent of expanding considerably on the Epilogue (which was, I admit, perfunctory), but still giving little more than a framework of events with a somewhat superficial commentary. In part I baulked at the complexity of the task, and the prodigious amount of material needing digestion: about a third of all the Balliol people there have ever been are still alive. But I am also very aware of my inability to be objective about the recent past, because my own life has been so intimately integrated with the College's since 1961. And while glasnost is a fine thing, there are inevitably inhibitions about people one has known, loved (many), or loathed (few). Although the facts stated in the extended Epilogue are, I hope, the truth, they are not always the whole truth; and in case any bias or prejudice is found in my commentary, I confess it now.

Ronnie Bell (my sometime Tutor), Richard Cobb, Jack de Wet, and Sir Edgar Williams—all of whom have died recently—were my main unofficial sources of information about Balliol affairs in the forties, fifties, and early sixties. It was a privilege to have known these very different great men. For my own time, I have largely relied on my own memory of how things were and felt, as opposed to how they are recorded, but some thoughtful letters from Howard Marks helped me to form a clearer view of the mid-sixties.

Sir Anthony Kenny, Master 1978–89, was the *onlie begetter* of the first edition, and contributed a handsome foreword to it; Baruch S. Blumberg, Master 1989–94, urged me with irresistible enthusiasm to prepare a second edition; and Colin Lucas, Master from 1994, readily agreed to write a new foreword. For these and other kindnesses, I thank all three of them.

I owe warm thanks to all at Oxford University Press who have been involved with either or both editions, especially Anne Ashby.

In August 1994 I visited Buittle in Galloway, where, in 1282, the pious Dervorguilla sealed the College's first Statutes. I am grateful to Alistair Penman for giving me an on-the-spot account of his excavations there, to Daphne Brooke for background on the history of the region, and to Jeffrey and Janet Burn for entertaining me so hospitably. A major work on Barnard Castle by David Austin is on the verge of publication: in 1990 he most kindly sent me a draft chapter which gives rich detail about the Balliols and Barnard Castle. I was also privileged to be allowed by Richard Oram to obtain a copy of his PhD thesis (St Andrews, 1988), on the Lordship of Galloway *c*.1000 to *c*.1250, which gives further valuable background information. Finally, I recall with great pleasure a couple of days in August 1990, when I was the guest of Tony and Simone Hervey at Fontaine-sur-Somme near Bailleul-en-Vimeu, where it all began.

J.H.J.

Balliol
28 January 1996

PREFACE TO THE FIRST EDITION

THIS is the second attempt at a full-length history of the College in modern times. H. W. C. Davis was responsible for the first, which was published as one of the F. E. Robinson series of college histories in 1899. Davis himself drew heavily on the work of others, especially Henry Savage's *Balliofergus* (1668), Frances de Paravicini's *Early History of Balliol College* (1891), and the Balliol chapter by R. L. Poole in *The Colleges of Oxford* (1891). The 1899 history was revised in 1963 by Professor R. H. C. Davis and the late Dr Richard Hunt, for the College's septcentenary celebrations. Coverage was then extended to 1949, with the addition of new chapters by Sir Harold Hartley and Sir David Lindsay Keir, but much of the 1899 text was left untouched. Only a limited amount of new material could be added, although a more sympathetic account of Balliol in the late eighteenth century was appended. Many relevant publications have appeared since 1899, and extensive new documentation has become available, both in the College Archives and in collections elsewhere. Furthermore, the 1963 edition has been out of print a long time. I hope, therefore, that this new account will not be thought superfluous. Although I differ frequently from Davis and his 1963 editors in matters of fact and judgement, this is only because I have enjoyed access to richer original sources than they did. I contradict Davis from time to time, but I do not intend to disparage. His book remains a remarkable achievement for a very young scholar (he was only twenty-five when it appeared); I have made constant reference to his framework, as set out in the septcentenary edition of his work. Dr Hunt never knew of the present enterprise, but encouraged me with great kindness during an earlier less ambitious exercise in revisionist Balliol history. I salute his memory with affectionate respect. Professor Ralph Davis, the only survivor of the principal contributors to the 1963 history, freely gave his blessing to my plans before work began. I am grateful to him for this, and must also thank Messrs Basil Blackwell, who kindly renounced their 1963 copyright in the College's favour.

I am deeply grateful to the Master and the late Professor Lionel Stones for their interest and encouragement. Both of them took great pains with my first draft, and made many valuable comments. Mr Vincent Quinn and Dr Penelope Bulloch, successive College Librarians, and their colleague Mr Alan Tadiello, have been unfailingly helpful over many years. For new material, stimulating conversations, and diverse practical assistance, I am indebted to many other Balliol friends, especially Dr Christopher Hill, Canon Peter Hinchliff, Mr James Irvine, Brigadier D. W. Jackson, Dr Maurice Keen, Mr Ray North, Mr Lionel Peart, and Mr John Prest. Also close at hand, I am grateful to the staff of the Bodleian and Westgate Libraries (especially Mr Colin Harris and Dr Malcolm Graham respectively), and to Miss Ruth Vyse of the University Archives. In the course of my research, I have had correspondence with the custodians of more than thirty collections outside Oxford. They were patiently co-operative in providing photocopies and answering my questions, and enabled me to make use of widely dispersed original sources, which my other commitments denied me the time and opportunity to inspect personally. I am particularly appreciative of the trouble taken by Mr N. H. Bennet, Dr M. E. Finch, and Mr C. M. Lloyd of Lincolnshire Archives office; Mr E. J. Cornelius, Librarian of the Royal College of Surgeons of England; Dr D. Crook of the Public Record Office; Mrs Christine Fyfe of the Library, Keele University; Miss Sue Hubbard and Mr J. D. Warner-Davis of Hereford Record Office; Mr Hugh Jaques of Dorset County Record Office; Mr P. I. King of Northamptonshire Record Office; Ms Mary L. Robertson of the Huntington Library, California; Mr N. H. Robinson, Librarian of the Royal Society; Dr R. C. Smail of Sidney Sussex College, Cambridge; Miss M. M. Stewart of the Library, Churchill College, Cambridge; and Miss Mary E. Williams of Bristol Record Office. Miss Joan Johnson gave me some valuable leads to new material which I should otherwise have remained quite ignorant of, both through her *Princely Chandos* (1984) and other works, and by a most helpful correspondence. All the typing was expertly done by my secretary, Miss Claire Cheshire, who showed exemplary patience with my tendency to draft and redraft incessantly. My brother-in-law Mr G. P. Hebdon examined the final draft with a very critical eye, and my copy-editor, Mr Richard Jeffery, not only detected a mortifying number of slips but also made a lot of useful suggestions. To all these, and to many other kind people who are too numerous for me to list individually without appearing to spread my thanks too thinly, I am heartily grateful. On the other hand, I must at the same time also absolve them all from any blame for the mistakes and defects in this history; the responsibility is mine alone.

Special thanks are due to Mr T. O. Beachcroft and the Revd Prebendary F. Vere Hodge for the illustrations showing Theophilus Leigh and John Davey respectively. No other representations of these two Masters are known to me. I am grateful to the Rector and Fellows of Exeter College for permission to reproduce the portrait of Joseph Sanford, and to the President of Corpus Christi College, Oxford for permission to reproduce that of Richard Fox. The impression of Robert Abdy's brass is reproduced by permission of the British Library.

The access I had to several unpublished (but nevertheless polished and scholarly) studies was a great advantage: the Revd Andrew Clark's exhaustive lists and notes concerning Balliol, both in the College Library and in the Bodleian; H. P. Smith's notes on 'The Contribution of Balliol to the Making of the Tradition of Extra-mural Education', in the College Library; L. K. Hindmarsh's works on Balliol benefactors and Balliol heraldry, in the College Library; C. M. Lloyd's calendar of seventeenth-century bishops' visitation papers at Lincolnshire Archives Office, which he kindly provided a copy of; and Mrs Gwen Beachcroft's papers and collections concerning the Mastership of Theophilus Leigh, which are deposited in the Bodleian.

When asked about their profession, real historians are apt to admit the importance of facts reluctantly, as theoretical chemists sometimes are about experiments. Abstract interpretation on a grand scale is the thing. By such lights this book is not proper history, because its primary concern is with facts at the local level. Explanations are offered here and there, but diffidently and hedged about with many a 'perhaps', 'possibly', or 'probably'. Some allusions to the wider world are made, to put the College's fortunes into rough context, but I am well aware how inadequate the background given is. For this is an archivist's account, rather than a historian's and I hope to be forgiven for my preoccupation with parochial matters. The chapters on the early years, for which the surviving records are sparse, are relatively thin: I have been loath to fill gaps by extrapolation from the records of other institutions. In the century covered by the last five chapters the converse problem presents itself, with a couple of tons of original material, and well over a hundred relevant printed books. I have not allocated space in proportion. On the contrary, because so much has been published about 'modern' Balliol since the time of Jowett, I have not tried to give more than a superficial survey of the principal events and changes which have taken place. In particular, reference to the careers of individuals admitted after 1833 is only made occasionally. Such data are freely available from the printed College Registers, and are surveyed in Sir Harold Hartley's *Balliol Men* (1963). It is paradoxical that the College Archives are unhelpful in most periods on the very *raison d'être* of the place—the academic activities of its members. This is partly because the Bursars have, until recently, been the principal record generators and keepers, and partly because academic work has always been a more individual than institutional thing. Occasionally, personal sources (letters, diaries, memoirs) go some way to meet the deficiency, but a complete picture cannot be painted. This is, therefore, the area for which coverage is least adequate. The reader who would dig deeper in it should turn to the treatments, based on evidence drawn from all the colleges, which will be found in the eight volumes of *The History of the University of Oxford*.

All the special material for which no location is indicated is in Balliol College Archives or Library. Exact dates are Old Style where appropriate. Dates given by year only are according to modern practice, but there have been manifold confusions on this score in previous lists of Masters, Fellows, etc., and it is feared that some may have slipped through again. Biographical details and sources are in general only given for important College figures (Masters, long-serving Fellows, major benefactors, etc.) who do not have entries in the *Dictionary of National Biography* (*DNB*) or the printed College Registers. Reference to these and other authorities, such as J. Foster's *Alumni Oxonienses*, will in most cases amplify the data given considerably, but this has usually been taken to be so obvious that they are not cited specifically. In the same way, A. B. Emden's monumental *Biographical Register of the University of Oxford* is the source of most of the facts given about pre-Reformation members, but it would have been monotonous to point this out every time. PRO = Public Record Office; PCC = Prerogative Court of Canterbury; *OED* = *Oxford English Dictionary*; OU = Oxford University; Bt. = Baronet; *VCH* = *Victoria County History*; JCR = Junior Common Room; OUDS = Oxford University Dramatic Society; ICS = Indian Civil Service; WEA = Workers' Educational Association. A detailed survey of the diverse printed and manuscript sources used is given in Appendix G. Quotations have been edited lightly where clarity seemed to demand it. Where emphasis is indicated in a quotation, it is present in the original; square brackets are occasionally used to insert a missing word or clarify an obscure one. Omitted material is indicated by three dots, ..., whatever its extent. Medieval personal names which related men to places have, where the identification seemed secure, been turned into their modern English equivalents. An author with a taste for minutiae is bound to be tempted to burden a book such as this inordinately with notes. I have tried to keep the number down, by citing source material precisely only when the point seemed of particular interest. In cases where a document had been printed, in general I used and therefore cite the printed source (e.g. H. E. Salter's *Oxford Balliol Deeds*, 1913). Where it was possible to do so, I have relied on the availability of other works (see Appendix G) which specify their authorities exactly and exhaustively, instead of repeating all the references. Chapter 8, for example, is heavily dependent on A. [J. P.] Kenny, 'Reform and Reaction in Elizabethan Balliol 1559–1588', in J. [M.] Prest (ed.), *Balliol Studies*, 1982, and the reader who seeks the original material for this period will find an admirable guide there: it has more copious and detailed notes than would have been reasonable here. I have therefore given notes to Chapter 8 only when there is something to add, and I have even reproduced some of the Master's quotations without comment. Similarly, exhaustive footnotes for Chapter 14 would have been superfluous, because my own 'Sound Religion and Useful Learning: the rise of Balliol under John Parsons and Richard Jenkyns 1798–1854' (also in *Balliol Studies*) covers the same ground and gives access to chapter and verse. Again, with Chapter 15, the excellent index of the well-known biography of Jowett by Abbott and Campbell (on which Faber's biography is to a large extent a commentary) enabled references to be kept to a minimum. I hope that these policies will not irritate too much any students of detail who want to trace my footsteps. The papers, correspondence, photocopies, and all the rest of my material concerning this book, have been placed in the College Archives.

J.H.J.

Balliol
2 July 1987

CONTENTS

LIST OF ILLUSTRATIONS

Frontispiece

The College Arms, as used since about 1900, drawn by Mr Alvin Ferris.

Figures

Plans

Plates

The portraits and other works of art reproduced all belong to the College except where otherwise indicated. Details of the artists, etc. are in most cases given in Mrs R. L. Poole [Rachael Poole], *Catalogue of [Oxford] Portraits . . . ,* ii, part I, 1925. See also J. [H.] Jones, *The Portraits of Balliol College. A catalogue*, 1990. The photographs for Plates 1, 3, 11, 13, 16, 18, 21, C1, C5, C14, and C16 were all taken by Thomas-Photos, Oxford; the others are by various photographers, including Mr John Peacock, Dr Reza Gandjei, Mr Chris Honeywell, Mr Norman McBeath, Mr Colin Webb, Dr Mark Wood, and the author.

Black-and-white

Colour

between pages 102 and 103.

I

The Foundation of the College

THE University of Oxford was not initiated by the considered act of any individual or institution. There was no grand design, and there are no Founders to honour. On the contrary, it evolved unplanned, from humble and ill-defined origins. Academic activity of an uncoordinated and rather informal kind began in the city well before the year 1200. A loosely organized self-perpetuating system soon grew from this, and a democratic structure with officials and regulations crystallized in the early thirteenth century. The University had little to do with the domestic arrangements and discipline of its members in these early days. They found what accommodation they could, and lived according to their own inclinations. This worked whilst they remained few in number, but the student population expanded, creating economic pressures for itself and social problems for the city. Rents rose and tensions developed. Outbreaks of violence became commonplace. Some controls of the rents exacted from students on the one hand, and of their behaviour on the other, were essential. Restraints were gradually imposed by the University and the King. The pattern which emerged was one in which most students lived together in small groups in lodging-houses or halls, which were subject to rent control and run by resident principals. These halls, however, fell far short of anything which could be termed a college. They were small, with limited facilities. Lacking endowments, they had no pretensions to be permanent or independent corporations. The movement to establish true colleges, which sprang from Paris, did not begin in Oxford until the late thirteenth century. To the rich and pious who provided the money, the foundation of a college was an aid to their souls' salvation—both through the merit of the charity in itself and by imposing on the beneficiaries the duty of having masses said in perpetuity. To the ecclesiastical authorities, a college was an attractive means of establishing an organization which was not only eleemosynary, but which also enabled some control to be exercised over the behaviour and education of the students in it. The Church's concern was partly paternal because they were very young, partly disciplinarian because they were very unruly, and partly to do with theology and politics because nonconformist thought was liable to develop in the uninhibited atmosphere of the University at large.

Few families in the ranks of the northern nobility could claim precedence over the Balliols of Barnard Castle. They held extensive lands in England and in France,[1] and to these possessions John de Balliol, the head of the family at the time in question, had added power in Scotland by his marriage to Dervorguilla of Galloway. In the district around Barnard Castle, he ruled like a petty sovereign, but he could not browbeat his neighbour Walter Kirkham, the Bishop of Durham. Kirkham was a man to reckon with. 'Little in body but great in mind', as the Lanercost Chronicle describes him, he commanded the respect of the most powerful in the land. According to the legend which has been spun from the Lanercost and other chronicles, Balliol had persistent differences with the Bishop. They came to a head around 1255–60. Kirkham had excommunicated a number of Balliol's retainers for taking over some lands which he claimed as the property of his see. Balliol's response was violent. He laid an ambush for the Bishop, subjected him when captured to some indignities, and carried off part of his retinue. The Bishop laid a complaint before the King (Henry III), obtaining a writ which condemned the outrage in the strongest language and demanded instant reparation. The offender submitted, and the people of Durham enjoyed the spectacle of the haughty baron prostrating himself in penitential garb before the doors of their cathedral, the Bishop chastising him personally. The Bishop also imposed the further penance of a substantial act of charity, in the form of a perpetual endowment for the support of scholars at Oxford.

Thus the legend.[2] The truth may be a little less colourful, but no doubt also has at its nucleus the fact of John Balliol being induced to favour Oxford by Walter Kirkham. This must have taken place before August 1260, when Kirkham died, although his successor Robert de Stichill (Bishop of Durham 1260–74) probably helped to carry the matter through.[3] In obedience to the mandate, or willingly—only an evidently

---

[1] The family sprang from Picardy (not Normandy, as was at one time maintained), taking its name from Bailleul-en-Vimeu. See: A. R. Wagner, *English Genealogy*, 2nd edn., 1972, p. 58; W. Greenwell, 'The Baliols of Bywell and Barnard Castle', in J. C. Hodgson, *A History of Northumberland*, vi, 1902, p. 14; G. A. Moriarty, 'The Baliols in Picardy, England, and Scotland', *New England Historical and Genealogical Register*, cvi (1952), 273; G. Stell, 'The Balliol Family and the Great Cause of 1291–2', in K. J. Stringer (ed.), *Essays on the Nobility of Medieval Scotland*, 1985; K. J. Stringer, *Earl David of Huntington*, 1985; and D. Austin, *Acts of Perception: A Study of Barnard Castle in Teesdale*, London, English Heritage, HMSO (forthcoming). The main Balliol castle was on the high ground to the south of Bailleul-en-Vimeu. No superstructure survives, but the massive earthworks on which it stood can still be found in the dense Bois de Bailleul (part of the Château Coquerel estate). An expedition partly under the auspices of the College surveyed and studied the site 1923–5. The present author visited it in 1990 (MISC 95–7, 221).
[2] See, for a critique of the legend, J. H. Burn, *A Defence of John Balliol*, n.d., *c.*1970, privately printed.
[3] To judge from his appearance in the *Rotulus Benefactorum*: A. B. Emden, *Balliol College Record*, 1967, Supplement.

prejudiced and embellished chronicle makes him reluctant—Balliol hired a house in the suburbs of Oxford, near the church of St Mary Magdalen. This was used as a hostel for the accommodation of sixteen poor Scholars, to whom he made an allowance of eightpence a week each. The early existence of this community, from which the present-day College descends directly, is confirmed by a royal writ dated 22 June 1266: on that day, Henry III ordered the Mayor and bailiffs of Oxford to advance £20 to John Balliol out of moneys owing to the Crown, 'for the use of the Scholars whom he maintains in the said town'.[4]

The house hired by John Balliol, which belonged to the University, stood in Horsemonger Street (the modern Broad Street), facing the moat and the city wall. On the west it was flanked by tenements belonging to St Frideswide's Priory and other parties, which extended to the corner of the street; on the east by eight small houses, the most remote of which was roughly where Staircase III now is, in the corner of the Front Quadrangle. Behind the houses there was a labyrinth of small gardens, groves of trees, and pathways. The arrival of the original Balliol Scholars can hardly have attracted much attention, for there was little to distinguish them from the informal societies in the existing halls. There were no Statutes; the Scholars made their own rules and elected their own Principal. Their weekly dole was paid to them by John Balliol's agents; this was their only income and they had no capital. But their benefactor was making plans to put them on a permanent footing. In his will he assigned a sum of money for the purchase of income-yielding land.[5] Soon after John's death in 1268, his eldest son Hugh bought the right to certain rents at Stamfordham in Northumberland,[6] and it appears from the records of a dispute of 1273 that at least some of these were by then vested in the 'Convent of the Scholars of John de Balliol'.[7] The Scholars also had books in common ownership at a very early stage: Peter de Cossington, who died before May 1276, bequeathed a copy of Boethius, *De musica*, which is still in the College Library. There was clearly a degree of corporate identity, despite the lack of Statutes to formalize it.

John's son Hugh died in 1271, and although he had other sons they either died or took no part in completing the Foundation, the credit for which belongs to John's widow Dervorguilla. She took up the task with vigour. 'Dervorguilla of Galloway, Lady of Balliol' was a great lady in her

---

[4] *Calendar of Documents relating to Scotland*, i, ed. J. Bain, 1881, p. 476.

[5] John Balliol's will does not survive, but it is mentioned in several deeds of his executors: the wording of Balliol College Archives E.4.2 is especially clear in showing that it was his stated wish that the College should be endowed.

[6] E.4.1.

[7] *Northumberland Pleas from De Banco rolls 1–19*, ed. A. Hamilton Thompson, 1950 (*Surtees Soc.* clviii), p. 18; PRO, CP 40/3, rot. 9d. In Trinity Term 1273, 'Walterus de Fodryngg' unus de conventu scolarium Johannis de Balliolo' appeared before the Court of Common Pleas at Westminster, concerning the Stamfordham property.

4

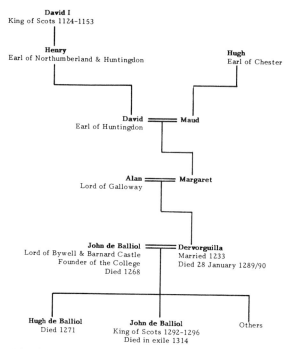

Fig. 1. The descent and family of Dervorguilla of Galloway, Lady of Balliol.

own right (see Fig. 1). The nobility of her blood is proclaimed by the heraldic devices on her seal. Its reverse is of special interest, because it shows the lion of Galloway and orle of Balliol impaled as in the College arms of the present day (see the frontispiece).[8] She ruled by hereditary right over one of the most uncouth and lawless districts in Scotland, but she had been educated in England at the court of her grandfather, David, Earl of Huntingdon, and she was a devout and cultured person. During her widowhood, she was preoccupied with good works to perpetuate her husband's memory. In Galloway she built Sweetheart Abbey as a resting-place for herself, and for his heart. In Oxford she set out to consolidate his venture. Andrew de Wyntoun's Chronicle gives a poetic account:[9]

[8] The present arms (Azure, a lion rampant argent, crowned or, impaling Gules, an orle argent) were only adopted and used consistently by the College from about 1900. The same orle and lion were combined in several other ways during the nineteenth century. Amalgamations of the Balliol orle and the arms of Scotland (Or, a lion rampant within a double tressure flory and counterflory gules) are also found on nineteenth-century items. The arms generally employed by the College (e.g. to mark silver) before that were simply Gules, an orle argent.

[9] Based, with minor liberties for the sake of clarity and rhythm, on the versions given by W. Huyshe, *Dervorguilla, Lady of Galloway*, 1913, p. 46, and F. de Paravicini, *Early History of Balliol College*, 1891, p. 52.

When the Balliol that was her lord,
That spousit her, as they record,
Had sent his soul to his Creator,
Ere he was laid in sepulture,
His body she gert open tite
And gert his hart to be tane out quite.
And that ilk hart, as men said,
She balmèd it and gert be laid
Into a coffyn of evore,
The which she gert be made therefor,
Enamellit, parfitly dicht,
Lokkit, and bunden with silver bricht. . . .

And always when she ga'ed to meat,
That coffyn she gert by her set,
Richt as her lord were in presens,
And to it she did reverens. . . .

She ordanit in her testament,
And gave them bidding verament,
That his hart they should then ta'
And lay between her pappis twa,
When they suld make her sepulture;
To her lord did she this honour. . . .

She founddit then in Galloway,
Of Cistew's order, ane abbay,
Dulce cor she gert them all,
(That is, Sweethart) the abbay call.
And now the men of Galloway
Call that stead the New Abbay. . . .

And in the University
Of Oxenfurde she gert be
A College founddit. That Lady
Did all her dedis dewotely.
A better lady than she was nane
In all the ile of Mare Brittane.
She was richt plesande of Bewty;
Here was gret takynns of Bownty.

If the College, as we shall now call it, was to be permanent, a constitution was required. In 1282 Dervorguilla addressed a code of Statutes, in the form of a letter, to Brother Hugh of Hartlepool and William de Menyl; the latter was an MA in the University, the former a Franciscan friar residing in the Oxford convent. They may have been the agents (*procuratores*) by whom the Balliol dole had been distributed up to that point.

The Statutes which the Procurators were instructed to put into force are not exhaustive. In some matters they imply that the College is already governed by customary rules, and they leave the Scholars to settle many questions for themselves. In all probability some parts are little more than a formal statement of usages which had prevailed from the beginning— e.g. the authority of the Principal is to be according to their customs and practices ('secundum statuta & consuetudines inter ipsos usitatas & approbatas'). The points upon which they are silent, however, are curious. The time for which a place on the Foundation was tenable is not defined, although we know, from the record of a dispute which took place forty years later,[10] that the Scholars were restricted to the Faculty of Arts. The curriculum of the Arts Faculty comprised the *trivium* (grammar, logic, and rhetoric), the *quadrivium* (arithmetic, geometry, astronomy, and music), and the three philosophies (moral philosophy, natural philosophy, and metaphysics). Members had to leave if they wanted to study in other faculties (Theology, Canon and Civil Law, Medicine). The majority probably left on attaining the MA degree, or soon after.[11] It seems very unlikely that the Arts limitation depended on informal regulation: it was surely codified. More telling still, nothing appears about the appointment of Scholars. On this we remain ignorant, as the only contemporary allusion to the procedure is in the confirmation of Dervorguilla's Foundation which her son John made in 1285,[12] to the Principal and his colleagues and to their legitimate successors ('eorum successoribus per legitimam eleccionem societatem illam intrantibus'). This is ambiguous, as *eleccionem* here might refer to choice by some external authority or democratic election by the Society itself. Whatever the process was, however, we would expect clear guide-lines to have been laid down for it. The Foundress and her advisers would hardly have left such a fundamental matter uncontrolled. It is difficult to evade the conclusion that there were further Statutes unknown to us—a deduction which is corroborated by other equally explicit references[13] to restrictions in Dervorguilla's Statutes which are not in fact to be found in the code she sealed at Buittle Castle, on 22 August 1282. The entire document is translated in Appendix A.

The only subjects the surviving Statutes do deal with in any detail are the authority of the Procurators, the office of the Principal, and the daily life of the Scholars. The Scholars were to attend divine service on Sundays

---

[10] H. E. Salter, *Oxford Balliol Deeds*, 1913, p. 285.

[11] Previous accounts have supposed that attaining the MA degree terminated membership, but E. B. Fryde and J. R. L. Highfield (*Oxoniensia*, xx. 40) have pointed out that four Regents are numbered as Fellows in 1321. Furthermore, the commission cited in n. 13 below mentions three years' grace after graduation. Limitation to the Faculty of Arts was the critical matter.

[12] Salter, op. cit., p. 10.

[13] In a papal commission of 1364, for example: see Salter, op. cit., p. 299.

and feast days, and every year to celebrate three solemn masses for the souls of the Founders. On ordinary days they should attend lectures at the Schools, and pursue their studies according to the Statutes of the University. Within the house their conversation should be in Latin; once a week all were to meet together for a disputation on a subject announced by the Principal. The disputations were academic exercises something like formal debates, designed to teach students how to marshal their arguments; one of them would be assigned to put each side of a case, and their performances would be critically assessed by a senior member in his 'determination' of the disputation. Two meals a day were to be provided at the common table. If in any week the cost of the common table were to exceed the allowances, then the Scholars were to be charged by the Procurators in proportion to their means, for the payment of the deficit; those in financial difficulty were not to be called upon for more than a penny in any week. There was always to be a poor student maintained upon the crumbs of the common table. The Principal was elected by the Scholars from among their own number, but his election was only valid when it had been confirmed by the Procurators. He was responsible for enforcing discipline within the house. He presided at table and at the weekly disputations. He could suspend those who disregarded his instructions from the society of the common table; such offenders were to be served separately and after all the rest. Although the Statutes imply that the Principal's functions were to be purely internal, he was the leading figure in estates and financial matters from the very start. The *Principalis* who features in the Statutes and other documents emanating from Dervorguilla is not clearly distinguishable from the *Magister* (occasionally *Custos*) who appears in other sources during the first quarter-century: these terms are, for practical purposes, synonyms for the individual functioning as Head of House. A sentence of expulsion could only be pronounced by the Procurators, who acted as Visitors, being charged to hear all complaints. They were to be obeyed in all matters concerning the order and well-being of the Society. Their authority and role would seem to have been somewhere between those of the Master and the Visitor of the modern constitution. The ordinary members are always designated Scholars (*scolares*) in these Statutes. The alternative term Fellow (*socius*) soon begins to creep into use, but carries no implications of superior status or authority until very much later.

Nothing is said in the Statutes about the College buildings, but it is obvious that the dining-hall was the focus of social life. For divine service the Scholars resorted, until a little later, to the nearby parish church of St Mary Magdalen. Its north aisle was repaired by Dervorguilla, and fitted up as an oratory dedicated to St Catherine. Dervorguilla had a special devotion to St Catherine, the virgin martyr of Alexandria,[14] who naturally became the College's patron saint.

The next step the Foundress took was to increase the endowment. About the end of 1283, she assigned certain lands and rents in Stamfordham and Heugh (Northumberland) to the Principal and Scholars of the College and their successors, wherever they might settle.[15] There had been a wholesale migration of students to Northampton about twenty years before, and it was still far from certain that Oxford would be the University's permanent location. But although Dervorguilla allowed for the eventuality of a removal, she worked on the assumption of permanence, and gave her Scholars a house of their own in Oxford. In 1284 she purchased a block of three tenements lying a little to the east of their rented lodgings, converted it into a single house suitable for the needs of a student community, and moved them into it, stating that it should be known as the 'House of the Scholars of Balliol'.[16] New Balliol Hall, as it was in fact called to distinguish it from the previous accommodation (which became known as Old Balliol Hall), was located as shown in Plan I.

In making these arrangements, Dervorguilla was advised by Richard de Slikeburne. He was, like Hugh of Hartlepool, a Franciscan. Tradition

---

[14] In Bishop Oliver Sutton's statement approving Dervorguilla's Foundation, he noted that it was 'to the honour and praise of the supreme and undivided Trinity; of the most glorious Virgin Mary, Mother of the only Son of God; of the Blessed Virgin and Martyr Catherine; and of the whole Court of Heaven' (Salter, op. cit., p. 280). According to legend, St Catherine of Alexandria was a learned and noble lady who was martyred in the early fourth century; see S. Nevanlinna and I. Taavitsainen (eds.), *St Katherine of Alexandria*, 1993. Her symbol is a spiked wheel; it appears in several places around the College and on some College silver. She is patron saint of scholars, among others. The wooden statue (carved *c*.1635) which is now in the Old Library (it was formerly the centrepiece over the door of the Chapel screen) is probably meant to represent her; the book the figure holds alludes to her learning, but the usual spiked wheel symbol is lacking (perhaps lost).

[15] E.4.2.

[16] This name—'Domus scolarium de Balliolo'—is found in many early deeds and is on the first common seal. It was sometimes shortened to 'Domus de Balliolo', a form the College was enjoined to perpetuate when the Statutes were revised in 1340, and which survives in the toast of loyal alumni. 'Aula de Balliolo'—Balliol Hall—is the commonest title in the fourteenth century: the term *Collegium* appears late in that period, but does not oust all others for two centuries more. The name in English has also varied, and became so corrupt ('Bayley Colledge', 'Bailif Colledge') in the sixteenth century that the Founder's name might have been forgotten but for the stability of Latin. The current full proper corporate designation originates from the royal charter of 1588: 'The Master and Scholars of Balliol College in the University of Oxford'. The name Balliol gets garbled even today. Balloil is a common corruption. A few minor streets etc. are named after the College, but the only well-known eponyms were aircraft: the Balliol and the Sea Balliol trainers. The Balliol Business Park (Wolverhampton) was named after them; it has nothing to do with the College. The Balliol Business Park (Longbenton) is on land long owned by the College. The connection of the racehorse Balliol Boy is obscure. *Superform Races and Race Horses*, Flat Edition 1996, notes him as a 'nice sort with scope' who 'goes well fresh'.

holds that he was her confessor, but there is little to support this conjecture in the documents from which our knowledge of him is derived. The first of these is a letter addressed to him by Dervorguilla in 1284.[17] After an opening in which she says that she has decided to continue her husband's charity to the Scholars, she asks him to help her. There are expressions in the letter which imply a close sympathy between him and her. She calls him her 'dearly beloved brother in Christ' and speaks of 'our complete confidence in your discretion and devotion'. He continued to exercise his trust for several years. In 1287, for example, he is described as Rector of the House, and we find him involved in a transaction whereby the outstanding debts which were due to John Balliol at the time of his death were assigned to the College.[18] These amounted to a very substantial sum, but some of them were of twenty or thirty years' standing, and although the Principal pursued the debtors with great energy, he was not completely successful. Dervorguilla also empowered Slikeburne to choose Procurators for the House. We do not know upon whom his choice fell, but it is likely that one of the two posts was reserved for his Franciscan brethren. This tradition was enduring: we have proof that it was being observed in 1325, 1415, and 1433.[19]

Walter of Fotheringhay was probably the first Principal elected according to Dervorguilla's Statutes.[20] A native of one of her main residences, he appears to have enjoyed an unusual measure of her confidence, and she made him one of her executors. He was a Fellow of the College in 1273 and Principal by 1284. In 1298 he was collated to a prebend at Lincoln, doubtless through the favour of the Bishop, Oliver Sutton. The Foundress had been careful to secure for her Scholars the protection of their diocesan (Oxford was then in the diocese of Lincoln): the new Statutes and arrangements were confirmed by Bishop Sutton in the year 1284. Not content with this, she contrived to ensure that no question as to the legality of the Foundation could ever be raised, by having her son John (now described as her husband's heir because of the deaths of his older brothers) confirm it in a charter which was witnessed by Bishop Sutton, together with the Bishop of Durham, the Chancellor of the University, and the Archdeacon of Oxford. No medieval corporation could be considered fully equipped

---

[17] Salter, op. cit., p. 279.

[18] Ibid., p. 283.

[19] B.22.38, D.4.8 (Salter, op. cit., p. 285), and D.4.10 (Salter, op. cit., p. 302).

[20] This was first stated in print as a definite fact by Henry Savage in *Balliofergus*, 1668, and it has been repeated by all subsequent College historians. However, Robert of Abberwick appears as 'Custos domus scolarium Oxon. de Balliolo' in June 1283 (Fine Roll, 2 Edward I, m. 14: PRO, C 60/81). This is before the earliest reference to Walter of Fotheringhay as Head of House, but we cannot tell whether Robert of Abberwick was elected under the 1282 Statutes or took office earlier. In either case he is the first Head of House who can be named. He was no doubt Walter of Fotheringhay's immediate predecessor, as he was a Fellow of Merton from 1284.

without a common seal, and it seems likely that the design of the College's seal was approved by Dervorguilla herself as a finishing touch: it has all the main heraldic devices shown on her own seal. The original matrix, a beautiful example of the seal engraver's craft, is still in the possession of the College.[21]

Dervorguilla died in January 1289/90;[22] she was buried in Sweetheart Abbey near Dumfries, with her husband's heart on her bosom.[23] She left a legacy of £100 to the Principal and Scholars, but despite the fact that the Principal was himself one of the executors, it proved difficult to persuade the Balliol family to discharge the obligation. The College sued the son of their benefactress in Chancery, but part of the sum remained unpaid until the year 1330; it was from her grandson, Edward Balliol, that satisfaction was eventually obtained.[24] Fortunately the financial position of the Society was sound, and they do not appear to have suffered materially

---

[21] The earliest surviving example of the use of this matrix is dated 1341 (E.1.20), but a common seal ('sigillum commune') is mentioned in 1307 (B.9.2); its latest known use is in 1575 (D.15.3). The matrix of a smaller 'sigillum ad causas', of early but uncertain date, also survives, but no example of its use is known. The Bursars' accounts for 1588 show expenditure of 30s. 'for the newe seale'. Two matrices of the second seal, which was in use from 1588 (A.16.18) until recently, exist.

[22] The exact date was 28 Jan. 1289/90. At the 'inquisitio post mortem' following a writ dated 4 Feb., 18 Edward I, it was stated that she had died on the Saturday after the Conversion of St Paul. The Septcentenary was observed (*Balliol College Record*, 1990, p. 65) on 21 January 1990 because the Lanercost Chronicle records (*Scottish Historical Review*, vii, 1910, pp. 56–7) that she died on the Feast of St Agnes (21 January); but this does not contradict the official record—the author of the Chronicle probably meant the Nativity of St Agnes (28 January).

[23] Her tomb probably stood before the high altar, but no trace of the original monument remains. A new tomb was made in the sixteenth century, in table form, with her effigy resting on it; fragments of this tomb were reassembled in the south transept of the ruins in 1933 (J. S. Richardson, *Sweetheart Abbey*, HMSO, 1951). The College had an inscribed stone placed nearby in 1966. It has been suggested (J. R. Scott, *Memorials of the Family of Scott*, 1876, p. 52) that John Balliol's heart was removed to Brabourne in Kent during the early fourteenth century, Sweetheart Abbey being in an insecure state through war and poverty. This is plausible, because Brabourne church had close connections with the Balliols, and a heart shrine of the period survives in it. It is not supported by any evidence, however, and B. J. Scott (*The Norman Balliols in England*, 1914, p. 275) states, albeit without giving any authority, that the Brabourne shrine was made for the heart of Aymer de Valence, who died in 1324.

[24] For the genealogy of the Founders' descendants (who have, however, never had any special rights in the College, like Founders' Kin at some other colleges), see J. R. Scott, op. cit., B. J. Scott, op. cit., and A. Sinclair, *Heirs of the Royal House of Baliol* and *Remarks on the Tables of the Heirs of the Royal House of Baliol*, Edinburgh, n.d., c.1880. The family name Balliol was extinct in England and Scotland by 1400. The senior representative of the family in 1986 was, by his own claim (MISC 74), Ursel Baliol Scott, who died on 20 January 1989, without issue.

from this delay. For some years after Dervorguilla's death they continued to add to their land and property, partly through purchases and partly through gifts from former members of the House. By 1310 the whole of the site of the present Front Quadrangle had passed into their hands, but it is unlikely that they used the whole of the area themselves. Small as it was, New Balliol Hall offered accommodation enough for the sixteen Scholars. The newly acquired tenements would for the most part have been treated as investments, and rented out. In other parts of the city, the College acquired Hert Hall (1310) on a site which is now part of Merton College garden; Chimere Hall (1310) on a site between the present Canterbury Gate of Christ Church and the lodgings of the President of Corpus Christi College; and several houses (including St Hugh's Hall) in School Street (1310–17). This street ran from the west end of the University Church past Brasenose Hall as far as the city wall. Near the top of the street, on the left-hand side, Balliol held a block of four tenements, which were let for academic purposes, and commonly known as the Balliol Schools. The land on which they stood is now occupied by a part of the Divinity Schools.[25] In the same period the College acquired its first living—St Lawrence Jewry—which it received from Hugh de Vienne in 1294, together with some associated property in London. The College was deprived of the advowson in 1951, and it was assigned to the Corporation of the City of London, but the long connection is marked by a stall in the church which is reserved for the Master of Balliol, and the Corporation still pays a corn rent in respect of part of the Guildhall site.[26]

The most important of the bequests made to the College at this time has a complex history.[27] Oxford had a large Jewish colony, whose ghetto was in St Aldate's parish. The whole of its property fell to the King when he expelled Jews from England in the year 1290, and from the spoil he gave to William Burnel, Provost of Wells, the synagogue and some adjacent houses. Burnel and his more famous uncle Robert (Bishop of Bath and Wells; Chancellor to Edward I; died 1292) may have intended to found on this site a college of their own, but if so the scheme was abandoned, and in 1304 William bequeathed all the property he had

---

[25] The College's records of these early Oxford property transactions are printed and analysed in Salter, op. cit.

[26] The College Archives are very rich in material concerning St Lawrence Jewry (see especially B.19, B.20, and B.22; B.22.1, a deed of about 1200, is the oldest item in the Archives). On the Guildhall connection see C. M. Barron, *The Medieval Guildhall of London*, 1974. The Balliol property was between the church of St Lawrence Jewry and the Guildhall, on the west side of Guildhall Yard, over the site of Roman Londinium's amphitheatre: see N. Bateman, *Current Archaeology*, cxxxvii, 1994, 164, and MISC 206.

[27] Salter, op. cit., p. 91.

acquired in the area to the College. Legal complications delayed matters for a decade, however, and the executors could not grant good title until 1313. It was clearly stated that the rental income from the property should be used by the College to swell its ranks ('ad augmentacionem numeri scolarium domus eiusdem'), but whether this was done is doubtful. The core of the benefaction was still known as Burnel's Inn a hundred years later, when Richard Clifford (Bishop of London, died 1422) leased part of it and maintained some students there. 'London College' was also ephemeral, but that name survived for a further century, until the whole of Burnel's gift was swallowed by Wolsey's agents for Cardinal College (see Chapter 6).

John Balliol's Foundation rose from the ranks of the mere boarding houses in a single generation. Although still a weakling compared to its contemporary Merton, which had been conceived on a grander scale and nourished with greater wealth, it had all the essential features of a college by the beginning of the fourteenth century: a house of its own, modest endowments, and the right of self-government within the limits of a formal constitution.

Fig. 2. Dervorguilla's agent Hugh of Hartlepool. A rubbing from the life-size effigy on his gravestone at Assisi.

2

Constitutional Change and Expansion in the Fourteenth Century

THE restriction of the Scholars to studies in the Arts inhibited both the ambitions of individuals and the development of the Society. Those who aspired to the more advanced faculties were obliged to leave soon after taking the MA degree, so there were never many of any great seniority or external influence in the College. It seems that there was a move in 1325 to bend the rules, and enable students to take up other subjects in the spare time left by their Arts work. But the Visitors took the view that this would be a fraud on the Foundation, and would not condone it. After a formal hearing before the entire community, they ruled that no Scholar could attend or devote any of his energies to any faculty other than that of Arts, whether in full term or vacation. Though no doubt a severe blow to those affected, the decision seems to have been in line with the customs of the House, as it was confirmed by several former Scholars who were present at the hearing.[1] The Scholars continued to leave the College soon after graduating as MAs. Many promising young men, including several who rose to be the most notable thinkers of their age, were lost by the College in this period, often to Merton. An account of them is given in the next chapter.

The principal event of the years immediately after 1325 was the erection of a new College Chapel. Some sort of chapel, described as a *cantaria* or *oratorium*, had been in use from 1293, pending the establishment of a permanent chapel with the help of Ela, Countess of Warwick.[2] This is known from the licence approving the arrangements, which was issued by the Bishop of Lincoln, Oliver Sutton: it was he who had approved Dervorguilla's Foundation in 1284. He was a prelate well disposed to students, and the licence was a special concession to enable them to combine worship and academic activity with minimal interruption to the

---

[1] H. E. Salter, *Oxford Balliol Deeds*, 1913, p. 285. The two Visitors, previously called Procurators, are termed External Masters for the first time in this document; in the next century they are alluded to as Rectors.

[2] This identification is confirmed by her appearance in the *Rotulus Benefactorum*: A. B. Emden, *Balliol College Record*, 1967, Supplement.

latter.[3] Succeeding bishops renewed the licence, until the College's right
to a chapel of its own became traditional. The office of Chaplain was
endowed by Hugh de Warkenby and William de Gotham in 1310. It was
further endowed, or possibly duplicated, by Richard de Hunsingore in
1312. Hugh de Vienne, a wealthy public figure who probably died about
1296, also contributed to the new Chapel with a bequest of 50 marks,
stipulating that it was to be built to last, of stone with a leaded roof. The
building, which was almost certainly on the site of the present Chapel,
was dedicated to St Catherine. The work progressed slowly because it
proved difficult to obtain the money from Hugh de Vienne's executors.[4]
It was under way in 1309 and it must have been nearing completion in
1328 when Nicholas of Whaplode, Abbot of Reading, gave £26. 13s. 4d.
for the fabric, together with a glass window worth £10 and timber and
lathes, using funds put in his hands for charitable purposes by Adam le
Politer, burgess of Reading.[5]

There was a steady influx of precious manuscript books throughout the
fourteenth century. Some of these are still in the Library; others are
recorded in wills. No catalogue has survived, but inventory numbers are
entered in some of the extant manuscripts, from which it can be calculated
that by 1385 the number of volumes was at least 155. At any given time
some (perhaps most) of these would have been on extended loan to
Fellows, if we can safely assume that normal collegiate practice was
followed. Other volumes would have been in pawn. Chests, from which
loans secured by the deposit of valuables such as books could be obtained,
were a fundamental part of the financial structure of the University. Ample
evidence of the use of the Balliol books in this way survives in the
inscriptions still found in them. MS 89, for example, was pledged by the
Master and six Fellows for twenty-one marks in 1375; the pledge was
subsequently renewed and supplemented many times by their successors,
but the book was eventually redeemed and brought home, where it has
remained. There was always a risk of loss in this process—no doubt this
is why some were inscribed with prohibitions, as in MS 257: 'Iste liber
est domus de Baliolo anathema sit quicunque alienaverit.' In the very early
days books not in pawn, or out on loan, would probably have been stored
in chests. The first properly laid-out library was not constructed until
the fifteenth century, but the identical contemporary inscriptions in the
volumes bequeathed by William Rede, Bishop of Chichester, in 1385,

---

[3] Salter op. cit., p. 314; *Lincoln Record Soc.* lii. 83, 94, 97, and 132. On Sutton and the
University of Oxford see R. M. T. Hill, *Trans. Roy. Hist. Soc.*, 4th series, xxxi. 1.

[4] Salter, op. cit., p. 336; Hugh de Vienne's executors were having troubles of their own
collecting debts due to his estate: *Calendar of Chancery Warrants 1244–1326*, i, 1927, p. 264.

[5] Salter, op. cit., p. 315.

suggest that by then there was some kind of library room with chained books: 'Liber aule Balioli Oxon. in communi libraria eiusdem et ad usum communem sociorum ibidem studencium cathenandus.'

There were also fresh endowments. In the year 1340 Sir William Felton, a Northumberland knight,[6] with the consent of the King and the Pope, assigned the tithes and glebe of Abbotsley, in Huntingdonshire, to the College. The revenues accruing therefrom, estimated at something less than £40 p.a., were to be expended in relieving the most pressing needs of the Scholars. Part was to be used to raise the weekly allowance by half; with another part, books relating to the various faculties, for common ownership, were to be purchased. Out of the remainder, the allowances of those who had graduated as MAs were to be continued, until they could obtain adequate ecclesiastical preferment. The requirement that members should leave after graduating had sometimes driven them to take up manual work to support themselves.[7] The extension of support for those waiting for a benefice was probably linked to the acquisition of the advowsons of Fillingham, Brattleby, and Riseholme, through the agency of Thomas Cave and William Brocklesby, in 1343.[8] In fact it was several years before the College actually received the Felton benefaction, because it was necessary to wait until the existing Rector of Abbotsley vacated the benefice, which did not happen until 1361. In that year the Scholars, following directions from Rome, made an agreement with the Bishop of Lincoln for the maintenance of a vicar. The Bishop drove a hard bargain. All the small tithes and sixty acres of the glebe were reserved for the vicar; the College furthermore undertook to build him a parsonage, to pay him an annual pension of five shillings, and to keep the chancel of the church in repair; little of the £40 p.a. can have remained when these requirements were satisfied. After all the preliminaries had been duly transacted, the Master took possession in the prescribed form. He rang the bells of the church, touched the paten upon the altar, and took possession of the Rector's house—trivial details which are of more interest when we note that the Master in question was John Wyclif.

The reforms for which the Felton funds were intended were initiated

---

[6] There was a succession of knights of this name; the Balliol benefactor is the one who died about 1359, and is buried in Edlingham church. For details of his life, see J. C. Hodgson, *A History of Northumberland*, vii, 1904, p. 113.

[7] The details are recited in the Pope's licence, which is transcribed in Salter, op. cit., p. 299, and translated in F. de Paravicini, *Early History of Balliol College*, 1891, p. 168.

[8] E.5.1–10. Thomas Cave and William Brocklesby were also busy at this time helping the College to extend its boundaries a few yards to the east. In 1337 they acquired St Margaret Hall, the tenement between Old Balliol Hall (which belonged to the University) and Dervorguilla's New Balliol Hall. In 1342, they conveyed it to the College by a deed which was witnessed by Sir William Felton: Salter, op. cit., p. 25.

long before it was actually received. This was made possible by the
liberality of Sir Philip Somervyle, a knight who was Lord of the Manor
of Wichnor in Staffordshire, but who also had strong Northumberland
connections.[9] In October 1340, just a few months after Felton's benefaction, Somervyle gave the advowson of Long Benton in Northumberland,
with two plough-lands in the same parish, to the College. As the purposes
of the gift, and the conditions attached to it, were complicated, the College
authorities were persuaded to accept a new code of Statutes. The original
manuscript of these Statutes has long since disappeared from the Archives,
but we fortunately have a contemporary copy.[10]

The Northumberland connection is the only evident link between
Felton and Somervyle, but the coincidence of timing, and similarity of
purpose, point to a common influence on them and their benefactions.
Richard of Bury, Bishop of Durham, was probably the prime mover. He
was the principal witness to Somervyle's new Statutes, which established
the Bishop of Durham as the ultimate authority set over the College, and
enacted that masses were to be said in perpetuity for his soul, along with
those of Somervyle and his family. The analogy between the original
foundation and the thirteenth-century refoundation—for that is what the
Felton–Somervyle reforms amounted to—is very close. In both cases a
Bishop of Durham was instrumental in persuading knightly neighbours
to provide endowments.

The size and composition of the Society were altered fundamentally in
the new scheme. In future there were to be six places, filled by election
from the House, subject to the approval of the Visitors, for graduates
who would study theology. In making an election the Scholars were to
choose men who were 'upright, pure, peaceful, humble, having ability for
the pursuit of learning and a desire to make progress'. These were to be
provided for out of the existing endowment. The Somervyle income was
to be employed partly in raising the allowances of the existing members
as Felton had intended, but to elevenpence a week, not a shilling, with
augmentation by a further fourpence in times of scarcity or festival. The
rest was to provide new places. There was to be an additional Chaplain,
nominated by the Somervyle family, or in their default by the College: he
was to enjoy all the domestic privileges of the Scholars, with life tenure
of his office. Six new Scholarships were created for students in Arts, who
were put on the same footing as the sixteen of the old Foundation. The

---

[9] For information about Sir Philip Somervyle, see M. H. Dodds, *A History of Northumberland*, xiii, 1930, p. 409, and J. Hodgson, *A History of Northumberland*, i, part 2, 1827,
p. 315.

[10] The Statutes are far too long-winded to reproduce again: they are transcribed in Salter,
op. cit., p. 286, and translated in de Paravicini, op. cit., p. 184.

right of electing them was vested in the College, subject to the limitation that natives of the Long Benton area were to have preference over those from other parts of the country. They were to 'excel in poverty, ability, and manners' and nobody was to be admitted under pressure from any great man.

The new inmates necessitated some important adjustments in the constitution of the College. Somervyle did not go so far as to destroy the old offices of the Principal and Procurators, but he made the former nugatory by providing for the election of a graduate Master whom all members of the College were to obey, and he introduced the Chancellor of the University, together with the Warden of Durham College, as colleagues of the Procurators, who appear throughout as External Masters (*magistri extrinseci*). Over and above the visitatorial board, the Bishop of Durham was empowered to intervene, if he thought it necessary, and enforce the Statutes. The exact distribution of powers among the various authorities cannot be determined from the new Statutes: confusion and strife were inevitable. The Visitors no doubt disagreed among themselves and with the College. The Principal and the Scholars of the old Foundation could claim that they were under no obligation to obey the new Master, because Somervyle had provided that if anything in his Statutes was contrary to the ancient Statutes, then the older rule should prevail. If this principle had been consistently applied there would have been under the same roof two distinct communities, with different leaders, enjoying separate endowments. Things never came to this pass. In 1363 the College addressed a petition to Pope Urban V at Avignon, in which they represented that the new Statutes, 'though they are reasonable and useful to the College, and made, as it is believed, with a pious intention, are yet very contrary to the earlier Statutes, a thing which in many ways troubles and disquiets the consciences of the Scholars, causes dissensions, and acts as an incentive to quarrels'. At the Pope's command, Simon Sudbury, Bishop of London, undertook to 'modify, correct, withdraw, or change' those of the Statutes which appeared to be contrary to the intentions of the original Founders.[11] Although there is no copy in the Archives of the revision thus made, it is likely that Sudbury put an end to arguments by abolishing, on the one hand, the complex visitatorial arrangements of Somervyle, and on the other the office of Principal. The Procurators, or External Masters, who from this point are usually termed Rectors (*rectores*), regained most of their old powers, except that supreme authority in College affairs seems to have passed to the Bishop of London. Although the tradition that one of the Visitors should be an external secular MA,

---

[11] Salter, op. cit., p. 299.

and the other a Franciscan, was to be perpetuated, the power of electing its own Visitors was vested in the College itself from this time. Their role was also clarified, and probably reduced: they were to be responsible for general oversight of College affairs, the confirmation of elections and admissions by the College, and the enforcement of the Statutes.[12] From a formal point of view the authority of the Master remained substantially as it had been fixed by Somervyle, but in practical terms it was enhanced, because the parties to whom he was answerable had been reduced in numbers and influence.

The forms prescribed for the election of the Master have in part come down to the present day. The votes were received and written down secretly by the Principal (or, later, the Senior Fellow, who took on the mantle of the Principal when that office was abolished) and two Scrutators, who were themselves chosen from the MAs. Before voting, all had to take an oath before the Senior Fellow that they would, 'faithfully and without any respect of persons and with no consideration of past or future reward', speak for him they knew 'to have the most knowledge, most ability, and most zeal for advancing the affairs of the House'. On election, the new Master also took an oath before the Senior Fellow, that he would observe all the Somervyle Statutes. He was then sent to call upon the Lord of the Manor of Wichnor (Somervyle's estate), who was bound to confirm the election without further demur. On his return to Oxford, two of the senior Fellows took him and introduced him to the Visitors.

In virtue of his station, the Master was to have the privilege of a private room, with a serving-boy, probably a poor student, assigned to him. As it would often be necessary to entertain strangers coming on business, the Master might have 'a table in no way luxurious at the common expense' prepared for him, in the privacy of his own apartment. Once a year he ought in person or by deputy to make a progress round the College estates, and prepare for the audit-meeting an exact account of their condition. He received the rents, defrayed all current expenses, and handed over the surplus to the Treasurer, by whom the chest was kept. Apart from the custody of the chest, the only financial duty which he was able to delegate was that of paying the allowances due to the Somervyle Scholars. They were paid by 'their Masters'. We have here the first hint of something like a tutorial system. Apparently, each of the six additional Scholars was assigned as a pupil to one of the six theologians.

The Master could be deposed if his accounts were found unsatisfactory at the audit-meeting, or if he were 'useless or negligent in fulfilling his

---

[12] Some of Sudbury's ordinances are summarized in papal commissions of *c.*1500: these are transcribed in Salter, op. cit., p. 309, and translated in de Paravicini, op. cit., p. 234.

office or luxurious or notoriously vicious'. If the College wanted to be rid of him, the Principal or Senior Fellow would convene an indignation meeting, which could resolve to deliver a solemn warning. After three such warnings the Master might, if still incorrigible, be denounced to the Visitors, who were then bound to eject him from office.

Disciplinary matters were to be dealt with by the Master and two of the 'older and more discreet Scholars of the Society'. They were charged to act without commotion or delay, arbitrating in personal quarrels and imposing appropriate penalties for misbehaviour. Contumacious offenders might be deprived of their commons for a fortnight, and when this punishment had been thrice inflicted without result, expulsion might ensue. Every Scholar took an oath on admission that he would never dispute a sentence of expulsion in a court of law, but the sentence of expulsion might be reversed if signs of contrition were remarked. Among the venial offences listed as being within the jurisdiction of the senior triumvirate are the practice of shirking lectures, disputations, and church services, hanging about idly in the city at unlawful times, misbehaviour at table, and rudeness to a senior. But conviction of perjury, sacrilege, murder, adultery, theft, or disgrace by a grave sin of the flesh, led *ipso facto* to perpetual exclusion.

The Felton and Somervyle benefactions increased the allowances of the Scholars, but the intention was to remedy former poverty, not provide luxury, which is condemned in the Statutes. If the revenues were increased by good fortune or further benefactions, the surplus was to be used to establish new Scholarships, not to enhance the value of those already existing. No Fellow could have an external income of more than £5 p.a. and retain his place. But the Master's limit was £40, and he was also allowed to hold another office in plurality, presumably to make the Mastership more of a career post.

Somervyle's Statutes use the terms Scholar and Fellow interchangeably, and we have followed them above in their inconsistency. It is clear, however, that a hierarchy based on seniority was recognized. Its existence is also shown by the fact that in the few surviving early deeds which name several members, they are always, so far as we can tell, recited in order of seniority. Elections were to be organized by a group of elders, and discipline was similarly controlled; some at least of the younger members were subordinate to a group of seniors. There was no clear constitutional distinction between the two age-groups in many matters. All would have had a vote in elections, for example, although even here some were more equal than others, as (in accordance with medieval custom) it was decreed that on indecisive occasions the votes of the seniors were to prevail. A stratified society was emerging, with Somervyle's Statutes placing control largely in the hands of the experienced and relatively permanent seniors. They were, in their turn, under the guidance of the Master. By the end of the fourteenth century the constitution was already a skeletal model for the present day.

3
The Early Members

No pre-Reformation accounts, registers, or other records of internal administration, from which the medieval roll of the College might be reconstructed, survive. Only muniments of title to property, which often name Fellows acting for the College, and passing references to Balliol affiliations in the records of other institutions, enable us to identify the early members. The names of some fifty who were admitted before 1400 are known with certainty, and another thirty or so with reasonable confidence,[1] but this is probably only 10–20 per cent of the total. Nor are those we know representative, because the means by which we recognize them, in most cases, mark them as men who achieved seniority in the College or preferment after leaving. Those who died young, or never rose from the obscurity in which they had been born, are the majority. They have no memorial, and are perished as though they had never been.[2]

Of those who joined the College in the thirteenth century we are only permitted a few glimpses. Robert of Abberwick (Northumberland), the first known Head of House, for example, appears only once on the scene in connection with the College, in 1283.[3] Then for a couple of years he was a Fellow of Merton, before returning to the North Country, where he had his main career. He was Dean of the Collegiate Church of Auckland (County Durham) 1293–1304, and then Provost of Beverley (Yorkshire) until his death about 1306. There is little to put any flesh on the skeletal life which the records of his appointments mark in such tantalizing outline, apart from a few folios of a manuscript in the Library:[4] *De generacione et corrupcione secundum magistrum* R. *de Alburwic*. This is the earliest known work by a member of the College which is preserved.

Master Robert's migration to Merton is the earliest proven instance of

---

[1] The principal authority is A. B. Emden, *Biographical Register of the University of Oxford to A.D. 1500*, 1957–59, but see also id., 'The Last Pre-Reformation *Rotulus Benefactorum* and List of Obits of Balliol College', *Balliol College Record*, 1967, Supplement, and [R.] J. [A. I.] Catto, 'The First Century of Balliol Men, 1260–1360', in J. [M.] Prest (ed.), *Balliol Studies*, 1982.

[2] See, however, the rest of Ecclesiasticus 44: 1–15, the traditional lesson in Chapel in Gaudy time.

[3] See Ch. 1, n. 20.   [4] MS 313, fos. 160–6.

what was to become regular practice. The strict and exclusive adherence to the Faculty of Arts in Balliol drove its members elsewhere, if they were minded to take up advanced studies. Few were inclined to stay for long, even Heads of House. Walter of Fotheringhay's long and apparently unbroken residence (Fellow in 1273, Head in 1284 and until at least 1292) is very much the exception to the rule. Merton was the commonest destination of emigrants from Balliol, although other colleges accepted them occasionally. No regional ties were written into the Balliol Statutes, but the Founder's associations with the North naturally induced a slight bias, which was increased by the Felton and Somervyle benefactions. It became quite pronounced in the middle of the fourteenth century. This we can tell from the surnames of the members, which, in the manner of the times, often proclaim their origins—e.g. Hugh of Corbridge (Northumberland), three at least 'of Wakefield' (Yorkshire), William of Ferriby (Humberside), and many more. It was not so in the very early formative years, when we also find names of the Lincolnshire, Huntingdonshire, and Northamptonshire region, probably men following in the footsteps of Walter of Fotheringhay (Northamptonshire), who was a canon of Lincoln after leaving Balliol. More remarkable still, there was a trio of Cornishmen around 1300: Stephen of Cornwall, John of St Germans, and Hugh of St Ives. The West Country had no college of its own at this stage, and uncommitted Balliol embraced them. But when they had to leave because they had finished with the Faculty of Arts they would not have fitted easily into any other existing college. Master Stephen went to Paris to study medicine; John and Hugh joined the Benedictines and studied theology. The foundation of Exeter College, in 1314, gave the men from Devon and Cornwall a natural home, and those parts, which were to dominate Balliol in the eighteenth century, were not represented in it again for three hundred years.

The principal source of evidence for the early membership of Balliol comes from the deeds by which properties were conveyed to the College. Fortunately for us, title was in many cases passed from one group of Fellows to another a number of times, before coming to rest in the name of the College itself. Thus about 1303 Peter de Bradele, probably because he was resigning his place, formally transferred his share in some tenements to his colleague (*consocius*) William de Gotham; the transaction was witnessed by five who are named, and others who are not.[5] The study of other documents shows that two of those named were members, and also that it was normal practice to recite names in order of seniority. This enables us to speculate, with the aid of other scraps, that the five were as

---

[5] H. E. Salter, *Oxford Balliol Deeds*, 1913, p. 141.

follows:

Pontefract, Thomas of. MA; Franciscan; Visitor.
Burley, Adam de. MA; probably Visitor, but possibly Head of House.
Cornwall, Stephen of. BA; probably Head of House; he was by 1307, when he appears[6] as 'Stephanus de Cornubia, magister domus scolarium de Balliolo': this is the first use of the title Master.
Campsall, Richard of. BA; Fellow. See below.
Tendring, Geoffrey of. BA; Fellow.

Peter de Bradele, Adam de Burley, and Richard of Campsall are all known as active philosophers, and Dr Jeremy Catto has argued ingeniously that circumstantial links between the first two and the great Walter de Burley make Walter a Balliol man too.[7] William de Bonkes is yet another philosopher of this generation whose association with Balliol is recorded,[8] as a result of the part he played in real estate manœuvres to extend the College site. But these sightings are all accidental and incomplete. Only once in medieval times are we allowed to know the names of all the resident members. This is in 1321, from an agreement which recites the entire membership of the Society, from the Visitors down to the most junior Sophister.[9] The memorandum of a meeting to discuss the Statutes held only four years later[10] also enables us to identify a group of distinguished ex-members, because they attended this meeting as the College's elder statesmen. The College roll for 1321 which can be compiled from these, and other sources, is given below:

THE COLLEGE ROLL, 1321

Visitors

Lutterell, John. Chancellor of the University 1317–22. A controversial figure, ejected from the Chancellorship. Theologian. Nicholas of Tingewick had succeeded him as secular Visitor by 1325. Died 1335.
Reading, John of. Franciscan. Theologian; disciple of Duns Scotus. Robert of Leicester had succeeded him as Franciscan Visitor by 1325.

---

[6] Salter, op. cit., p. 117. He was subsequently an MD of Paris; his codex of the works of Galen is in the College Library (MS 231).
[7] Catto, op. cit., p. 10.
[8] Salter, op. cit., pp. 17–18.
[9] E. B. Fryde and J. R. L. Highfield, 'An Oxfordshire Deed of Balliol College', *Oxoniensia*, xx, 40.
[10] Salter, op. cit., p. 285.

Head of House

Waldeby, Thomas de. *Principalis*. MA. Henry de Seton had succeeded him by 1324. Still living 1359.

Masters of Arts

Seton, Henry de. Head of House (*custos*) by 1324, probably until 1327.
Felthorpe, Thomas of. Theologian. Still living 1343.
Retford, Richard de. Vacated his Fellowship by 1325. Fellow of University College in 1340. First Provost of The Queen's College, appointed by the founder, 1340. Died 1369.
Drayton, Robert of.

Bachelors of Arts

Severley, John de. Fellow of Merton by 1323. Ecclesiastical lawyer. Still living 1356.
Essholt, Henry de.
Bradwardine, Thomas. Fellow of Merton 1323. Distinguished theologian, philosopher, mathematician, and diplomat. Archbishop of Canterbury 1349; died of the plague four days after receiving the temporalities of the see.
Staveley, John of. Fellow of Merton (to which he left a notable collection of books) in 1323, still in 1335. Follower of Bradwardine, and student of St Augustine.
Barwe, William de.
Leverton, William of. Foundation Fellow of Oriel College 1326; Provost 1332–48. Doctor of Medicine by 1335. Died 1348.
Pipewell, Adam de. Fellow of Merton by 1325. Wrote on Bradwardine's theory of mechanics.
Luceby, Nicholas de. Head of House (*custos*) in 1328, but vacated by 1329.

Sophisters

Wakefield, Robert of. Fellow of Merton by 1324, still in 1338.
Brechowell, Maurice de.
Bokton, John de.

Distinguished Old Members

Burley, Walter de.[11] Born about 1275. Probably Fellow about 1295. Fellow of
   Merton by 1301. Distinguished and prolific philosopher. Still living 1344.
Campsall, Richard of. Fellow by 1304. Fellow of Merton in 1305, still in
   1326. Philosopher and theologian. Buried in Merton Chapel.
FitzRalph, Richard.[12] Fellow, vacated by 1321. Theologian, philosopher,
   and trenchant preacher; opponent of the Friars. Chancellor of the
   University 1332–4. Archbishop of Armagh 1346. Died 1360.
Horkstow, Walter of. Fellow before 1307. Fellow of Merton 1307, still in
   1324. Theologian. Buried in Merton Chapel.
Tingewick, Nicholas of. MA and beneficed by 1292. Visitor, and thus
   probably an old member, in 1325. Theologian and physician. Chief
   physician to Edward I, who once said that he owed his recovery from
   a long illness 'next under God, to Tingewick'.[13] Died by 1339.

Walter de Burley, Thomas Bradwardine, and Adam de Pipewell were
members of a school of natural philosophy (i.e. science) which was pre-
eminent in the first half of the fourteenth century.[14] Works such as Walter
de Burley's *De primo et ultimo instanti* and Bradwardine's *De proportionibus
velocitatum* laid the foundations of the thought from which the ideas
of Galileo and others eventually emerged. Because Walter de Burley,
Bradwardine, and most of the others associated with this school were of
Merton, it has often been called the Merton School. But this obscures the
fact that many of them were also Balliol men. Richard Swineshead,[15] for
example, was a Fellow of Balliol in 1344; his book *Liber calculationum*
earned him the title 'Calculator'.[16]

[11] Catto, op. cit., p. 10; C. Martin, 'Walter Burley', *Oxf. Hist. Soc.*, NS, xvi. 194.

[12] K. Walsh, *A Fourteenth-Century Scholar and Primate; Richard FitzRalph ...*, 1981. This
is a detailed and authoritative study, but it must be pointed out that the statement (p. 3)
that he was, with three others, compelled to resign in 1325 is erroneous. The document
in question (printed in Salter, op. cit., p. 285) makes it clear that they were quondam
Fellows by that date. FitzRalph had resigned his Fellowship before 2 Aug. 1321 (see Fryde
and Highfield, op. cit.). See also the *DNB*, etc.

[13] Emden, *Biographical Register*, entry for Tingewick. For additional references, see C. H.
Talbot and E. A. Hammond, *The Medical Practitioners in Medieval England*, 1965, pp. 229–31.

[14] E. D. Sylla, 'The Oxford Calculators', in N. [J. K.] Kretzmann, A. [J. P.] Kenny, and
J. Pinborg (eds.), *The Cambridge History of Later Medieval Philosophy*, 1982, p. 540.

[15] There was also a John Swineshead, and a Roger Swineshead, both of whom were
active in the same period as Richard Swineshead, leading to some confusion: J. A.
Weisheipl, 'Roger Swynshed...[16] ', *Oxf. Hist. Soc.*, NS, xvi. 231. The Swineshead who is
mentioned in Balliol deed B.1.12 (1344) was definitely Richard (Salter, op. cit., p. 26).

[16] Simon Bredon, a noted writer on arithmetic and medicine, is a further example. He
was a Fellow of Balliol before proceeding to Merton, and he left three of his books to
Balliol (R. A. B. Mynors, *Catalogue of the Manuscripts of Balliol College Oxford*, 1963, p. xiii).

An alleged portrait of John Wyclif hangs in the Hall. It is but a copy
of a work of imagination. Even if his likeness was ever taken, it is unlikely
that it could have survived, bearing in mind fifteenth-century persecution
of his followers and desecration of his grave. Master Richard Jenkyns had
it made and hung to assert his Protestant opposition in the face of the
beginnings of a Roman revival in 1828.[17] Wyclif was a BA Fellow of
Merton in 1356, but within the next four years he became an MA, and
Master of Balliol.[18] His is a unique example of migration from Merton to
Balliol, in sharp contrast to the many contrary instances. It has been
thought that his election to the Mastership implies that he had been a
member of Balliol before 1356, but there is nothing to corroborate this,
which would in any case still leave the puzzle of his appearance at Merton
in 1356 unexplained. In the early summer of 1360, 'Magister Johannes de
Wyclif magister domus scolarium Aule vocate la Baillolhalle de Oxon'
made a court appearance concerning a dispute over the rent of a St
Lawrence Jewry tenement.[19] The following year he carried through the
impropriation of the Rectory of Abbotsley by the College. The deed
appointing him the College's representative in the matter was executed in
the Chapel on 7 April 1361:[20] a related document of the following day
describes him 'magister sive custos Collegii Aule de Balliolo'.[21] A month
later he was admitted Rector of Fillingham on the College's presentation,[22]
and he probably resigned the Mastership then, although his successor
John Hugate does not show himself as such until 1366. In 1363 Wyclif
obtained an episcopal licence to return to the University notwithstanding
his parochial responsibilities, and he rented a room at The Queen's College.
Archbishop Islip appointed him Warden of Canterbury College in 1365.
This new college had recently been established for the higher education
of both the secular and regular clergy. The first warden (1362) was a
monk, but the arrangements were a failure because the seculars and
regulars quarrelled. The constitution was revised and Wyclif was put in
charge, but the regulars were reluctant to accept him. When the Ben-
edictine Simon Langham became Archbishop in 1366, he moved to get
rid of him. There was a prolonged dispute. Wyclif appealed to the Curia,

[17] Bodleian MS Finch d. 10, fo. 47; Richard Jenkyns, writing to Robert Finch (1783–
1839, Balliol 1802; *DNB*) on 9 April 1828, mentions that he had lately given 'the
College a Portrait of Wycliffe copied from a supposed original in the possession of Lord
Denbigh'.
[18] A. [J. P.] Kenny, *Wyclif*, 1985; A. [J. P.] Kenny (ed.), *Wyclif in his Times*, 1986.
[19] E.7.14; see also B.22.60.
[20] E.7.9.
[21] E.7.12. For other documents mentioning Wyclif see E.1.38B, E.7.10–11, 13, and
15–16.
[22] Emden, *Biographical Register*, entry for Wyclif.

IHON
WICKLYF

1. John Wyclif, Master about 1360.

but the final decision from Rome in 1370 went against him. Throughout this upheaval he was establishing himself as Oxford's leading philosopher and theologian. His philosophical writings belong to this period. The *Summa de ente*, which was finished about 1372 and is his major work, comprises two books. The first is concerned with being and man; the second with the attributes of God. In the second book he crosses the boundary (scarcely discernible to the layman) from philosophy into theology. At about the same time as he was turning to theology, he began to have influence beyond the academic world. Through the commendation of John of Gaunt, he entered the service of the King in 1371 or 1372, and was drawn into Church–State controversy—in particular over papal claims to rights of taxation and appointment in England. His views found favour at court, but his writings became ever more direct in their attacks on the Church. He denounced its wealth, its corruption, and its indulgences for sin given at a price; he proclaimed some of its doctrines, like that on transubstantiation, philosophically indefensible and idolatrous; and he condemned the Papacy and its trappings. He was accused of numerous errors by the Church authorities in 1377. The Chancellor of the University declared that his 'theses were true enough though they sounded badly to the ear', and Wyclif survived, but in 1380 his teaching on the Eucharist was pronounced heretical by a commission and he retired to his rectory at Lutterworth.

One of the principal treatises of his theological *Summa* was 'De veritae scripturae', 'On the truth of Scripture', in which the authority of the Bible and its freedom from error are laid down. It was a logical development from this, and his views on Church authority, to the idea that all must have access to the teaching of the scriptures for themselves, a principle which in turn meant translation from the language of the clergy into that of the masses: 'The language of a book, whether Hebrew, Greek, Latin or English, is the vesture of the law of God. And in whatever clothing its message is most truly understood by the faithful, in that is the book most reasonably to be accepted.'[23] It is as the first English translator of the complete Vulgate that he has been practically canonized by Protestant writers. In fact his responsibility for it was somewhat more distant than this simplified popular view supposes, but it was his thinking and leadership which gave it birth. He died, and was buried, at Lutterworth in 1384. Such was the power of his ideas, and the threat to the Church of the Lollard movement which they began, that his opponents condemned him posthumously, dug up his body, and burnt it, scattering his ashes into the river Swift. His doctrines spread to Europe, especially Bohemia.

[23] Kenny, *Wyclif*, p. 65.

They were an important influence on the Hussites, and eventually on Martin Luther. In England Lollardy lingered on until the sixteenth-century, when most of the reforms Wyclif had urged were carried out, and the established religion fell into line with his teachings.

4

The Fifteenth Century

IN 1386 Richard II gave a licence for the conveyance to the Master and Fellows of three tenements and a garden which were contiguous with their house (*mansus*), 'for the enlargement of their said house'.[1] The properties concerned were to the north-west, and the transaction was part of the piecemeal territorial expansion which continued for the next hundred years, at the end of which the southern half of the present site of the College was wholly in its hands. With a little more space at its disposal, Balliol could now aspire to grander buildings like those of Merton and New College, and around 1400 it began to lay out a quadrangle. Although no part of this quadrangle survives intact and two-thirds of it has been altogether replaced, the dimensions and general plan of the present Front Quadrangle were settled by 1480. Our knowledge of the buildings is very hazy, being based very largely on observations made considerably later. The chief witness is Anthony Wood, writing about 1660,[2] but we also have a sketch of 1566 by John Berebloc, and a very detailed engraving by David Loggan, showing the College in 1675. All of these saw a quadrangle with a relatively new Chapel, but otherwise things were probably still essentially as in the late fifteenth century.

The east range, a simple residential block, was probably the first to be built. The west side, comprising the Hall, etc., was complete by 1430, when former Master Thomas Chace, Chancellor of the University, gave a window for the Hall. Robert Wombwell and Thomas Barry, both quondam Fellows, were also commemorated in stained glass, which no doubt signified financial or practical contributions. In Wombwell's case it may have been the latter, as he was one of the Visitors (*rectores atque visitatores*) whilst the building works were in progress, and in that capacity had to help adjudicate a dispute in 1415.[3] A College Meeting (*concilium*) had been convened in the Chapel because the College was in debt, and it

[1] H. E. Salter, *Oxford Balliol Deeds*, 1913, p. 71.

[2] A. Wood, *The History and Antiquities of the Colleges and Halls in the University of Oxford*, ed. J. Gutch, 1786, p. 70.

[3] B.22.38. This document provides a unique record of an early College Meeting. Such meetings were probably always held in Chapel. The word used for the meeting—*concilium/consilium*—was reintroduced into College jargon about 1895, for the informal College business meetings held on Wednesday evenings in term time.

had been necessary to pledge certain valuables—most likely books, although the College did also have a little plate which it might have used.[4] The debts had arisen partly from the building programme and partly from legal expenses. The Meeting had decided to delegate power to take such steps as they thought fit to Master Thomas Chace and Bursars (*thesaurarii*) Robert Acclum and John Warthill. The matter had come to the Visitors because a dissident party, claiming the proxy of an absentee, objected to the creation of a committee. The majority decision was confirmed and the matter was left as originally resolved. Unfortunately, the record of this dispute is an isolated document. There are no accounts or memoranda of corporate decisions to throw further light on College affairs until well into the sixteenth century.

The west side of the quadrangle, although completed structurally by 1430, was embellished later, at the expense of George Neville (Archbishop of York 1464–76) and William Gray (Bishop of Ely 1454–78), whose arms were part of the decoration. Gray was responsible for the oriel window of the solar (now the Master's dining-room) over the old Buttery: his arms appeared on the three corbels beneath the window, and were repeated there in the nineteenth-century restoration. Another striking feature which survives is the ornate arch which framed the entrance to the passage at the south end of the Hall: its principal features were preserved in a new arch over the Chapel passage opening when the Hall was modified about 1792. Otherwise only the shell of the west side remains, with vestigial indications here and there of the original details.[5] The Hall was much modified in the late eighteenth century and abandoned to the needs of the Library in the nineteenth, the transmogrification being completed within living memory by the insertion of a mezzanine floor.

Of the south range which made up the forefront of the College, little can be said. It was predominantly residential, with the gatehouse tower as its centre-piece. The porch had a vaulted roof into which the insignia of various benefactors were worked. The arms of Thomas Kempe, Bishop of London 1450–89, were seen there by Wood, who also noted that 'over the gate are carved in stone, under the ridge which parts the upper chamber from the roof, two bells, and another at the top of the tabernacular works over the pedestal'. The bells were thought to be a play on the name of William Bell, Master about 1483–95, and point to the completion of the

---

[4] For example, William Rede, Bishop of Chichester, bequeathed (*inter alia*) a cup, presumably of precious metal, in 1385: R. A. B. Mynors, *Catalogue of the Manuscripts of Balliol College Oxford*, 1963, p. xiv.

[5] The original Buttery arches, which had been blocked up and plastered over by about 1792, were exposed during Library conversion work in 1959: one of them can be seen at the south end of the Lower Library. Another original arch is still *in situ* just inside the present College Office door.

building having taken place in his time. The whole building was demolished in the nineteenth century,[6] but many aspects of it were transmitted
to its successor, from the grander features, such as the vaulted porch and
tower above, down to the repetition of the Bell rebus high above the gate
on the quadrangle side.

The Library, at first-floor level with chambers beneath,[7] ran between
the Hall and the Chapel, on the north side of the quadrangle. It was built
in two phases. The bays nearest the Hall were credited to Thomas Chace
by a legend in one of the windows.[8] The other side-windows also commemorated benefactors,[9] and at the east end there was a window, showing
the Master and Fellows kneeling before St Catherine.[10] The date on Chace's
window was 1431, but the west end may have been nearing completion
in 1423 when Roger Whelpdale, sometime Fellow, and Bishop of Carlisle
1419–20, made his will, leaving the College six books and money to
provide a set of Library keys for the Fellows.[11] A generation later the
Library was extended eastward by Robert Abdy, Master about 1475–83,
who added several more bays, following Chace's design.[12] Only the walls
and windows remain. Externally a crenellated parapet and new low-
pitched roof were imposed in the late eighteenth century, and at about
the same time bookshelves of the modern kind replaced the last of the
medieval two sided lectern-desks. There was originally a series of these

[6] The stonework immediately over the gates, and some of the bosses from the porch
vaulting, were preserved by assembly into a tomb-like decoration in the centre of the
Fellows' Garden.

[7] These chambers are now the Old Common Room complex; there was a communal
room here in 1676, and perhaps even as early as 1459, when deed B.22.48 was transacted
'in quadam bassa camera subtus librariam collegii'.

[8] 'Condidit hanc edem Thomas Chace ... ' The window contained not only his arms,
but also those of the University, because he was Chancellor. The panel showing the
University arms survives: it is their earliest known representation.

[9] The early buildings of the College were liberally adorned both inside and out with the
arms and symbols of its many benefactors, many of whom were not otherwise recorded.
Much of the heraldic glass survives, although it has been moved about a great deal, and
many inscriptions are lost. The admirable practice of documenting armigerous benefactors
in this way was copied by nineteenth-century architects, with the result that there are well
over a hundred different heraldic shields and other devices to be found about the College.
An exhaustive analysis was made by L. K. Hindmarsh in 1949: see the Hindmarsh
manuscripts.

[10] This window, unfortunately very incomplete, is now in the Chapel.

[11] Mynors, op. cit., p. xix; the inscription in MS 210 proves Whelpdale to have been a
Fellow.

[12] There was an inscription in the window nearest the Chapel on the north side which
is given by Wood as 'Orate pro bono statu et anima Magistri Roberti Abdy Magistri hujus
Collegii, qui istam partem Bibliothece construxit anno ...'. Abdy's will was proved at
Oxford on 12 July 1483 (*Surtees Soc.* xlv. 284). He was buried in the church of St Mary
Magdalen, where there was a memorial brass, which is now lost.

2. Robert Abdy, Master about 1480: an impression of his memorial
brass, which was formerly in the church of St Mary Magdalen,
Oxford.

on each side of the Library, at right angles to the walls and alternating
with the windows, which were designed to throw as much light as possible
on the reading areas. Each desk housed perhaps a couple of dozen volumes,
on shelves beneath the sloping surface, chained to the desk in such a way
that only a few could be brought up and consulted together. To a
considerable extent these details are conjectural, but they are corroborated
by many fragments of evidence and by the various dimensions of the
place, all of which point to conformity with the usual pattern of late
medieval libraries, except in orientation. A north–south alignment was
generally favoured, because this gave the best early morning light. The
east–west site which was in fact chosen may have been picked so that the
Library could have clear ground belonging to the College on both sides
for light, security, and peace. The suburban area in which the College
stood was noisy and squalid;[13] the further from the main thoroughfare the
better.

The cost of all this architectural activity was borne by many benefactors.
Chief among them was a select category of alumni—men of noble birth
who had been taken into the College as boys for the completion of their
education. These were never 'on the Foundation'—receipt of a charitable
dole would have been beneath them even without the disqualification of
their wealth—but were much more by way of being paying guests. To
begin with it was no doubt an occasional matter of a spare chamber or
two being used in this way, when there was an opportunity of generating a
little extra revenue, and of raising the social tone. Occasional opportunism,
however, became self-perpetuating practice. Some of those thus brought
into the fold became firmly attached to the College, repaying with interest
the hospitality and friendship extended to them in their student days. Only
four can be named with certainty. William Gray, and his kinsman George
Neville, were benefactors of this class who have already been mentioned.
To them can be added Robert Beaumont[14] and Edward de la Pole.[15]
Seventeenth-century antiquarians extrapolated boldly from these
instances, on the thinnest of evidence, and assumed a Balliol attachment
for a number of other distinguished figures who had been associated with
the University but for whom no other College seemed to make a claim.

---

[13] About 1380, for example, it was necessary for the College to petition for closure of a
slaughterhouse nearby (on the corner of present-day Broad Street and Magdalen Street)
because the clamour of the animals was interfering with their studies, and the decomposing
offal which was being thrown into the street was filthy, smelly, and infectious: *Oxf. Hist.
Soc.*, NS, iv. 254.

[14] Probably of Balliol in 1421, when he was Senior Proctor. Of noble birth. Died about
1460. Benefactor: B.14.12. His name appears in the *Rotulus Benefactorum*: A. B. Emden,
Balliol College Record, 1967, Supplement.

[15] Nephew of Edward IV. Probably resided 1481–2. Died 1485. Benefactor. His name
appears in the *Rotulus Benefactorum*: Emden, op. cit.

Those thus wished uncritically upon the College include four whom it would be gratifying to accept: Humphrey, Duke of Gloucester;[16] Cardinal John Morton;[17] Sir Thomas More;[18] and John Tiptoft, Earl of Worcester.[19] Unfortunately, the best that can be said about these assignments is that if they did have a connection with Balliol, then it was slight. Certainly they did not make a mark to compare with William Gray's. He kept the College in his sights for nearly fifty years, and was perhaps the most important single figure of its history in this century.

William Gray was born about 1412–15, the third son of Sir Thomas Gray of Heaton in Northumberland, by Alice, a daughter of Ralph Neville, the first Earl of Westmorland.[20] Thomas Gray was executed in 1416, but his brother, another William Gray, became Bishop of London (1426) and took his namesake nephew under his wing. About 1430 he was sent to study at Oxford and took up residence at Balliol, which may have been chosen partly because of its Northumberland connections, and partly because of his uncle's *ex-officio* role as its supreme Visitor. He graduated as a Master of Arts in due course, but retained his rooms in College until 1442, holding office as Chancellor of the University 1440–2. During this time he began to collect and commission manuscript books, showing an early humanist interest in having some of Duke Humphrey's very new donations copied. Late in 1442 he left for the Continent, matriculating at the University of Cologne on 1 December of that year, together with

[16] His arms were shown in a Library window, but with an inscription implying that he had made his contribution as a memorial to John Patrick, his 'quondam Valette de Wardroba' (see Wood, op. cit., p. 94). Duke Humphrey might have been persuaded to do this by Thomas Chace, who was his chaplain for a period. The tradition that Duke Humphrey was educated at Balliol seems to have been stated first by J. Bale, *Scriptorium Ilustrium maiori Brytanniae, nunc Angliam & Scotiam Vocant: Catalogus*, Basle, 1557, p. 583.

[17] His membership seems to have been generally accepted, but is not corroborated. His arms were nevertheless incorporated in the decoration of the lodge porch in the nineteenth century.

[18] It would be easier to accept that he was a member of the College if proof of Cardinal Morton's connection were evident, as More spent some of his boyhood in Morton's household. More's birth near the Balliol parish of St Lawrence Jewry, the fact that he is known to have lectured there, and his close association with Cuthbert Tunstall (who was definitely a Balliol man), are the only other circumstantial props which can be found. Furthermore, there is a conflicting (albeit also weak) tradition that he was a member of Canterbury College (now Christ Church): W. A. Pantin, *Canterbury College Oxford*, iv, 1985 (*Oxf. Hist. Soc.*, NS, xxx), p. 99. On More see the *DNB* etc., and A. [J. P.] Kenny, *Thomas More*, 1983.

[19] It is actually well established that he resided at University College 1440–3, although he did have Balliol connections. George Neville was his brother-in-law, and he was closely acquainted with both William Gray and John Free.

[20] For detailed accounts, with references, of William Gray and the other Balliol humanists, see the *DNB* (under Grey, William), Mynors, op. cit., and R. Weiss, *Humanism in England*, 2nd edn., 1957.

Nicholas Saxton and Richard Bole, two Fellows of Balliol who were registered as his *familiares*. They stayed there about two years before Gray moved on to Italy in pursuit of humanistic studies, visiting Florence, Padua, and Ferrara in turn. Saxton, and possibly Bole as well, travelled on with him. In 1445 Gray was appointed the King's representative at the Roman Curia, a position which was to keep him in Italy for most of the next decade. All this time Gray was collecting manuscripts, and he must have had a substantial library by the time he returned to England in 1453. He was appointed Bishop of Ely in 1454, holding that office until he died. Although active and conscientious in the affairs of Church and State, he retained his scholarly interests, accumulating yet more books, and maintained his Balliol links by helping numerous Fellows of the College with patronage and preferment. Richard Bole was one who benefited.[21] It is not known when Bole returned from Italy to England, but he did so well ahead of Gray. By 1449 he reappears as a chaplain to the Archbishop of York, and in the summer of 1450 he must have been in or near London, because in July Balliol appointed him to act on its behalf in some business to do with the City living of St Lawrence Jewry. After Gray's consecration as Bishop of Ely, Bole's name begins to turn up in his sphere again. In 1467, Bole was appointed Archdeacon of Ely, a dignity he held until his death in 1477. He was buried in Wilburton Church near Ely, where his memorial brass survives. His manuscripts he gave or left to Balliol. Only about a dozen can now be identified, but they are enough to reveal that he was a bibliophile and scholar with the same humanistic leanings as his great patron. Three are written in his own hand, as can be seen by the personal touch with which he concluded one of them: 'Finit Salustius in Jurgurtino per R. Bole 20 Februarii Anno 1460.' Robert Thwaytes,[22] Master about 1450 and Chancellor of the University in 1446, was another protégé of William Gray's; but the best known of the Fellows helped by him was John Free, who went to Ferrara in 1456 at Gray's expense in order to study at the school of Guarino da Verona, and stayed in Italy, becoming a notable humanist scholar. Although not the first member of the College to be passionately interested in the new learning, he was the first Englishman to contribute significantly to it by his own writings, and a pioneer in the study of Greek literature in Greek.

It was no doubt kinship which brought George Neville to Gray's college: he came into residence about 1448. By 1453 he was Chancellor of the University, and was soon advanced to the See of Exeter, becoming Archbishop of York in 1464. Popular accounts of him have dwelt on the

---

[21] Mynors, op. cit., p. xlvi.

[22] His will was proved on 31 Oct. 1458 (*Surtees Soc.* cxvi., 53). William Gray was one of his executors, and was no doubt instrumental in passing his books to the College: several can be identified (Mynors, op. cit., p. xx).

prodigiously extravagant banquet[23] he threw to celebrate one of the upward steps in his meteoric career, but he deserves a better remembrance. He was a prominent humanist patron and, like Gray, a major Balliol benefactor. Through his generosity and good offices the financial security of the College was substantially reinforced, by the acquisition of property in Oxford, Moreton (near Thame), and London.[24]

Towards the end of his life, Gray arranged for his collection of manuscript books to pass to the College. Perhaps he had a hand with Robert Abdy in extending the Library to accommodate the collection in his lifetime; perhaps he bequeathed the manuscripts in his will and the extension was Abdy's work alone. He died in 1478 and was buried in his cathedral of Ely. The ornate canopied tomb erected over him has long since disappeared, but his literary monument survives with few losses. Nearly two hundred manuscript volumes of his are still in the College Library. The majority of his extant gifts contain theological treatises, but he also gave a rich collection of classical and humanistic works. Most of them bear the inscription 'Liber domus de Balliolo in Oxon. ex dono Willemi Gray Eliensis episcopi': every one a better memorial than a tombstone.

[23] H. Savage, *Balliofergus*, 1668, p. 105. The bill of fare reported stretches the credulity a little. More than thirty thousand creatures are supposed to have perished for the feast, including eighty fat oxen, three thousand geese, four thousand woodcock, three hundred pike, four thousand rabbits, and four porpoises, all washed down with more than a thousand hogsheads of beer (over half a million pints) and four hundred and sixteen hogsheads of wine (at least a hundred thousand modern bottles).

[24] On Neville, see the *DNB*, etc. His name appeared in the pre-Reformation *Rotulus Benefactorum* (Emden, op. cit.) but was overlooked, along with several others, when the Bidding Prayer in current use (see the Epilogue) was composed. This was probably only about a century ago, although it has been revised from time to time by the addition of the names of modern major benefactors.

Fig. 3 The arms of William Gray, on the masonry supporting the oriel window of the Master's dining room.

5
Bishop Fox's Statutes

SIR PHILIP SOMERVYLE 's Statutes, as amended by Simon Sudbury (acting on a papal commission), guided the College through the fifteenth century. It will be recalled that this code was a conservative one, incorporating many features of Dervorguilla's.[1] Regarding the subjects which might be studied by members, it was restrictive. The College was placed under the supervision of two Visitors, who in this century were called Rectors. They were not the supreme authority in College affairs, however: Sudbury had reserved this for his successors in the See of London, who were also invested with the authority of making further alterations in, or additions to, the Statutes. They used this discretion at least twice, in 1433 and 1470,[2] but only to make modest adjustments in the regulations for the Mastership and for disputations. In other respects there was no change. The Rectors were chosen by the College, but it was prescribed that they should be outsiders—one a Franciscan, and the other an ordinary senior member of the University (i.e. a secular person, not belonging to a religious order). About 1500, the Master and his colleagues complained to the Pope about them, and asked him to order a complete revision of the Statutes. The Rectors had, it was alleged, attempted to enforce the observation of obsolete regulations, which had resulted in the *de facto* expulsion of some members. It was intolerable that strangers had interfered in matters which were really none of their business. The assertion that the Rectors were strangers is difficult to understand, in view of the fact that they were appointed by the College itself—and on at least two occasions it had appointed ex-members to the secular post. Robert Wombwell (ex-Fellow) and Richard Rotherham (ex-Master) are known to have been Rectors in 1414 and 1433 respectively.[3] Neither the petition to Rome, nor any direct records of the discord which provoked it, have yet been discovered, but the gist of the College's complaint is recited, by way of introduction, in the response which Pope Julius II made on 13 August 1504:[4]

---

[1] See Chapter 2.
[2] H. E. Salter, *Oxford Balliol Deeds*, 1913, p. 102.
[3] B.22.38; Salter, op. cit., p. 302.
[4] Transcribed in Salter, op. cit., p. 310 and translated in F. de Paravicini, *Early History of Balliol College*, 1891, p. 238.

... A petition lately presented to Us, on behalf of Our beloved sons, the Master and Scholars of the College Hall or House of Balliol, in the University of Oxford and Diocese of Lincoln, stated that Simon, Bishop of London, of blessed memory, by virtue of a certain Apostolic Letter ... decreed and ordained, among other things, that whenever a new Master of the Scholars of the said College was elected, he should, immediately after his election, enjoin upon all the Scholars or Fellows of the said College the election of two Rectors (viz. one of the Order of Friars Minor and the other a secular Master of the said University but not a member of the said College); and that though this Statute and Ordinance was drafted, so it is believed, with pious intentions, yet the said Rectors thus elected interfere in many matters which do not pertain to them, and often grievously wrong the Scholars of the College, pestering and disturbing them, and endeavouring to compel them to observe certain Statutes which are so old that no man remembers when they were first made and which have already passed into disuse ...; and that they have ... unjustly expelled *de facto* from the said College certain Scholars, who were obliged to withdraw from the study of philosophy and theology despite being admitted into the said College for that purpose; and that ... it is necessary for the peace and tranquility of the Scholars aforesaid that the said Statutes should one and all be revised, reformed, corrected, and amended ...

This is discreetly vague, like a bad character reference. No names, dates, or other details are given for the rumpus which led to the petition, and specific accusations are avoided. The Rectors are blamed, but three years later it was alleged that 'a certain Visitor' had thrown the Master and Fellows into such confusion that 'the College would have collapsed into final and everlasting ruin, had not someone applied healing hands in time'.[5] The Visitor (*visitator*) in this instance might have been one of the Rectors, but if so why was the Bishop of London not called in? He had previously acted as overlord, but he is not mentioned anywhere in the Pope's answer to the petition and, as we shall see, his role was abolished altogether in the new Statutes which eventually emerged. It seems probable that the truth is that the College felt oppressed by the whole of the visitatorial system to which it was subject—no other college had threefold supervision to contend with. When a particular Bishop of London made a special nuisance of himself, this was the last straw and the College decided to go over his head to the Pope for constitutional reform. This is unfortunately as far as we can take our speculation with any confidence, as we do not know the exact date of the dispute, and there were three Bishops of London in quick succession at about the right time.

The Pope granted the College's request, and appointed the Bishops of Carlisle and Winchester to examine all the Statutes given to the College

---

[5] See the preamble to the 1507 Statutes, printed for the Royal commissioners, 1853.

over the years. They were allowed sweeping powers to make whatever changes they thought desirable, or even to draft completely new Statutes. Of the Bishop of Carlisle we hear no more. Bishop Richard Fox of Winchester took on the task alone, choosing to put aside all previous Statutes, and set the College up for a fresh start with new ones.

Little is known about Richard Fox's early years, but there is a consistent tradition that he was educated at Magdalen College. His first definite appearance is at the age of about thirty-five in 1484, when Richard III sought to bar his institution to the Vicarage of Stepney, on the grounds that he was abroad with the rebel Henry Tudor. After Bosworth Field, Fox rose rapidly to be one of Henry VII's most trusted and powerful ministers, receiving in turn the bishoprics of Exeter (1487), Bath and Wells (1492), Durham (1494), and Winchester (1501), in recognition of his support. He was politically active until 1516, but from about 1500 he was much engaged in educational matters. He was elected Chancellor of the University of Cambridge in 1500, was Master of Pembroke College, Cambridge, 1507–18, and, as an executor of Lady Margaret Beaufort, had a hand in the foundation of St John's College, Cambridge.[6] In Oxford he was *ex officio* Visitor of Magdalen and New College, but is best known as the founder of Corpus Christi College, his principal memorial, in 1517. He was not himself the author of any major work, but he was thoroughly in sympathy with the new learning of the Renaissance, and had amicable contact with several of its leading figures. He died in 1528, active in the consolidation of his newly founded college until shortly before his death, despite blindness and increasing infirmity.[7]

Fox was clearly well qualified to undertake the revision of the Balliol Statutes. Three years elapsed between the Pope's commission and the completion of the job. Much debate and consultation were involved. It is likely that Fox's friend, John Claymond of Magdalen, later to be the first President of Corpus Christi, acted as his agent throughout these discussions.[8] No doubt there was also much study of the statutes of other colleges. Fox would already have been familiar as Visitor with the statutes of New College and Magdalen—especially the latter, as Magdalen was unsettled at this time and his active intervention was necessary in 1506. It is also known that in 1506 he was interested in the statutes drawn up by

---

[6] There is a present-day alliance between St John's College, Cambridge, and Balliol under whch the two colleges extend hospitality to each other's members from time to time. This pleasant arrangement has no ancient basis, however: it was established this century (College Meeting minutes, 4 Nov. 1931 and 12 Nov. 1944).

[7] *Letters of Richard Fox 1486–1527*, ed. P. S. and H. M. Allen, 1929; T. Fowler, *The History of Corpus Christi College*, 1893 (*Oxf. Hist. Soc.*, xxv), chapter 1.

[8] Salter, op. cit., p. 312.

3. Richard Fox, author of the College Statutes, 1507.

Bishop John Fisher for Christ's College, Cambridge.[9] It might therefore be expected that one or more of these colleges would have provided Fox with a model for Balliol, but this is not so. Nor can many similarities be found between the statutes he gave to Balliol in 1507, and those he formulated for Corpus Christi a decade later. Although the new Statutes are completely coherent and original, they are a radical adaptation of earlier Statutes to meet changed circumstances, rather than an unfettered novelty.

The new Statutes came into effect soon after 16 July 1507,[10] when Fox sent a mandate for the members of the College to take an oath before John Claymond to observe them.[11]

After a brief preamble summarizing the circumstances of the revision, Fox launched into an elaborate metaphor, in which the College is represented as a human body. The Master is the head and centre of the senses. The Fellows are the abdomen and thighs, giving the body weight; the Chaplains are the ribs, enclosing the vital organs; the Senior Fellow is the neck, providing the natural link between the head and the rest. The Deans are the shoulders, where burdens can be put; the Bursars, as the men of business, are the arms and the hands. The servants are the body's feet and must go wherever they are bidden. The Scholars are closely linked to the Fellows, but must also do as they are told and perform some menial tasks, so they are between the Fellows and the servants, i.e. the legs. The metaphor reappears again and again throughout the Statutes.

The collegiate body was seen by Fox as complete without any Rectors, who, in his most fundamental change, vanish completely. In place of them and the Bishop of London, the College was given the unqualified right of electing a single Visitor itself. Furthermore, this Visitor was only entitled to appear in the College once a year unless he was expressly invited. In the anatomical metaphor he is cast in the role of the physician who is called in when the body is afflicted. Fox himself was the first Visitor under the new Statutes.[12]

The Master, who had to be more than thirty years old, learned in theology, and in priest's orders, was to be elected by the Fellows, the Senior Fellow convening the election in the Chapel. The procedure, which was very similar to that dictated by Somervyle's Statutes, was specified in great detail. Other things being equal, one who was, or had been, a Fellow was to be favoured: 'eumque extraneo praeferant, caeteris paribus, qui in

---

[9] Allen and Allen, op. cit., p. 35.

[10] The Statutes of 1507 were transcribed and printed for the Royal Commissioners, 1853, and extracts are translated in de Paravicini, op. cit.

[11] Salter, op. cit., p. 312.

[12] Thomas Cisson, for example, was presented to him for confirmation as Master in 1511.

dicto Collegio Socius nutritus et exercitatus fuerit.' If the votes were equally divided between two candidates the most junior Fellow's was to be discounted. The election made, the new Master was to be presented to the Visitor and sworn in. His duties and powers were carefully defined. Residence for forty days of each term was obligatory except by leave of the Visitor, but the office was made more attractive by allowing the Master to hold a College living to augment his stipend of forty shillings. He had general oversight of all College business, studies, and discipline. Fellows and Scholars alike were admonished to show him filial obedience and he, for his part, was to be a good father ('bonus paterfamilias').

Until this date the terms *socii* and *scolares* had been used more or less interchangeably for all the twenty-eight members supported by the Foundation as redefined by Somervyle. Fox reduced the number of Foundationers to about twenty (which enabled the allowances for commons to be increased) and divided them into two clearly defined groups: the ten Fellows (*socii*), as before, and the Scholars (now called *scholastici*).[13] Vacancies in the Fellowship were to be filled by election, each existing Fellow having one vote and the Master having two, with the same provision for equally divided voting as in the election of a Master. Candidates had to be born in wedlock ('de legitimo thoro natus'), of good character, and in need of financial support. Normally they should have taken the BA degree, but this qualification was to be waived if they were Scholars of the House, who were also to be given preference, other things being equal ('si quisquam e Collegii Scholasticis moribus et scientia aequari extraneo poterit, is in electione praeponatur').These stipulations apart, elections to Fellowships were to be open and based on academic merit. Regional and personal connections were not to be taken into consideration, and any candidate attempting to procure a place by bribery or influence was to be *ipso facto* ineligible. All new Fellows were to serve a year's probation, although this seems to have been a mere formality. Two of the Fellowships could only be held by men in priest's orders who served as Chaplains, and all Fellows were under an obligation to take orders within four years of graduation as MA, which was not to be delayed.

Scholars were to be less than eighteen years old on admission, and accomplished at plainsong and grammar ('in plano cantu et grammatica eruditi satis'). Otherwise there were no restrictions on eligibility. The Master and Fellows each had a Scholar assigned to him, and the Scholars

---

[13] The number of Scholars has been stated by many previous writers as ten. The number is not actually stated in the 1507 Statutes, but it is explicit that the Master and Fellows were to have one each. Since there were to be ten Fellows, eleven Scholarships must have been intended initially. In any case, the Statutes provided for the number of Foundationers to be adjusted according to income.

had to wait on them at table, in return for which the broken victuals
were theirs. They were probably also meant to receive an allowance for
commons, although this is not stated. It seems from later accounts to have
been set at half the Fellows' rate. When a Scholar left, or was promoted,
the senior member to whom he had been attached had the right of
nominating his successor.

It was evidently a community organized on medieval monastic lines
which Fox set out to perpetuate. The Scholars, and presumably the Fellows
too, were to wear clerical garb and be tonsured. Attendance at the divine
offices was rigidly prescribed. A passage of scripture was to be read aloud
during dinner. Conversation was to be in Latin. Prayers and masses for
the Founders and benefactors were to remain the College's duty. The
conduct and behaviour of all members was to be firmly regulated. The
gates should be locked at eight in winter and nine in summer, and the
keys put into the custody of the Master until the next morning. Nobody
was to spend the night in the town. Arguments and quarrels were to be
avoided and no arms of any kind were to be carried within University
limits, except on leaving for, or returning from, a journey outside the city.
Bows and arrows were allowed for recreation, however.[14] Members were
forbidden to enter taverns or alehouses except when invited by a distinguished visitor who could not be refused. Extravagance was frowned
upon and limits were set on expenditure at feasts. Diversions such as
entertainments given by travelling players or jugglers were specifically
prohibited. Minor transgressions were to be dealt with informally by the
Master and one of the Deans. Serious offences—that is, breach of any of
the rules mentioned above, conviction of a crime, adultery, fornication,
etc.—were to be brought before a court comprising the Master, a Bursar,
a Dean, and two other senior Fellows, which had the power to fine, or
expel.

It was expected that Fellows of the College would be 'devoted to study
and learning', working only at logic, philosophy, or theology, except that
they could take up canon law during the long vacation, Leave was severely
restricted, to eight weeks in each year (the regulation was the same for
Scholars). The ordinary allowance for a Fellow was raised from eleven
pence to sixteen pence a week, with an extra fourpence in festival weeks
as before. In addition they were to receive small annual stipends according
to their degrees: twenty-eight shillings and eightpence for an MA, eighteen
and twopence for a BA. Over and above this they would have received

---

[14] Lionel Jackson, a Fellow who died in 1512, had among his personal property 'on bow
with xxi arows': A. B. Emden, 'The Last Pre-Reformation *Rotulus Benefactorum* and Lists
of Obits of Balliol College', *Balliol College Record*, 1967, Supplement. Edmund Burton, a
Fellow who died in 1528, also owned a bow: OU Archives, Register EEE, fo. 299ᵛ.

honoraria for attendance at endowed masses, and perhaps payments for private tuition. An income of more than £5 p.a. was incompatible with continued tenure. They were to 'give and attend lectures, dispute, and respond in the schools of the University'. Very detailed regulations were laid down for College disputations, which were to be held twice a week in term-time. These were (it seems) primarily for the graduate members, although the rest were probably encouraged to join the audience. Little is said about the exercises or teaching of undergraduates. Scholars seem to have been expected to participate in the disputations only if they had begun the study of logic. Attendance by those for whom these functions were appropriate was to be obligatory. Absence and inadequate performances were to be punished—graduates with a fine, Scholars with a beating.

College officers, who were paid small stipends, were elected from among the Fellows every year in the autumn. The duties of the Bursars (*thesaurarii, bursarii*) were broadly the same as those of the Domestic and Estates Bursars of today, although they seem to have been jointly responsible for everything rather than dividing up the business. The Deans (*decani*) were the officers charged with supervision of the Scholars. They were to see that they were taught and made progress, and to exercise disciplinary control over them in consultation with the Master. In addition, the Senior Dean was Librarian, with the duty of maintaining everything in good order, and control of access. Visitors were to be excluded unless they were brought in by the Master or a Fellow. The Junior Dean (*decanus secundus*) was responsible for the vestments, plate, and other property of the Chapel.

Previous Statutes contain no provision for associates of the College who paid their way without any subsidy from the Foundation. However, as related in the last chapter, there were certainly a few residents of this kind in the College during the late fifteenth century, normally young men from the higher reaches of society. This category appears in Statutes for the first time in 1507, but only relatively briefly, from which we may deduce that they were still but a detail of the full picture. The term actually used for them is paradoxical—*extranei*, outsiders, who nevertheless are spoken of as being 'admitted' or 'expelled': 'extranei qui non sunt de corpore, ad cohabitandum ex consensu Magistri sive vicarii et majore parte Sociorum admissi.'[15] The special expression 'Commoner' (*communarius*) is not found in Balliol records until later in the century. Fox's regulation for these so-called *extranei* was simple: they were to be required to bind themselves by oath to observe the Statutes in almost all respects like Fellows. It seems to have been taken for granted that this category would

[15] The term *extraneus* is also used elsewhere in the Statutes, in contexts which show that it could embrace real outsiders as well as Commoners.

in most cases continue to comprise sons of noblemen or young men of that status. One important concession was made to them. They were not confined to the study of logic, philosophy, and theology, but were expressly given permission to read civil law, canon law, and other subjects in private.

Fox did not disdain minutiae, and very few eventualities are unprovided for. The honesty of the Cook, payments during sickness, the allocation of chambers, and much else of a minor nature are all carefully dealt with. The only obvious major omission is that there are no rules governing the financial relations of members with the College. Some details had to be clarified, reiterated, or amplified by subsequent Visitors, and there were a few additions, but the core of the 1507 Statutes survived for the next three and a half centuries.

6

The Second Chapel and the Reformation

A MEDIEVAL fog has obscured our view of the College so far, and will not clear for another generation, but it begins to thin out in the early sixteenth century. From the brief glimpses of activity we are allowed, we can tell that the reconstruction of the Chapel loomed large in College affairs. It had already been planned by 1495, when the Master, William Bell, made his will, leaving ten marks, and as much more as his executors could contrive, to be used 'circa novam capellam'.[1] Perhaps a start was made at this time, but further benefactors were needed for completion of the scheme. Fortunately several were forthcoming. Thomas Harrope was the next we know of. He was probably an ex-Fellow of the College: at the time we hear about him, he was the Rector of Great Haseley, near Thame. Around 1515 he acquired in stages various properties in Old Woodstock, Wootton, and elsewhere in Oxfordshire, conveying them to a body of trustees headed by Cuthbert Tunstall. They held the properties for the benefit of the College, to which the title was passed later.[2] Tunstall (1474–1559) was the most distinguished Balliol man of the period. He was a scholar of some note, with command of many disciplines, and he was also a successful prelate politician, first as Bishop of London and then of Durham. A member of Sir Thomas More's circle, he remained passively faithful to the Roman tradition through the ecclesiastical upheaval of Henry VIII's reign, without losing his head or his status, and was an executor of the King's will. Deprived of office under Edward VI, he was restored on Queen Mary's succession. He kept aloof from the Marian persecutions, but he was deprived again by Elizabeth. Tunstall's connection with Harrope, if there was anything more than their common membership of the College, is not obvious, but their relative ages suggest the possibility that Harrope was Tunstall's tutor.

Harrope's benefaction established a firmer financial base to work from, and in his will of 1521[3] he gave further specific and practical assistance for the rebuilding of the Chapel: 'I bequeath the tymbre of xx^tie okes lyinge

---

[1] H. E. Salter, *Oxford Balliol Deeds*, 1913, p. 335. Bell's will was made on 4 May 1495. He requested burial in St Mary Magdalen church.

[2] See especially A.21.56 and F.8.44–55.

[3] Oxfordshire County Record Office, MS Wills Oxon. 180, fo. 151.

in my heycroft to bayley college to the buyldinge of their chapell.' He also left a 'greate sledge' together with other gear for the transport of the timber. Major works were soon under way.[4] In 1522 William Eist, 'mason, of Burfurth', was engaged for the stonework of the south wall and windows. A certain amount of stone was already available, but he was to provide more from Burford as required. Eist had been one of Bishop Fox's master masons for the Corpus Christi buildings,[5] and may have owed the Balliol commission to that connection. Six years later the Balliol works were in the hands of John Lobbens, 'mason of my Lordes work', and William Jonsons, both of whom were in Cardinal Wolsey's service, working on the construction of Cardinal College.[6] Their contract was 'to werke or cawse to be wroghte iii heides of wyndos of iii lyghtes, and one of iii lyghtes of the northe syde and the heid of the eiste wyndow of v lyghtes, evry wyndow to be wroughte w^t vousers and chawmerantes'.[7]

The College had every reason at this point to keep on the right side of Wolsey's men. Two years earlier, it had parted with several houses on the site of the projected Cardinal College, in return for a mere verbal promise of payment, or real estate in lieu, but nothing had been forthcoming. The deal had been made by the Senior Fellow, John Bradley, 'being lefte in the said College in the tyme of sickness, the maister and other of the Colledge being then in the cuntry'. In a petition to Chancery many years later it was alleged that Bradley 'by secret meanys unawares unto the maister and the Company did get out there commen seale and therby did geve and graunte' the properties to John Higdon, Dean of Cardinal College. This was no doubt a use of litigants' licence in order to strengthen the petition, but it is clear that Bradley had made a very insecure bargain. His College was still living in the hope of receiving its due when Wolsey fell in 1529, throwing the plans for Cardinal College into confusion. The building work was halted abruptly, and for a while the King's anger seemed likely to extend to demolition, in order to obliterate Wolsey's ubiquitous insignia. But his wrath abated, and in 1532 Cardinal College was refounded, under the royal name and patronage. Unfortunately for Balliol, neither King Henry, nor the authorities of his new foundation (the present Christ Church), were the least bit moved by its attempts to obtain satisfaction. This was a major financial setback, as the properties

---

[4] For the best previous outline, and sources not specifically cited here, see *VCH*, Oxfordshire, iii. 90.

[5] T. Fowler, *Corpus Christi*, 1898, p. 37.

[6] *VCH*, Oxfordshire, iii. 228. Lobbens and Jonsons are both quite well known: J. Harvey, *English Mediaeval Architects*, revised edn. 1984 (under Lebons, Johnson).

[7] i.e., voussoirs (arch-stones) and chamfers (mouldings).

had been worth more than £10 p.a.—about an eighth of the College's total annual income.[8]

Wolsey's disgrace was not, however, an unmitigated disaster for Balliol. It happened just as the masonry of the Chapel windows was completed, and much of the glass which was put in them can be linked with Cardinal College. The apparent collapse of Wolsey's scheme left a number of his circle with good intentions unfulfilled, and perhaps even glass already made for it. Their generosity was diverted to Balliol, possibly with thoughts of making some amends for their patron's default over the purchase-money for the houses he had razed. John Higdon, Laurence Stubbs, and Thomas Knolles, successive Presidents of Magdalen, were these donors. They all had close ties with Wolsey, and some of the glass they gave is in the style of James Nicholson, a glazier who is known to have worked for Cardinal College in 1528. The common factor in all of this was Laurence Stubbs. On the one hand he had an intimate association with Balliol through his brother Richard, Master 1518–25, and on the other his role as one of Wolsey's household chaplains gave him close ties with all aspects of the arrangements for Cardinal College.[9] The importance of his contribution was commemorated by an inscription in the great east window:

Orate pro anima Magistri Laurentii Stubs sacrae theologie professoris et istius collegii specialis benefactoris qui hanc fenestram procuravit sumptibus suis. AN DNI MDXXIX.

A good deal of this window has survived, despite removal and mutilation when the Chapel was rebuilt in the nineteenth century: it was reset as the present east window in 1912. Its main theme is the Passion, Resurrection, and Ascension of Christ. It includes portraits of Laurence Stubbs, and his brother Richard. The glass now in the window on the south side nearest the altar was given by them jointly. It is the only other reasonably complete survivor from the period, telling the legend of St Catherine's martyrdom in lively colours. The rest of the early glass is in a very incomplete and muddled state, although portraits of John Higdon and Thomas Knolles can still be seen. Remnants of two more windows which were given about 1530 are also preserved in the present Chapel. They are ascribed to Sir William Compton and Thomas Leson. Compton had been a page to Henry VIII before his accession, and held many offices under him, but had no link with the College and was regarded as one of Wolsey's rivals. Finding his name among the benefactors would therefore be a puzzle, but for the

[8] For the documents, and an account of this affair, see Salter, op. cit., p. 127. See also ch. 11 n. 6.

[9] *VCH*, Oxfordshire, iii. 228.

fact that Leson was in his service, and an executor of his will when he died in 1528: Leson's curriculum vitae and gifts to the College on his own account make it probable that he was an alumnus.[10]

The Chapel was probably complete in essentials by 1536, when John Kitson, sometime Bursar, died. He left seven pounds to the College in his will,[11] in which he also wrote that 'after Mr Wryght and I have made our countes for the receiptes and expenses about the buylding off the chapell, I suppose veryly that the coledge wilbe found in my debtt aboute v^li, the which I do geve clerely unto the coledge, besides the vii^li abovesayd, to be prayd for, and to have my name sette in the rolle among the benefactors'. Two important peripheral features were not finished until several more years had passed, however. The Vestry, a secure annexe doubling as a Treasury or muniment room, to which access was obtained through the Chapel by a door on the right of the altar, was mentioned in William Eist's contract of 1522, but there was presumably still work to be done on it in 1539, when Thomas Leson bequeathed £10 to the College 'to the making of ther vestrie there'.[12] The project, which had been conceived a full half-century before, was only given its finishing touch, a 'turrett' at the west end, in 1544;[13] Nicholas the Cook earned himself an extra fourpence in 1545 by clearing away the last of the sand, stone, and clutter left by the builders.[14]

The Benefactors' Roll on which John Kitson was so anxious to be accorded a place was a long one by his time, with more than a hundred and fifty names on it.[15] Enumeration there was not a matter of vanity but of prudence, because it meant that one's soul would be regularly prayed for. In Thomas Harrope's case additional provision was also made, establishing a special commemoration on his anniversary every year, and ensuring a good turn-out by payments of eightpence each to every Fellow who attended.[16] Arrangements like these were doomed to be frustrated: prayers for the dead were part of an old order which was soon to be swept away by the Reformation. Indeed, the process had already begun before the new Chapel was finished.

By 1527 the King had resolved to divorce Catherine of Aragon, but he

[10] *VCH*, Oxfordshire, iii. 90.

[11] OU Archives, Register EEE, fo. 384.

[12] PCC will, 32 Dyngeley (1539).

[13] Bodleian MS Top. Oxon. e. 124/9, fo. 4. No tower of any kind appears on the Chapel in Berebloc's drawing (1566), although a little tower with a spire is shown by Loggan (1675) and later artists.

[14] Bodleian MS Top. Oxon. e. 124/9, fo. 11.

[15] A. B. Emden, 'The Last Pre-Reformation *Rotulus Benefactorum* and List of Obits of Balliol College', *Balliol College Record*, 1967, Supplement.

[16] Emden, op. cit.

was unable to get the decision he wanted from Rome, or much support from the English clergy. Determined to have his way, he set about making himself master in his own land, bullying the clergy into co-operation, and using Parliamentary legislation to erode and finally abolish the authority of the Pope in England. In 1534 the Act of Supremacy established the King as the 'supreme head on earth of the Church of England'. The members of all colleges and similar corporations were required to make a formal acknowledgement of this principle, and nearly a hundred and seventy submissions from across the land survive. Balliol's[17] is unique in bearing a reservation, written boldly in abbreviated Latin between the pro forma declaration[18] and the College seal:

We have appended our seal to this deed and signed our names having maintained that we intend nothing to prejudice divine law, the rule of the orthodox faith, or the doctrine of Holy Mother Catholic Church.

By me William Whyte, Master of Balliol College
By me Walter Brown
By me William Wryght
By me John Kytson
By me John Foster
By me Thomas Parke

Had any of them been public figures, or the College other than small and insignificant, some stir would surely have followed this aberration, but it passed unnoticed.

The surrender of all documents depending on Papal authority was demanded next. The College Register records that on 11 June 1537, in the presence of the Master and all the Fellows, five papal bulls (concerning the Statutes, etc.) were solemnly taken from the muniment chest, to be handed to the King so that they could be 'reformed'. As an attempt to revise history, this was a complete failure, because the Fellow who chronicled the event also transcribed all the offending documents in full before they were given up. The copies are crossed through, but only lightly and symbolically, so that very few words are lost.

The break with Rome enabled anti-clerical and Protestant activists to advance, bringing further controversy. Changes were erratic, reaction alternating with reform, unsettling England and its institutions. We know very little of Balliol's internal affairs in the decade following the Act of Supremacy, but the signs are of a strained atmosphere, reflecting the mood of the country at large.

[17] PRO, E25/102+; summarized in J. Gairdner, *Letters and Papers Foreign and Domestic ... Henry VIII*, vii, 1883, p. 439.

[18] The wording is exactly the same as spelt out by the King for Oriel: G. C. Richards and H. E. Salter, *The Dean's Register of Oriel 1446–1661*, 1926, p. 382.

William Whyte, the Master who had led the 1534 protest, decided to resign in 1539. This was apparently of his own volition, but we may safely conjecture that he found the encroachment of Protestant principles on the orthodox faith uncomfortable. He would certainly not have been much in sympathy with Thomas Cromwell, the King's chief minister 1534–40. Cromwell was a fervent reformer. His powers gave him the last word, short of the King, in ecclesiastical matters, and he intruded in College affairs with assumed visitatorial authority. On hearing of Whyte's intention to step down, he sent instructions that the College could and should, without 'any cytations delayes or other like solempnyties of the law', proceed to the election of a Master without 'any parcyalitie or corruption', provided a majority of Fellows were present.[19] This freedom only led to intrigue. George Cotes, a former Fellow, conspired with Thomas Parke to deceive the rest of the electorate into thinking that Whyte's resignation was conditional upon Cotes's election. They, 'cawlyng to memory how unkynde a parent owre olde master Whyte was to hys company', were glad to seize any opportunity to be rid of him and agreed upon Cotes.[20] The Bishop of Lincoln, the rightful Visitor, was alarmed and wrote to one of Cromwell's staff:[21]

Master doctor, I beseche you remember the mater of baylive colledge, that ther maye be an indyfferente good man ther chosen. For if Cootes shulde obtaine itt, I reckon the colledge undone. And so I beseche you shewe my lorde the man is so wilful, headye parcyall and factyous that within breffe tyme ther shulde be fewe in that house butt of his countreythe and some of those that are nowe there shulde have little quyette.

This view was contradicted by Owen Oglethorpe, President of Magdalen,[22] who reported that 'his judgement in scripture is very well amended and is not addicte to manis doctrine nor scholemannis phantasies, but only to godds worde', and that he was a very suitable candidate. Cromwell urged the Visitor to accept Cotes, promising to assist with his ejection if he misbehaved,[23] and duly confirmed the election himself shortly afterwards. The deception was exposed to him in 1540, and he made an attempt to impose William Wright instead,[24] but Cromwell was himself

---

[19] R. B. Merriman, *Life and Letters of Thomas Cromwell*, ii, 1902, p. 240.

[20] PRO, SP1/158, fo. 162; summarized in J. Gairdner and R. H. Brodie, *Letters and Papers Foreign and Domestic … Henry VIII*, xv, 1896, p. 181.

[21] PRO, SP1/154, fo. 141; summarized in Gairdner and Brodie, op. cit., xiv (Part 2), 1895, p. 171.

[22] PRO, SP1/154, fo. 154; summarized in Gairdner and Brodie, op. cit., xiv (Part 2), p. 177.

[23] Merriman, op. cit., p. 241; summarized in Gairdner and Brodie, op. cit., xiv (Part 2), p. 190.   [24] See n. 20, above.

arrested and executed before anything could come of it. Wright did eventually succeed Cotes, but not for several years, and in the interim the latter had many disputes to cope with. In 1542 rumours were circulated that he had been guilty of regional partiality in an election. This was the very fault the Bishop of Lincoln had warned of, and Cotes felt it necessary to exonerate himself by examining all the Fellows on oath in the Chapel, as to whether they would accuse him: they all declined to do so.[25] A fortnight later, on 31 October 1542, the Visitor declared that in the election of Fellows the College was to consider only the ability and character of the candidates, not their origins or family connections:[26] '... in sociis eligendis solum considerent virtutem et aptitudinem discipline ac bonorum morum et non patriam aut consanguinitatem ...' In addition, there were never to be more than four Fellows from any one county. The Visitor also took the opportunity to pronounce on some other points not dealt with explicitly by Richard Fox, including dealings with women—ever a delicate issue, but especially so at this time, as the marriage of priests was part of the prevailing controversy. Nobody was to bring a woman into the College on pain of expulsion, except that a lady of noble birth, or the mother of a member, might be entertained at the Master's table if at least two Fellows were present. Even laundresses were to be kept out: linen was to be handed to them in the porch beneath the gate-tower, beyond which they were forbidden.

Four at least of the Fellows were in active opposition to Cotes— William Wright, William Francis (who had reported the election scandal to Cromwell), John Smythe, and John Nowell. The last two were so rebellious that Cotes had to get injunctions from the Visitor requiring them to submit to his rule. Smythe remained recalcitrant, and a year later was fined for the remarkable offence of making off with the Master's breakfast.[27] Cotes gave way to Wright in 1545, reappearing on the public scene as one of Queen Mary's bishops in 1554. Wright had control for a couple of years until the death of King Henry in 1547, but then stepped aside for James Brookes, who held office until Wright was called back in 1555.

Four fellows of Corpus Christi College were reported to the authorities in 1535 for obstructing the 'extirpyng of ungodly and papisticall doctrine'.[28] One of them was James Brookes, an ardent Romanist—but one who had learned to keep his head down. Shortly after he became Master of Balliol, a national campaign of radical Protestant reform began.

---

[25] Latin Register, translated in F. de Paravicini, *Early History of Balliol College*, 1891, chapter 11.

[26] Salter, op. cit., p. 320.

[27] Latin Register, de Paravicini, op. cit.

[28] J. G. Milne, *The Early History of Corpus Christi College Oxford*, 1946, p. 29.

Royal visitors came to Oxford in 1549, bent on clearing away the trappings of the old religion. Their trail remains in the Bursars' accounts for that year:[29]

to a painter for obliterating images beside the altar	8d
for wine to the present Visitors	8d
to a poor man for cleansing the Library when the King's Visitors were here	2d
to 2 workmen, 1 day, removing altars	8d
to the King's visitors for their pains in University business	30s 0d
to their scribe for his office	6s 8d

Two years later there is an entry for dismantling the organ, and an English Bible was bought. At about the same time the Library was, like others in the University, purged of 'superstitious' works, and something like a third of its manuscripts were thrown out. A careful Bursar, quick to make a few extra pence, sold the resulting scrap paper and parchment to a local butcher, who no doubt used it to wrap his joints. Mercifully, many treasures which might have attracted the attention of the zealots survived. The Library could have fared worse, and the windows in the Chapel escaped. The seal matrix given by Dervorguilla was untouched—its Virgin and Child image would surely have condemned it if it had been noticed. Some ancient practices survived as well. The entries which appear in earlier accounts for 'exequies', the special offices for the souls of benefactors, do not disappear. They remain, thinly disguised as expenditure on 'gaudies'. In any case the blast of reform was short-lived, and the pendulum swung quickly to the other extreme, on the accession of Mary Tudor in 1553. New service-books were bought for the Chapel, the altars were refashioned, and in 1555 the English Bible was sold. Gifts of new sacramental silver and vestments were received,[30] and there is every indication of an enthusiastic return to Roman ways.

Brookes was consecrated Bishop of Gloucester in 1554, but remained as Master until the end of 1555. He was still Master when, as the Pope's personal representative, sitting on a ten-foot-tall 'solemn scaffold with a cloth of state very richly and sumptuously adorned' in the University Church, he opened the proceedings for heresy against Archbishop Cranmer, Bishop Latimer, and Bishop Ridley. Bishop Jewel, who would have been in the dock himself had he not fled abroad, thought Brookes a 'beast of impure life and most impure conscience', but he was a man of some scholarship. His behaviour at the trials, though severe, was without the ranting characteristic of some of the Marian extremists. Cranmer,

---

[29] The quotations and information which follow are taken from the Bursars' accounts, as transcribed and englished by Andrew Clark: Bodleian MS Top. Oxon. e. 124/9.

[30] Latin Register, de Paravicini, op. cit.

Latimer, and Ridley were condemned to the stake, and on 16 October 1555 the last two were taken to be burned 'on the north side of the town in the ditch against Balliol College'. As the fire was kindled at Ridley's feet, Latimer said to him 'Be of good comfort, master Ridley, and play the man. We shall this day light such a candle, by God's grace, in England, as I trust shall never be put out.' This drama was enacted in the middle of Broad Street, near the front door of the present Master's Lodgings. A stone cross set in the road marks the place. Ashes and fragments of bone were found there when the road was dug up in 1838.[31] Cranmer perished similarly in 1556, on or near the same spot, in equally steadfast style.[32]

Elizabeth's Protestant regime followed Mary's persecutions in 1558. It dealt swiftly with the likes of Brookes, who was deprived of his bishopric on refusing to take the requisite oath acknowledging the royal supremacy and denying the Pope's jurisdiction. He was cast into prison and died there not long afterwards.[33] It was easy enough for the new Government to select and deal with prominent individuals; lesser men and institutions clinging to popery were a more elusive proposition, as the history of the College in the following generation was to show.

[31] The precise location of the Martyrdom is discussed by H. Hurst, *Oxford Topography*, 1891, p. 123. The fact that the ashes were discovered in the year 1838 must make one a little cautious about the report. There was at that time a violent controversy in Oxford over the revival of Roman Catholic traditions, the 'Oxford Movement'. One of the tactics of the opponents of the Movement was to harp upon Marian persecution—hence the erection of the Martyrs' Memorial in St Giles' Street, near the back gate, in 1839. The discovery of the Martyrs' ashes at the very height of the controversy would seem a little too good to be true.

[32] This paragraph is largely based on *The Acts and Monuments of John Foxe*, ed. G. Townsend and S. R. Cattley, vii and viii, 1838.

[33] It is confidently stated in many places that Brookes was deprived in 1558 or 1559 and imprisoned, dying in February 1559/60, but it must be noted that Archbishop Pole's register records that the See of Gloucester was vacant from 1558 'per obitum bone memorie domini Jacobi Brokes ultimi episcopi': D. M. Smith, *Guide to Bishops' Registers of England and Wales*, 1981, p. 91.

7

Elizabethan Balliol: College Life and Administration

T H E second half of the sixteenth-century has a special fascination for the College historian, because it is the earliest period for which a reasonably detailed picture of the administration and daily life of the College can be pieced together. Up to this time, the surviving documentation is almost entirely confined to matters of statute and title to property. Practically nothing about the domestic routine and activities of the medieval College has come down to us. The very names of most of its members are unrecorded, and we can only conjecture that their life-style was like that in other collegiate societies about which more is known. All this changes around 1540. The office of Notary, or Secretary, to the Master and Fellows was established in 1538,[1] the Latin Register of elections and other corporate acts which had been maintained in desultory fashion for a generation becomes more systematic, and records of all kinds become progressively more copious. Regular Bursars' accounts first appear in 1544,[2] perhaps an incidental result of a 1542 series of Visitor's injunctions[3] which, among other things, tightened up financial controls in several respects. The Latin Register and the Bursars' accounts, augmented here and there by a letter, a will, or a lawsuit, bring the College to life for us at every turn.[4] We can identify more easily with a society in which it was often difficult to account for all the beer the Butler bought; and trivial scraps, such as the 'gytterne

[1] Latin Register, p. 44.
[2] The original accounts only survive from 1568, but Andrew Clark's detailed notes on an earlier volume (now lost) running from 1544 are in Bodleian MS Top. Oxon. e. 124/9–10.
[3] H. E. Salter, *Oxford Balliol Deeds*, 1913, p. 320.
[4] Unless otherwise stated, all facts given hereafter in this chapter derive from entries in the Latin Register or the accounts. Most of the entries used are found between about 1570 and 1600, but a little liberty has been taken with the term 'Elizabethan', one or two domestic facts being taken from years a little before or a little after Queen Elizabeth's reign. Precise authorities are given only for items of particular interest, but notes which should enable all the relevant entries to be located have been deposited in the Archives. The period was one of inflation, but wages may be taken as a rough yardstick of money values. The rates paid for casual labour by the College were usually about a shilling a day for skilled men (carpenters, masons, etc.), 8*d.* a day for labourers.

the brydge being off',[5] listed among a dead man's effects, or the six shillings spent on a cushion for the Master to sit on in Chapel, or the need to keep the kitchen salt-tub locked, all enrich our appreciation of what life was really like, more than endless poring over formal estates transactions ever could.

John Berebloc's 1566 woodcut gives an impression of the appearance and extent of the principal buildings, but implies, by omission, that the College was more compact and organized than was actually the case. By this time it owned the whole of the southern half of the modern site (see Plan IV), and had extended its territory into the street, establishing a partially enclosed yard planted with trees in front of the main gate.[6] Although the tenements on the west, facing the parish church, were leased out, the tenants can often be shown to have been College servants or tradesmen with close links. Even the 'Catherine Wheel' Inn was not completely alienated: there was probably some sharing of stable facilities, and College guests were frequently entertained there instead of in the College proper. The rest of the site was a confusion of gardens, paths, trees, and outhouses: privies, a charcoal store, an oven-house, stables with a watering-place for the horses, a well and pump, an ashpit, a place for chopping wood and stacking faggots, and so on. The gardens seem to have been mainly to the north of the Chapel and Library, with the privies near by, although these were moved from time to time, as it became necessary to fill in and re-dig. The stables were over towards the back gate by the 'Catherine Wheel'; the oven-house (and probably the charcoal store and faggot stacks as well) stood conveniently by the kitchen. 'New Lodgings' ('Hammond's Lodgings'—see below), sufficient to accommodate two Fellows and their pupils, were built on the south side, between the Corner House and the Master's Lodgings, towards the end of the sixteenth century, but the College did not otherwise stray outside the buildings shown by Berebloc for residential purposes in this period.

In the University census of 1552,[7] which is the earliest quantitative evidence available, the College is reported as having some twenty-six academic members, comprising the Master (James Brookes), six MAs, six BAs, and thirteen undergraduate students. Since there were ten Fellowship places, and about ten Scholarship places, most of the residents must have

---

[5] In other words, a broken guitar: Alyne's Inventory, 1561, OU Archives, Chancellor's Court Inventories.

[6] References in the accounts to work concerned with this yard, its elm-trees, seats, etc. are frequent. It was enclosed in 1675 (Final Accounts, £40. 8s. 6d. spent on the 'Wall and Gates before the elms, and for Pitching the Way before the Wall'), and the public path through it was closed in 1683, but it was lost under the Mileways Act of 1771: see Salter, op. cit., p. 26. St John's College still has a forecourt.

[7] *Register of the University of Oxford*, i, ed. C. W. Boase, 1885, p. xxiii.

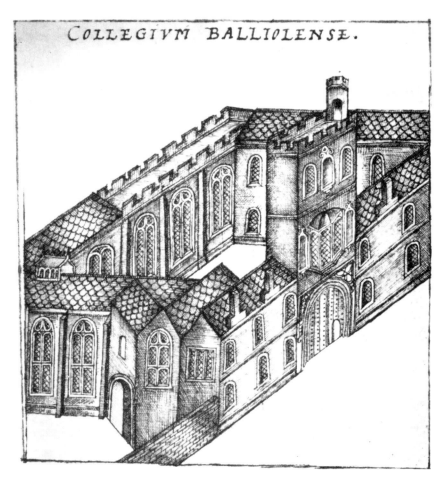

COLLEGIVM BALLIOLENSE.

4. Balliol in 1566, by John Berebloc.

been 'on the Foundation' and there could only have been a handful of undergraduate and senior Commoners. The number of places on the Foundation was fixed by custom and income, but the number of Commoner residents who could be taken in was limited only by demand, and domestic facilities. In a situation where room-sharing was the norm, there must always have been room for just one more undergraduate, so the physical capacity of the College was, within reasonable limits, no problem. It was possible to meet and profit by the sharp rise in the demand for University education which took place between 1550 and 1580, after which there was a levelling off or slight decline.[8] In 1576, which is the first year for which a reasonably reliable estimate can be made from the Bursars' Books, there were forty-two undergraduates in residence, a threefold increase since 1552. The undergraduate numbers fluctuated rather wildly at this sort of level for the rest of Elizabeth's reign, ranging between twenty-four (1586) and eighty-three (1594): see Appendix E. The signs of expansion to be found in the accounts are fewer than might have been expected. There is no obvious increase in the number of servants, for example—no doubt because a fair proportion (10–30 per cent) of the undergraduates were Servitors working their way. The indications of an expanding community we do find are few but fundamental, as in 1596–7, when several payments were made for 'inlarging the privyes'.

No Balliol admissions registers are available until well into the seventeenth century, but the University matriculation records give us some information about new members. Their age at entry was very variable, ranging from twelve, or even less, to twenty or so, but most were between fifteen and eighteen years old, so that on average they were somewhat younger than the freshers of today. They came from all over the south of England, but a bias in favour of Gloucestershire, Worcestershire, Herefordshire, Warwickshire, and Shropshire is discernible. It seems to have been common for those of tender years to be sent up with the protection of a servant, or in the company of an older cousin or brother: between 1580 and 1583, for example, no less than nine pairs of related simultaneous entrants are identifiable, out of a total of only just over fifty new undergraduates.

Each resident Fellow had a Scholar-pupil, who was required by the 1507 Statutes to be, nominally at any rate, his servant. He also had in his care a share of the Commoners and Servitors which was determined by his popularity. The financial arrangement between him and them for their tuition was a matter of private contract. There were about twenty[9]

---

[8] L. Stone, 'The Size and Composition of the Oxford Student Body 1580–1909', in L. Stone (ed.), *The University in Society*, i, 1974, chapter 1.

[9] A list of rents enabling a count appears, e.g., in the Bursars' accounts for 1572–3.

chambers that were generally assigned only to Fellows, former Fellows, and other senior members (of whom there were usually a few),[10] who then sublet space to their pupils. From 1561 this was regulated by a College resolution, which laid down that every Commoner living in a Fellow's chamber who had no room of his own was to pay sixpence a quarter to the College, and sixpence to his Tutor (*socius preceptor*). At times the Latin Register hints at overcrowding, as in 1571 when Robert Persons (a very popular Tutor) was assigned a single room for his pupils, on the condition that he installed not fewer than three of them in it. The Master was, of course, set aside from the Fellows by his unique and privileged constitutional position, but from a domestic point of view his situation was not sharply distinguished from theirs until after about 1570. Until then he is found being assigned chambers just like the Fellows. In 1559 there is a reference to the 'cubiculum orientale vulgo cubiculum Magistri'; this chamber was where Staircases II and III now are, and the 'Great Chamber' which is now the Master's dining-room was not restricted to the Master.[11] Allusions to 'our Mr his lodgings', which were near the kitchens,[12] and included the Great Chamber, appear soon after this, however, and the Master's Lodgings have been there even since. It became conventional from this stage for Masters to be married. Adam Squire (Master 1571–80) was married by 1587, when John Aylmer, Bishop of London, alludes to him as 'my lewd son-in-law' in a letter, although there is no evidence that he ever kept a wife in Oxford.[13] Edmund Lilly (Master 1580–1610) and

[10] Martin Culpepper is a notable example. He was never on the Balliol Foundation, but he resided and paid rent 1568–73 between being a Fellow of New College and returning there as Warden. Senior Commoners could also sublet: in 1550 the College agreed with John Howe, who was not a Fellow, to 'let to farme unto the said John Howe clerk all that their greate chamber with all other chambers and studies ... or his assynes beynge scolers or students only', for a rent of 26*s.* 8*d.* p.a. (D.13.19).

[11] In addition to the case of John Howe mentioned in the preceding note, we find (in the Latin Register) Anthony Garnet assigned to the Great Chamber both well before (1557) and long after (1571) his Mastership (1560–3); it is also recorded that Robert Hooper died in the 'cubiculum orientale', soon after resigning as Master in 1570.

[12] The location is proved by a 1597–8 accounts entry for 'a locke to the door between the Mr his lodging and the kitchen'. The Kitchen and Buttery were at the south end of the Hall. It has been suggested by J. Newman in *The History of the University of Oxford*, iii (ed. J. McConica), 1986, p. 624, that, as in other colleges, the Head had the oriel-windowed chamber over the gate, with the Treasury above him in the top storey of the tower. But Balliol's Treasury is known to have been by the Chapel in the early sixteenth century, and so far as the Master is concerned the suggestion is conjecture.

[13] J. Strype, *Historica. Collections of the Life and Acts of ... John Aylmer*, 1701, p. 189. Squire had at least two children by Aylmer's daughter, but one of them was described as 'little John' in 1594 (Strype, op. cit., p. 173), so the marriage may not have taken place until after Squire's resignation.

his wife Mary were probably the first couple to live in College *en famille*.[14]

The rooms were provided by the College practically bare except for bed frames; other furnishings were the responsibility of the tenant. Only communal places and the Master's Lodgings had tables, chairs, and cushions out of the common purse. In the 'Inventarye of alle suche goodes as were founde in the chamber of Mr Alyne of baylie Colled' in 1561, the only furnishings and decorations listed are:[15]

> ij fetherbeadis ij bolsters, and a pylloo wth a pyllobeyre
> a payre of shetes
> a blanckett ij coverlettes
> a red capett
> ij chayres
> a table with a Frame
> a Joyned Forme
> a case with a pictor of christ in hym
> a sheett
> a sheete
> a pylloobeyre
> a old deske
> a boxe without a cover wth old papers in hym
> one othr box without a cover
> certen paynted papers hanging about the chamber
> a teaster for a bead paynted

Hardly the trappings of luxury, and even with his thirty-odd books and few personal chattels, Alyne's room would have appeared spartan by modern standards. The painted papers hanging about the chamber sound like a half-hearted attempt to achieve a little cosiness. This must have been difficult, as the walls were mostly just whitewashed at the time, although the piecemeal installation of wainscot panelling around the College, which was to continue over the next half-century, had begun. Nor is it certain that the windows would have been fully glazed: the frequency and wording

[14] The childish signatures 'Nicklous Lillie', 'Edus Lillie', and 'John Lillie' appear on the inside of the front cover of the oldest Statute Book, and 'John Lilly, Jane Lilly, and Mary Lilly, children of Edmund Lilly ... and Mary his wife' are mentioned in an indenture of 1597 (Lease Log Book, p. 26). A Katherine Lilly is named together with Jane and Mary in the Latin Register, p. 170 (1595). Three sons and three daughters, apparently all minors, were living when Edmund Lilly made his will in 1602 (PCC, 52 Wingfield, 1610). Mary Lilly's maiden name was Wenman; her brother Thomas was a Fellow of Balliol (A. Clark, *The Life and Times of Anthony Wood*, i, 1891, p. 39).

[15] OU Archives, Chancellor's Court Inventories. A 'pylloobeyre' was perhaps a device for supporting a pillow; a 'teaster' = a tester, a bed canopy. Mr Alyne's status is not clear. A slightly later inventory, of the effects of an MA Fellow (George Holland, 1596), is printed in *The History of the University of Oxford*, iii (ed. J. McConica), 1986, p. 633.

of the many entries for glazing in the accounts suggest that some of the work was first-time glazing.

Little passages called 'entries' led from the rooms into the quadrangle. Payments for paving the entries are shown in the accounts from time to time and it is probable that bare hard-packed or gravelled earth was gradually disappearing. Purchases of gravel for paths in the quadrangle and gardens were made occasionally, and the drainage ditches ('gutters' and 'sinckes') had frequent attention, but it was no doubt a losing battle against mud and puddles. Only a few areas, such as around the Chapel and the water pumps ('plumpes'), were paved. There were two wells with pumps, one in the backyard and one in the quadrangle. They were very complicated contraptions, requiring a lot of maintenance. The one in the quadrangle must have been a very striking feature, as there was a large painted lion on top of it. This lion was regularly repainted, and carefully repaired when necessary—a symbol of corporate pride, like the Founder's arms painted over the main gate.[16]

1576–7	Item to the smith for mending the plumpe when the lion fell downe at the greate winde	v^s ii^d
1579–80	Item for a grene elme for the pumpe	vi^s
1585–6	Item for plankes and boring the pumps in the quadrangle together with a newe shoe, and certeyne iron plates	vi^s x^d
1592–3	Item for a new pyn to the plumpe in the backe syde	xvj^d
	Item for settinge up the plumpe in the quadrangle	xxviii^s viii^d
	Item for new payntinge and mendinge the fan and the lyon upon the plumpe	vii^s vi^d
1606–7	Item for canvas tallow clacks and nayles and one new shoe and verne and gable for both the plumpes	iii^s vi^d
1608–9	Item for newe painting the plumpe and the lion	6^s

There was little else in the quadrangle to catch the eye, but behind the Chapel and Library was an enclosed ornamental garden with an arbour, summer-house, and seats overlooked by elm-trees:

1582–3	Item a gardin dore key for the gardiner	v^d
	For making the seates in the Gardin	vi^s
1584–5	Item for rose trees	vi^d
1586–7	Item to Morris for 4 yong apple trees and other worke which he did in the garden	ix^s
1590–1	Item mendinge the locke of the little house in the garden	iii^d

---

[16] The accounts for 1604–5 include the entry 'Item to a painter for the diall and for armes on the foregates and for Dervorguilla her picture 10s'.

1595–6   Item for graveling the walkes in the garden   iii^s vi^d
         Item for poles for the arbor   ii^s viii^d
1608–9   Item for plantinge 8 yonge elmes in the backside   7^s 2^d

The 1561 regulation about the rent of Commoners which has already been mentioned was an early move in a campaign to introduce more control over this class, and to integrate them more fully into the College, as required by both the letter and the spirit of Bishop Fox's Statutes. In that year it was decreed that anyone who wished to use the College's facilities as a Commoner should be required to live on the premises and participate in academic exercises, conducting himself in all respects like a member of the Foundation. This was a reiteration of the Statutes. The screw was tightened in 1571, when it was enacted that everyone in College of less than BA status was to be assigned to the Master or a Fellow as his Tutor. This key principle was made statutory in 1574: 'Nullus communarius sit in collegio non gradatus sine tutore Socio aut Magistro Collegii.' It was also decided in 1571 that in future senior Commoners would only be accepted in special cases. An oath of loyalty to the College was to be required, and admission fees were to be levied, ranging at first from ten shillings for a *domini filius* to half a crown for a *plebeii filius*. The academic pace also quickened. There were to be twice-weekly lectures on natural philosophy in Hall, which were obligatory for all BAs; attendance at the Saturday philosophy disputations in Chapel was to be required of all BAs and Fellows; Praelectors in Greek, rhetoric, and logic were enjoined to lecture at least four times a week. Academic discipline was enforced by fines; disruptive behaviour could result in corporal punishment. In 1570 the Senior Bursar, Robert Benson, complained that Scholar Thomas Haddon had accused him of perjury, by which he no doubt meant insincere oath-taking in connection with the Act of Supremacy. The insult was aggravated by being pronounced in Chapel. Haddon admitted his guilt, and was sentenced to confess it before getting six of the best (*sex plagas*) from the Dean, all publicly in the Chapel. Thomas Woode, who had incited Haddon, was sentenced similarly at the same time, but he refused to submit and was expelled. Fellows were also liable to fines if they failed to fulfil their academic duties, or quarrelled among themselves. In 1599, for example, the Senior Bursar and Senior Dean were deprived of their commons for two weeks for exchanging 'contumeliosa verba'. Main meals were taken in the Hall, which was furnished with separate tables for the Fellows, Scholars, and Commoners, and benches for them to sit on. It had walls which were partly panelled and partly whitewashed. The Kitchen and Buttery were right by the entrance, where the Butler had a desk for his account book, with an abacus to keep track of the battels charges incurred. There was a fireplace too, and a lectern from which the Scholar to whom the duty fell would read from the Bible, or some other improving work.[17] The basic commons provided on ordinary days were rather plain. It is clear that there were regular purchases of bread, beer, cheese, butter, eggs, and spices, but references to other foodstuffs are uncommon. This was partly because some needs were met by the College itself. The cook had his own kitchen garden and a run for fattening capons. Two dozen apple-trees were planted in 1562–3, and ten plum-trees in 1583–4. In 1559 a pasture was sublet on condition that the College retained grazing rights for half a dozen sheep, which would be slaughtered one by one as required for its own use.[18] Fish was bought from time to time, but red meat appears in the accounts rarely. Real luxuries are only mentioned in connection with special occasions—a peacock given for the St Catherine's Day dinner in 1549, figs and almonds when the Master returned from a journey in 1555–6. If everyday fare was plain, feast days were frequent—more than a dozen in the year. The St Catherine's Day feast[19] was the biggest event in the calendar. There was a special allowance over and above normal commons: as a rule this was exceeded, but the excess was still charged to the House. Just before the great day there was a general clean-up in the Kitchen. The 1589 and 1604 entries are typical:

1589–90	For scouring vessel at St Katherens tide	xviii^d
	For St Katherens feast	xiii^s iii^d
	Item for the overplus thereof	xxx^s
1604–5	Item trenchers for the haule at St Katherines tyde 4 doz	16^d
	Item for the loane of dishes at St Kather: tyde	8^d
	Item gawdies at St Katherines feast	xiii^s iii^d
	Item pro excessu	xxi^s vii^d

In most years there is no breakdown, but we can see that in, for example, 1558, special purchases were made including wine, which hardly ever features in the accounts otherwise, except for Holy Communion. Such a grand affair was more than normal resources could cope with, and extra help, tableware, and linen had to be organized.

---

[17] A new regulation concerning this practice, which is prescribed by the 1507 Statutes, was made in 1560, and the accounts for 1600–1 contain an entry for 'binding the hall bible'.

[18] Latin Register, p. 84.

[19] The St Catherine's Day (25 Nov.) feast would originally have been for the Foundationers and guests only. The present-day tradition of St Catherine's Day Dinners, to which as many members of all ranks as can be accommodated in Hall are invited, began in 1897 at the suggestion of E. J. Palmer: H. Jones and J. H. Muirhead, *The Life and Philosophy of Edward Caird*, 1921, p. 222.

According to a note of College customs made in 1564, parties were also part of the regular social round: 'On midsomer even, synt peters even, magdalin even and saynt james even, the mr and felowes wear wont by a laudabel custom to have an hores drinkinge with fyne caks and good ale, and wear wont being then together to sing som himpen or anthem ...' Three payments for 'musitians cominge to the colledge' were made in 1575–7, but music generally played only a small part in College life. Of other amusements we have only a few hints, such as the seventeen shillings spent on 'the first making of the boulinge alley' in 1582–3. This sounds genteel enough, but more robust pursuits were not unknown: in 1597 two young Commoners were taken in Shotover forest, and reported for killing one of the King's deer and assaulting the keepers.[20]

Hospitality to guests provided further diversions. Anyone bringing money from a distance could expect a good evening in the 'Catherine Wheel', and there were heavy expenses from time to time when distinguished visitors inflicted themselves on the College. The most memorable event of this kind was the Queen's visit to the University in 1592. It is unlikely that she herself paid any attention to the College, but her associates did, and the whole affair was rather costly:

Item for the entertaynment of strangers and Courtyers that resorted to the College when the Court was here	xxx[s]
Item for the gloves[21] that were given to Noblemen from the College	l[s]
Item for the entertaynment of the quene which the coll was assessed to paye and toward the charges of the university	xxx[s]

The normal pattern of life was also disrupted every few years by a more sinister visitation: the plague. At least three times (1563, 1571, 1604) the College decamped, or dispersed, for a term or more. Regulations for corporate migration to avoid epidemics appear in the 1507 Statutes. Permission was given for them to move to a 'place with purer air, not more than twelve miles from the University' and follow normal College routine as far as they could. From September 1563 to October 1564, they took refuge in a house at Handborough rented from John Palmer. They settled in there to the extent of holding the annual College Meeting for elections in November, and entertaining the neighbours in February. In May 1571 there was a 'crudelissima febris pestilentialis' and the College was dispersed for several months. Those 'qui ob pestis periculum fugerant' were allowed an adjustment in room rent when it reassembled. In the summer of 1604 they resorted to a house on the outskirts of Woodstock.

[20] Royal Commission on Historical Manuscripts, *Calendar of Salisbury Manuscripts*, vii, 1899, p. 174.

[21] It was customary for a pair of gloves, usually of value between 5s. and 15s., to be presented to any visiting grandee.

The King was then in residence there and they caused some consternation at the possibility that infection would be carried to the Royal Household. Although it was recognized that the danger was slight because they were all in good health and had left Oxford before having any contact with the disease, Thomas Sackville, the Lord Treasurer and Chancellor of the University, wrote to confine them to their lodgings:

I wishe and requier you that during such tyme as his Majesty or the Queen shalbe pleased to remaine at Woodstock, everyone of you who are now abiding in or neere the said town as aforesaid do containe yourselves within the privity of your owne howse and feilds adjoining without resorting into the towne or in anie wise shewing or presentinge yourselves in the Court.[22]

The Bursars had responsibility for most of the practical aspects of College life. They were assisted by a small permanent staff comprising the Manciple (*Obsonator*), the Butler (*Promus*), a Cook, and an under-cook. These four were fully part of the College family, being entitled to commons and other perquisites, and they sometimes actually lived in College. The under-cook had the status of an apprentice and was regularly provided with basic clothing. Payments for wages to a laundress, a barber, and the Master's servant also appear in every account. By the end of the century a gardener, a tiler, and a carpenter had been added to the regular payroll. Other craftsmen were employed on a casual basis as needed: a plumber for the lead-work about the windows and roofs, a smith for chaining books in the Library, a tinker, a locksmith, a glazier, and so on.

The Manciple and the Butler were the Bursars' right-hand men. They did not usually receive any stipend: all they had direct from the College in most accounts were their commons and allowances. They must have collected much of their income through battels payments, and other fees not passing through the Bursars' books, and no doubt depended on the profits they could make out of the control they had over supplies and battels. As they were liable for losses, it would only have been logical to give them a share in any profits. Because they handled large amounts of

[22] For more detail and sources see J. [H.] Jones, 'Balliol and the Plague', *Balliol College Record*, 1983, 32. Charitable payments for the relief of plague victims appear in other years, e.g. 1582–3, 1594–5, and 1605–6. In 1606, travelling expenses were paid for journeys to Woodstock 'about our removinge in tyme of sickness', but it is not clear whether the College actually fled from Oxford or not. The house on the outskirts of Woodstock, where the refugees stayed in 1604, was probably 'Praunce's Place' in Old Woodstock, which was College property. It had been leased out in 1589 with the reservation that they should have the use of enough rooms for the accommodation of the Master and twelve other members when there was 'plague or any infectious disease' in Oxford (F. 1.5). Praunce's Place, later known as the Old Manor House, still stands on the east side of the main road, immediately north of the Black Prince public house. On Praunce's Place see: *VCH*, Oxfordshire, xii, 1990, pp. 425–7; and J. Blair and I. Baxter, *Oxoniensia*, lvii (1992), 349.

College money, and were in the front line for many kinds of business, the College was very dependent on them. As an insurance against their default they were required to provide bonds on appointment. In 1597 Thomas Smith, an illiterate baker who supplied much of the College's bread, and Joseph Barnes the printer, jointly made themselves liable for up to £100 in the event of Richard Finnings failing in his responsibilities as Butler, which were set out in detail.[23] Such bonds were not always an effective safeguard. The College had to bear an £18 'loss in the buttery by the butlers departure' in 1585–6, and he left his books in a mess as well. Fourteen years later it was necessary to sue another Butler, because he owed more than £40 for losses. He was made to pay what little he could in instalments until 1613, when he was finally forgiven the balance 'in respect of his years and poverty'. The boot could be on the other foot, however: in 1556 judgment against the College was given in a Chancellor's Court suit for debt brought by the Manciple, Edward Little. The Bursars also had a personal stake in their duties. In 1556 the College agreed that they could have the profits on the sale of bread, provided they accepted responsibility for the battels of the Commoners. The principle was reiterated in 1571, now including profits on beer as well. This became too much of a good thing as the number of Commoners grew, and in 1574 it was decided that profits on bread and beer should go to the College, the Bursars receiving additional remuneration in lieu. They were also released from the liability for Commoners' battels, but they could still be held personally responsible if they landed the College in difficulty by negligently failing to pay creditors or collect money due. Laurence Keymis had cause to regret his Junior Bursarship in 1585–6 on this score. When the accounts for that year were audited he was obliged to sign an acknowledgement that he was chargeable with unpaid bills and uncollected battels amounting to more than £34. He settled part of this, but he still owed over £22 in 1588, and the College's patience eventually ran out. In 1589–90 one of the accounts he had left unpaid had to be cleared, and legal proceedings were initiated: the business was still unresolved two years later.[24]

1589–90   To Smith for an old debt which Mr Keymis should
        have payed   xviii^{li} xviii^s

[23] F.9.7. Finnings was to 'behave himselfe Diligentlye faithfully and trulye in his office of the Butlershippe', presenting up-to-date accounts to the Bursars regularly; he was responsible for 'all stores of breade beare butter chese egges spyce mercerye ware or anything els that cometh to the use of the said Colledge and Commoners'; he was to report all losses and meet them; he was expected to 'safe and orderlye kepe all plate lynen and other the College goods' which were in his hands.

[24] See the accounts cited, and A.16.18. The Keymis affair was not unique. Robert Persons and James Stancliff, Bursars in 1572–3, were denounced for negligence; Thomas Wenman resigned half-way through his 1597–8 Bursarship, leaving a trail of debts and complications.

	For our suite in the court against Mr Keymis	xxix^s vii^d
1590–1	Item to Smaleman for warning Mr Keymis to the court	vi^d
	Item to hym the second tyme	iiii^d
1591–2	Item to the Registers man for wrighting the cytation for Mr Kemise to apere	ii^s

The evasive Keymis disappears from Balliol affairs at this point, taking up the life of a maritime adventurer, as one of Sir Walter Ralegh's inner circle.

The Bursars presented two accounts for audit in each financial year, the first in early July and the second on or about St Luke's Day (18 October), which was also the traditional day for the election of new officials and Fellows. It would be quite misleading to describe any year as typical, as there were erratic variations, but the accompanying table giving approximate figures for the year 1577–8 will serve to illustrate the scale of things in a relatively normal year.

	1st Account	2nd Account
Income from estates	£61	£42
Other income	£15	£5
Total income for the year: £132		
To the Master, Fellows, and Scholars	£47	£19
To the servants	£10	£3
Other expenditure	£24	£9
Total expenditure for the year: £112		

The income from College houses and lands was more or less stable, in the region of £80–100 a year, until about 1590. With the exception of major estates at Long Benton in Northumberland and Abbotsley in Huntingdonshire, and a smaller one at Beeston in Bedfordshire, all the property concerned was either reasonably close at hand, or in London.[25] Estates administration was thus fairly straightforward,[26] and apart from

---

[25] Locally there was property abutting the College and elsewhere in Oxford; at Moreton near Thame; at Nethercote; at Oddington; at Steeple Aston; at Woodstock; and at Wootton. In London there was property in the parishes of Clerkenwell, St Lawrence Jewry, and St Margaret Pattens.

[26] For a detailed account of the College estates and their administration in the period 1500–1640, see G. D. Duncan in *The History of the University of Oxford*, iii (ed. J. McConica), p. 559.

frequent difficulties in exacting prompt payment—resort to the distraint of tenants' goods was necessary several times—no serious problems were met. In 1576 an Act of Parliament had provided for the rents on estates owned by Eton, Winchester, and the Oxford and Cambridge colleges, which had previously been fixed for long leases, to be tied to the price of corn.[27] This proved greatly to the advantage of these corporations, including Balliol, because bad harvests in the 1590s caused a sharp increase in the price of cereals. In that decade the College's estates income rose by nearly half to an average of about £150 p.a. Although it was a time of inflation, costs generally rose less than the rental income. Complaints in the Bursars' Book at the 'great price of beer' were out of place; the factors which had pushed the price of beer up were also responsible for enabling the College to raise its standard of living.

The income from other sources was much more variable. Profits from the sale of bread and beer, and room rents, appear regularly. Admission fees—usually entered as 'pro vasculis argentibus' or 'plate money'—are given regularly from 1582, when their collection became the Bursars' responsibility. In several accounts, charges for renewing leases ('fines') are listed, and there is no indication that these were yet being absorbed by division among the Master and Fellows, as became the practice later. Benefactions received were also sometimes answered for in this section, together with payments from long-standing debtors and, occasionally, income from the sale of surplus and scrap, as in 1585–6, when the sale of 'the windfallings of the wallnut trees' and 'old rotten wood left at the removinge of the cole house' raised nine shillings and sixpence.

On the expenditure side, the stipendiary payments and allowances to Fellows and servants seem very modest. A Fellow had a little more than a pound a year from the College. Although this was additional to his commons allowance, which had risen from the sixteen pence a week set by the 1507 Statutes to twice that amount by 1600, he would have had battels for days when he exceeded his allowance, and room rent to pay as well. We might conclude from this that he was hard up, but we should not overlook the fact that he was receiving tuition fees and rents from pupils in his chamber, and very likely other payments and advantages not shown in the accounts as well. In some years any surplus remaining in the Bursars' hands at the end of a year can be seen to have been carried forward to the next, but its fate is not always evident. The first explicit indication of a dividend being made is at the end of the accounts for 1595–6, when £14 (practically all the year's surplus) was distributed among all

[27] *Oxf. Hist. Soc.* lviii. 190.

members on the Foundation, including the Scholars.[28] College officers
only received small statutory stipends of six shillings and eightpence a
year each, but from 1575 the Bursars also shared the £15 a year which
was allocated in lieu of bread and beer profits. Except for a few fees and
dues payable externally, the rest of the expenditure is under the single
heading *Expensae minutae*, whether large or small. All manner of maintenance and administrative expense is charged here, in haphazard order.
Much of it is as we would expect, but there are a few surprises. For
example, there is not a single book purchase in the whole period, although
Library maintenance (cleaning, chains, glazing, binding, locks) does
appear. It is probable that there were no accessions except by gift. Another
telling absence is any sort of charge to do with a mechanical clock. On
the other hand, there are many entries showing a preoccupation with
matters which do not loom at all large in our own lives, like litigation,
which was part of the normal pattern of life, and at times a risky strain
on the College finances. The benefaction of William Hammond[29] is an
extreme but not isolated case, which stands out from a constant background of minor disputes. In 1572, Anthony Garnet, who had been Master
1560–3, persuaded Hammond to increase the College's endowments, and
provide for additional places. In his will, which was proved in 1575,
Hammond allocated £1,400 of his estate for this purpose, appointing three
feoffees to deal with the project. The feoffees were Viscount Montague,
Mr John Browne, and Garnet, who was the most active. A number of
modest sums were paid over by the feoffees in the next few years and
Garnet also obtained for the College the lease of a new house, between
the Master's Lodgings and the house on the corner of the street. This
house was used as residential chambers: known first as the 'New Lodgings',
it became 'Hammond's Lodgings' later. The financial arrangements of the

---

[28] The practice concerning dividends was erratic for some years. In 1608–9 there was
a surplus of £96. Of this, £40 was carried forward as a float to the next year, £5 was
deposited in the Treasury to be saved for work on the Chapel roof, and the rest was
'devided amongst the companye of the mr. and the rest of the bodie of the house according
to the Statute of the Realme in that behalfe provided'. This is an allusion to the 1576 Act
regarding college leases and corn rents, which enjoins in one section that surplus income
should be 'expended to the use of the Relief of the Commons and Diett of the saide
Colledges'. It appears that the surplus, if any, was used to augment the commons of all
Foundationers for some years, and the custom of sharing it between the Master and
Fellows as a money dividend did not evolve until later.

[29] William Hammond of Guildford, a clothier, was Mayor of Guildford in 1550, 1558,
1564, and 1571; he was a major benefactor of Guildford Grammar School. At one time
he planned to endow a college to be called the 'College of the Holy Trinity in Guildford',
but was persuaded by Anthony Garnet to divert the money intended for this purpose to
Balliol. His will was proved in the PCC, 19 Pyckering (1575). The extensive documentation
of the dispute over his benefaction is in B.6 and B.8.

benefaction were very complicated, many parties with conflicting interests being involved, and Garnet either embezzled or mismanaged some of the funds. Legal argument, costing the College more than £250, dragged on for more than twenty years and the College never did obtain all the legacy. Garnet's ultimate fate is not known, but he was still protesting his innocence from Marshalsea prison in 1597. Whether he owed his confinement to the Hammond affair or to his conviction for recusancy[30] does not appear.

Regulations aimed at ensuring prompt payment of battels were kept under constant review. In 1554 an order, which was confirmed by the Visitor, laid down that no member was to remain in debt to the College for more than fifteen days after the end of each term. Defaulting Fellows were to be deprived of commons until the debt was cleared; lesser members were to be expelled. Furthermore, all junior members were to provide the College with a financial guarantee. It is probable that in many cases the necessary responsibility for a man's battels was accepted by his Tutor, whose arrangement with his father would cover domestic charges as well as tuition. An addition to the Statutes in 1571 confirmed that Fellows were to be guarantors for their Scholars, but for Commoners this practice was forbidden in 1563, when it was decreed that in future they would be required to provide some external security for payment of their battels. Many examples of the written guarantees obtained for this purpose survive.[31] In almost all cases the guarantor was a local man of business, who was presumably paid a premium for the risk he undertook. The defences were not watertight, but did ensure that relatively few bad battels debts fell on the College.[32]

Except for minor details, the accounts presented by the Bursars are well organized and follow the same rules consistently, but it is nevertheless impossible to draw broad conclusions about the financial health of the College from them. This is partly because some features are inscrutable, but mainly because they are only complete in their own terms. Their purpose was to account for Foundation moneys handled by the Bursars,

---

[30] *Catholic Record Soc.* lxi. 103.

[31] A series is found, for example, at the back of the Bursars' Book of Battels for 1589–98. These guarantees were replaced by the 'caution money' system early in the seventeenth century. Under this system members had to deposit with the Bursars on admission a sum which was forfeited if they defaulted on battels later. The system was not abolished until 1983.

[32] Arrears of rent and battels are listed at the end of the second account in some years. These debts were sometimes several years old and the running total was hovering around £100 at the end of the century, but most of the money seems to have been collected eventually. The list at the end of 1602–3 shows total debts of more than £120, but less than £40 proved irrecoverable in the long run.

no more. Two major sectors of the overall situation are omitted. First, battels transactions only appear as selected net results—certain profits and losses, with no indication of how these were computed. Dealings balanced by the Manciple or Butler are not shown. Secondly, nothing is said about reserves in the form of cash or plate. Cash reserves were kept with the muniments in the Treasury, which was a secure vestry, off the Chapel. The 1507 Statutes gave control of the Treasury to the Bursars, acting with the Master, but in 1574 it was laid down that all the Fellows in residence should be present when its massive and many-locked door was opened. This is as much an indicator of the mutual distrust prevailing in the Fellowship as anything else, but it also implies that there were significant cash holdings. Unfortunately, although a few transfers between the Treasury and the Bursars' accounts are recorded, the balance in the Treasury chest is at no time stated, and it is apparent that some large movements of funds took place without being noticed by the Bursars' accounts at all. The accounts for 1602–3 show two shillings and ninepence 'bestowed uppon Mr Clark and Mr Whitten that brought Mrs Dunchs 100^{li}', but they do not show the hundred pounds itself—it presumably went straight into the Treasury.

An impression of increasing confidence and developing competence in business matters emerges, in spite of the obscurity of the accountancy and the failings of individuals. As the end of the century approaches, the care with which the accounts are kept improves, and the standard of living rises. The average expenditure on Foundationers' commons and feasts increases by more than the inflation of foodstuff prices in the period, and the accommodation becomes more comfortable as panelling replaces whitewashed stone. The *ad hoc* approach to the running of the establishment, with much employment of casual labour, slowly gives way to a more organized regime with a larger permanent staff. In 1550 the College was a tiny, diffident society still very much cast in a medieval mould: by 1600 it had grown in size and vigour, and the ancient Foundation was but the nucleus of a more complex organism with capacity for further evolution.

8

'Suspicion of Papistrie'

ELIZABETH succeeded her Catholic half-sister Mary in November 1558, and a reaction in favour of Protestant views was inevitable. By the following spring, an Act of Supremacy had established her as 'Supreme Governor' of the Church. An Act of Uniformity imposed the services of the Book of Common Prayer. The mass, and other ancient ceremonies, were once more banished. Royal agents were sent to Oxford so that there could be no evasion. William Wright, the Master, resigned. On his second admission as Master in 1556—for he had the unique distinction of holding the office twice—he had shown his colours by presenting an elegant *theca* (a sacramental accessory) for use in the Chapel at festivals.[1] Ostensibly, he stepped down of his own free will, but in reality he was driven out by Queen and conscience.[2] Francis Babington of All Souls was 'elected' into his place, but he did not stay long. He migrated to take up the Rectorship of Lincoln in the following year, and enjoyed some prominence in the University for a while. As a scholar he had a considerable reputation, and his books show him to have had wide interests.[3] But he soon came under suspicion as a crypto-Papist, and he fled the country in 1565. When he left Balliol on 27 October 1560, on which date he had already been Rector of Lincoln for two months, he 'resigned the office of Master or Warden into the hands of the Fellows', handing over the Statute Book and the keys of the chest to the Senior Fellow. Its corporate autonomy thus restored, the College elected a former Fellow, Anthony Garnet, as Master. At the time he held an appointment as chaplain in the household of Thomas Percy, Earl of Northumberland, a Catholic who had been favoured by Queen Mary. Garnet's sympathies are thus clear,[4] but he seems to have avoided trouble for three years, and he was allowed to live in College after his resignation. His replacement by Robert Hooper, an internal candidate

---

[1] *Theca*: a sheath, case, or box—either a reliquary or a container for the corporal (a linen cloth for the elements to be placed on during the Eucharist). If the latter, not to be confused with burse (folder), which has only been in use since the seventeenth century.

[2] *Catholic Record Soc.* i. 20, 43.

[3] V. H. H. Green, *The Commonwealth of Lincoln College*, 1979, p. 128.

[4] Furthermore, many of the Garnet family were Catholics, and Anthony himself appears as a recusant in later life. He was also closely associated with the Catholic Viscount Montagu.

although never a Fellow, was very quiet. Hooper guided the College through difficult times until 1570, without leaving any trace of his character or affections behind him; he died in College soon after relinquishing his post.[5] John Piers was 'elected and nominated' Master on the very day of the vacancy; the unusual formula 'electus et nominatus est' is probably a subtle signal from the Notary (Robert Persons, of whom more later) to tell us that external authority was intruding. This we may also infer from the fact that Piers was a complete outsider. Furthermore, Hooper's 'free and spontaneous resignation' in the Register is suspiciously defaced. The Visitor knew that something irregular was afoot, and sent his man to stop the election, but by the time he arrived and fixed the formal inhibition to the Chapel door, it was all over. Piers was formally admitted Master a week later; less than a year afterwards he accepted the Deanery of Christ Church, a staging-post on his way to the Archbishopric of York.

The Visitor frustrated by Piers's appointment was Nicholas Bullingham, Bishop of Lincoln. It was not his first attempt to obstruct a College election. The Master and Fellows had been all set to proceed with their annual elections on 29 November 1565, when they received a letter from Bullingham requiring them to desist. They were divided about what to do. A voting majority (the Master, Richard Shaghnes, and Adam Squire) took the convenient view that the Statutes were above the Visitor, and that in any case they could choose their Visitor themselves and Bullingham had never been elected by them. John Atkinson, Robert Hammond, and George Godsalf objected impotently, and the proposal to make Probationers John Tunckis and Thomas Coventry full Fellows was carried. The Bishop asserted his authority, and after some argument the College had to accept that the Bishop of Lincoln was Visitor *ex officio*. But the promotions were allowed to stand. Tunckis held his Fellowship until 1573. Coventry soon departed to begin a distinguished legal career, which led to his appointment as Justice of the Common Pleas, and a knighthood, in 1606.

The politics underlying the contretemps over the 1565 elections are inscrutable. Bullingham was a decidedly Protestant reformer, but the three Fellows who appeared to back him up, and who were declared contumacious as a result, were not at all of his persuasion. Perhaps they were just opportunist trouble-makers. A month later Godsalf was arraigned for carrying arms within the College precincts, disobedience to the Vicegerent, and perjury—by which it was meant that he was a suspected Papist. He was expelled, but his colleague Hammond refused to be a party to his disgrace, and stormed out of the College Meeting in

---

[5] An inventory of his goods was taken on 12 Jan. 1570/1: OU Archives, Chancellor's Court Inventories.

Chapel. This drew on him a second public warning for contumacy, but he survived it until 1570. Atkinson left a more secret and poignant pointer to his Catholicism. Prayers for the dead being part of the old order, there was a danger that past promises to pray for the souls of the benefactors would be forgotten, so he carefully recorded their names and their 'obits' in the back of the College Register,[6] signing with a proud flourish 'By me John Atkinson, Fellow of Balliol College 1568', but protecting himself from censure by drawing very light cancelling strokes through the list of obits.

In 1566 the Bishop of Lincoln appointed a committee of three to visit the College on his behalf, to purge it of Romish practices. They made ten decrees to be 'perpetually observed'.[7] There were to be Communion services according to the Book of Common Prayer at least three or four times a year, and everyone of 'lawful yeres and discretion' (reminding us that many students were mere boys) was to receive the sacrament, on pain of a fine of 3s. 4d. Those attending Chapel were to behave themselves in 'such godly manner that they hinder not the worde of god to be redde or songe, or disturbe others'. Absence from morning prayers by under-graduates was to be 'punished with stripes'. English was to be used, and Latin service-books were to be destroyed. Prayers in Chapel and grace before meals were to be 'without invocation of sayntes or prayer for the deade'. The Master was to take all members with him to hear University Sermons.

George Godsalf went abroad after his expulsion. He was ordained at Cambrai, returning to England as a missionary priest in 1577. Possibly the first Balliol man to take that perilous path, he was arrested in 1581, and banished after he had languished in the Tower and Marshalsea prison for four years. There were to be many like him. The best known is Robert Persons or Parsons. He came up in 1564, to St Mary Hall in the first place. He was drawn to Balliol by a Scholarship a couple of years later. The Scholarship led naturally to a Fellowship, and he rapidly established himself as a lively and successful Tutor with many pupils. Exactly what the colour of his religion was at this stage of his career is unclear. When he took his BA in 1568, he had to take an oath acknowledging the Royal Supremacy. In later life he claimed to have forsworn the oath in his heart and been a consistent Catholic. He was probably vacillating between the old and the new way. After 1569, indecision became more difficult. A Catholic rebellion in the North smashed hopes that the people would

---

[6] A. B. Emden, 'The Last Pre-Reformation *Rotulus Benefactorum* and List of Obits of Balliol College', *Balliol College Record*, 1967, Supplement.

[7] The text of the ten 'Iniunctions' is printed in full in F. de Paravicini, *Early History of Balliol College*, 1891, p. 291.

forget about the Church of Rome, and a papal edict *Regnans in Excelsis* (1570), which released Catholics from their allegiance to the Queen, made them all into potential traitors in Government eyes. More determined moves than before were made to root popery out of the University. Another commission was sent to Oxford. In Balliol, Persons's close friend Richard Garnet was expelled from his Fellowship and imprisoned.[8] He managed to escape abroad, and would have been ordained, but he got 'entangled in an unexpected marriage'. It is as a member of the recusant laity that he is noticed subsequently, in poor circumstances together with his wife and children.

Adam Squire, elected Head of House in 1571, is the least engaging of all the Masters of Balliol. His name first appears in the accounts in 1557, as the Junior Scholar. In 1559, still an undergraduate, he was elected to a Fellowship. He held it until 1568, when he resigned but kept his name on the books. As a Fellow he was never out of College office (Junior Dean 1560, 1563, and 1566; Notary 1561, 1562; Senior Dean 1564, 1565; Senior Bursar 1567) and he was also Proctor in 1567. In religion he was most definitely Protestant, as can be seen from the disputation topics he chose for his 1576 inception in theology:

> Does purgatory exist? No.
> Should prayer be made for the dead? No.
> Does the Holy Spirit desert the elect when they sin? No.

Henry Savage noted in 1668 that he was a 'great Mathematician', but contemporary references to him have nothing to say of his scholarship, and are uniformly damning about his character and honesty. Quarrelsome, dissolute, lewd, lecherous, prodigal, hypocrite, spendthrift, filthy liver, and fantastical are among the terms used. He attracted ridicule for insisting on preaching the sermon at his own wedding. He brought his tenure of the Mastership into jeopardy by dabbling in astrology, and conning some gamblers into paying him for magical assistance.[9] A good deal of this sorry testimony is derived from hostile Catholic sources. But it cannot be dismissed as part of the slander and character assassination which was customary between the opposing parties, because it is borne out by the correspondence of his most Protestant father-in-law Bishop Aylmer. Aylmer was Bishop of London, and when his daughter married Squire,

---

[8] This Richard Garnet was no doubt closely related to Anthony Garnet; he was brother to Henry Garnet (executed after the Gunpowder Plot, 1606) and father of Thomas Garnet (martyr, 1608).

[9] K. V. Thomas, *Religion and the Decline of Magic*, 1971, p. 231; B. Capp, *Astrology and the Popular Press*, 1979, p. 143.

... to enhance his daughter's position had made him Archdeacon of London. This man, while on a visitation of his district, was caught by the magistrates with another man's wife. This having been brought to the notice of the father-in-law, the son-in-law, in order to induce him to take a more lenient view of the matter, was willing to add to his offence. So he forged, in his wife's name, a letter full of passion, to a certain knight, and pretending that he had intercepted it, produced it to his father-in-law as an excuse for his lapse. The latter was extremely distressed, but when he found out afterwards that the whole affair had been invented by his son-in-law, he flew into a passion and is said to have given the Archdeacon a tremendous thrashing, not with the pastoral staff, but with a butcher's cudgel.

No other Master of the College has been taken in adultery and assaulted by a Bishop.

Soon after he became Master, friction began to develop between Squire and Robert Persons. This probably had its origins partly in religious differences, but it was also a clash of personalities. Persons had a reputation as an extrovert: 'The fellow was much noted for his singular impudency, going in great barrel hose, as was the fashion of the hucksters in those times, and drawing also deep in a barrell of ale.' Articulate, arrogant, academically successful, he irritated Squire, who set out to bring him down. He seems to have been strongly supported in this by the recruitment to his faction of Christopher Bagshaw, who was destined to be Persons's lifelong enemy. There was a major row between Persons and Squire in 1572–3 over the College accounts. Persons was Senior Bursar, and it was rumoured that he had taken advantage of his weak (if not simple) Junior Bursar colleague, James Stancliff, and falsified some entries. Severe criticisms were voiced at the interim audit in 1573, although they stopped short of direct charges of dishonesty. Persons and Stancliff continued in office, achieving balanced accounts by the end of the year. Three decades later Bagshaw was still accusing Persons of cooking the books. By this time, Persons was the leading English Jesuit; Bagshaw had also embraced Catholicism and attained prominence, but as an anti-Jesuit, and Persons's conduct as Bursar was handy ammunition.

At Christmas 1573, with Persons away in London, Bagshaw poached one of his special pupils, a young undergraduate called James Hawley. Persons's version of what transpired was that Hawley had been persuaded by Bagshaw to go with him to 'certayne commedies' which Persons had forbidden; having led him into this heinous crime, he offered him protection from Persons's wrath, and took him over as his own pupil. A College Meeting was convened to resolve the quarrel, but it led instead to a further airing of the earlier dispute over the accounts, accusations of religious deviance, and a concerted effort by the majority to get rid of Persons. The possibility of using a statutory technicality was considered, and it was alleged that he was disqualified by illegitimacy from holding a Fellowship—Fox's Statutes, it will be recalled, enjoin that no bastard may be a Fellow. The charge could not be sustained, however, and was almost certainly false. But the stratagem was not necessary anyway. A sufficient proportion of the Governing Body was resolved to throw him out by more direct means if necessary. He was urged to resign voluntarily, in which case he would be allowed to depart with dignity after three months' grace, and told that if he would not do this '... they would violently ioyne together to have him out with all his schollers ... and that they would, that very night, cast out by force and fury both his and all his schollers stuff without the College ...'. He agreed to step down in the face of this pressure, asking that until he actually went 'he might keep his scholars, chamber &c and be reputed a fellow in the house, the matter being concealed from all the boys and the younger sort ...' He duly entered his resignation in the Register, according to the customary formula, but instead of recording that he was acting 'sponte et non coactus' (freely and not under coercion) he wrote 'sponte et coactus'. We cannot tell whether this oxymoron was a slip of the pen or a subtle belligerent gesture. Although the minutes show that it was agreed at the same time that he should retain his rooms, Scholars, and rights to commons for the time being, Squire was too spiteful to allow him to conceal the reality of his expulsion:

When Parsons was expell'd, he was one of the deans of the colledg, and so by his place was to keep corrections in the hall on the Saturdays. The next time therefore of correction, which was on the day of Parsons his expulsion, or soon after, Dr Squire causeth Parsons to go into the hall as dean, and to call the book and roll &c, and then commeth Dr Squire himself in, and as if it had been in kindness to countenance him (but in truth more profoundly to deride him) he calleth him at every word, Mr Dean, and desireth him often to have a strict care to the good government of the youth; and not only for a fit, but all the time of his year that he was to continue in office. Some of the commoners knew all this pageant, and laught the more sweetly.

Persons did not actually leave until 1574, when another rumpus—this time over the consumption of flesh during Lent—provoked the Fellows who had combined against him the year before to publish his 'resignation' and have it celebrated by the ringers of St Mary Magdalen. Within a few months Persons had left England, and he soon joined the Jesuits. In 1580 he returned as a Catholic missionary, moving furtively about the country hearing confessions, and saying mass secretly. But what was missionary zeal to the Catholics was sedition to the Government, especially in Persons's case, because he was also circulating propaganda run off on an illicit printing-press. He was able to elude capture, and continue moving from one safe manor-house to another by night, although his printing-press was discovered at Stonor. He eventually slipped away to exile. Persons and his colleagues are known to have been active elsewhere in Oxfordshire, and Holywell Manor could well have been on their itinerary. It was held at this time by the Napiers, who were staunchly Catholic, and was provided with a priest's hole in case of searches.[10] Others were not so lucky or clever as Persons. One such was his former pupil Alexander Brian or Briant,[11] who had been a Scholar under him at Balliol at the time of his final expulsion. He had then migrated to Hart Hall for a while before travelling to the Douai seminary. He was one of the first wave of missionary priests to return to England. Persons's father was among the lapsed Catholics he visited and reconciled to their Church. But he was taken in April 1581 and tortured in the Tower:

And because he would not confess where he had seen father Parsons, how he was maintained, where he had said mass, and whose confessions he had heard, they caused needles to be thrust under his nails; whereat Mr Brian was not moved at all, but with a constant mind and pleasant countenance said the psalm *miserere*, desiring God to forgive his tormentors ... After this he was, even to the disjointing of his body, rent and torn upon the rack, because he would not confess where father Persons was, where the print was, and what books he had sold ...

He was hanged, disembowelled, and quartered at Tyburn on 1 December 1581, together with Edmund Campion and Ralph Sherwin. His name is on the list of Forty Martyrs of England and Wales who were canonized by Pope Paul VI in 1970. He is the only Balliol man to have been accorded this ultimate veneration, but at least one other was martyred, and is revered for his constancy. Thomas Pylcher was elected a Fellow of Balliol in 1576 and served as Bursar in 1579.[12] Like St Alexander Briant, he studied at the Douai seminary. Undeterred by the latter's fate, he came to help with the English mission in 1583; he was banished in 1585 but returned, only to

[10] Mrs Bryan Stapleton [Mary H. A. Stapleton], *A History of the Post-Reformation Catholic Missions in Oxfordshire*, 1906, p. 211. The Blessed George Napier (martyred at Oxford, 1610) was born in the Manor House.

[11] Alexander Briant is listed as a Scholar of Balliol in 1573, but he matriculated from Hart Hall in 1574. Both migration and late matriculation were common in the sixteenth century. His membership of the College is confirmed by a number of explicit references to him as a Balliol pupil of Persons. At the end of the *Expensae minutae* in the accounts for November 1580 to July 1581 there is an entry 'Itm. mro. Brian pro veteri debito xx^{li}'—i.e. 'To Mr Briant on account of an old debt, £20.' He was suffering in the Tower at this time, and the entry probably arose from a covert attempt to do something for him. That the College really owed him £20 seems improbable.

[12] An exhaustive collection of information about the Blessed Thomas Pylcher (who was beatified at Rome together with a large group of English Martyrs, 22 Nov. 1987) has been published by L. E. Whatmore, in *The Southwark Record*, in parts, Sept. 1964–Dec. 1965.

be apprehended and condemned; he was executed at Dorchester on 21 March 1587.

So many Balliol men became involved with the forces of Catholic reaction that the College acquired notoriety for it.[13] Even Christopher Bagshaw, who had been so active in the Master's Protestant faction a decade before, left to go to the seminary in Rheims in 1582. For the first but not last time in its history the College, small though it was, came to the notice of the authorities as a breeding-ground for trouble-makers and political opposition. A Privy Council informant wrote to his masters:

That Balliol Colledg hathe not been free from the suspicion of papistrie this longe time it appeareth by the men that have been of the sayme house, namelye, Brian and Parsons. With Parsons and since his departure from the colledg hath Turner, Bagshaw, Staverton and one Pilcher been fellowes: all which were grevously suspect of religion. And certaune it is that this Pilcher is gone this year from thence to Rhemes, looking dailye for Bagshaw as he did report ... Staverton is in like manner departed the colledge, and it is thought that both Bagshaw and he be gone over the sea. It is said that Turner also either is gone or shall goe beyond the seas with a physician, to whom the Q. Majestie had geven leave to passe and to take one with him. It is thought some of these have lefte their resygnation of their fellowship with theyr schollars whom they have trayned up, as Bagshaw to Elis his schollar, and Staverton to his scoller Blunt, which two yf they be fellows, the College will remain in its deserved name of suspicion of papistrie. This may be forseen in causing the Master ... to place those which be knowne to be zealous and godly. The election is at Saynt Katherine's day or after presentlye.

The election was successfully influenced. Elis and Blount were diverted to Fellowships at Lincoln and Trinity respectively; the safe new Fellows elected instead included Thomas Sanderson, later one of the translators of the Authorized Version of the Bible. During the next few years, Balliol cleansed itself of the taint of popery and began to earn a Puritan label under the influence of Edmund Lilly as Master, backed up by Fellows like the future Archbishop of Canterbury, George Abbot, and his brother Robert. But they felt insecure. Their recent history gave them no claim on Government sympathies, and their ancient muniments stemmed from papal authority. In particular, their corporate status was not clearly established or defined. They therefore set out to obtain a new Charter. After

---

[13] In addition to George Godsalf, who has already been mentioned, William Staverton (Fellow 1576), Richard Yeomans (Servitor 1575), and Simon Fennell (Commoner 1572) were all missionary priests; George Turner (Fellow 1572) had a very successful practice as physician, and earned royal favour in later life, despite his 'backwardness in religion': see the *DNB*, etc.

much trouble and expense,[14] in 1588 they obtained one from the Queen reaffirming their institutional integrity, and purporting to establish the College anew with herself as Foundress. Complete with her Great Seal attached, it is an ornate and imposing document.[15] But they still felt uneasy, and, royal protection apparently not enough to reassure them, they also petitioned William Cecil for a promise of his support if the Charter should ever be called into question.[16] His response is not recorded, but in any case their fears were unfounded. No more was heard of the matter, and the College settled ever more confidently into political and religious conformity.

In one domestic area the College was fortunate to escape continued suspicion. The 'Catherine Wheel', which stood on the west side of the present Garden Quad, was leased out, and on the face of things not Balliol's responsibility, although the accounts show considerable intermingling of College affairs with it. It shared stables and probably some employees with the College, and Fellows often entertained visitors there. During the late 1580s the subtenant was Alice Boyden, 'a pious catholic widow'. In 1589 a midnight raid resulted in the arrest there of two missionary priests and a Catholic gentleman, together with one Humphrey Prichard. Prichard was a servant at the 'Catherine Wheel', 'who for twelve years had done signal services to the poor afflicted persecuted catholics in those evil days'. All four were ceremoniously hanged and butchered in the usual way.[17] But this does not complete the account of the involvement of the College and 'Catherine Wheel' with Catholic underground activities. In January 1606–7, Robert Wyntour, one of the Gunpowder Plot conspirators, confessed to the Lords Commissioners[18] that he had been at the 'Catherine Wheel' about a year before and had there, after a solemn oath of secrecy, been told of 'the proiect of the powder' by Robert Catesby. The air in that corner of the College must be conducive to hare-brained schemes. In the eighteenth century Southey and Coleridge planned their 'Pantisocracy' on the same spot. Today the members of the Junior Common Room hold their debates there.

[14] There are several debits in the accounts for gloves presented to major officers of State in 1587. In 1588 there is an entry 'for the final discharge of our suitte for our Corporation and the Seale'.

[15] D.7.8.

[16] British Library, Lansd. 59, item 6.

[17] Bishop [R.] Challoner, *Memoirs of Missionary Priests*, Philadelphia, 1840, i. 147.

[18] PRO, SP14/216, item 169.

9

The Early Seventeenth Century

DERVORGUILLA'S Statutes said nothing about regional affiliations. Somervyle's were also silent on the subject so far as the core of the Foundation was concerned, but, for the places he added, introduced a preference for men from the vicinity of Long Benton. Fox's code did not preserve this modification, and explicitly forbade any consideration of origin in College elections. As related in Chapter 6, this principle was the subject of some argument in 1542, with the result that the Visitor reasserted it rather firmly. The spirit, if not the letter, of the regulation was nevertheless soon undermined by the benefaction of John Bell, sometime Bishop of Worcester. When he died in 1556 he left his London house in Clerkenwell to the College, directing that part of the rental income derived from it should be used to support two Exhibitioners from the diocese of Worcester.[1] They were to be accomplished in grammar, and capable of starting on logic: 'duos scholares sive studentes in grammatica expertos, idoneos, habiles et sufficientes pro introitu ad disciplinam sive scientiam logicam sive dialecticam.' A significant bias in favour of the diocese grew from this, assisted by the fact that an early Bell Exhibitioner, from 1582 to 1585, was Henry Bright. He was briefly a Fellow, and then made a very successful career as a Worcester schoolmaster, sending many of his boys to Balliol.[2] The Bell Exhibitioners were, when resident, paid fifteen shillings a quarter. They were appointed by the Master, whose personal pupils they were, and they enjoyed the status and privileges of the Domus (i.e. Foundation) Scholars. Other benefactors followed John Bell's example. Thomas Browne, a former member, endowed by the will he made in 1586 a small Exhibition of a shilling a week for 'one poor towardly scholar' from Hampshire, with special preference to his own kin and the parishes of Basingstoke and Kingsclere.[3] The more substantial Dunch Exhibition

---

[1] The regulations for the Bell Exhibitions were printed with the College Statutes for the Royal Commissioners, 1853. There is a list of holders 1559–1852, compiled by A. Clark, with related notes by him, in the Archives.

[2] H. Savage, *Balliofergus*, 1668, p. 114. See also his epitaph in the north aisle of Worcester Cathedral.

[3] There is a transcript of Thomas Browne's will in the Scholarship and Exhibitions Register 'Conventa Collegii de Balliolo'. The regulations were amended somewhat by his executors. There is an incomplete list of holders of the Browne Exhibiton 1608–1821,

of £8 p.a. was established in 1605, in accordance with the wishes of Sir William Dunch's widow Mary.[4] The right of nomination alternated between the Dunch family and the College, with preference, when it was the College's turn, to a boy 'of the free school of Abingdon ... if there shall be then any Scholar in that School fit to be chosen'. The Dunch Exhibitioners in the College were to be 'chamber free there, and ordered, ruled and demeaned as touching their discipline, exercises, and bringing up, in such manner as the Exhibitioners of Doctor Bell and other the Scholars of the said House are'. They were also to share with Scholars their advantages, *ceteris paribus*, in Fellowship elections. It appears, in fact, that the Exhibitioners supported by all these schemes were additional Domus Scholars in all but name. In later years actual Domus Scholars are found holding Exhibitions in plurality. The arrangements were advantageous not only to the recipients but also to the College, since in every instance part of the Exhibition endowment income went into the College corporate account. In the case of the Bell Exhibitioners, for example, the Clerkenwell property yielded £10 p.a., of which the College received £4 and the Exhibitioners £6 between them, except that in cases of vacancy or absence the stipend reverted to the College. The numbers and sums involved in these modest schemes were not large enough to have a drastic effect on the composition or wealth of the College, but they paved the way for more ambitious proposals which did.

Peter Blundell was a wealthy clothier who had risen from humble Devon origins to great opulence as a London merchant. Tradition says[5] that he was

... at first a very poor lad of Tiverton, who for a little support went errands for the carriers that came to that town, and was tractable in looking after their horses and doing little services for them as they gave him orders. By degrees, in such means, he got a little money of which he was very provident and careful; and bought therewith a kersey[6] which a carrier was kind enough to carry to London gratis and make him the advantage of the return. Having done so for some time he at length got kersies enough to lade a horse and went up to London with it himself. Where, being found very industrious and diligent, he was received into good employment by those who managed the Kersey trade ...

compiled by A. Clark, with related notes by him, in the Archives. The Exhibition was dependent on a rent charge imposed on lands at Rotherwick, Hampshire.

[4] The composition by which the Dunch Exhibition was regulated was printed with the College Statutes for the Royal Commissioners, 1853. There is a list of holders 1604–1744 compiled by A. Clark, with related notes by him, in the Archives. The Exhibition was dependent on an annuity of £10 derived from property at North Moreton in Berkshire.

[5] *Donations of Peter Blundell*, Exeter, 1792, note A.

[6] A kind of coarse woollen cloth.

At the end of his life, worth some thirty or forty thousand pounds, he was able to call on his 'righte deare and honorable Friende Sir John Popham, Knighte, Lord Chief Justice of England' to help his feoffees carry out his wishes.[7] He died unmarried in 1601. In his will he made a large number of bequests to individuals at all levels of society (including the son of the carrier who had helped him put his foot on the first rung of the capitalist ladder), and for various charitable purposes.[8] He founded a free Grammar School at Tiverton, and also left £2000 to be used by Popham in the 'establishing of six ... students in Divinity in the university of Oxford or Cambridge or both for ever'. Popham was given a free hand to negotiate arrangements for the six places as he thought fit, but it was stipulated that once a scheme had been set up, the students were to be selected by his feoffees 'with the advice of the Schoolmaster there for the time being out of the said Grammar School of Tyverton, and not else where'. Blundell's purpose in endowing places at the universities was clearly stated in his will as 'the Increase of good and Godly Preachers of the Gospel'—a typically Puritan sentiment. In Cambridge Popham approached Sidney Sussex College and Emmanuel College, both new and frankly Puritan foundations. In Oxford he turned to Balliol, which also had Puritan leanings, and was his own college as well. Emmanuel declined involvement, but interim arrangements were soon made for Balliol and Sidney Sussex to have two and four Blundell places respectively, on a similar basis. A definitive agreement between Balliol and the Blundell feoffees was made in 1615, Popham having died meanwhile. The College was given £700 for the purchase of lands in Woodstock as the endowment for the scheme, which was to support one Blundell Scholar and one Blundell Fellow simultaneously. They were to receive stipends of £8 and £15 respectively, with the same rights and obligations as their colleagues on the ancient Foundation. When Blundell Fellows had graduated as MAs, they were to 'apply and addict themselves to the study of Divinity' and were to 'enter the Ministry, and become preachers of the word of God' as soon as possible, although a Fellow could hold his place for ten years from becoming an MA, or until he 'accepted a benefice with cure of souls, or charge of school'. The Scholar, chosen from the school at Tiverton as laid down by Blundell, succeeded the Fellow automatically when a vacancy occurred, whereupon the feoffees presented a new Scholar. The object of

[7] Five executors, five overseers, and twenty-seven feoffees (two of them infants) were named in the will as well as the Lord Chief Justice. The feoffees or trustees were left property in Devon to hold for the school and other purposes connected with Tiverton; provision was made for them to be a self-perpetuating body.

[8] There is a full contemporary copy of his will in the Archives (C.20.1). The will has been printed (*Donations of Peter Blundell*), 1792, but there are many minor discrepancies between the printed version and the Archives copy.

the scheme was to secure the permanent presence in the College of two Tivertonians. This required some finesse. On the one hand, it was clear that when a Scholar was ready to take on the status of Fellow, the Fellow might not be ready or willing to resign. On the other hand, a Fellow might vacate his place by death, marriage, or taking a benefice before the Scholar was of sufficient standing to be promoted. Two special provisions were therefore made. If a Blundell Scholar had been a BA graduate for a full year, but found the Blundell Fellowship occupied, he was allowed to claim the next Domus Fellowship to fall vacant, and to hold it until the Blundell Fellowship was free for him to be transferred into it. If a Fellowship vacancy arose too soon for the incumbent Scholar to take it up immediately, the feoffees could send a second Scholar. The scheme was to be expanded later, and became in time the subject of much acrimony, with complaint that it was an imposition and even a fraud on the ancient Foundation. It is difficult at this remove not to be critical of the College's attitude. Originally, despite protests over the years to the contrary, it was a good bargain for the College. The Woodstock estate which the Blundell money was invested in gave an increase in rental income of nearly £40 p.a., comfortably sufficient to meet all the expenditure associated with the Blundell students—especially as stipendiary payments were made only when they were actually in residence. It seems, in fact, to have been a handsome settlement by the feoffees. If, in later times, the endowment was inadequate, that was due to bad luck or mismanagement, not parsimony on the part of the benefactor's representatives.

Lady Elizabeth Periam's benefaction was both more straightforward and more generous. She was the eldest daughter of Sir Nicholas Bacon, Lord Keeper under Elizabeth I, and half-sister to Francis Bacon. She married, as her third husband, Sir William Periam, Chief Baron of the Exchequer, who died in 1604. When she made her will in 1618,[9] she arranged for some property in the Buckinghamshire parishes of Hambleden and Medmenham to be put at the disposal of her 'honorable freinde' the Archbishop of Canterbury, 'to be bestowed on Charitable uses in some Colledge of Oxford either in felowshipps or schollershipps as his grace shall thinke fitt'. The Archbishop of Canterbury at this point was the former Fellow of Balliol George Abbot, of whom more is said below. He advised that Balliol would be an appropriate college for the benefaction, and in fact Lady Periam lived to approve the arrangements personally in 1620.[10] Declaring herself minded 'to procure in some measure the promoting and increase in learning and religion', she promised to have the lands she had earmarked for the purpose conveyed to the College for the

---

[9] PCC will, 34 Dale (1621).

[10] The indenture was printed for the Royal Commissioners, 1853.

support of an extra Fellow, and two additional Scholars. They were to be known as Lady Periam's Fellow and Lady Periam's Scholars, but were to be otherwise practically indistinguishable from those on the ancient Foundation. She reserved the right to make the appointments herself while she lived, but after her death the patronage was to become the College's. The initial nominations were made or approved by her, but she died in 1621.[11] Thereafter, one of the Scholars was appointed by the Master, and the other by the Periam Fellow.[12] The Fellow was to 'undertake the tuition or tutorship of her Scholars and read unto them freely, without expecting any salary or reward for the same'. The Scholars were to have an allowance of £4 p.a. each, but the Fellow was simply to be 'received in omne jus Socii', having 'commons, diet, stipends, fines upon leases, dividends and allowances as other Fellows shall or do enjoy'. There was to be an annual commemoration feast, and a special sermon preached by the Periam Fellow on the First Sunday in May, but no other strings were attached. Lady Periam also gave an extra £50 for additional accommodation to be built. Tradition has it that the Periam Lodgings, which were somewhere near the site of the present Junior Common Room, eventually gave way to latrines, whence the once well-known Balliol euphemism 'Visiting Lady Periam'.[13] When the lavatories were moved to the other side of the Garden Quadrangle in 1912, the name followed them. The conveyance of the Periam endowment to the College was achieved in a roundabout manner via Archbishop Abbot and others, and not completed until 1628.[14] The Medmenham component of the property was exchanged for lands at Princes Risborough during this process. It all seems to have been above board, but Henry Savage, writing about thirty years afterwards,[15] thought the College was cheated by Lady Periam's executors: 'Thus our Pious Benefactrix beteem'd her Scholars reasonable Messes of Commons, but her cooks licked their own Fingers in dividing them.' Whether there is anything in this carping we cannot tell, but the fact is that the overall endowment income of the College was increased by more than £60 p.a., which was more than Lady Periam had promised, and easily enough to cover all the costs of the expansion.

George Abbot was also involved in another proposal which would have had far-reaching effects if it had been allowed to take root properly.

[11] There is an imposing monument to her in the church of St Mary the Virgin, Henley-on-Thames.

[12] There is a list of Periam Fellows and Scholars compiled by A. Clark, in the Archives, with related notes by him.

[13] J. Riddle, *Up the Cistern*, 1984, p. 14; J. S. Neaman and C. G. Silver, *A Dictionary of Euphemisms*, paperback edn., 1984, p. 69.

[14] E.12, E.15.

[15] Savage, op. cit., p. 85.

He was the senior member of a group of trustees to whom Thomas Tisdale of Glympton left £5,000 when he died in 1610, 'for the maintenance and sustenation of thirteene Schollers in Balliol Colledge in the University of Oxford, if there they may be conveniently placed and entertained according to the purpose of this my will; and if not then in some other Colledge within the University'. Tisdale was a rich trader and farmer, who had been brought up in Abingdon and who had made much of his fortune there. His scheme would have supported thirteen members, of whom six were to be of Scholar status and seven were to be Fellows. Preference in appointments to these places was to be given to his own kin and boys from Abingdon School, with the power to decide being partly with the college concerned and partly with the Abingdon authorities. To begin with, there seemed no obstacle to settling the scheme on Balliol, and soon after Tisdale's death the College received £300 of the benefaction. Some of this money was used to lease some tenements belonging to Christ Church which were on the north side of the College. This property included a building known as Caesar's Lodgings, which was for the accommodation of the Abingdonians (the lease was renewed by the College from time to time until 1773, when the freehold was purchased, extending the freehold site of the College northwards almost as far as the present-day limits). After an unexplained delay, Tisdale men were admitted to the College around 1620, but no detailed contract was made for the long term. The College hesitated, because it was reluctant to enter into an agreement which would result in a fundamental change in its composition, but terms were eventually agreed informally with the Abingdon corporation. Unfortunately, whilst this was pending, Richard Wightwick, Rector of East Ilsley in Berkshire, offered to augment the Tisdale endowment. It then occurred to the trustees (who still held by far the greater part of the money), and also to the corporation, that there was sufficient capital to form the basis of a separate institution, instead of grafting Tisdale's scheme on to an existing college which was proving less than enthusiastic. The outcome was that the trustees asked for their money back, and in 1624 they proceeded to set up Broadgates Hall as Pembroke College, named after the Earl of Pembroke. The five Tisdale Scholars at Balliol promptly migrated to Pembroke, and were named as Foundation Scholars in its charter. This was a severe blow to Balliol, because the £300 advanced by the trustees as an interim payment had already been spent. The College considered making a fight of it at law, but all parties agreed to submit to the arbitration of Archbishop Abbot. He ruled that the £300 should be repaid in instalments over the next few years. This was done, but every time an instalment fell due Abbot paid from his own pocket. The net result of the whole affair so far as Balliol was concerned was thus that it acquired the lease of a substantial contiguous property, which it did not really want at the time, but at no expense. The College felt swindled, and at a loss to understand its misfortune. The Balliol claim on the Tisdale money was apparently overwhelming. Thomas Tisdale had indicated a preference for Balliol explicitly in his will, and his widow had even recorded that he had been 'lyberally benificiall to Balliol Colledge' on his memorial in Glympton church, where her hollow praise can still be read. Furthermore, not only was George Abbot a Balliol man, but Richard Wightwick was too, and so was Thomas Clayton, the Principal of Broadgates Hall who became the first Master of Pembroke. It seems that Balliol had simply overplayed its hand, and prevaricated to a degree which exasperated the trustees enough to make them receptive to the idea of establishing a new college on their own terms instead of haggling over the arrangements any further. The last straw, perhaps, was the violent death of a Tisdale man at the hands of a Balliol Scholar in April 1624 which is related below: Pembroke's charter was sealed in the following June.[16]

On 3 June 1624, Scholar Ferriman Moore[17] was indicted before the Vice-Chancellor, the Mayor, and other Justices of the Peace, charged with assaulting Tisdale Foundationer John Crabtree[18] 'with a certen knyfe to the value of Sixe pence', 'giving the said John with the said knyfe one mortall wound in the bellye'. Moore pleaded not guilty, but was convicted of 'homicyde and manslaughter', whereupon he 'prayed the benefit of his clergie to be graunted unto him'. As he 'was a Clerk and did reade', this was allowed and branding was to have been his punishment. The Justices, however, were moved by the circumstances to petition the King for a pardon. Moore and Crabtree were both young and had had no quarrel previously, the Justices pointed out. There had been some 'childishe words' between them 'at a Beaver [bever—a snack, light refreshments] time in the said Colledge'. Crabtree, the senior and a BA although still under twenty, had not only taunted Moore with being a mere under-graduate (he was only sixteen) who should not presume to drink with a BA, but had also 'offered him violence several tymes, kykt him, pulled him by the haire and eares'. Moore had turned away from the Buttery hatch to go to his chamber, but when Crabtree followed him he drew his

[16] Most of the information in this section is derived from D. Macleane, *A History of Pembroke College Oxford*, 1897. See also Savage, op. cit., and MBP 13a.

[17] Ferriman Moore was elected a Scholar of Balliol on 11 March 1623/4. He matriculated from Exeter College as the son of Eustace Moore, aged seventeen, on 16 July 1625.

[18] John Crabtree took his BA from Balliol in 1623. The assault took place on 22 April 1624; his burial four days later is recorded in the register of St Mary Magdalen.

knife in self-defence, and wounded Crabtree in the confusion of the ensuing brawl. The Justices had taken pity on Moore in his misfortune and, in anticipation of a pardon, had granted him a reprieve 'from his burning in the hands', thinking that if branded he might 'turne his affection from his Colledge and his studdie'. Moore, who was 'well bredd in Learning, a youth of good hopes and come of godlie parents', was duly pardoned,[19] but he abandoned his Balliol Scholarship. He vanished from the scene for a year or so, and then resumed his education at Exeter College.

Accidental homicide provides a curious link between one of the College's most junior members and its most distinguished alumnus of the time, Archbishop George Abbot. On a deer hunt in July 1621, Abbot missed his target and killed a gamekeeper with a crossbow bolt. A Scholar in 1579, he was a Fellow from 1583 to 1597; later, he was Master of University College. Of Calvinist views, he was Vice-Chancellor in 1600, 1603, and 1605. In this capacity he once committed over a hundred undergraduates to prison, for sitting in his presence with their hats on. It was also as Vice-Chancellor that he had his first clash with William Laud, then a Proctor. Theological and political wrangles amounting to a feud between them lasted for the rest of Abbot's life. Laud was of the Arminian school, which, in its attitudes to ceremonial, and in some doctrines, leant towards Rome in a way which was anathema to the Puritans. Abbot remained dominant for many years, and through the patronage of the Earl of Dorset, Chancellor of the University, obtained royal favour. He was made Bishop of Lichfield and Coventry in 1609, and was translated to London in 1610. In the following year he was appointed Archbishop of Canterbury. As we have already heard, he was a good friend to Balliol for the next decade, but the fatal accident and resulting controversy of 1621 accelerated the decline in his influence which had already begun. As Abbot's power diminished, Laud's fortunes and theology prospered, and Laud had been the principal political and ecclesiastical force in the country for several years when he finally succeeded Abbot as Archbishop, on the latter's death in 1633.[20]

It was the influence of his younger but more distinguished brother which procured the election of Robert Abbot as Master of Balliol, when

---

[19] The circumstances of Crabtree's death are detailed in the petition for Moore's pardon, which survives in PRO, SP14/175.

[20] P. A. Welsby, *George Abbot. The Unwanted Archbishop 1562–1633*, 1962; H. R. Trevor-Roper, *Archbishop Laud 1573–1645*, 1940. For an exhaustive survey of works by or about Abbot, see R. A. Christophers, *George Abbot ... A Bibliography*, Charlottesville, 1966.

Edmund Lilly died in 1610.[21] Of Lilly's character and achievements not much is known beyond Henry Savage's remarks:[22]

He was an excellent Divine, universally read in the Fathers, all whose Opinions he would reckon up upon any Question in Divinity Disputations in the colledge; and that with such volubilitiy of Language and rivers of Eloquence, as made all covet to hear him, and his very enemies to admire him. He was Chaplain to Q. Eliz. and had been preferred by Her, had not his long-winded Sermon displeased her, when State-business occasiôned Her to enjoyn him brevity.

Of Robert Abbot, on the other hand, a great deal more is known. The contemporary biography,[23] though effusive, presumably has a foundation of fact:

... as a carefull and skilfull Gardiner he set his nurserie with the best plants, making alwayes choyce of the towardliest young men in all Elections, and when he had set them, he took such care to water and prune them that in no plat or knot in the famous nurserie of the University of Oxford, there appeared more beautifull flowers, or grew sweeter fruit than in Baliol Colledge whilst he was Master ... his diligent reading to his owne Schollers, and his continuall presence at publicke Exercises ... both countenanced the Readers and encouraged the Hearers.

That there was a strict attitude to College teaching under him is confirmed by a resolution of 1613, which gave Moderators and Praelectors the power to impose fines for negligence at disputations and lectures. He was a disciplinarian in religious observance as well, and never missed Chapel himself. Faced with excuses for absence from evening prayers because of its inconvenient time, he changed the hour from five o'clock to eight, and gave instructions for 'the gates to be lockt to prevent, or at least discover, all Noctivagators'. 'He every weeke viewed the buttry booke, and if he found lavish expence upon any mans name he would punish him severely for it.' At the same time he earned a reputation for kindness to those in difficulty, 'and if any were visited with sicknesse, he tooke care of them as if they were his owne children'. A conciliator in internal disputes, he was a vigorous controversialist outside the College. Soon after his election, he preached a virulent attack on 'The Old Waye'[24]—criticism by

---

[21] Robert Abbot acknowledged his younger brother's influence in his election in the dedicatory preface to his sermon 'The Old Waye' (1610), which he described as '... the first fruits of my return to this famous Universitie, whereof the chiefest protection under his most Excellent Majestie, belongeth to your Grace, and wherein through your Grace his commendation, though to a forward and wel-willing companie, I am now become a Head, where I lived sometimes an inferior member'.

[22] Savage, op. cit., p. 115.

[23] D. Featly, in *Abel Redevivus*, compiled by T. Fuller, 1651. Two engraved portraits are known to the College (for one, see Plate 5); there is an oils on panel portrait in the Maidstone Museum and Art Gallery: see MISC 202.   [24] See n. 21, above.

5. Robert Abbot, Master 1610–16.

6. The monument to Lady Elizabeth Periam (Benefactress, died 1621), in the parish church of St Mary the Virgin, Henley-on-Thames.

implication of Laud and his party, whose influence was on the increase. As Vice-Chancellor, he harangued Laud from the pulpit more specifically to his face in 1615:[25]

What art thou, Romish or English? Papist or Protestant? ... A Mungrel or compound of both: a Protestant by Ordination, a Papist in point of Free Will, Inherent Righteousness, and the like. A Protestant in receiving the Sacrament, a Papist in the Doctrine of the Sacrament? What, do you think there are two Heavens? If there be, get you to the other, and place yourselves there, for into this where I am ye shall not come.

These were spirited terms for the Master of Balliol to use against a neighbour, for Laud was President of St John's at the time. Although he complained privately at being obliged to sit and suffer abuse in public, Laud made no response. He would have his day later. In 1617 Robert Abbot was made Bishop of Salisbury, and he gave way as Master to John Parkhurst, who presided for the next twenty years. Parkhurst had no previous connection with the College, but was a protégé of Archbishop Abbot. More to the point, he was linked by marriage to the Tisdale family, with whom the College was negotiating for Thomas Tisdale's endowment. Savage described Parkhurst as a man of 'singular Learning, Gravity and Piety, frequent in Preaching and vigilant in the Government of this Colledge', but he does not seem to have made much of a mark in academic affairs. He had unrestricted leave of absence, and probably resided most of the time with his family at his Rectory of Shellingford, where he is buried.[26]

Soon after Robert Abbot's election, a new Statute was made providing for the admission of Fellow-Commoners:[27] 'Anno Domini, 1610, Novembris 22, ordinatum est unanimi consensu Visitatoris, Magistri et omnium Sociorum, liberum fore eidem magistro, aut ejus vicario, et majori parti Sociorum, extraneos quoscunque, quos vulgo appellant communarios, ad mensam et convictum Sociorum admittere ...' They were to be subject to the same personal, religious, and academic discipline as humbler students, with the slight advantage of a warning from the Dean in private when they transgressed. If such warnings were ineffective, however,

[25] P. Heylyn, *Cyprianus Anglicus*, 1671, p. 62.
[26] John Parkhurst (*DNB*) was baptized at Holy Trinity Church, Guildford (which was also the birthplace of the Abbot brothers), in 1563. He was presented to the Rectory of Shellingford in 1602, was married there on 22 Aug. 1611 (to Sarah Brooks, widow, daughter of Anthony Tisdale of Abingdon), had several children baptized and/or buried there 1612–39, and was himself buried there on 29 Jan. 1638. He bequeathed £20 to the College for the Library: his will is printed in V. M. Howse, *Shellingford. A Parish Record,* 1978, p. 119.
[27] Printed for the Royal Commissioners, 1853.

offenders were to be dealt with according to their ages and offences, without deference to rank. For their social privileges they were to pay an admission fee of £5 in books or plate. They were not a new class. Informal arrangements enabling the occasional rich man's son to study at Oxford for a year or two had existed since the fifteenth century. The new regulations merely recognized, took advantage of, and encouraged, the increased demand for such places from the upper strata of society. The Fellow-Commoners were to remain an important component of the College until towards the end of the eighteenth century. Their presence was financially advantageous to the House, because of the fees they paid, and the domestic profits made out of them. For the Fellow lucky enough to be Tutor to one of them, there were fat pickings from tuition charges (which were a matter of private contract), as well as the prospect of preferment if he could ingratiate himself with an influential family. More subtle, and in the long run more important to the College, was the slow creation of a pool of well-disposed and wealthy benefactors.

John Evelyn[28] confirms that the Fellow-Commoners were subject to the same academic regime as other students. In April 1637, he tells us, he 'was admitted Fellow-Communer of Balliol Colledge upon the 10th in the Chapell there, taking an Oath to be conformable to the Statutes, and Orders of that Society', noting that 'Fellow-Communers in Balliol were no more exempted from Exercise than the meanest Scholars there'. Later the same year he duly performed as required: 'December 9, I offerd at my first exercise in the Hall, and answered myne Opponent: and upon the 11th following declaymed in the Chapell before the Master, Fellows, and Scholars according to the Custome. The 15th after, I first of all Oppos'd in the Hall.' From his Tutor, George Bradshaw, Evelyn says he got little help, learning more from the company of his friend James Thickens. For the first year Bradshaw controlled Evelyn's money as well as his studies, this being a normal part of a Tutor's duties *in loco parentis*. Fellow-Commoners were probably not accommodated in any great luxury, either. Room-sharing was still the usual thing. It had to be, with around eighty residents to be packed in. Several of the attics or cock-lofts had been converted into rooms during the early years of the century,[29] in response to rising student numbers, but this did little to relieve the pressure. There were about eighty rooms by 1640, but many of these were 'studies', which were probably little more than cubicles. They were intended as working spaces, and only a few contained beds. Of proper 'chambers' there were only about thirty. The furniture inventory of 1640 from which these

[28] *The Diary of John Evelyn*, ed. E. S. de Beer, 1955.
[29] See the accounts for 1609–10, for example.

figures are derived also shows that there were fewer beds than residents.[30] The most plausible way of making the equation balance is to suppose that the younger students slept in pairs in the truckle-beds which were found in all the Tutors' chambers. In Henry Savage's case, there was a press or folding bed as well as the truckle-bed, which would have been pushed under the main high bed during the day.

> In Mr Savage his Chamber
> One high bedstead   one Truckle bed   one settle
> One Court Cupboard   one large Mappe of the World
> One large Table with leaves
> Two large Wainscote Chaires   one Imbroydered Chaire
> One large Presse   one presse bed
> One pair of Andirons
> One fire shovell
> One plate Locke
> One Wainscott Covering for the chimney

The chambers not allocated to Fellows were probably assigned to Fellow-Commoners and other senior members of the society, but it is likely that all of them had to share. That Evelyn did so appears from a note he makes of his brother Richard coming in 1640 'from schole to be my chamber-fellow at the University'.

Evelyn's disparaging remarks about his Tutor were grossly biased: Evelyn was a Royalist, looking back after the Civil War in which Bradshaw had been for Parliament, and thinking (probably wrongly) that he was related to Bradshaw the regicide. In any case, it is clear that there were many active and successful Tutors in early Stuart Balliol. Thomas Good, for example, was a resident Fellow from 1629 until the beginning of the war, when he had thirty-six pupils, 'bearing up the credite and reputation of that colledge'.[31] Edward Wilson was another. He was Tutor to Thomas, second Lord Coventry, who 'profited in vertue and good letters' under him. Wilson was for many years Senior Fellow, probably resident in College. Henry Savage records several more, such as Thomas Chambers, 'the greatest Tutor at that time in this Colledge'. The College Lecturers too took their duties seriously, if not recklessly, as in the case of Thomas Wilkinson: 'He read the Logic Lecture with that vigour, eloquence and prolixity, that drew on every scholars admiration, and his own death.' Nor was the College lacking in Fellows inclined to private scholarship,

---

[30] This unique inventory, 'A Note of such utensills that are in every particulare chamber in Ball. Coll.', is found at the beginning of Plate Records 2. It appears to be a complete room-by-room survey of College furniture. The purpose for which it was made does not appear.

[31] Lincolnshire Archives Office, VV 2/4/22.

despite its equally fatal consequences in the case of John Wood, an early Blundell Fellow: 'A Man of singular Parts and Learning. His head would, and did endure study several whole days and nights together, which his Body could not long doe: and this occasioned a lameness in his leg, upon which he dyed.'[32]

The official College teaching was largely in the hands of the three Praelectors (rhetoric, Greek language, and logic), with, in some years at least, a Catechist to teach divinity, reinforcing the frequent and lengthy sermons. The Master supervised the whole operation: in Abbot's case minutely, in Parkhurst's probably from a distance. We know very little about the private work of the Fellows as personal Tutors. No doubt this depended on the whim of the Tutor and the needs of the pupil. Remedial Latin and Greek would probably have been necessary in some cases, and private instruction in religious matters would certainly have been given by conscientious Tutors. Beyond that, all is conjecture, but it seems reasonable to suppose that general topics outside the College syllabus were introduced, especially into the teaching of those who were preparing for the Inns of Court, and lives as men of affairs. Geography and history, for example, are likely to have been taught at an elementary level—hence Henry Savage's 'large Mappe of the World'.[33]

The College also had in this period a number of prominent resident senior members who were not Fellows. Thomas Clayton, Regius Professor of Physic and later first Master of Pembroke, took his MD from Balliol in 1611. He was one of several medical men on the books. Edward Sylvester ran a small but very successful private grammar school in All Saints' parish, where he prepared boys for the universities. He was well known not only for this but also for his command of Greek language and literature, which was not yet a strong subject in Oxford. He had much in common with a remarkable trio from the Greek Orthodox world who came to the College in his lifetime. Christopheros Angelos arrived in England as a refugee about 1607, and was received first at Cambridge, but migrated to Oxford, for his health's sake, a few years later. Loosely associated with Balliol, he lived in Oxford, teaching Greek for most of the next thirty years. He also published a number of pamphlets in Greek, together with Latin or English translations—perhaps the first works written and printed in Greek in England. No doubt it was in part because of Balliol's links with Sylvester and Angelos, that Metrophanes

---

[32] Savage, op. cit., p. 116 ff.

[33] See above. Thomas Chambers (Fellow, died 1628) also had a 'great map' (OU Archives, Chancellor's Court Inventories); George Holland (Fellow, died 1596) had 'a greate mappe of the world with curteans' as well as 'seven lesser maps' (*The History of the University of Oxford*, iii (ed. J. McConica), 1986, p. 634).

Kritopoulos applied to the College about 1617, but Archbishop Abbot also had a hand in his admission. He had been sent to England by Cyril Lukaris, a senior member of the Greek Orthodox hierarchy, to see and hear something of the doctrine and ways of the Church in England, and to learn English. He would have had letters of introduction to the Church authorities, perhaps to Abbot himself, who would naturally have thought Balliol a very appropriate place for him. He stayed about five years, with Sylvester acting as his interpreter when necessary. By 1636 he had risen to be Patriarch of Alexandria. The third and last in this succession of members from the edge of Asia was Nathanael Konopios. He too was an associate of Cyril Lukaris, then Patriarch of Constantinople, but Lukaris was assassinated in 1638, and Konopios fled to England. Archbishop Laud gave him patronage, and directed him to Balliol about 1639. He attracted the attentions of his contemporaries as a man of culture and learning in literary Greek, and also because of the strange music he composed, for the musical traditions of the Orthodox Church depended on scales and conventions which were unfamiliar to English ears. A peculiarity of more lasting significance was recorded by John Evelyn: 'He was the first I ever saw drink Coffè, which custome came not into England til 30 years after.' The era was one of gradually awakening interest in Greek and oriental studies. The College clearly played its part in Oxford, and two at least of its alumni made names for themselves in the wider world as orientalists. William Seaman (1606–80) was in the service of the English Ambassador at Constantinople in the 1630s; he later published the first translation of the New Testament into Turkish, and a Turkish grammar. His near contemporary John Greaves (1602–52) is best known as a mathematician and astronomer, but he too travelled extensively in the Near East, surveying the pyramids, and collecting coins, gems, and oriental manuscripts.[34]

In the time of Elizabeth, there were few notable members of the College outside theological and ecclesiastical circles. Admiral Sir William Monson (1569–1643) and Lord Chief Justice Sir John Popham (1531–1607) are the principal exceptions. In the next generation, however, Balliol men begin to appear and distinguish themselves in more diverse fields. Sylvester, Seaman, and Greaves are examples we have already mentioned. Humphrey Davenport (1566–1645), Robert Mason (1571–1635), Francis Popham (1573–1644), Thomas Coventry (1578–1640), and John Wilde (1590–1669) were all prominent politicians. Dud Dudley (1599–1684) was an inventive ironmaster, who was probably the first to use coal instead of charcoal for

---

[34] The information in this section is mostly derived from Savage, op. cit., de Beer, op. cit., and A. Wood, *Athenae Oxonienses*, ed. P. Bliss, 1813–21. On Angelos, Kritopoulos, and Konopios, see R. Browning, 'Some Early Greek Visitors to England,' in *Essays in Memory of Basil Laourdas*, Thessalonika, 1975.

smelting iron ore. This was technically more complicated than it sounds, and of great economic and environmental significance, because the iron industry was consuming the country's trees, in some areas, much faster than nature could replenish them. William Barlow (Archdeacon of Salisbury, died 1625) was an early student of magnetism. John Rouse was Bodley's Librarian from 1620 to 1652: he managed to keep the Library open and intact through the upheaval of the Civil War, and had the courage to refuse to lend King Charles I a book in 1645. But every flock must expect to produce a black sheep from time to time. Richard Vennar (died 1615) was something of a writer, but his main claim to a place in the *Dictionary of National Biography* rests on an imaginative fraud or practical joke. In 1602 he advertised the premier performance of a non-existent masque entitled 'England's Joy' and sold a houseful of seats before making off with the takings. Fortunately for him the Balliol judge he appeared in front of when he was caught (Sir John Popham) took it as a joke, but he never lived it down. His luck went from bad to worse, and he ended his days in a debtor's prison.

Precarious solvency was the College's financial status when James I came to the throne. For the year 1604–5 the accounts show a credit balance of only £8, which had perforce to be carried forward as part of the float for the next year. Nothing could be laid up in the Treasury, or shared out among the resident Foundationers to augment their commons. Over the next fifteen years things took a turn for the better in several ways. Student numbers and domestic profits rose hand in hand, benefactions giving increased rental income came in, and there were occasional windfalls from the sale of stone out of the College quarry at Headington.[35] Student numbers fell off again somewhat after 1620, but financial security was by then more firmly established. The years 1604–5 to 1642–3 all showed a surplus, but the surplus was largely absorbed by increases in the standard of living. Twice in the period it was necessary for special steps to be taken so that large extraordinary expenses, in both instances on the Chapel, could be met. By 1606 it was clear that the roof needed re-leading, and a fund was opened for the purpose. The work was undertaken in 1610–11, when about £75 was spent on it. The scale of the operation may be judged from the fact that it cost eighteen pence, a good day's pay for a labourer, to have the new lead shifted from its delivery point at the back gate to the Chapel, and an 'engyn' had to be borrowed to raise the lead to the roof. The second programme, one of embellishing the Chapel interior a quarter of a century later, was much more expensive. For this, an appeal

---

[35] The College went to a great deal of legal trouble and expense to establish its claim to this quarry about 1610. It was claimed successfully that the quarry had been 'time out of mind in the possession of our Colledge'. The quarry was to the east of one owned by Magdalen College. See the accounts 1605–12 and Savage, op. cit., p. 82.

was launched. Over £300 was raised, much of it subscribed by former Fellow-Commoners. Sir John Popham[36] gave £100, the largest single amount. This was used to provide panelling and a richly carved screen, which was surmounted by the large effigy (probably St Catherine) which is now in the Library. Peter Wentworth and Richard Atkins gave new windows showing Philip and the eunuch, and the illness of Hezekiah. These windows, which are by Abraham van Linge, survive in the present Chapel, although both are now divided into two parts. The brazen eagle lectern which still stands as the Chapel centre-piece was given by Edward Wilson at the same time, and the present pulpit also dates from this campaign.

Adorning the Chapel was no luxury in the 1630s. What the Puritans would have regarded as foolish and superfluous was little more than the requirement of elementary decency to those who followed William Laud, which in 1636 meant practically everyone in the University, whether they liked it or not. As John Evelyn put it, 'for then was the University exceedingly regular under the exact discipline of William Lawd, Archbish: of Canterbury then Chancelor'.[37] Laud was elected Chancellor of the University in 1630. He was at that time still Bishop of London, but had already eclipsed George Abbot and his party in both power and royal favour. A man of strong views and energy, with the ability to control a great variety of complex business, he was not easily deflected from any course on which he set himself. Reform of the University was his mission. He was already active behind the scenes before his election, as in 1628, when squabbling over proctorial elections made necessary the promulgation of new regulations. Laud was instrumental in procuring the King's sanction to a system under which the right to nominate moved among the Colleges in a cyclical fashion. Colleges were allocated turns according to their relative importance: Christ Church six turns in the cycle of twenty-three years, Magdalen five, New College four, Merton and five others three turns each, Trinity and three others two, but Balliol only one, in the humblest group together with University College, Lincoln, Jesus, and Pembroke. On becoming Chancellor, he lost no time in making his intentions clear, demanding a weekly report on University affairs from the Vice-Chancellor, and pressing forward with work on the preparation of a comprehensive set of University Statutes. The Laudian Statutes, as they came to be known, were approved by the King in the summer of 1636. Their most fundamental novel feature was the introduction of examinations for degrees. But Laud's vigilance extended also to the detail of

---

[36] Son of Sir Francis Popham; entered as a Fellow-Commoner in 1618; not to be confused with Lord Chief Justice Sir John Popham (1531–1607), his grandfather.

[37] De Beer, op. cit., ii.19.

daily life, and few aspects of religion, study, dress, or conduct escaped his attention. For a while after his election, members of the Calvinist opposition could be heard protesting against him. Balliol's Giles Thorne (Fellow, elected 1617) was one who spoke out in 1631, possibly thinking that he would be protected from the worst effects of any official wrath by the fact that the Visitor, Bishop John Williams of Lincoln, was an opponent of Laud's. Thorne was one of three who were hauled before the King for preaching defiant sermons. He had aggravated his offences by appealing to Convocation when the Vice-Chancellor attempted to deal with him. The Proctors were sacked for not backing up the Vice-Chancellor; Thorne ('whose contumacy was notorious and his sermon base') and his friends were banished from the University.[38] Thorne went, but kept his dignity, entering his resignation in the College Register personally, and recording in the traditional form that it was 'sponte et non coactus'.

John Parkhurst resigned the Mastership in 1637, and Thomas Laurence was elected to succeed him. Laurence was a royal chaplain through Laud's influence, and his election was in all probability procured by Laud, who had been able to intrude himself as Visitor because Bishop Williams was suspended from office and imprisoned in the Tower. He had a reputation as an 'excellent Preacher, exquisite in the Elegancies of the Greek and Latin Tongues'; in Balliol he was a disciplinarian, but John Evelyn would not reproach him for his severity, 'considering that the extraordinary remissenesse of discipline had (till his coming) much detracted from the reputation of that Colledg'.[39]

The increasingly oppressive regime provoked an exodus of groups from all over the country, seeking freedom in New England from enforced conformity. The Puritan complexion of the College in the early seventeenth century would lead us to expect some Balliol men to be among these American pioneers. There were at least four. Roger Ludlow was a lawyer who sailed from Plymouth to Massachusetts Bay in 1630.[40] He was active in Massachusetts for a while, but threw in his lot with the Connecticut colonists about 1635. He probably drafted Connecticut's Fundamental Orders, its first constitutional document, in 1638, and he certainly

[38] A. Wood, *The History and Antiquities of the University of Oxford*, ed. J. Gutch, ii, 1796, p. 375.

[39] Savage, op. cit.; de Beer, op. cit., ii. He retained the Mastership until 1648 (see the next chapter), retreating to Colne in Huntingdonshire afterwards. In his will (PCC, 1658, 585), he requested burial in the same grave as his recently deceased wife, in the chancel of Colne parish church. He had several children, and was by no means a poor man when he died, as stated in the *DNB*. He may have practised as a surgeon, because he left his 'Barbers case with all Instruments therein' to his eldest son Thomas.

[40] J. M. Taylor, *Roger Ludlow*, 1900.

drew up its first Code of Laws before returning across the Atlantic during the Interregnum. The other three were all clergymen. Edward Norris emigrated about 1636, and was a leading moderate minister in Salem 1640–59;[41] Robert Jordan went to Maine and settled there in 1640;[42] John Bishop served as Pastor of the First Congregational Church, Stamford, Connecticut, 1644–94.[43] Nor was it leadership and pastoral care alone which they contributed to the shaping of America. They also gave their genes: John Bishop, for example, has been estimated to be the progenitor of over half a million descendants, most of them citizens of the United States.

[41] *Dictionary of American Biography*, xiii (ed. E. Malone), 1934, p. 552.

[42] He was Minister of the Episcopal Church at Casco Bay 1640–8, and preached at Casco Bay occasionally 1648–75; he married Sarah, daughter of Governor John Winter of Lygonia; he was active in various public affairs; he died at Newcastle, New Hampshire, in 1679. Information from Mr H. V. Jordan, of Kearsly, Bolton, 1985, and Dr J. B. Bell, of New York, 1986. See also T. F. Jordan, *The Jordan Memorial. Family Records of the Rev. Robert Jordan and his Descendants in America*, Boston, 1882.

[43] Information from Mr John Bishop IV, of Cambridge, Massachusetts, 1985.

10

The Civil War and Interregnum

NATIONAL unrest erupted into civil war during the summer of 1642. The University was generally strong for King Charles, and before the end of August a volunteer force of over three hundred academic enthusiasts was strutting about, playing at soldiers:[1]

> ... they marched downe through Halywell; and so, thorough a gate neere Mr Napper's house, they entred in to Newe Parkes; where by their commaunders, they were devided into foure squadrons, whereof two of them were musketers, the third was a squadron of pikes, the 4th of hallberdes; and after they had byn reasonably instructed in the wordes of commaund and in their postures, they were put into battell arraye, and skirmished together in a very decent manner ...

Mr Napper's house was Holywell Manor, and the New Parks were fields to the north of it. There was much confused coming and going before the King rode into the city in late October, after his battle with the forces of Parliament at Edgehill. Oxford was to be the Royalist capital for the next four years. Preparations for a siege began at once. Earthworks were thrown up in the fields near Holywell Manor, to protect the exposed north flank.[2] A labour force was conscripted from both Town and Gown, with a levy on institutions for wages, tools, and materials. Payments of this tax are the only direct allusion to the war in the Balliol accounts: debits totalling more than £25 for the erection of the ramparts ('pro aggeribus struendis') appear between 1642 and 1644. Enough shovels, spades, pick-axes, and hedging bills to equip a work-force of over three hundred men were issued from the military stores for the 'workes att Holliwell',[3] and at times the parish must have been like an anthill. The results were still clearly visible early in the last century, and vestigial ditches and banks yet remain here and there. The present Master's House is named 'The King's Mound' after one such bank—perhaps the site of the 'battrye at Hollywell' for which ammunition was supplied in 1643.[4] No major action took place in the sector, but it was not all military engineering and patrols. In December 1643 a Captain Hurst was shot there by order of the King, for

[1] A. Clark, *The Life and Times of Anthony Wood*, i, 1891, p. 54.
[2] R. T. Lattey, E. J. S. Parsons, and I. G. Philip, *Oxoniensia*, i. 161.
[3] I. Roy (ed.), 'The Royalist Ordnance Papers', *Oxfordshire Record Soc.* xliii and xlix. 187.
[4] Roy, op. cit., pp. 263 and 281.

stabbing a superior officer in an argument. The execution took place by 'Mr Napper's barn', an ancient great barn which used to stand over the road from Holywell Manor, where the Martin and Dellal Buildings of 'Holywell Minor' now are.[5]

The common soldiers and junior officers were billeted around the city wherever there was room, in private houses or inns like the 'Catherine Wheel', which also served as a reception point for supplies being brought in from the county.[6] The King established himself in Christ Church, the Queen at nearby Merton. The rest of the court, and the senior officers, took rooms in the other colleges. Balliol housed about thirty of them, including at various times the Earls of Clare and Cork, the Bishop of Ossory (Griffith Williams), Sir Ralph Clare, Sir Robert Poyntz, and Sir Thomas Lyttelton. All of them were in some way prominent in the Royalist cause, but only Lyttelton was a full-blown matriculated Balliol man. On the other hand they were all in residence for a fair time, and had their names entered in the Buttery Book to enable them to battel like the College's Commoners, so they all have some claim to be considered members—a point which becomes of some interest when we notice that there were women among them. The swagger and boisterous life-style of these guests were quite unlike anything the College had seen before. It was the same for the neighbours, and—not for the last time—Balliol people added to their problems, as a Trinity man recorded:[7]

Our Grove was the Daphne for the Ladies and their gallants to walke in, and many times my Lady Isabella Thynne (who lay at Balliol College) would make her entry with a Theorbo or Lute played before her. I have heard her play on it in the Grove myself, which she did rarely; for which Mr Edmund Waller hath in his Poems for ever made her famous. She was most beautifull, most humble, charitable, etc, but she could not subdue one thing. I remember one time this Lady and fine Mris Fenshawe (her great and intimate friend, who lay at our College) would have a frolick to make a visit to the President. The old Dr quickly perceived that they came to abuse him: he addresses his discourse to Mris Fenshawe, saying, Madam, your husband and father I bred up here, and I knew your grandfather. I know you to be a gentlewoman, I will not say you are a Whore; but gett you gonne for a very woman.

Mris Fenshawe was wont, and my Lady Thynne, to come to our Chapell, mornings, halfe dressd, like Angells. The dissoluteness of the times, as I have

---

[5] F. J. Varley, *Oxoniensia*, ii. 141; I. G. Philip (ed.), 'Journal of Sir Samuel Luke', *Oxfordshire Record Soc.* xxxiii. 222.

[6] M. Toynbee (ed.), 'The Papers of Captain Henry Stevens', *Oxfordshire Record Soc.* xlii. 14. In 1644, Commissioners from Parliament came on a safe conduct to negotiate with the King, and were accommodated in '... a mean inn, the sign of the Katherine Wheel ... which house was little above the degree of an alehouse': B. Whitelock, *Memorials ...*, Oxford, 1853, i. 332.

[7] *Aubrey's Brief Lives*, ed. O. L. Dick, 1962, p. 260.

C1.   The Lady Dervorguilla's seal, as on her Statutes, 1282.

C2.   The ruins of Sweetheart Abbey, by Alfred Waterhouse, 1870.

C3. The first common seal of the College: a modern impression and the corresponding original matrix, which probably dates from 1282.

C4. The second common seal of the College, as used from 1588 until recently: a modern impression and the corresponding matrix.

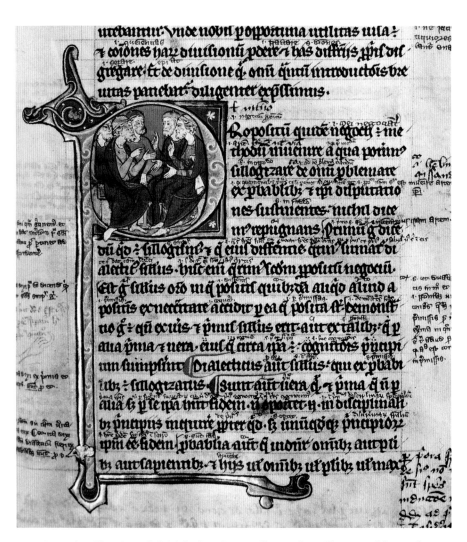

C5.   An illuminated initial showing a disputation. From a thirteenth-century manuscript in the College Library.

C6.   The burial of St Catherine. From a sixteenth-century window in the
Chapel.

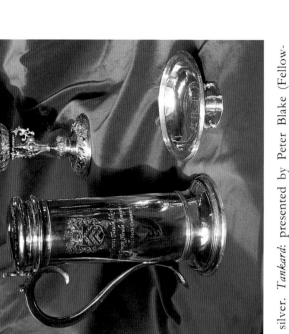

C7. Some seventeenth- and eighteenth-century College silver. *Tankard:* presented by Peter Blake (Fellow-Commoner), 1693. *Tankard with lid:* capacity 3½ pints, made in 1669, presented by John Kyrle (the 'Man of Ross'). *Two-handled cup and lid:* made in 1715, possibly for Sir Christopher Wren, and bequeathed by Robert Finch in 1830. *Flagon:* made in 1607 and presented by Henry Turvile, William Davenport, and Robert Horton (Fellow-Commoners) and George Holland. *Chalice:* probably originally a steeple cup for use at High Table, made in 1607 and presented by Thomas Sanderson in 1614, modified for Chapel use in 1618. *Paten:* no hallmark, probably made out of the Sanderson steeple-cup cover in 1618, possibly at the expense of John Price (Fellow-Commoner).

C8. Theophilus Leigh, Master 1726–85.

C9. The Broad Street front and forecourt, about 1770.

C10. John Parsons,
Master 1798–1819.

sayd, grieving the good old Doctor, his dayes were shortened, and he dyed and was buried at Garsington.

The supply of new entrants almost dried up at the beginning of the war, and the number of students in residence dropped abruptly. For the few who remained the whole atmosphere was wrong, and they were liable to be 'debauched by bearing Armes, and doing the Duties belonging to Soldiers as Watching, Warding and sitting in Tipling-Houses for whole Nights together'.[8] Despite manifold distractions, academic appearances were maintained. Elections were held, the accounts were kept and audited, College Lecturers were paid, and St Catherine's Day was celebrated according to ancient tradition. But the veneer of normality was thin, and grew thinner as the College slid slowly towards financial ruin. On 1 July 1642, £210, probably most of the cash reserves, had been 'lent to his Majestie out of the Treasurie by the unanimous consent of the Master and fellowes'.[9] With the onset of the war, although estates income apparently remained largely unaffected (remarkably if really so, since most of it was derived from distant and hostile parts),[10] takings and profits from residents fell, and expenses rose, because of contributions to the war effort. The situation was aggravated early in 1643, when the College had to give up its plate to the Royal Mint, which was temporarily housed in New Inn Hall. Eighty-two pounds of silver and twenty-six pounds of silver gilt were surrendered.[11] This was not just a sacrifice of the decencies of the common table. The College plate was also its only realizable asset, and there was no other financial reserve. A little later, fifty-three pounds of brass was given in, probably for ordnance purposes. Seizure of Chapel utensils would have been sacrilegious, and they were exempt. The chalice presented by Thomas Sanderson (Fellow 1582; one of the translators of the Authorized Version of the Bible), which is still in use, owes its survival to this, and so does the Chapel's brazen eagle lectern. The College was otherwise swept clean, and left without any financial security at all. The money and valuables put into the King's hands were quite clearly loans, but no recompense or repayment has ever been made. Valiant efforts by the Bursars to conduct business as usual slowly broke down as the Royalist organization collapsed, and the accounts finally peter out completely in 1645–6.

In the small hours of the morning on 27 April 1646, the King slipped

---

[8] Dick, op. cit., p. 23.   [9] Treasury Book 1.

[10] H. W. C. Davis (in *A History of Balliol College*, revised by R. H. C. Davis and R. Hunt, 1963, p. 115) makes much of the loss of rents. The accounts are incomplete, but it appears from those which we have that the losses were small. In 1644–5, for example, the total income entered under the heading *Reditus Recepti* is £243, the same as in the years immediately before the war. On the other hand, the College's financial problems in the 1660s were then blamed, in part, on uncollected rents during the war.

[11] F. L. M. Willis-Bund, Appendix II in Davis, op. cit.

out of Oxford in disguise. Within a few days the Parliamentary Army, under Sir Thomas Fairfax, closed its lines about the city. To avert a bloody and destructive siege, Fairfax offered honourable and generous terms, remarking 'I verie much desire the preservation of that place (so famous for Learning) from ruine, which inevitably is like to fall upon it except you concurr.'[12] The garrison of three thousand men marched out on 24 June, 'well armed with colours flying and Drums beating',[13] to disperse outside the city. The Royalists left the University and colleges with the integrity of their buildings, privileges, and constitutions guaranteed by the Articles of Surrender, but no individual's place was secure. All that was promised was that dismissals would not be precipitate, and even this assurance was qualified with the ominous reservation 'that this shall not extend to retard any Reformation there intended by the Parliament'.[14] Most of the academics had been loyal to the Crown throughout, and could hardly expect to be left undisturbed.

Within a few days of the Parliamentary take-over, academic autonomy was suspended. No elections or admissions were to be made, or leases sealed, 'until the pleasure of the Parliament be made known therein'. Shortly afterwards, a squad of Presbyterian divines was sent down to preach at the University. There was a good deal of theatrical pulpit rhetoric, but nothing much actually happened until a board of Visitors was set up, nearly a year later, 'to reforme and regulate the aforesaid Universitie'.[15] Even then the pace was slow, as the leading figures of the University proved ingeniously obstructive. The reformers were patient but resolute. Vice-Chancellor Samuel Fell was declared 'guilty of high contempt and denyall of authoritie of Parliament', stripped of authority, and ordered to move out of his Deanery at Christ Church. More than orders were required: his wife and children had to be carried out by troops. Most of the other heads of houses were ejected as well. Thomas Laurence, still Master of Balliol, kept a low profile, but was displaced as Lady Margaret Professor. He submitted to the Visitors shortly afterwards 'without any salvo or reservation', promising 'to observe the Directory in all ecclesiastical administrations, to preach practicall Divinity to the people, and to forbeare the preaching of any of those opinions which the Reformed Churches have generally condemned'. He was one of the few men of consequence in the University to submit, and he might have been

[12] A. Wood, *The History and Antiquities of the University of Oxford*, ed. J. Gutch, ii, 1796, p. 480.

[13] Ibid., op. cit., p. 485.

[14] Ibid., op. cit., p. 484.

[15] The Register of the Visitors has been edited by M. Burrows (*Camden Soc.*, 1881), and much further detail is given by Wood, op. cit.

tolerated as Master, but he seems to have been ashamed of the whole business, as he promptly resigned and slipped away to a country living. George Bradshaw, a Fellow who had assisted the Visitors from their first appearance, was appointed to succeed him as Master by an Ordinance of Parliament on 21 July 1648. According to John Evelyn,[16] Bradshaw 'had parts enough' but had been at odds with Laurence since before the War to an extent which 'tooke up so much of his tyme that he seldom or never had any opportunity to discharge his duty to his scholars'. Bradshaw was one of the Balliol trio among the 'divers worthy Gentlemen' who were appointed 'Delegates to the Visitors' in September 1647. The others were Thomas Good, who nevertheless prospered after the Restoration and ultimately became Master, and Anthony Palmer, to whom the payment of Fellowship emoluments was ordered by the Visitors in 1651, despite his recent marriage. He had, they recorded, 'continued in the said colledge one whole year after his marriag at our spetiall instance and request, that he might be an assistant unto the Master'—a unique exception to the celibate tradition.

With a thorough shake-up among the University's dignitaries under way, the Visitors turned to the lower strata. In May 1648 they began a systematic examination in the colleges, asking each member in his turn if he would submit to the authority of Parliament. The answers they received were very varied. The Balliol replies, which are exemplified below, span the whole range from abject subordination to bloody-minded refusal, but most pleaded conscientious grounds for declining or gave evasive responses:

James Pitt: Till I am further satisfied I cannot submitt.

Francis Fitzherbert: I conceive I ought not in conscience to submitt to this Visitation.

Richard Smith, Cooke: I humbly submitt to the authoritie of parliament in this visitation.

Thomas Throkmorton: I will not be soe traiterous to my Kinge as to acknowledge the pretended right and authority of his enemies.

Those refusing to submit, or failing to appear for examination, were expelled. The loyal Throgmorton nevertheless managed to hold his place and make a nuisance of himself for nearly another year, when the Visitors were provoked into reiterating their sentence:

Ordered: That whereas Thougmorton in Balioll Colledge in Oxon, haveinge beene formerly (by an order of the Committee of Lords and Commons) expelled the Universitie for his high contempt of the authoritie of Parliament, and haveinge also since behaved himselfe (in many perticulers) contemptuously towards the

[16] *The Diary of John Evelyn*, ed. E. S. de Beer, 1955, i. 13, ii.17.

Visitors in neglectinge their comaunds, and disregardinge their indulgence and favor which they shewed him in hope of his Reformation, and also affronted the Government of this Universitie. That hee shall therefore be expelled the Universitie, and forthwith depart the same upon his perill.

Only one Fellow was examined in this first round. The College Register showed that Robert Feilden had been absent in the service of the King in 1645, and neither his refusal to submit nor his dismissal can have surprised anybody.

There was plenty of expostulation and obstruction, but little practical resistance to the military reality of the situation. One of the few instances was a plan by the remaining Cavaliers to start a local counter-revolution in July 1648. The garrison and Visitors were to be surprised while at their Sunday devotions, and after the Cavaliers had joined forces with similar groups in other towns, an attempt would be made to relieve Colchester, where a number of Royalists who had taken up arms again were besieged. The conspirators met in the 'Catherine Wheel'. An alehouse in the suburbs was a convenient rendezvous, but drink was their undoing. Some of them 'discoursed of their design in their cups' and gave the game away. Only three were captured, and one of these escaped. The other two, a barber called Adams and a musician by the name of Curteis, were made to cast lots in prison for the roles of hangman and victim. On 4 September they were marched to the 'Catherine Wheel', where preparations were made for Curteis to hang Adams from the inn sign. The condemned man climbed the ladder, delivered his final speech, and was poised to die, when the presiding officer reprieved him. He was later pardoned. A melodramatic tale, but it really happened, in the street now overlooked by the Junior Common Room windows.[17]

Eight more Fellows were ordered to be expelled *en bloc* in August 1648, for failing to appear before the Visitors, but the sentences were not put into effect immediately. Only James Thickens and Richard Spurway were actually ejected, two months later. The submissions of Thomas Good and Anthony Palmer were probably taken for granted, despite their absence, because they had previously collaborated with the Visitors. The rest managed to retain their places anyway, simply by keeping their heads down until the purge was over.

Foundation vacancies were filled by the Visitors with men who held acceptable political and religious opinions, mostly chosen from the 'great rabble of new faces, scraped out of Cambridge and the Country' who were brought in to establish 'a new plantation of Saints'. One at least of their nominees, George Swinnock, must have pleased them: he became a

---

[17] Wood, op. cit., p. 602.

well-known Nonconformist writer. Another, however, let them down. Matthew Poore, who was put in during 1648, was admonished by the College and reported to the Visitors for misconduct in May 1650. They found the 'many Articles of foule and scandalous nature' alleged against him proved, and expelled him from the College and University. About a dozen appointments were imposed on the College by the Visitors in the period 1648–50, after which self-government was allowed again, and elections were once more made according to the Statutes.

The Fellowship of 1650 thus comprised a mixture of intruders and survivors. Several of the latter are of particular interest. Nicholas Crouch,[18] elected in 1640, had slipped away from Oxford at the end of 1645, reappearing without any fuss in June 1649. He was at heart a Royalist, as the note in his diary for 30 January 1649 shows: 'Rex Barbarè capite Truncatus'. But the cause was lost, so he opted for a quiet and apolitical life, whilst taking a very active part in the domestic business of the College. He took up the study of medicine, perhaps to avoid controversy, and practised the profession in a limited way. The Library has his medical notes and prescription books. Smitten with antiquarian interests, he spent much of his time transcribing, analysing, and arranging the College Archives. Many of the sources for this history owe their survival to him. Henry Savage, also an undoubted Royalist, was of a less retiring nature. Within two years of his nominal expulsion, he had put on enough of the Puritan for the Visitors to judge him 'eminent for piety and learning, and fitt for Government', and they appointed him Master when Bradshaw's resignation was exhibited to them on 20 February 1650. It was later claimed that Bradshaw had in fact been ousted to make way for Savage, Thomas Good being the prime mover.[19] Good himself, as already noted, had collaborated with the Visitors from their first appearance, and he held his Fellowship without interruption from 1629 to 1658, but he was a 'peaceable, moderate' man and an 'honest and harmless puritan';[20] he avoided controversy by being absent for much of the last decade or so of his tenure. His kinsman[21] and sometime Scholar, John Good, also held

---

[18] See MSS 334–6, 339, 355. MS 355 is his diary; its entries are few, brief, and mainly concerned with his own movements, but some are gems not recorded elsewhere, e.g. 27 May 1660, 'Dns: Edm: Fortesc: Matrimon: Comisit in sacello Coll: de Bal:' the first known marriage in the Chapel. The bride, Margaret Sandys, was related to the Master's wife.   [19] Lincolnshire Archives Office, VV 2/2/30 and 2/4/22.

[20] A. Wood, *Athenae Oxonienses*, ed. P. Bliss, 1815, iii. 1154.

[21] That Thomas Good and John Good were related is implied by the circumstances, although the relationship is unclear. There were at least six of the name Good admitted to the College in the seventeenth century, but their genealogy has yet to be unravelled. There were two main branches with Balliol connections—one centred on the City of Oxford, and another with its base in Worcestershire and Shropshire.

his Fellowship right through these troubled years. His election as a Probationary Fellow was the last recorded by the College before the city fell; his appointment as a full Fellow was the Visitors' first. He remained in residence until his death in 1676. Commonly known not as 'John Good' but as 'Tutor Good', he had a reputation as a 'scholastical retired and melancoly man'. He entered into a pact with some friends that the first to die would appear to one of the others, and prove the immortality of the soul, if he could. This happened in 1654, when a 'resemblance' of a recently deceased friend appeared in John Good's chamber and 'said to him with a trembling and faint voice *Sors tua mortalis, non est mortale quod opto*'.[22]

A recent Master has made the maelstrom of the English Revolution and its intellectual undercurrents the main themes of his writings.[23] From a different vantage point, a Balliol poet of the time bemoaned 'the sceane turn'd topsie turvie' in verse:[24]

> The world is a great Bedlam, where men talke
> Distractedly, and on their heads doe walk,
> Treading antipodes to all the sages,
> And sober-minded of the former ages....
>
> No teaching now contents us the old way,
> The lay-man is inspired every day,
> Can pray and preach *ex tempore*: the priest
> With all his learning is despis'd and hist
> Out of the Church, and some have lately sed,
> He should be shortly brought to beg his bread....
>
> Dost see my muse the world turn'd upside down,
> The prince on foot, whiles mounted is the clown;
> The beggar now a purchaser, and hee
> That was worth thousands, brought to beggerie? ...
>
> Dost thou behold all this, and canst be mute?
> Come take thy bow and arrowes, aim and shoot
> The sharpest of them, cast thy keenest dart

[22] A. Wood, *Fasti Oxonienses*, ed. P. Bliss, 1815, part 1, cols. 387–8. It has been alleged that the 'wraith of an old Fellow in eighteenth-century costume' has been seen in the Fisher Building (Davis, op. cit., p. 152), and ghostly figures of young men dressed in 'nineteenth-century infantry uniform' and the 'style of the early twentieth-century' were seen by credible witnesses on Staircase XVI, during 1974 and 1980 respectively (*Balliol College Record*, 1982, 67).

[23] J. E. C. Hill, Master 1965–78: a bibliography of his writings up to 1977 is given in *Puritans and Revolutionaries*, ed. D. H. Pennington and K. V. Thomas, 1978. See also G. Eley and W. Hunt (eds), *Reviving the English Revolution. Reflections and Elaborations of the Work of Christopher Hill*, 1988.

[24] Thomas Washbourne (1606–87): *The Poems of Thomas Washbourne*, ed. A. B. Grosart, 1868, p. 181.

At this mad age, and strike it to the heart;
Come dip thy pen in vinegar and gall,
And never leave til thou has vented all
Thy just spleen on it: if it stil grow worse,
Let it expect not thine but God's great curse.

What parts did Balliol men play in the affairs which Christopher Hill and Thomas Washbourne have observed so acutely? Although the College had its share of Royalist colonels, and was represented among the officials on both sides, none of them had a major influence on events. Its writers made more of a mark, but even they for the most part only merit footnotes to the intellectual history of the period. Tobias Crisp[25] was a radical theologian who preached that God's grace was for all men, not just a chosen élite: no sin so heinous that forgiveness would be denied. Harmless enough sentiments, these now seem, but such thinking was part of the drift towards ideas about equality, democracy, and communism which gathered momentum after Crisp's death in 1643. A lasting development in which Balliol men played a small part was the birth of the Royal Society. Timothy Baldwin and George Castle were both peripherally associated with the Oxford Experimental Philosophy Club, a group of 'virtuosi or wits' including Christopher Wren, Robert Boyle, and Robert Hooke, which met to discuss and experiment upon scientific topics in Oxford during the Commonwealth.[26] This club was part of the movement from which the Royal Society emerged after the Restoration. Two more Balliol men, Timothy Clarke and John Evelyn, were active in the same sphere. Both of them were named as council members in the Royal Society's first charter.

The Puritans worked hard to rid the University of Royalist opinion and to impose their own social mores, their own brand of godliness. Disciplined collegiate life was firmly enjoined, with orders enforcing common meals in Hall (at which only Latin or Greek were spoken). Only 'auncient weomen, and of good report' could be engaged for domestic help. Members of the University were told to forbear 'all excesse and vanitie, in powdering their haire, wearing knots of ribands, walking in boots and spures and bote-hose-tops'. Attendance at academic exercises and Sunday services was to be obligatory. All religious observance should be plain in form, without ritual or ceremony. Tutors were to be hand-picked, and required to exercise tight control. As well as controlling the money, behaviour, and studies of their pupils, they were to say prayers with them daily. Regular sermons, long ones by modern standards, were to be delivered, and junior members might be examined on them to prove that

---

[25] [J. E.] C. Hill, 'Dr Tobias Crisp, 1600–1643' in J. [M.] Prest (ed.), *Balliol Studies*, 1982.
[26] C. Webster, *The Great Instauration*, 1975; Clark, op. cit., p. 201.

they had been attentive. All this is known from the Register of the Visitors. How effective the measures were in Balliol is difficult to tell, but the few glimpses of College life we catch in the 1650s all point to the survival of Cavalier attitudes and sympathies. The first year's accounts after the resumption of normal business show a donation of ten shillings to a 'poore gent formerly in the King's service'. In 1654 the ardent Royalist John Evelyn was welcomed back with special hospitality.[27] Gentleman-Commoner John Holt's behaviour would no doubt have passed unrecorded but for the fate it brought him. 'This Holt upon a frollick had been merry at Heddington' and on his way home at three in the morning he had a contretemps with an ex-Parliamentarian. He fell off his horse and was trampled to death. A disorderly end was followed by a disorderly funeral in the church of St Mary Magdalen, after which the preacher was punished for 'profanation and abuse of scripture, tending much to the palliation of and extenuation of gross miscarriages, to the strengthening of the hands of the wicked, and sadning of the hearts of the godly'.[28] Gaudies continued uninhibited, and the summer 'Act Supper' described by Hannibal Baskerville sounds positively convivial:[29]

... a custome they have in Balliol Coll., where they keep an eminent Act Supper,[30] which once I sawe, being invited thither to take part of their good Cheer, some years before the Kings restauration. And that was in the middest of the hall in the fireplace they had planted an Oak ... with all his green boughs and leaves flowrishing upright, but the bark of the body was taken off. This strange sight, it being hard to conceive how they got it into the roome, with the musick and good Cheer to boot, made the entertainment very pleasant.

Counterbalancing indications of the tone the Puritans were trying to create are quite lacking.

When the Restoration of the Monarchy came in 1660, almost all the members of the College who owed their places to the Visitors were long gone. The change is hardly noticed in the College records. There were no ejections, interrogations, or administrative discontinuities. James Thickens was restored to his place by a writ from the Crown, but the only other signal of political change in the College Register is the resumption of the practice of designating years by regnal number: 1660 is declared, in

[27] De Beer, op. cit., iii. 105.

[28] Clark, op. cit., p. 184; Burrows, op. cit., p. 370.

[29] Bodleian MS Rawl. D.810, fo. 35.

[30] The Act was an annual event in early July, originally intended to mark the conclusion of the academic exercises for graduation. By the late seventeenth and early eighteenth centuries it was the principal social occasion in the University's calendar, but it was 'overshadowed by the entertainments and general junketing which accompanied it' (V. H. H. Green, 'The University and Social Life' in *The History of the University of Oxford*, v (ed. L. S. Sutherland and L. G. Mitchell), 1986, p. 350).

Nicholas Crouch's distinctive hand, to be the twelfth year of the reign of King Charles the Second.

Initially, a tolerant attitude towards Nonconformity prevailed, but opinion soon hardened. The Act of Uniformity reimposed the Church of England with a vengeance. In Chapel on 31 August 1662, Henry Savage solemnly made the declaration which was now required by law.

I Henry Savage Mr. of Balliol Colledge Oxon. doe by these presents declare mine unfeigned assent and consent unto and approbation of the 39 articles of Religion mentioned in the Statute made in the 13th year of the Reign of the late Queen Elizabeth, and of all and every thing conteyned in the said articles, according to the literall and Grammatical sense thereof. And I doe here declare my unfeigned assent and consent to all and every thing conteyned, and prescribed in and by the Book intituled the Book of Common Prayer and Administration of the Sacraments and other Rites and Ceremonies of the Church, according to the use of the Church of England, together with the Psalter or Psalms of David, pointed as they are to be sung, or said, in the Churches; and the forme or manner of making ordeyning and consecrating of Bishops Priests and Deacons. In witnese where of I have hereunto subscribed my hand this 31th day of August Anno Dni. 1662, according to the Act of Uniformity of Anno 14to Caroli secundi Regis.

Hen. Savage.

The College was to remain firmly in the grip of the Established Church for most of the next two centuries.

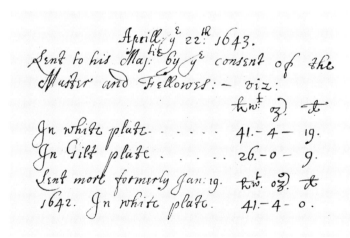

Fig. 4. The College's record of its loan (which is still outstanding) to the King, reproduced directly from the Treasury Book.

BALLIOFERGVS,
OR A
COMMENTARY
UPON THE

Foundation, Founders and Affaires,

OF

Balliol Colledge,

Gathered out of the RECORDS thereof,
and other ANTIQUITIES.

With a brief Description of

EMINENT PERSONS

Who have been formerly of the same House.

Whereunto is added,

An exact Catalogue of all the Heads of the same
Colledge, never yet exhibited by any.

Together with

TWO TABLES,

One of ENDOWMENTS, the other
of MISCELLANIES.

By *HENRY SAVAGE*, Master of the said Colledge.

OXFORD, Printed by A. & L. LICHFIELD, Printers
to the University. 1 6 6 8.

7. Henry Savage, Master 1651–72.

8. The title-page of Henry Savage's *Balliofergus*, 1668.

II

Penury and Recovery 1660–1720

W E have already made frequent reference to *Balliofergus*,[1] the history of the College which Henry Savage circulated in manuscript soon after the King's Restoration. It was printed in 1668. The Oxford antiquary Anthony Wood had helped him in a small way, but did not think much of it. A scratchy professional scholar, Wood was jealous of the dabbling amateur: 'But the Author having no natural Geny to the study of Antiquities and History, ... hath committed many foul Errors therein.'[2] It is true that holes can be picked in Savage's work with ease, and his style is patchy. Sometimes he meanders, like an old man after dinner, moving by degrees away from his theme until he forgets what he meant to say. But when in his stride he has a memorable turn of phrase. His resounding dismissal of uncritical historians is typical. In the previous century Bishop Lesley had persuaded himself, and others had repeated, that the College had been founded and endowed by John Balliol, King of Scots, who was of course actually the Founder's son, and a mere child when the College was established.

These are meer Empusas, having no more to go with but one leg, which is the imagination of their Author ... I confess 'tis a common, but almost impardonable Error of Historians, to pin their Faith on other Mens sleeves when they cannot, or will not, take the pains to finde out the truth ... Five or six more besides Lesley, write the same with him, deriving it by tradition one from another, or else all from some single Author of credit amongst them, which becomes like a Dog of good creance in the Pack, which at a loss, no sooner spends, than all the rest follow him with open mouths without ever laying their noses to the ground ...[3]

---

[1] H. Savage, *Balliofergus*, 1668. MS 255 is an earlier version dated 1661; MS 429 comprises various drafts and notes including some provided by Anthony Wood. For bibliographical details, see F. Madan, *Oxford Books*, ii, 1912, p. 222.

[2] A. Wood, *Athenae Oxonienses*, ii, 1721, p. 499.

[3] Savage, op. cit., p. 12. *Empusa* = hobgoblin or spectre; *spends* = barks on picking up the scent. The mistaken idea that the College was a 'Scotch Foundation' established by John Balliol, King of Scots, was very persistent, and even now resurfaces from time to time. It led to the Warner Benefaction, which in turn led to the Snell Benefaction (see later in this chapter), which between them gave substance to the originally false tradition. In the nineteenth century, the College became so confident in its Scottishness that the arms of

He does not entirely avoid running with the pack himself, and despite his strictures occasionally repeats the unjustified fancies of others in his own work. He is least reliable on the identification of early alumni. But Savage was breaking new ground. No history of the College—or indeed of any college—had been attempted before, and he had to work from a poorly organized accretion of original documents. The transcriptions printed in his book are full of minor slips, but the history of the College's foundation, constitution, and estates which he reconstructed by examining all the relevant deeds he could find has been borne out by subsequent re-investigations. He does not appear to have overlooked anything of significance which survives in the College Archives. Conversely, it is gratifying to report that all the deeds he does cite can still be found. As well as providing an outline history of the College's first four centuries, Savage's book has many personal touches throughout, especially in his comments on notable members he had actually known.

Balliofergus is not an essay in *pietas*, historical scholarship, or idle curiosity, although all these elements are present. There is much harping on the College's financial problems, which are usually ascribed to the fraudulence and caprice of parties long since dead. Maladministration and imprudence were in fact at the root of the College's difficulties, compounded by bad luck and the hard times experienced by all the colleges. This picture, however, did not suit Savage's purpose, which was to provoke sympathy, and attract benefactors. The principal dedicatory epistle, to Archbishop Sheldon (of Sheldonian Theatre fame), was, beneath its veneer of fulsome praise, a begging letter. The list of over a hundred distinguished living members which is given prominence at the beginning is surely a cry for help. Some copies also have a dedication to the Earl of Lauderdale, with an explicit plea for assistance because the College was 'the mockery of Fortune'.

Whilst this slightly pathetic appeal was being hawked about, the financial situation of the College went from bad to worse. Property yielding about one-fifth of the total rental income was razed in the Great Fire of London, and weak administrative practices allowed the College to slide badly into debt to its bakers, butchers, and brewers, largely because of increasing uncollected battels arrears. Apparently blind to the looming crisis, the College became factious instead of uniting and taking decisive action to avert collapse. Two Fellowships were suspended, with the Visitor's approval, immediately after the Great Fire.[4] Some plate was

Scotland (Or, a lion rampant within a double tressure flory and counterflory gules) were displayed on College book-plates, notepaper, and on at least one building (the Library Tower).

[4] Latin Register, 1666.

sold,[5] and Savage was able to raise several substantial donations.[6] But by 1670 the College's debts still amounted to at least £500, more than two years' corporate income. About half could be offset on paper by battels arrears, although it would have been more realistic to write most of these off as irrecoverable.[7] It was time for the Visitor to intervene.[8]

Bishop William Fuller of Lincoln took the College's affairs in hand during July 1670, visiting in person for several days, and assuming his statutory powers, which were absolute. He called for all the accounts and College books, but he did not restrict himself to financial matters, and also asked many questions about teaching, religion, and conduct. He had been primed for the proceedings by Thomas Good, who had written to him beforehand with detailed suggestions about what should be probed, and urging him on: 'Beseeching Almighty God to direct you in your intended visitation, that al things may be carryed on to his Glory, the increase of good literature, and for the happiness and prosperity of that auntient and almost ruinid foundation.' It will be recalled from an earlier chapter that Good was a moderate Puritan who had been a Fellow of the College many years before. He had long since been without any formal position in College affairs, and wrote from his Shropshire parsonage, but he was in close touch with the Balliol situation, and evidently influential with the Visitor. At the end of his investigation, the Visitor expressed dissatisfaction with what he had found, and recorded 'That in his perusing the Accounts and State of the Colledge he found a great neglect and miscarriage, both in the Master and Fellows, which he cannot pass over without some reprehension and admonition'. For the time being, however, he contented himself with referring the detailed auditing of the accounts to a committee of college heads, and adjourning his visitation pending their report.

[5] Silver to the value of £52 was sold to Mr Porter, goldsmith, in 1668, to help reduce the debts. It had all been given since the Civil War. See the First Latin Register, p. 332, and Plate Records 2.

[6] A schedule of donations, somewhat confused, is inserted in Benefactions Book 1.

[7] The total debt was estimated even in 1672 at £600 (Lincolnshire Archives Office, VV/2/4/22), and some progress towards reducing it had already been made by then. As well as debts for provisions, the figure of £600 includes returnable caution money deposited by members, which had been spent. See also F.12.3, which confirms the total debt in 1671 as around £550, having been over £800 in 1667, when £463 was owed to the butcher alone.

[8] The papers of the Bishops of Lincoln as Visitors of Balliol 1621–87 survive at Lincolnshire Archives Office, reference VV/2. They are an extensive and rich source, especially for the period 1670–4. As well as financial papers, visitation questions and answers, etc., they include a long series of letters from Thomas Good. Except where otherwise indicated, the following section is based on these papers. An excellent calendar of them has been prepared by C. M. Lloyd.

The conclusions of the auditors are not known, but the Visitor reactivated his inquisition in 1671. This time some of his questions were rather more pointed. The exact questions, and three sets of answers to them, survive. They are signed respectively by (*a*) Henry Savage, (*b*) Senior Bursar Thomas Allam, with William Good and George Burton, and (*c*) Junior Bursar William Beach. Four of the Articles of Enquiry, and the corresponding replies, will suffice to illustrate the degree of discord existing:

Article 4.   Do the Deans and Bursars perform their duties according to the Statutes?

Savage: 'They have (for ought we know) done nothing flatly against Statute in things relating to their offices purely, but Mr Allam hath since his bearing his office done things which any modest intelligent and honest man would be ashamed of.'

Allam et al.: '... the Bursars doe justly and statuably execute their office, the Deans doe not.'

Beach: 'Prayers and exercise are not exactly observed by the Deans. Neither have the Accounts been punctually audited heretofore by the Bursars.'

Article 6.   Are the Statutes read publicly as required, and what of lectures etc.?

Savage: 'The Statutes of the College are publickly read twice every year as alsoe Divinity lectures but other lectures are not read, yet in liew thereof the Lecturers doe moderat in disputations which are duely performed. And the Mr. did for diverse years give an able Grecian 4 lib. per annum to read a Greek lecture which was performed in the Hall accordingly.'

Allam et al.: 'Part of the Statutes are read publiquely twice every year. Divinity and other Lectures are not, disputations in the Arts and Sciences are not performed.'

Beach: 'The Statutes are duely read. Lectures and Disputations are not duely observed.'

Article 7.   'What Tutors are there in the College, be they of sober conversation, exemplary in their lives, diligent in reading to their pupils, not only the Arts and Sciences but alsoe the Articles of Religion, exhorting them to a serious practise of piety and Religious duties.'

Savage: 'Most of the Fellows are Tutors, and we suppose they doe theire respective duetyes.'

Allam et al.: 'All the Fellows are Tutors, two excepted, and to the other part of this Article they are present to answer for themselves.'

Beach: 'Most of the Fellows are tutors. But all of them doe not so diligently read to their pupills as tis to be wished.'

Article 9.   Are the servants chosen according to the Statutes, and 'did any one give money or other reward for theire places?'

Savage: 'The servants are (as we conceive) statuably chosen; nor doe we know that any of them gave anything for their places.'
Allam et al.: No, and 'there has bin money given and received for places'.
Beach: 'The underbutler or porter was not statutably admitted, for the cooks place there was a reward promised, if not already given.'

Many other issues and allegations were debated, some very hotly. The Master denied that the Cook's place had been sold, but it was generally believed that his wife had done just this. In vain he protested that servants had been bribed to say so, and in any case he was also accused of other improprieties—taking Exhibition money for his non-resident son, holding two livings contrary to the Statutes, and so on. The estates were being mismanaged, and there were hints that there had been deals favourable to individuals but injurious to the College. The College's debtors included the Master and Senior Fellow. The Scholars were being charged for tuition instead of being taught gratis. Allam had put unreasonable charges on battels, which, Savage said, 'seems to the Undergraduates a great burden and occasiond complaints'. Attendance in Chapel was irregular. The former scandalous practice of women visiting Fellows in their chambers had ended, but two Fellows lodged in the town, and one was even said to be a married man with a child. Only on the basic practical facts of the situation was there any accord. They were agreed about the essentials of their plight, if not the apportionment of responsibility. Virtually the only satisfactory thing to emerge was that the collegiate buildings were in a reasonable state. On this the Master had answered in 1670: 'The Chappell and other buildings of the Colledge are for the most part in sufficient repair ... and we have a constant survey taken of all decays and they are mended as soon as with convenience they may be.' Nobody was able to contradict him then, or in the following year. This was the only aspect of his stewardship to escape criticism. That the buildings had been well maintained was vitally important. An unexpected heavy expense in that department would almost certainly have proved the *coup de grâce*.

His investigations complete, the Visitor issued instructions covering all the deficiencies which had been exposed. The Statutes were to be publicly read, lectures were to be given, Chapel services were to be more regular, and absence or lateness was to be punished. Tighter administration was to be introduced all round. Individuals in whom he found fault were specifically dealt with. The Master was 'admonished to be more careful of the Observance of the Statutes', and ordered to pay into the Treasury the £20 he had received from the Cook. Allam's treatment was curiously contradictory: an admonition recorded in the College Register for running down the Master with rude words and gestures was cancelled, but at the same time he was mentioned by name in a general admonition to be more respectful to the Master. Thomas Hodges was ordered to resign within a year, probably for holding benefices incompatible with his Fellowship. Even Nicholas Crouch, whom Thomas Good thought 'honest and ingenuous', with a 'candide disposition', was not spared. He was to hand back £6 he had accepted for a Scholarship place, and put an equal sum into the Treasury from his own pocket. The Visitor's views on the sale of places and on the attitudes and conduct of the Master and Fellows were thus made plain. Two features of the College's financial system which had been exposed without being condemned now seem rather shady. The first was that the College did not receive room rents: practically the entire site was divided up into territories assigned to the Fellows, which they could and did sublet for personal profit. The practice was no doubt thought acceptable because the basic emoluments of Fellows were so meagre—half a crown a week for commons plus various statutory small sums, amounting in all to only £7. 13s. 1d. a year. The second practice which might have been reformed with advantage was by this time customary throughout the University. When a lease was renewed, a lump sum or fine was paid which did not relate in a fixed way to the rent. Now the rent was paid every year or half-year into the corporate account, from which stipends, commons, and general expenses had to be met. The fine, on the other hand, was a payment made once only, when the renewal of the lease was granted; it was usually simply divided among the Master and Fellows (with a share to Domus, i.e. the College corporation) at the time. This placed them in the position of choosing between immediate personal gain and corporate income for their successors. A tenant might be willing to pay a large fine (which was nice for the present) in order to secure a long lease at a low rent (which would impoverish the future). The system also carried the risk of bickering among the members of the Governing Body, because there was flexibility over the timing, except with leases which had actually expired. In fact tenants usually negotiated for renewal long in advance of expiry if they could, because this gave them the upper hand in the discussions.[9]

The Visitor withdrew from the battle-front after the second round of examination and deliberation, but did not officially wind up his visitation, and he kept in touch with the College's affairs. His principal informant was still Thomas Good. In September 1671 Good wrote to say that he

---

[9] The Lease Log Book, or Fine Book, contains a detailed analysis of leases granted, with discussion of the calculation of fines and rents. It was begun by Nicholas Crouch and kept up to date by his successors. The period covered is roughly 1600–1800.

had heard from Balliol

... that the affairs of that unfortunate colledge are still declining; that the master and his party fearing a removal are calling upon the tenants to renew their leases with al possible speed & tis feard they wil set Robin Hoods pennyworths [i.e. dishonestly low prices] unless they be immediately preventd; that elections of officers at St Lukestide, of Fellows at St Katherinestide will be carryed on by the master (or rather by the mistresse) and her party to the great detriment of the Colledge ... I wish (if it may) that there were a decree made that for the future noe master might be marryed, and that this present Lady (by your Lordships strict iniunction) might never come within the colledge gates any more ...

Two months after this, he wrote 'the manciple and the new cook (as I am informed) doe shark upon the schollars', and reported that there was unrest over elections. But the College's fever, no doubt eased by Allam's death and Beach's resignation, did begin to subside, although there was still much to be done when Henry Savage died on 2 June 1672.[10] Only three days later, the Privy Council was advised that it would be inappropriate for a mandamus to be issued for the vacancy, 'there being but one man, Mr Good of Hereford, likely to come into the place with affections suitable to its necessities'.[11] Shortly after this, Good wrote to the Visitor from Shropshire:

Though I was unwilling to accept of the Masters place of Bal. Coll whilst my old friend and colleague was alive, yet the place being now void by his death I doe modestly desire it, not for any great advantage that may accrue to myself, but for the publick good of the poore colledge, of which I am more tender than any private concerns of my owne.

Good also thought he would have a majority in any case, and that it would be advisable to let the electoral process take its course. The Visitor decided to avoid all uncertainty. Because his visitation was only adjourned, the power lay in him to appoint a new Master, and he installed Good in

---

[10] He was buried in the Chapel on 5 June, at the bottom of the steps going up to the Altar (Latin Register; A. Clark, *The Life and Times of Anthony Wood*, ii, 1892, p. 247). His will was proved in the Chancellor's Court (OU Archives, Chancellor's Court Wills). There is a portrait of him in the Hall. He had several children. His troublesome wife was Mary, sister of William Lord Sandys, with whom Savage is said to have travelled in France in 1642, probably as his tutor (*The Complete Peerage*, xi, 1949, p. 447). Only about a dozen Chapel burials are recorded altogether. Senior Fellow George Powell was the last to be laid to rest there, in 1830. The normal burial place for members who died in residence was the parish church of St Mary Magdalen. Further burials in the Chapel were prohibited in 1855 (D.10.5).

[11] PRO, SP29/310, fo. 188.

Savage's place forthwith. The election by the College took place after-wards, and was pure formality.[12]

When he came into residence the following October, Good took firm control of the College's internal administration, and purposefully set about raising funds and recovering debts, writing to tell the Visitor his hopes and plans:

... I am now returned to the old colledge, where by the blessing of Almighty God I shal use my best endeavour for reducing it to its former splendour, though to effect that I must wrestle with divers difficultys ... however I shal not forbeare to solicite my friends and acquaintance whoe have had their educacon in this place to become benefactors to their old mother in her necessitys occasioned partly by the late wars, by the dreadful fire at London, by the neglegence of her children in poynt of accounts ...

The direct approaches he made to rich former members, like John Evelyn,[13] were very effective, and he managed to obtain payment of many outstanding battels accounts. With the help of the Visitor he secured a substantial donation from Dr Richard Busby, the great Headmaster of Westminster School, and he negotiated successfully with several external foundations, of which more will be said later.

The overall result of Good's efforts was that the College was solvent by the time he died in 1678,[14] but he did not have a particularly easy reign, as there was a minority among the Fellows who resented his reforms. In 1674 he complained to the Visitor that certain Fellows were opposing him out of pique: 'I have disannuld their sharking impositions and lazy customs which grew up in my predecessors sleepy government.' He was not deterred from persisting in his campaign, but he was hurt by the 'cross-capers' and 'continual oppositions ... by those Fellows which never obteined one farthing of any Gentleman towards the payment of our debts'. They might have shown some gratitude, he felt, especially as he had 'repaired some of the Fellows Chambers' and 'allowed them money

[12] The Visitor's instrument appointing Good as Master was drafted (Lincolnshire Archives Office, VV/2/2/35) and executed (D.3.16) on 14 June 1672. The 'election', however, took place on 16 June, 'unanimi consensu omnium sociorum' (First Latin Register).

[13] E. L. G. Stones (*Archives*, 16 (1983), 131) has given an account of a petition to King Charles II (preserved at Longleat House) in which he cites Good's correspondence with Evelyn and his other fund-raising efforts.

[14] He died on 9 April 1678; he was buried in Hereford Cathedral. His will was proved in the PCC (1678, 32). It appears that he had neither wife nor descendants living when he died. He made a bequest 'to Baliol colledge for the maintenance of a fyre in that house from Allhallowtide to Candlemas' and 'towards the maintenance of some ingenuous yong man to be chosen out of the Parish of Tenbury, Burford or Corely', but no signs of these subsidies have been found in the College accounts.

to make a hansome common roome'. His own estimate was that the grand total of money raised or recovered by him was about £2,000, a remarkable and practically single-handed achievement.

Comical anecdotes are fun, but can distort perception of their butt, because they linger longer in the memory than cold fact. The enduring image of Thomas Good as a silly old fool, so completely at odds with his performance as the College's saviour, seems to be based largely on one such well-known anecdote. It is a richly worded and amusing tale,[15] and it has indeed been rightly said that it is too good not to be quoted at length.[16] But it seems fair to preface it with the doubting reservation of the original raconteur:

There is another ridiculous story of him, which I doe not well beleeve; but however you shall have it. There is over against Baliol College a dingy, horrid, scandalous alehouse, fit for none but draymen and tinkers and such as by goeing there have made themselfes equally scandalous. Here the Baliol men continually ly, and by perpetuall bubbeing ad art to their natural stupidity to make themselfes perfect sots. The head [Good], beeing informed of this, called them togeather, and in a grave speech informed them of the mischeifs of that hellish liquor cald ale, that it destroyed both body and soul, and adviced them by noe means to have anything more to do with it; but one of them, not willing soe tamely to be preached out of his beloved liquor, made reply that the Vice-Chancelour's men dranke ale at the Split Crow, and why should not they to? The old man, being nonplusd with this reply, immediately packeth away to the Vice-Chancelour [Ralph Bathurst, President of Trinity]; and informd him of the ill example his fellows gave the rest of the town by drinkeing ale, and desired him to prohibit them for the future; but Bathurst, not likeing his proposall, being formerly an old lover of ale himself, answered him roughly, that there was noe hurt in ale, and that as long as his fellows did noe worse he would not disturb them, and soe turnd the old man goeing; who returneing to his colledge, calld his fellows again and told them he had been with the Vice-Chancelour, and that he told him there was noe hurt in ale; truely he thought there was, but now, beeing informed of the contrary, since the Vice-Chancelour gave his men leave to drinke ale, he would give them leave to; soe that now they may be sots by authority.

Good's correspondence seems to indicate a degree of paranoia about the evils of women and alehouses, and he was perhaps 'very often guilty of absurditys'. But it is better to judge him on the practical achievement of his Mastership, and on his own words. Whilst he was Master, his book *Firmianus and Dubitantius* was published.[17] Most of this is a laboured fictional dialogue on controversial subjects, but it begins with a list of

[15] 'Letters of Humphrey Prideaux . . .', *Camden Soc.*, NS, xv. 13.

[16] H. W. C. Davis, *A History of Balliol College*, revised by R. H. C. Davis and R. [W.] Hunt, 1963, p. 133.

[17] T. Good, *Firmianus and Dubitantius*, 1674.

aphorisms which summarize his views in pithy form, offering the advice
that readers 'will not altogether loose their time, if they shall please to
entertain these following considerations in their more serious thoughts'.
Thirty-four considerations are put forward, of which the following are
representative.

11. We must live by Scripture rule, which must be the measure of all our Actions;
    not the example of others, nor the common customs of the times, nor the
    Civil or Common Laws of the Country, which are too short and narrow, and
    crooked, to measure our Actions by.

14. Seriousness in business is the greatest wisedom, temperance the best Physick,
    a good conscience the best Treasure.

15. Drollery and foolish jesting renders a man unfit for any employment, Sacred
    or Civil.

16. The true definition of a Good-Fellow, is, that he is a pittiful thing, good for
    nothing.

18. Honesty is the best policy; every Knave is a Fool.

20. Business is the best Recreation; the mistimeing of innocent past-times, the
    immoderate and unseasonable use of them, the intemperate use of the
    Creature, as Meat, Drink, Tobacco, much Sleep, (things in themselves not
    sinfull) are the common occasions of great debaucheries, and sins against
    God, our neighbour, and our selves and families; they are apt to encrease an
    airy lightness in our discourse and carriage, some of them do much promote
    melancholly, which renders a man resty and inactive in the business of his
    calling, and especially in duties of piety.

22. Though some kinds of gameing (if due circumstances be observed) be not
    unlawful, yet when we spend more time upon them, than at our devotions,
    when they hinder us in the duties of our calling, when they are carryed on
    with a covetous desire of gain, when we stake our hearts as well as our
    money, when we grow passionate, curse and swear, at a bad cast, or game,
    they are exceeding sinful.

26. More kindness ought to be shew'd to a sober Non-conformist, than to a
    debauched profane Cavalier, who is the grand Non-conformist and adversary
    to our Church.

33. Tutors in the University that are not very carefull to bring up their Pupils in
    good literature, and religion especially, are grand Traitors to them, and betray
    that trust which is reposed in them, and such Pupils commonly return into
    their Country, a shame and reproach to the place of their education, where
    they will rail against, revile and curse, such wretched Tutors.

These are not the notions of a foolish old man. They vouch for a thoughtful
Puritan, but no bigot, with a slight tendency to radical views—an altogether more convincing character for the man who dragged the College
out of the mess it was in during the 1660s.

Although it was Good's immediate concern to rescue the College from
bankruptcy, it was also his intention and hope to improve the long-term

position, by obtaining additional endowments for places. Endowments unencumbered with conditions were of course straightforward improvements. Usually there were strings attached, but in such cases it was still possible to manipulate them to the College's advantage in various ways. If an external trust would take on the indefinite support of an existing post or posts, so that it could make future appointments, this would release income from the original endowment, so that the other Foundation places could have more generous emoluments. Alternatively, an outside body could in effect be sold a share of the establishment for a cash lump sum, in return for which its nominees would be guaranteed places and stipends in the future. Less obviously attractive, but at least tending to increase domestic turnover and profits, were endowments which simply provided for students who drew nothing from the Foundation. Contracts belonging to any of these three categories could of course be negotiated in such a way that there were other direct and indirect advantages to the College and its senior members.

The Blundell feoffees had shown, at an early stage of the financial difficulties, that they were well disposed towards the College, with a gift of £50; when Good discovered that they were minded to expand their provision for Blundell's boys at the universities, he began to negotiate with much larger sums in view. His efforts were complicated by the attitude of some Fellows, who made a point of being disagreeable to members of the Blundell Foundation, so that for a while it seemed that the feoffees might turn to Sidney Sussex.[18] In 1676 Good nevertheless struck a bargain.[19] Under it, an existing Fellowship and Scholarship were converted into additional Blundell places, for a consideration of £600. This was tantamount to the outright sale of Foundation places, and a breach of the Statutes by introduction of a regional restriction for what were, legal niceties apart, still places originally created by ancient endowments. Furthermore, although this doubling of the Tiverton representation in the College was the last formal concession to them, their increased numbers gave them greater confidence and influence, so that in the next century they were able to become dominant. The 1676 agreement was, for this reason, much condemned by nineteenth-century reformers and College historians, but Thomas Good would have seen it as a bold step enabling him to put the College back on its feet, sacrificing the independence of two places in order to preserve the viability of the rest. Freedom from regional restrictions on admission, desirable as it appears to us now, must then have seemed at best an eccentricity. Several of the colleges with closed foundations were flourishing. That Good himself had

---

[18] Lincolnshire Archives Office, VV/2/4/13/, 15, and 16.
[19] C.20.6.

no doubts about restricted Fellowships and Scholarships is shown not only by his eager acceptance of more Blundell places but also by his attempts, at about the same time, to raise funds for the exclusive benefit of Worcestershire students at Balliol. He had an open letter printed and circulated to the clergy of the county in which he had himself been born:[20]

I have had many sad thoughts concerning the unhappiness of my Native Country; ... that whereas almost all Counties in England and Wales have convenient Maintenance allotted for the Education of young students in one of the two Famous Universities of Oxford or Cambridge; Worcestershire is altogether destitute of any considerable Encouragement for Ingenious Scholars; whereby many that have had parts worthy of higher employment, have been condemn'd to inferior Callings; and others who might have been eminent in their generation, have been snatched away from those famous Nurseries unto poor Country Curacy's before their Beards were grown; where their lean and scandalous Sallaries have scarcely afforded them a short Canonical Coat to cover their nakedness.... May it please your Honours ... to ... consult together about the setling of two or more Fellowships and Scholarships in Baliol Colledge, (commonly known by the name of Worcester Colledge) for the Education of young Scholars, of that County: in so doing your Memories will be pretious in after ages, which will have just reason to celebrate your praises, and to bless Almighty God for such truly noble Benefactors and Patriots.

The assertion 'commonly known by the name of Worcester Colledge' is startling, but the college which now bears that name had not then been founded. If Balliol was really ever known as Worcester College, the fact has escaped all record save Good's appeal. It was probably an invention to draw attention to the strong—but unendowed—link which already existed between Balliol and the Worcestershire area. Nothing came of Good's scheme, perhaps because the goodwill of those parts had been exhausted earlier. Old members resident in Worcestershire had been prominent among those solicited successfully by Savage.

John Warner was a Fellow of Magdalen 1604–10.[21] In early life he enjoyed the patronage of Archbishop George Abbot, but he emerged later as a supporter of William Laud. Warner was appointed Bishop of Rochester in 1637. An outspoken Royalist, he was ejected from his see in 1643; he was restored in 1660. He was a Londoner by birth, but when he made his will he set up a scheme to support four Scots at Oxford. This was not out of any special affection for, or links with, Scotland, but in order to favour episcopacy there, by creating a means of indoctrinating young Scots with the ways of the Church of England. He approached his

[20] Balliol College Library, 670.e.6 (4).
[21] E. Lee-Warner, *The Life of John Warner, Bishop of Rochester 1637–1666*, 1901. This includes a transcript of Warner's will.

own college about his plan, but Magdalen declined to be associated with it,[22] and it was the 'Scotch Foundation' Balliol which he named in his will: 'I give out of my Manor of Swayton for the maintainance of four Schollars borne in Scotland eighty pounds yearly and for ever, which said Schollars shall be placed in Baliol Colledge in Oxford, there to enjoy their annuities or exhibitions until they are Masters of Arts and fitt to be admitted into holy orders according to the Church of England.' When he died in 1666 the College was dilatory, and nothing had been settled when Thomas Good became Master in 1672. He proposed to Warner's executors that they should endow two of the existing Fellowships, which would then be confined to Scots and subject to the conditions of the will; they would have associated with them two Scholarships also reserved for Scots.[23] This came to nothing, and eventually four Warner Exhibitions quite independent of the ancient Foundation were created. The first four 'Scotch Exhibitioners' were admitted to Balliol on 21 March 1672/3, thus beginning the strong connection which the College still has with Scotland. The scheme was never really successful. Complicated additional regulations had to be made to enforce the benefactor's intention, because several Exhibitioners defeated his purpose by not going back to Scotland after ordination. One of the first intake went as chaplain to the English factory in Lisbon; one of his colleagues became domestic chaplain in Lord Russell's house; another of the following year went to sea before settling in Essex. Relations between the Scottish Exhibitioners and the College were very cool for a long time, with mutual distrust over money. The College was said to overcharge; the Scots to welsh on their debts. Quick solutions to the problems were not forthcoming, and the scheme had not established a consistent tradition of its own when the Snell Trust appeared on the scene. This overshadowed, and practically absorbed, the Warner Exhibitions, which became in time little more than supplements to the Snell Exhibitions, because they were commonly held in plurality. Sir Orlando Bridgeman, Lord Keeper, was one of John Warner's executors. Bridgeman's seal-bearer and principal man of business was a Scot educated at Glasgow University, John Snell,[24] to whom he delegated some of the

[22] Lincolnshire Archives Office, VV/2/1/7; *VCH*, Oxfordshire, iii. 84.

[23] A detailed account of the early years of the Warner Exhibitions in the hand of Nicholas Crouch is to be found at the back of the Second Latin Register. There is an almost complete list of Warner Exhibitioners 1671–1888, compiled by A. Clark, in the Archives. Good's proposal to establish Fellowships for Scots out of the Warner benefaction was still under discussion in 1676, when all the Fellows signed a petition to the Visitor objecting, and protesting that Good had maligned them as 'factious and obstinate' whereas it was in fact a matter of conscientious judgement as to the interests of the College (D.22.9).

[24] [E.] L. [G.] Stones, 'The Life and Career of John Snell (*c.*1629–1679)', *Stair Soc.*, 1984, Miscellany II, p. 148.

details of the Warner negotiations.[25] Snell had personal links with Oxford through his wife,[26] and thus a double interest in Warner's scheme. He was a man of substance because of his association with Bridgeman, which gave many perquisites, but he had no son to whom he could leave his wealth, and when he came to make his own will in 1677, he modelled his principal provision on Warner's idea. The residue of his estate was to be used to support at Oxford a number of 'Scholars borne and educated in Scotland, who shall each of them have spent three years, or two at least, in the Colledge of Glascow in that Kingdome or one yeare there and two at least in some other Colledge in that Kingdome'; the students accepting this support were obliged to take holy orders and refrain from accepting any benefice in England, it being Snell's 'will and desire that every such scholar so to bee admitted, shall returne into Scotland, and there bee preferred and advanced as his or their capacity and parts shall deserve'. Snell died in 1679,[27] but life interests in the estate delayed the execution of his wishes for twenty years. No college was picked out in the will to be host to the Snell Exhibitioners, but the Master of Balliol was to be a trustee, together with the Vice-Chancellor, the President of St John's, and the Provost of Queen's. Balliol was perhaps thought the obvious choice because of the bogus Scottish tradition, now given substance and enhanced by the Warner Exhibitions. There is no sign that any other college was considered for, or sought association with, the Snell benefaction. In 1693 it was ordained, after Chancery proceedings, that Snell's estate at Ufton in Warwickshire should be conveyed to a group of senior members of the Governing Body (in effect the College itself, but technically a set of distinct and independent trustees). They were to manage the estate for the maintenance, at a rate of £40 p.a., of Exhibitioners nominated by the University of Glasgow and received into Balliol; their number was to increase up to a maximum of six, as income was released by the termination of annuities burdened on the estate. The Master of Balliol was to be paid £10 p.a. by the Trust, 'for his care and government of the said Scholars', and there was to be an allowance of £5 for an annual audit dinner. In addition, it was ordered that 'the overplus shall accrue to Baliol College, after the payments

---

[25] See Stones, op. cit., p. 175, and Lincolnshire Archives Office, VV/2/2/30, in which Snell is mentioned by name as involved in the Warner negotiations.

[26] He married Joan Coventry at St Clement Danes, London, on 8 May 1662; her sister Silvester was married to Benjamin Cooper, University Registrar. See Stones, op. cit.

[27] He died on 6 Aug. 1679, at his brother-in-law's house in Holywell. He was buried in the chancel of St Cross church, where there was a marble slab with an epitaph, but this seems to have been covered or destroyed in Victorian times. There is an imposing stone and bronze monument to him, erected by public subscription (unveiled 1919), at his birthplace: Almont, Pinwherry, in the parish of Colmonell (about 50 miles south of Glasgow).

aforesaid discharged, in consideration of those priviledges of the library and otherwise which the said Scholars are to enjoy'. This was the principal advantage to the College, because the estate was a valuable one, perhaps worth as much as £500 p.a.—well over the costs of the scheme.

There were twenty years of litigation over all this in the mid-eighteenth century. The epitaph for Snell's daughter, who died in 1738, complained bitterly that the estate could support several more students than it actually did, and implies that the surplus income being taken by the College was unreasonable. This accusation was eventually upheld, in 1759, when a limit of £20 p.a. was put on the transfer to general College purposes, coupled with an order that the balance of any surplus should be reinvested. Nothing was said about the profession the students were expected to follow. In fact, out of the first batch who were admitted in 1699, none was ordained: three took to medicine and the fourth became a professor of mathematics. The history of the Snell Foundation is scarred by repeated disputes over practically every aspect of it, but it survives in modernized form, and the stream of Glaswegian graduates, which has brought Balliol some of its most distinguished members, flows steadily to the present day.[28]

Thomas Good was succeeded by John Venn (Master 1678–87), who had been prominent in opposing him, especially over the Blundell agreement. Venn's election precipitated the first of many complicated wrangles with the feoffees, because it created a Fellowship vacancy which was claimed by a Blundell Scholar, citing the agreement of 1615 (see Chapter 9). This gave a Blundell Scholar of BA status the right to any Fellowship becoming void. Venn put up a spirited resistance to this attempt to apply 'an unreasonable composition'. His defence was devious in the extreme. The resignation of Henry Bayliffe in 1675 he held to be invalid, it having been sent in by his sister on his behalf because he was 'distracted', whereas learned opinion was that a madman could not legally resign his Fellowship. Since, on this premise, an election into Bayliffe's place had been made in error, he argued that there had been a supernumerary Fellow in the mean time, the situation only now returning to normal.[29] The affair eventually subsided because a Blundell Fellowship in any case became available for the impatient Scholar, but it is surprising that the feoffees did not ask for their money back. Anthony Wood's diary records Venn's election with a typical sneer: 'Apr.24, Th., John Venn, M.A., elected Mr. of Ball. Coll.; spent most of his time bibbing and smoking, and nothing of a gent. to carry him off.'[30] But this might well be a gross libel, and the sad fact is that

---

[28] The foundation of the Snell Exhibitions, and the litigation of the next two hundred years, are analysed in detail, together with biographical and genealogical summaries for the Exhibitioners 1699–1900, in W. I. Addison, *The Snell Exhibitions . . .* , 1901.

[29] Lincolnshire Archives Office, VV/2/5.

[30] Clark, op. cit., ii. 448.

9. Balliol in 1675, by David Loggan.

little is known of Venn's life and character, beyond the bare biographical bones.[31] The administration of the College seems to have followed a more settled pattern under him than before, and the only major financial perturbation was a Chapel improvement project which was begun in 1685. The floor was paved with black and white marble by Thomas Wood, 'lapidary or stone cutter'; the walls were covered with wainscoting, and a new ceiling of Flanders oak with painted beams was installed. This all cost about £250, which was raised by subscription among old members and well-wishers, including, once again, Dr Richard Busby, who gave another £50.[32]

Roger Mander (Master 1687–1704) was the College's second great benefaction-chaser of the half-century following the Restoration; he was also a benefactor in his own right. As a young Fellow in 1674, he had been one of a group opposing Thomas Good, who had asked the Visitor to suspend them from voting or holding office for two years: 'then they will keep their studys better, and not goe to taverns and Alehouses to make factions.'[33] Of his personality in later life, only glimpses can be found, as when John Evelyn records his relief that his Balliol grandson had recovered from smallpox. Mander had taken 'extraordinary care' and 'caused him to be brought out of his owne Chamber, & lodg'd in his owne Appartment, Bed & Bed-Chamber' and sent daily reports to the boy's family.[34]

In 1691 the College broke with long-standing convention and elected as Visitor one who was not Bishop of Lincoln: Dr Richard Busby.[35] This was a shrewd move. Busby, who was reckoned to be very wealthy, had already twice contributed very generously to Balliol appeals, and had for some years been thinking of endowing a post in the University.[36] In

---

[31] He was Vice-Chancellor 1686–7. He was born about 1647, the son of Simon and Jane Venn of Pyleigh, Lydeard St Lawrence, where he died on 8 Oct. 1687. John Venn the regicide was his second cousin. There are two table-top tombs close together in Lydeard St Lawrence churchyard, to the south of the tower: one of them is John Venn's. In his will, made a few days before he died (PCC, 1687, 70), he mentions his wife Katherine, but no children. She lived in Holywell until her own death, on 9 Dec. 1723 (*Oxf. Hist. Soc.* l. 141); she was a College Benefactress. See also J. Venn, *Annals of a Clerical Family. Being an Account of the Family and Descendants of William Venn, Vicar of Otterton, Devon, 1600–1621*, New York, 1904.

[32] These details are from insertions in Benefactions Book 1.

[33] Lincolnshire Archives Office, VV/2/4/14.

[34] *The Diary of John Evelyn*, ed. E. S. de Beer, v, 1955, p. 431.

[35] Although Busby's predecessor as Visitor was Bishop of Lincoln, the wording of the Latin Register record of Thomas Barlow's election on 26 May 1675 implies a genuine free election; he is rather pointedly described as President of Queen's, although he had been bishop-designate of Lincoln for more than three weeks (nominated 1 May 1675, consecrated 27 June 1675).

[36] Clark, op. cit., iii. 10, 21.

January 1694/5 he settled a Catechetical Lectureship on Balliol, and he confirmed the arrangements[37] in his will[38] shortly afterwards. The Lecturer was to be the Master's nominee; he was to deliver thirty lectures in Balliol a year, receiving £13. 6s. 8d. for his trouble; the lectures were to be devoted to the exposition of orthodox Christianity. It was unkindly said of Busby after his death that he 'tacked so many lectures to his gifts they will be dearly earned; he could not forbear being a pedant in his will, imposing exercises to the world's end'.[39] There was some truth in this, but from Mander's viewpoint it was a piece of patronage for him and his successors, as well as being a worthy innovation in itself; for the Fellows it was a means of increasing their low incomes in rotation.[40]

The College was very short of ecclesiastical patronage until the late seventeenth century, and the Fellowships were correspondingly unattractive. Roger Mander himself gave the advowson of Bere Regis, and was instrumental in arranging for the purchase (or procuring the gift) of several others which came into the College's hands in his time or shortly afterwards: Calstone, Duloe, Kilve, and Timsbury. In 1713 the Visitor, Henry Compton,[41] Bishop of London, gave five more:[42] All Saints and St Botolph's, St Leonard's, St Nicholas, and Holy Trinity, all in Colchester, and Tendring. The College thus became well endowed with livings, almost trebling the number in its gift in the space of a generation. The advantages of this to the College were indirect but significant, because the near certainty of a benefice in due course made the Fellowships much happier positions.

Mander was Vice-Chancellor 1700–2. The position was one of unaccustomed influence for the Master of Balliol, which was still a relatively insignificant college.[43] He used the office with ruthless partiality to promote its interests. His most notable success was in the year 1700, when he obtained separate gifts of £100 each from Bishop Compton, Dr John

---

[37] Printed with the College Statutes for the Royal Commissioners, 1853.

[38] Printed in G. F. Russell Barker, *Memoir of Richard Busby D.D. (1606–1695)*, 1895.

[39] Barker, op. cit., p. 141.

[40] There is an incomplete list of Busby Lecturers 1705–1859, compiled by A. Clark, in the Archives (Clark's Lists, x, at the end).

[41] E. Carpenter, *The Protestant Bishop, being the life of Henry Compton, 1632–1713, Bishop of London*, 1956. He was elected Visitor on Richard Busby's death in 1695.

[42] Second Latin Register, fos. 34ᵛ, 35.

[43] Balliol was placed in the poorest group of colleges for taxation purposes in 1681, assessed on £100 p.a.; cf. Christ Church, £2,000 p.a., at the other extreme (Clark, op. cit., ii. 565). A brief 1662 account of the colleges mentions fifteen by name, but overlooks Balliol (T. Fuller, *The Worthies of England*, ed. J. Freeman, 1952, p. 457); several visitors to the University have left detailed accounts which do not mention the College at all (e.g. C. Morris, *The Illustrated Journeys of Celia Fiennes 1685–c.1712*, 1982; W. H. and W. J. C. Quarrell, *Oxford in 1710*, 1928).

Radcliffe, and the corporation of Bristol.[44] Dr Radcliffe's gift was for unspecified rebuilding work; Bristol's was for the erection of new lodgings. The corporation had in its gift a number of Exhibitions to maintain Bristol lads at university, but had not found it entirely satisfactory to have the Exhibitioners dispersed randomly among the various colleges. Mander arranged for them to be taken in by Balliol, in return for help with his plan to erect a new building. The block of rooms now known as the Bristol Buildings was not in fact put up for some years,[45] but a fairly regular succession of the sons of Bristol citizens appears in the Admissions Book throughout the eighteenth century. Mander's second campaign on Balliol's behalf whilst he was Vice-Chancellor was ultimately a failure. It was known that Sir Thomas Cookes, of Bentley Pauncefote in Worcestershire, had earmarked £10,000 for the foundation of a new college which was to have strong ties to his home county. Mander, aided by his colleague John Baron, set about trying to secure this benefaction for Balliol. Gloucester Hall was also in contention, and was initially favoured, but there were difficulties. On 15 January 1699/1700 the Duke of Ormonde, Chancellor of the University, wrote to Cookes recommending Balliol as 'the fittest place for his charity'.[46] Cookes had earlier said that if he was frustrated over Gloucester Hall, he would settle his money somewhere else, and 'Balliol Colledg will stand as faire as any place'. The enlargement of Balliol by building in the garden was considered, and new Statutes were drafted, but all came to nothing despite Mander's efforts. After much acrimony and pamphleteering, Cookes' benefaction did settle on Gloucester Hall, which was renamed and incorporated as Worcester College in 1714.[47]

---

[44] Second Latin Register, fos. 19ᵛ–21A.

[45] The block now known as the Bristol Buildings is the oldest residential accommodation in the College (Staircases XII and XIII). Substantial payments to a mason called Townesend and others appear in the Final Accounts 1716–20; some or all of these may relate to the Bristol Buildings. The southern part of the site of the 'Catherine Wheel' overlaps that of the Bristol Buildings. The College bought in the remainder of the lease of the 'Catherine Wheel' in 1714. There is an entry in the second half-yearly account of 1714 for its demolition, but perhaps the northern part was left or rebuilt, as there are later references to it up to 1828 (H. E. Salter, *Oxford Balliol Deeds*, 1913, p. 360). The leases of the tenements on the site of the Fisher Building (Staircases X and XI) were clawed back in 1698–9 (Salter, op. cit., pp. 84–5). 'New Buildings' were erected there during the next five years (Salter, op. cit., p. 229; B.3.67) but were knocked down to make way for the Fisher Building later in the century. The timing suggests that these 'New Buildings' were in fact the result of contributions from the Bristol corporation and others in 1700. The name 'Bristol Buildings' has been in use for Staircases XII and XIII time out of mind, but is perhaps nevertheless a misnomer.

[46] 'The Case of Sir Thom. Cooks charity of £10000', Ince Papers.

[47] The affair is treated in detail in L. Sutherland, 'The Foundation of Worcester College,

When Nicholas Crouch died in 1690,[48] he left the College the choice of all his books, and £50 to be used as a float by the Bursar—he had himself been Bursar several times when money was short, and knew well the difficulty of working the College's finances with insufficient elbow-room. He also left to his successor in his rooms the 'income' (the initial payment for furnishings) which he had paid for them, with the proviso that they should thereafter remain free of income charges for ever. Fellows had to pay quite substantial sums, sometimes as much as £50, on this account when they were admitted or moved from one part of the College to another. It was a system which generated ill feeling and occasional hardship: Crouch's bequest was the first step towards its abolition.[49] Over the next few decades several other members followed the examples of Thomas Good and Nicholas Crouch, and remembered the College in their wills: Roger Mander,[50] Richard Greaves,[51] John Blagdon,[52] Richard Ellsworth,[53] John Newte,[54] and John Edgcumbe.[55] They all endowed closed Exhi-

Oxford', *Oxoniensia*, xliv. 62. Roger Mander's extensive file on the matter survives as the Ince Papers.

[48] He had lived in College most of his life; he was buried in the interior part of the Chapel on 23 July 1690. His will was proved in the Chancellor's Court a few days later (OU Archives, Chancellor's Court Wills).

[49] These payments were recorded in the Latin Register, because they were monitored by the College, but do not appear in the accounts, as they were transactions between individuals (e.g. on 5 July 1670 John Good paid £49 on moving into the chambers formerly assigned to Mr Bayley).

[50] He died on 21 Dec. 1704 and was buried in the Chapel. He had a wife Mary living when he made his will (D.20.15), but he mentions no children in it. He left his books to the College, with money for the endowment of an Exhibition restricted ('closed') to men from Somerset.

[51] Fellow 1675. He died on 24 September 1706. He left property at Siefton and Culmington in Shropshire (later exchanged for property at Llandeilo Graban in Radnorshire) as the endowment for two Exhibitions, closed in the first instance to Ludlow Grammar School, and then to Shropshire and Radnorshire. See D. J. Lloyd, *The Greaves Exhibition*, 1954 and *County Grammar School. A History of Ludlow G.S.*, 1977.

[52] Resident as an MA member, but not a Fellow; formerly of Wadham. His will was dated 7 October 1696 (A. Clark's Tables, ii, fo. 42; Scholarships and Exhibitions Book 1 ii, fo. 45). He left a property called 'Thorne(s)' in the parish of Stoodleigh, Devon, as the endowment for an Exhibition closed in the first instance to descendants of his sisters Joan Radford, Elizabeth Harris, and Sarah Bradford, then to persons of the name Blagdon, then to Devon.

[53] Fellow-Commoner 1709. He died on 5 Aug. 1714. In his will (D.22.2) he provided income (rent charges derived from property in the parishes of Timberscombe and Cutcombe) for two Exhibitions closed to Somerset, with preference to the parishes of Timberscombe, Catscombe, Selworthy, Wootton Courtenay, Minehead, and Dunster.

[54] Blundell Fellow 1676. By his will, dated 10 January 1715/6 (A. Clark's Tables, ii, fo. 65), he bequeathed a property called 'Lob Philip' in the parish of Braunton, Devon, to endow an Exhibition for pupils of Blundell's School.

[55] Servitor 1670. He gave or left property in the parishes of Tirley in Gloucestershire

bitions of essentially the same kind, with regional preferences which were sometimes specific and complicated, and also including in some cases 'founder's kin' preferences.[56] More were established by benefactors with no academic Balliol link—Charles Harris[57] and Mary Headlam.[58] Two of these Exhibitions live on,[59] albeit with greatly modified regulations, having survived the reforms and rationalizations of the last hundred and fifty years which swept away all the rest. The names of their Founders are now all but forgotten, and their endowments have been anonymously absorbed into the capital which subsidizes and encourages the students of the present day. But in their time the closed Exhibitions were of great importance to the College, and a major factor in determining its composition.

The financial well-being of the College improved steadily between about 1670 and 1720. From the indebted and disorganized state of 1665, when it had been necessary to borrow at interest to pay tradesmen, the College slowly moved over the ensuing fifty years to the other extreme, in which there was a cash reserve in the Treasury sufficient to permit investment by lending to tradesmen at interest.[60] The real value of the Fellowship dividend, which had by this stage evolved from the pre-war system of augmenting the commons allowances with surplus income into one of

and Chaceley in Worcestershire, as the endowment for two Exhibitions closed in the first instance to Hanley Castle School, then to Worcestershire.

[56] The Archives contain copious material concerning the closed Exhibitions established in this period, and the estates which supported them. There was litigation, in several cases, which delayed their award; there are lists of holders down to the nineteenth century, compiled by A. Clark, in the Archives.

[57] College Steward. By his will of 1713 (D.22.5), he assigned a rent charge imposed on lands at Lenborough in Buckinghamshire for the provision of two Exhibitions closed to sons of Oxford city freemen in the first instance, then to the city, and then to Oxfordshire, with preference to his own kin. He also gave money for a piece of silver; there is an elegant water-jug which bears his name (remade in 1797 from his original gift) in daily use in the Senior Common Room.

[58] Wife of the Revd Richard Headlam of Ipsden, Oxon. Her connection with the College, if any, has not been established. No identified relative was a member. She died about 1730, leaving provision for an Exhibition closed in the first instance to descendants of John Lydall, Elizabeth Springall (her sister), and Richard Lydall, Warden of Merton (her uncle). See D.22.6, Scholarships and Exhibitions Book 1 ii, fo. 37, and A. Clark's Tables, ii, fo. 58.

[59] The Statutes concerning the Newte and Greaves Exhibitions were most recently revised in 1985.

[60] In 1671 £250 was owed to a Mr Harris (F.12.13); payments of £15 p.a. interest ('pro faenore') to him appear in the accounts. In 1710 £100 was 'put to interest to Mr H. Clements Snr.' (Treasury Book 2); £5 p.a. interest was being received and used for Library purposes for many years thereafter. Clements was a well-known bookseller (Library Records: Dean's accounts 1694–1740).

cash payments, almost trebled between 1625 and 1720.[61] This was possible despite increased expenditure on higher living standards, and on the Library, which appears in the accounts regularly from this time. There were also some modest building works. These and the better standard of living were in part enabled by benefactions, but also by more efficient administration. Securing the benefactions was in itself part of the more businesslike approach to College affairs which began in earnest with Thomas Good. Closely coupled to financial recovery, the average number of members in residence rose rather jerkily from about 40 in 1665 to around 100 in 1720; the high proportion of Fellow-Commoners admitted—nearly one in five at the end of this period—was a particularly significant feature.

By 1720 the College was financially viable, full up, and provided with ample patronage for the advantage of its members at all levels. A college cannot flourish without sound finances, and patronage was also vital in the eighteenth century. But the character and fortunes of a college are determined at least as much by its members as its money, provided of course that there is enough of the latter; we turn to their lives, times, and politics in the next chapter.

[61] The excess of receipts over expenditure, as it appeared at the closure of the second half-yearly account, was divided into equal shares (after the allocation of a share, apparently arbitrary and usually small, to Domus), such that each Fellow received one share, and the Master two. In 1660–70 a dividend share was worth only a few pounds; it rose to around £12 in 1675 and, with fluctuation, increased to £30–£35 in 1720–5. The purchasing power of money changed little in this period. For collected data on dividends 1668–1840, see A. Clark's Tables, ii, fo. 89.

12

People, Life, and Times 1675–1725

I T was no doubt inevitable that the Visitor would eventually have actually to visit the College, and take action to avert financial collapse, but it was probably the scandalous and corrupt engagement of the new Cook which precipitated his drastic action in 1670. Why such a fuss over a lowly cook's place? The answer lies in the structure of the collegiate society at the time. It still rested on the principles established by Fox's Statutes. The Cook had not only an obvious practical function but also a statutory niche in the hierarchy, and he was just as much a member as the Master himself. The same was true, by Statute or custom, of all the non-academic people in the College. The appointments, failings, and deaths of the most prominent among them are recorded with all solemnity in the College Register, along with those of the Scholars and Fellows. On 14 July 1716, for example, Matthew Chancellor, the Cook, was formally admonished for negligence, by a full College Meeting in the Chapel. He was also suspected of fraud.[1] The University recognized college employees as part of itself for certain purposes, such as probate, and we find the wills of many of them proved, not in the Archdeacon's Court, like those of ordinary citizens, but in the University Chancellor's Court along with those of the academics. Not infrequently, they there revealed themselves to have been people of modest substance, with worldly goods comparable in value to those of their masters. A few of them can even be numbered among the College's benefactors, like Jane Wyatt. She is first mentioned in 1706, during the final illness of Thomas Wyatt, the Under-Butler, and she reappears from time to time as a College servant. Much later, probably when she died, she gave a piece of silver. This was remade in 1793, but the simple evocative inscription on it was presumably carried over from the original piece: 'D. D. Jana Wyatt hujus Collegii Famula 1738.'[2] It was quite commonplace for several members of a family to be employed at the same

---

[1] There was a similar case previously. William Smith, the Cook corruptly appointed in 1670, was formally admonished (but not dismissed) for fraud on 25 July 1673 (Latin Register); his estate was worth only a little over £20 in 1682 (OU Archives, Chancellor's Court Inventories).

[2] [D. W. Jackson], 'A Piece of College Silver', *Balliol College Record*, 1976, 52. Mag. Price, a College 'bedmaker', gave a zegadine, or two-eared cup, worth £5 in about 1640 (Plate Records 2).

time and there are several examples of a post being passed from father to son. When Thomas Wyatt senior died in 1706, his son was appointed Under-Butler 'in locum Patris sui' only four days later.[3] Similarly, on his death in 1695, Thomas Wood senior was succeeded as Butler and Manciple by his son Thomas.[4] When the second Thomas Wood himself died, his place was taken by Fanshaw Wearg,[5] whose father John had been Porter and Under-Butler;[6] a Thomas Wearg was College Barber. The network of close personal relationships extended to the local tenants, who are often found to be employees of the College, and who also included many of the small bakers, butchers, and brewers with whom the College dealt.

The grandest non-academic post in the College hierarchy was that of Steward, with functions somewhere between those of the modern Estates Bursar and College Solicitor.[7] Charles Harris, the benefactor mentioned in the last chapter, held this position. He was a gentleman who was very active in the affairs of the city, to which he was also a benefactor. The senior internal post was that of Manciple, which was often held together with that of Butler; the nearest modern equivalent is the Domestic Bursar. Under him there were the Under-Butler (with whom we might equate the present Master Steward), the Porter, and the Cook. There were a number of other statutory positions (Barber, Laundress, etc.), but these were part-time. Payments to named individuals for work about the buildings and gardens occur frequently in the accounts, but the people concerned were not, in this period, generally on the regular official payroll. The relationship of the Cook, the Under-Butler, the Butler, and the Manciple with the College and its members was no less complex than it had been a hundred years before. It involved much more than simple employment: there was a commercial element. Their stipends were low, even nominal, and they

---

[3] Latin Register.

[4] A. V. Simcock, *The Ashmolean Museum and Oxford Science 1683–1983*, 1984, p. 4.

[5] Fanshaw Wearg was nominated Butler and Manciple by the Master on 29 Feb. 1719/20 (Latin Register). He had served an apprenticeship as a kitchen clerk. Administration of his estate was granted in 1727 (J. Griffiths, *An Index to Wills proved in the Court of the Chancellor of the University of Oxford and to such ... Papers of that Court as relate to ... Causes Testamentary*, 1862).

[6] John Wearg was appointed Under-Butler in 1672 or 1673 (Latin Register), but he was described as Porter when the administration of his estate was settled in 1682 (Griffiths, op. cit.).

[7] Harris's post was described as 'Senescallus sive Pragmaticus (vulgo *Steward*)' when he was appointed in 1693 (Latin Register). His immediate predecessor Stephen Kibblewhite was described in exactly the same terms when he was appointed in 1684, but (like his own predecessor Hugh Ellis) as 'Attornatus et hujus collegii in rebus juridicis Pragmaticus' when he died in 1693 (Latin Register). They all became personally involved with College affairs (lending the College money at interest, obtaining leases of College property for themselves, and so on) to an extent which would now be regarded as thoroughly improper.

had to deposit substantial caution money as a guarantee against fraud or mismanagement, this device replacing the sworn bonds which had been required in earlier times. There were presumably profits to be made, but there was also a risk in the relationship: when Under-Butler Nicholas Winter died in 1668, debts to him by the College, some of them long-standing, amounted to more than £20, and he was also owed almost as much again in 'desperate debts', probably by members of College.[8] The senior domestic staff seem usually to have been literate men of some worth, and the post of Manciple, in particular, was one of considerable status. Indeed, the most distinguished member of the College in the late 1680s was its Manciple. The Thomas Wood who was appointed to the post in 1686 was one and the same as the 'lapidary or stone cutter', engaged in that year to install a new floor in the Chapel, but these descriptions disguise the fact that he was also a master mason and architect, with a flourishing business entirely outside the College. His best-known work is the Old Ashmolean, his masterpiece its elaborate portico facing the Sheldonian.[9]

The College currently employs the equivalent of about 85 full-time domestic and administrative staff, to support an academic community of about 600. This ratio of 7:1 is reckoned to be tolerably efficient, but it nevertheless contrasts rather sharply with that obtaining in 1700, when it was probably getting on for twice as great. The discrepancy arises not from a more luxurious existence now but from activities now (e.g. organized sport, systematic fund-raising) which were unheard-of then, and also from the fact that in 1700 many of the mundane chores, especially waiting at table, were performed by Servitors, young men partly working their way through the College. There were then between fifteen and twenty of them, paying low admission fees and caution money. A smaller number of 'Battelers' were between the Servitors and undergraduate Commoners (of whom there were 30–40) in status and fees; whether they had domestic duties to perform is not clear. Sometimes, when Servitors were admitted, they were assigned to serve individual Fellows, and Domus Scholars were almost always appointed to serve the Fellows to whom their places were annexed, in the standard form 'A.B. admissus est inserviturus Magistro X'. The Scholars were required to pay the same caution money as, and were thus probably regarded as on the same social level as, the Commoners, who did not have any menial duties to perform. It therefore seems likely that the service demanded from the Scholars was slight, although it was enough to cause at least one protest.[10] Even

---

[8] OU Archives, Chancellor's Court Inventories.   [9] Simcock, op. cit., p. 4.
[10] First Latin Register, between pp. 265 and 266: Ed. Dunch wrote on 4 April 1663 to complain that whereas his nominee (to a Dunch Exhibition, presumably) had 'expected a Scholarship, he reputes himself upon a service'.

the Servitors could not have been called on to work as waiters every day: there were so many of them that they would have spent most of their time falling over each other. Only one specific reference to the work done by a Balliol Servitor in this period has come to light, in the sad tale of John White's murder by a tailor called Thomas Hovell, in 1679.[11] The murderer's confession was that

... the aforesaid John White had brought him a coat to mend, and told him he had been to receive a parcel of money that came from his Father in Devon-shire, and that he was to pay it for taking the Degree of Batchelor the next day, and withal told him where he had put it in his study within his Chamber. These things lay broyling in his mind, that he did think it an easie matter for to Rob him. He therefore took an opportunity to carry his coat home just when the Schollar was to do his Duty, he being but a Servitor. So, coming when the murthered was going to Hall to wait at the Table, he came with the coat up stairs. The Schollar being in haste bid him sit down, and he'd be with him presently ... The Room being clear, he fell to renching the closet door open with a Hatchet, which himself had brought under his coat for that use ...

But White came back too soon, and caught the thief at his work. There was a fight and White fell to the ground. As he rose, Hovell picked up his hatchet and 'knockt him down with it, and followed his Blows so fast that he kill'd him'. He fled but was taken, and on 15 March 1679 he was executed in the College forecourt. Anthony Wood recorded his fate with relish:[12]

Mar. 15, Munday, Thomas Hovell that killed White a servitour of Ball. Coll. was hanged on a gallows against Ball. Coll. gate: died very penitent and hang'd there till 2 or 3 in the afternoone. The next day hanged on a gibbet in chaines on ... Bullingdon Greene. All his body gon by the beginning of 1686.

The Fellow-Commoners (*Socio-Commensales*), or Gentlemen-Commoners as they were sometimes called, had emerged as a definite special category of undergraduate early in the first quarter of the seventeenth century. By the last quarter they had become a more numerous, constant, and significant feature of College life. In the years around 1700, there were usually about half a dozen of them in residence at any one time. They were supposed to jump through the same academic hoops as other undergraduates, but few stayed long enough to take a degree. Paying higher fees than the rank and file at every turn, they were an important source of revenue.

[11] Anon., *A True Narrative of Three Wicked and Bloody Murthers* ..., 1680 (Bodleian 4° Rawl. 594). 'Mr' White was buried in the church of St Mary Magdalen, 5 Dec. 1679. He matriculated from St Alban Hall 30 March 1677, aged sixteen. The inventory of his estate records that he had £23. 19s. 4d., a substantial sum: OU Archives, Chancellor's Court Inventories.   [12] A. Clark, *The Life and Times of Anthony Wood*, ii, 1892, p. 483.

William Brydges was admitted as a Fellow-Commoner on 31 October 1701. He seems to have been a typical member of the class. His father, Francis Brydges of Tibberton, had been at Balliol before him, and the paternal homily he delivered when his son came up shows that he knew all about the temptations of student life. Much of his advice is timeless:[13]

... resolve against drunkeness, let the knowledge you have allready of that brutal sin suffice you. If you give yourself leave to drinke to bee hot headed you will certainly goe on to drunkeness, tis natural to doe so, & when you are in that condition you are lyable and prone to commit any vice or folly whatsoever; any madd pranke that shall be proposed shall be practicable & you may soon do that in a quarter of an hour which you can never make amends for in your whole life ...

Francis Brydges was comfortably off but not wealthy, and his blunt remarks about drink, lewd women, and sleeping in the town are laced with fervent hopes that William would look after his new outfit (especially the 'beaver hatt'), follow his Tutor's advice, equip himself for a self-supporting career, and save his money so that he was not 'overburdensome to a kind father'. A few weeks later William's Tutor (John Baron, soon to be Master) wrote well of his work, and reported that his battels were very modest:

... The tryal I have had of your son gives me great hopes concerning him. He is very well furnished with school learning, and relishes logicke better than I have known many freshmen ... His battles ... are 4.10.3. In that summe is contained what he pays his Servitor, Laundress, Bedmaker, barber, & chamber rent, so that he has nothing to pay farther but for Tuition, for cleaning his shoes and for books about thirty shillings ...

William kept his expenses at a reasonable level, although he found his allowance barely enough. At one point he had to borrow from his Tutor. His father was no doubt satisfied with the way his son emerged from a turbulent adolescence, and became very studious under Baron's care—he had been a troublesome schoolboy.[14]

Most of the Fellow-Commoners were from the upper reaches of the gentry and the lower levels of the aristocracy, but every so often came one with a nobleman's title. These were entered in the books as Noblemen-Commoners, with the formula 'A.B. admissus est Superioris Ordinis Commensalis' (or 'Socio-Commensalis'). From them large sums were extracted. The Master was quite open about this when replying to an admissions enquiry in 1723:[15]

[13] Hereford Record Office, Brydges Papers 81A/IV.
[14] See n. 13, above.
[15] Bodleian MS Rawl. Letters 45, fo. 172.

Sir James Harrington may, if he pleases, drop his title and be admitted a Gentleman Commoner of our College: and if he shall chuse to do so I will find him a Tutor for whose care of him I will be answerable. The expense will then be, with prudent management, abt. £20 a year.

If he shou'd keep his Title then I cou'd take the care of him myself and the expense wou'd be £200 a year. I shou'd not care to agree for less for his Tuition than Sir John Napier[16] pays me.

Harrington, the sixth Baronet of that name, chose the cheaper option: he was admitted in 1724 as an ordinary Fellow-Commoner, and described as a mere Esquire in the Register. But most noblemen were enrolled as such, and lived in the manner expected of them. James Brydges, first Duke of Chandos ('Princely Chandos', a distant relation of the Francis Brydges who has already appeared) would have been ashamed to let his son and heir apparent, the Marquis of Carnarvon, do otherwise. He sent him to Balliol in 1719. Chandos was 'very desirous He shou'd be kept close to his studies, and to the Publick Exercises of the College', so he 'wou'd not furnish Him with so much Money as to surfeit him with Plenty, & induce Him to take extravagant & ill courses'.[17] On the other hand, he did not want to put him on an inferior footing to others of his rank and quality. His compromise was £400 p.a., out of which he was to keep himself, his servant, footman, groom, and three horses. He was to live with the Master, John Baron, who presumably had general oversight of his affairs and behaviour, and he was to eat with the Fellows—the Duke did not approve at all of the new fashion among noblemen of keeping tables in their own rooms. Joseph Hunt, the Senior Fellow, who was to succeed Baron in 1722, was appointed Tutor, for a fee of £200 p.a. The young Lord Carnarvon stayed up for little more than eighteen months before going off on a Grand Tour of Europe, but he still managed to annoy his father by running up debts of £330. The Duke complained in pained tones of lax supervision, but nevertheless made Hunt a final present of an extra £200, as well as paying the expenses of his Doctor's degree. Baron's reward was 300 guineas for himself, with a further like sum to be spent for the College at his discretion.[18]

The College was a sharply stratified society, in which everyone knew his place. In the Hall and Chapel, for instance, this was literally true. Commoners ate with Commoners, and Scholars with Scholars. Each grade, from the Servitors upwards, had its own pews in Chapel; the Master and

---

[16] Sir John Napier, 6th Bt., was admitted as a Nobleman-Commoner in 1722.

[17] James Brydges to John Baron, 13 Oct. 1719: the Huntington Library, San Marino, California, Stowe Collection, James Brydges' Letter Books.

[18] The information given about Lord Carnarvon at Balliol is derived from James Brydges' Letter Books. See also C. H. Collins Baker and M. I. Baker, *James Brydges*, 1958.

Fellows all had their own special seats. Even the Master's Lady had a traditional place during services[19]—but the Chapel was a masculine preserve, and she was only allowed to peer down through the window at the east end of the Library, which looked directly into the Chapel. In their correspondence, members reveal their status-consciousness by continual references not to 'X' or 'Y' but 'X, a Commoner' or 'Y, a Servitor'. Although the divisions between the various categories were clearly drawn and frequently emphasized, movement from one to another was surprisingly easy. A Commoner could join the Fellow-Commoners—'put on a Fellow-Commoner's gown' was the expression used—simply by making up the difference in admission fees. This was not unusual. A step downwards was rare but possible: Charles Brent was admitted a Commoner in 1682, but in 1685 became a Servitor to reduce his expenses, because his father had died. The best examples of social mobility can be found among those who were taken in as Servitors. The most striking case is John Baron. He was admitted as a Servitor in 1686, his father's rank being entered as 'yeoman' in the College Register, 'plebian' in the University's. He was elected a Fellow in 1691. His humble origin does not appear to have disadvantaged him at all. He succeeded Roger Mander as Master in 1704, served as Vice-Chancellor in 1715, and was quite well-to-do when he died in 1722.[20]

Jeremiah Milles was an unremarkable Fellow of the College, elected in 1697. He had an utterly conventional and respectable career. He is nevertheless important for our present purposes, because he kept a private diary.[21] This survives for 1701–2, a period in which he served the University as Pro-Proctor and the College as Bursar. From it we can obtain a detailed impression of the life and daily routine of an ordinary Balliol don. His record of what he did during the first ten days of October 1701 is typical:

1 Oct. I took horse together with Mr Levet for Haley, & dined with Mr Fr. White, who was laid up with the Gout. We returned at 7 a clock, & spent the Evening together at the Katherine Wheele.

2 Oct. I drank Tea this morning as before, read half an hour, & then dined with M.W. [Wither, his pupil] with whom I spent the afternoon, we were at Mr Brathwaits Chamber. I read an hour in the Evening, & walk'd to the Taverns &c. but found few Schollars, except some seniors who are above order, as well as Statute, & I fear have outlived their consciences.

---

[19] D.3.19b, fo. 418.

[20] John Baron, the eldest son of John Baron, yeoman, of Hanley Castle, Worcestershire, was admitted as a Servitor, to serve Richard Greaves, in 1686. He died in College on 20 Jan. 1721/2, and was buried in the Chapel. His will (PCC) mentions many relatives, but neither wife nor descendants.   [21] MS 461.

3 Oct. I drank Tea this morning, as before, read 3 Lectures viz. to Mr Sharp, to Wither & Estoft, & King. I was at the Schools together with the Heads of Houses, as Proctor about addressing the King on the occasion of the Proclamation of the Prince of Wales.[22] The rest of the afternoon I studied & prayed. At night I supped with M.W. & stayed till 9.

4 Oct. I was with my Brother Tho. together with Wither & Estoft, then we open'd a dog, & considered the Heart, Lungs, Entrails &c. I was at the Coffee-house after dinner then with my Brother visited M. Rolf. The Evening I Spent wth Mr W. till 9.

5 Oct. This morning I drank Tea as before, & heard Dr Wake at Xt. Ch. [Christ Church]. I dined wth M.W. & heard the Provost of Oriel preach in the afternoon. After prayers I studied an hour & then was at the Coffee-house &c.

6 Oct. I was with Mrs Wither, & then with Mr Grabe at Xt. Ch. about some necessary business. We had a Convocation, & voted an address to his Majesty. I dined, & stayed with M.W. till 4. Then I read to Mr Sharp. & the Evening I was at Mr Barons Chamber with Mr Brickindon, Carter, Rogers of Oriel, & Mr Gale.

7 Oct. I drank Tea this morning with M.W. & then read a Lecture in Geography to W. & E. After dinner I read to Gibson, & then King. I studied an hour, & supped, & spent the Evening with Mr. Wither & Estoft.

8 Oct. I drank Tea as before, read to Mr Sharp &c. After dinner I was at Mr Estoft's Chamber & then read the Trial & last speeches of 6 Jesuites. At night I sup'd & was with Mr. W. till 9.

9 Oct. I drank Tea with M.W. & read to King. Then I dined wth M.W. & we went out to take the air in the Coach. I was at Mr Collins of Magdalen Chamber at night, where I played at Chess till 11 a clock.

10 Oct. I was with M. Wither, then read to Mr Sharp, & eating no dinner I meditated & read till 4, when my Brother came to me. I supp'd with M. Wither, & stayed there till 9. At 10 I walk'd over the Town, & found 3 Schollars wandering about the streets …

The day began officially with Morning Prayers, although Milles does not often mention attending. Chapel was in theory compulsory, at least for junior members, but in his advice to his son, Francis Brydges shows that he thought that the rule was not enforced strictly enough: '… lay an injunction on your self not to miss the Colledge prayers, the punishment that will be inflicted by the house I am satisfied is but little …'[23] A rather casual attitude to Morning Prayers is evident, too, in the fact that it was quite common for Fellows to appear in their dressing-gowns.[24] Milles

---

[22] William III was King at this date. He had no son to be Prince of Wales, but ex-King James II had a son called James who was still styled Prince of Wales. When ex-King James II died on 6 September 1701, James his son was proclaimed King ('James III'; 'the Old Pretender') by dissidents: it is this proclamation which Milles alludes to.

[23] See n. 13, above.

[24] D.3.19b, fo. 290.

never took breakfast as such, but usually refreshed himself on rising by drinking tea. Tea was increasing rapidly in popularity, but was still enough of a luxury for William Brydges to send away for half a pound to give as a New Year's present to his Tutor, for he was a 'mighty lover of it'.[25] There was hardly any need for a proper breakfast, because Hall dinner, the main meal and social event of the day, was served at eleven.[26] Even on St Catherine's Day, the festive meal was over by two. Evening prayers were at five, and a light early evening meal was provided in Hall, but people often supped out or in their rooms.

Milles filled the interludes between the day's events in a great variety of ways—University and College business, teaching, reading, trips to the coffee-house, visiting, and so on. He had about half a dozen private pupils in his care. They came to him alone or in pairs on average twice a week. These sessions were the nearest equivalent of the time to a modern tutorial, but the expression Milles uses is always 'I read to X', which suggests that the pupils were completely passive. On the other hand he was in their company informally for a high proportion of the time, dining with them quite often and occasionally riding out into the country for the day with them. He inevitably became very intimate with them. Following the death of one from smallpox,[27] he records making the arrangements for his funeral as if it was the most natural thing in the world for a Tutor to do. It was by no means an unrewarding, dull, or idle life. But he had no thoughts of permanency. Like most of the young Fellows, he was waiting and hoping for a benefice, which would enable him to leave, settle, and marry. He was already taking active steps to secure one through family connections by early 1701, but he had to wait until 1705: by then he was senior enough to claim the College living of Duloe in Cornwall.[28] He held it until he died in 1746.

Logic, ethics, classical literature, and divinity were, as of old, the principal subjects the Fellows read to their pupils, and lectured on in Hall or Chapel. They also provided the themes for disputations. These ancient

---

[25] See n. 13 above.

[26] The time of dinner was changed from 11 a.m. to noon about 1722: D.3.19b, fo. 226. In 1767 it was fixed at 2 p.m. (except on Sundays, when it was to be at 1 p.m.); at the same time supper was fixed at 8 p.m. (Second Latin Register, fo. 116A). In 1869 (English Register) dinner was moved from 5.30 p.m. to 6 p.m. In 1874 it was shifted to 7 p.m., at first during Trinity Term only.

[27] Smallpox cases are mentioned frequently in the diary.

[28] The advowson of Duloe was purchased by the College in 1701, with a view to augmenting the Mastership out of the income of the rectory and allowing the vicarage to be taken by a Fellow. In fact Milles, the first vicar put in by the College, was allowed the proceeds of the rectory and vicarage, subject to a payment by him of £50 p.a. to the Master (Second Latin Register, fos. 26–7).

academic rituals still took place regularly. Milles often notes that he acted as Moderator, and in February 1700/1 he records that he 'prepared for disputations, and opposed in the Chappel at 4 a clock, the question *An Sola Fides justificet?*[29] But the College 'Publick Exercises' were degenerating into arid formalities. The same was true of the stages in the University's graduation process, which gave little stimulus to the study of the traditional curriculum. Moreover, the period was one of intellectual awakening and diversification, which percolated down even to the undergraduate level. The subjects Milles read to his pupils thus ranged beyond the conventional syllabus, embracing geography, astronomy, modern history, biography, and natural philosophy. The College moved with the times by establishing official lectures in poetry and mathematics (1697), in addition to those already given in Greek, rhetoric, and logic. Payments to a Rabbi Abendana, which appear in the accounts at this time, suggest that Hebrew was also taught, and a Hebrew Lecturer was appointed from 1708. Particular care was taken over the framing of the course in mathematics, details of the topics intended to be covered being entered in the Latin Register.[30] There were to be two lectures of an hour's duration a week throughout the year, dealing with arithmetic, geometry, trigonometry, and algebra, including quadratic equations. Much of what we should call physics was taken in, with applications of mathematics to astronomy, optics, hydrostatics, mechanics, and the motion of projectiles. William Brydges attended these lectures, informing his father in 1704 that he had acquired 'Mercator's *Astronomia* (which is our mathematical booke in the hall)'. When a student wanted instruction in a fringe subject, but could not get it from his Tutor or College lectures, he might turn to a free-lance specialist teacher. There were several of these available in the University. William Brydges had some French from school, which his father wanted him to keep up, and he also set himself to learn Italian, writing home in 1703:

I received your letter this morning, and am glad that you approve my learning Italien. The gentleman's name is Mounsieur Conniers; he has been in Oxford 3 years, and is likely to continue much longer. He has abundance of schollars in our Colledge. Mr Ottley learns french of him. He has 10 shillings entrance and 10 shillings per month, and to come 3 times a weeke, which is 12 times, but he is not to have his money till 12 times are finished.

---

[29] That is, 'Does faith alone justify?' On a subsequent occasion the question was another chestnut of Reformation controversy: 'An liceat orare pro defunctis ut a purgatorio liberentur', i.e. 'Whether it is right to pray for the departed to be released from purgatory.'
[30] Second Latin Register, fo. 16.

He later reported that after a two-month course he found Italian easy and could turn French into Italian tolerably well. Another couple of months, he thought, would suffice for him to master it perfectly. At the same time he sustained an enthusiasm for mathematics, sending home for instruments, and announcing that he intended to 'goe out a measuring', confident that with practice he would make himself a 'master of measuring and surveying'. All this was additional to a wide range of general and classical reading. Even allowing for the fact that our evidence is from letters to a critical father he was anxious to please, we must conclude that William Brydges did not waste his time.

Just a little suspicion about the completeness of Brydges' reports is provoked by the absence of anything about non-academic pursuits, apart from a single embarrassed allusion to a tavern, and a rather earnest account of a sightseeing trip to Eton and Windsor. We know from Milles that there were lighter times as well. On 3 June 1703, for example, his diary says 'This morning Mr Baron & I, & all the Gent.-Comrs. &c were up· the water with the University Music. We dined at Godstow, & got home about 10 a clock.' The same small band of musicians had provided entertainment after dinner on St Catherine's Day the year before, when Milles had been responsible for the arrangements as Bursar: 'This being S. Katharine's day, & our chiefe festival, I was busy in preparing necessaries, & sending to invite strangers. After dinner we were in the Common Room, & had the University Musick. At night we play'd at Cards till past 12.' Milles was a great lover of cards and chess, and he also went quite frequently to musical occasions in other colleges, and at the Sheldonian Theatre. Evidence of athletic activity by members of the College is very sparse: there was a ball court (probably for a game akin to fives) near the back gate in 1675–95,[31] and Milles mentions a few sessions of 'vaulting', both alone and with his pupils. Otherwise exercise and fresh air were taken at a gentle pace, riding and walking; Milles was fond of strolling in Paradise Garden with his friends. The College, unlike many others, had no bowling-green, and so for that popular game it would have been necessary for Balliol men to resort to a public green. There were at different times two not far away in Holywell. One was roughly where Eastman House now stands, the other down past the Manor House. Such places were centres for drink, gambling, and boisterous company, and were quite different from the genteel surroundings associated with the modern game of bowls. There was a cockpit in Holywell too, quite close to the Manor

---

[31] H. E. Salter, *Oxford Balliol Deeds*, 1913, pp. 90 and 363; the court is shown on a plan of 1695 (*VCH*, Oxfordshire, iii, facing p. 92).

House.[32] Other occasional distractions included travelling entertainers and curiosities, bull-baiting on Gloucester Green, and horse-racing on Port Meadow. And, of course, the city had many taverns. In his capacity as Pro-Proctor, Milles spent many evenings on the prowl for tippling undergraduates: he triumphantly records against 18 February 1701/2, that he 'walked to public houses & took about 25 Schollars'. Next morning he interviewed the offenders, and handed out impositions. Milles himself was not averse to an evening's drinking in the tavern with his cronies, among whom we must number his Fellow-Commoner pupils. The newly fitted-out Common Room[33] (the room nowadays called the 'Old Common Room') gave them a more comfortable private place where they could club together for wine or enjoy one of the frequent 'treats' expected of Bursars on appointment, graduates on graduating, Fellow-Commoners on leaving, and so forth.

In 1673 Sir Thomas Wendy,[34] a quondam Fellow-Commoner, made the College his residual legatee, so far as his agricultural property was concerned. In fact nothing of this nature was ever received from his estate, but in 1677 his large and valuable library came into the College's hands, presumably in lieu. This accession of more than two thousand volumes revitalized the Library. Extensive work was necessary to accommodate the books, a special shipment of 72 dozen chains, of various lengths, to secure them being ordered from Birmingham.[35] The sudden expansion appears to have stimulated a general reorganization, with the writing of catalogues, and the initiation of an active purchasing policy. Previously the Bursars' accounts are completely lacking in records of book purchases. Additions were still almost entirely by gift. From about 1680 this changes and irregular expenditure of Domus funds on books can be traced. Thus we find under 1681, immediately before a payment for work in the quadrangle and clearing filth from the kitchen, that fifteen shillings (more

---

[32] See J. H. Jones, 'The Development of Holywell between 1700 and 1900', *Top. Oxon*, 22 (1978), 9.

[33] Alterations and furnishings when the Common Room was fitted out cost more than £45 (Final Accounts, 1676–7). Shortly after this, miscellaneous expenditure—pipes, tea, utensils—begins to appear on account of the Common Room. The room was used for College business (such as auditing the accounts) as well as social purposes, but Chapel remained the place for formal College Meetings. There are also occasional references to a Bachelors' Room (e.g. Latin Register, 1720); the Bachelors' Common Room was discontinued in 1828 (English Register).

[34] On Wendy's life and family, see the Hindmarsh Manuscripts, and L. K. Hindmarsh, 'Sir Thomas Wendy and his Family', *Notes and Queries*, 196 (1951), 287–90 and 354–6.

[35] One consignment of 16 doz. ell chains (@ 2s. 10d. per doz.), 16 doz. yard chains (@ 2s. 4d. per doz.), and 16 doz. three-quarter chains (@ 2s. 0d. per doz.), weighing 147 lb. in all (carriage 6s. 0d.), was received on 16 April 1678: Final Accounts, at the end of 1677/8.

than a fortnight's wages for the labourer in the following entry) was laid out on Dugdale's book about the recent wars:

Pro Libro impresso in Theatro pro Bibliotheca, cui Titulus est A Short
   View of the Late Trouble in England. Per D. Gul. Dugdale   00 15 00
Laboranti Abraham Marchant pro 3 diebus in Quadrangulo, et pur-
   gatione Colluv. in culina   00 03 00

From 1694 separate Library accounts were kept, by the Senior Dean, who collected fees on graduation, and spent the money on binding, chains, and books. In the first year of the new system the fees amounted to £7. 10*s*., accounted for as follows:

> Paid for the use of Ball. Coll. Library from
> Oct. 1694 to Oct 1695. Mr Pain Sen. Dean.

Paid the widdow Doe for binding Dr Wallis's works	0.04.0
for binding the Acts of Parliament	0.02.0
for binding Dr Gregory's opticks	0.00.6
for binding the Ph. Transactions for 94	0.01.0
Paid for Dr Wallis's works in sheets	1.16.0
Paid for the New Body of Geography Engl.	0.16.0
Paid Henry Clements per Bill	4.00.0
Paid for the carriage of [illegible] and to the Coll. Smith for chains and worke	0.10.0

Summa tot. sol.   7.09.6

The income of the Library fund was augmented, in 1696, by £1 p.a. derived from John Blagdon's benefaction (see also the previous chapter). More importantly, Blagdon provided £4 p.a. for the payment of an 'under librarian', and it appears that from this time many of the tasks associated with the expanding Library were undertaken by paid undergraduates. For the students so favoured, the access they got to the Library may have been a valued additional perk, because in general it was reserved for senior members only. The College did, however, make some provision for them, and maintained an 'Undergraduates' Library' or 'Little Library'[36] throughout the eighteenth century. It ran on admission fees—as with the main Library, the Dean was responsible for it—but the holdings seem to have been small and basic.

There are fragmentary main Library loan registers for some years around 1700. These show that the interests and studies of the Fellows were very varied. In his diary Milles notes at various times reading works on geography, history, logic, theology, and science; for light relief he

[36] See J.[H.] Jones, 'The Eighteenth-Century Undergraduates' Library', *Balliol College Record*, 1980, p. 61.

favoured travellers' tales. The impression is left, however, of a dilettante approach, lacking in concentrated effort or application. When we move from what they read to what they wrote, the conclusion that the Fellows were not very serious scholars is confirmed. Between 1675 and 1725, 53 Fellows were elected. Of these only nine are known to have published anything,[37] and their combined works only number about two dozen. These include but two with pretensions to scholarship. One was largely by a certain John Jones: it was a translation from the Greek, into tedious English verse, of 'Oppian's Halieuticks', published with the Vice-Chancellor's imprimatur in 1722.[38] The list of subscribers to the volume, which Jones dedicated to Lord Carnarvon, contains many Balliol names. The other was an edition by Joseph Hunt of a classical work on geometry, which he dedicated to three Balliol Fellow-Commoners, no doubt his pupils.[39] Perhaps we should not dismiss William Chilcot's *Practical Treatise concerning Evil Thoughts*[40] out of hand completely. This was a substantial work, which was valued enough to be reprinted in the nineteenth century. But all the rest of the published writings of the Fellows in our sample are forgotten sermons, or brief discourses on controversial subjects.

The Library subscribed to the *Philosophical Transactions* of the Royal Society from the very first issue, and several of the Fellows, including Milles, perused it regularly. But when it came to experiments, Milles was a butterfly. One afternoon he is 'upon the Schooles Tower with a magick Lanthorn, prisms &c'. Not long afterwards he has a squeamish adventure into vivisection—'we opened a dog alive, which I take to be a piece of cruelty, & will avoid it for the future'.

The College's reputation in the period is saved by a succession of distinguished mathematicians and astronomers, beginning with David Gregory. Formerly a professor at Edinburgh, he was appointed to the Savilian Professorship of Astronomy at Oxford in 1692, on the recommendation of Newton, and was elected FRS shortly afterwards. He needed a college base, and was attached to Balliol as a senior Commoner. He was a Scot, so this choice would have been the natural one. The widely held

[37] John Baron, William Best, William Chilcot, Theophilus Downes, Thomas Chamberlayne Coxe (admitted to Balliol as plain Thomas Coxe), Joseph Hunt, John Jones, John Newte, and Samuel Newte. William Lux is credited with some poems in the Bodleian Library catalogue, but the attribution seems to be based on an annotation in the Bodleian copy which could signify ownership rather than authorship.

[38] *Oppian's Halieuticks ...*, trans. William Diaper and John Jones, Oxford, 1722. Diaper (Balliol 1699, died 1717) began this work, but it was completed by Jones: see Diaper's entry in *DNB, Missing Persons*, ed. C. S. Nicholls, 1993.

[39] *Theodosii Sphaericorum libri tres*, ed. Joseph Hunt, Oxford, 1707. This work is wrongly credited to Thomas Hunt by H. Carter in *A History of the Oxford University Press*, i, 1975, Appendix, p. 452; Carter also implies that there is no copy in the Bodleian Library, but there are at least two: Savile J. 19 and 8° I. 55. Linc. (catalogued under *Theodosius, Tripolita*).

[40] William Chilcot, *Practical Treatise concerning Evil Thoughts ...*, Exeter, 1698.

misapprehension that the College was a 'Scotch Foundation' had been greatly consolidated by the Snell and Warner schemes. Gregory was an early Newton enthusiast. He is usually credited with being the first university teacher to lecture on Newtonian natural philosophy. John Keill followed from Edinburgh, close on Gregory's heels. He was admitted at Balliol, also as a senior Commoner, and allocated a Warner Exhibition in 1692. The syllabus for the College course in mathematics was probably devised by him, in consultation with Gregory. Keill became very well known in the University as a teacher of Newtonian principles, and his *Introductio ad Veram Physicam* ..., first published in 1702, but refined and translated later, was generally regarded throughout the eighteenth century as the best introduction to modern natural philosophy. He was also a frequent correspondent of Newton's, and became thereby the pivotal figure in a protracted and fierce controversy over the discovery of the differential calculus. Leibniz had accused Newton in 1705 of plagiarism. Keill set out to refute this and establish the opposite, that Leibniz had in fact derived his ideas from Newton, and merely changed the terminology. Newton believed this to be the truth of the matter, and encouraged the defence, but the issue was still not properly settled when Keill died in 1721. As a diversion from the main dispute, in 1715, Leibniz sent a complex problem in the properties of a certain kind of hyperbola to mathematicians in England, by way of a challenge. Before long, Keill was able to write to Newton to say that he had a solution, adding that 'Mr Sterling an undergraduat here has likewise solved this problem.'[41] The precocious undergraduate was James Stirling,[42] a Snell and Warner Exhibitioner of several years standing.[43] He must already by this time have been working on his *Lineae tertii ordinis Newtonianae* ... (1717), a commentary on Newton's enumeration of curves of the third degree. In it he gave proofs of several results which were merely stated by Newton, and he was also able to report four species of cubic not included in the maestro's catalogue of 72 (there are, in fact, 78 in all). He reached even greater heights in 1730, with a treatise on infinite series which was a major advance in that area. His name is associated with a number of important discoveries.[44] James Bradley, the last of this group, and the only Sassenach,

[41] *The Correspondence of Isaac Newton*, vi, ed. A. R. Hall and L. Tilling, 1976, p. 282.

[42] C. Tweedie, *James Stirling*, 1922; I. Tweddle, *James Stirling*, 1988; J. Dougall, 'James Stirling', *J. Glasgow Mathematical Assoc.* i, 1937, p. 33. The *DNB*, etc., assume that Stirling was a member of the University of Glasgow, but this is not so. The instrument nominating him makes it clear that he was an Edinburgh student (Second Latin Register, fo. 203ᵛ).

[43] In a comparable intellectual feat by an undergraduate in modern times, H. C. Longuet-Higgins (Balliol 1941) wrote an essay for his Tutor R. P. Bell in 1942, in which he proposed a hydrogen-bridged structure for diborane, long a thorn in the side of valency theory. The proposal was refined, substantiated, and published before the end of his second year: H. C. Longuet-Higgins and R. P. Bell, *J. Chem. Soc.*, 1943, 250.

[44] In particular, 'Stirling's Formula' for an approximate value of $n!$ when n is large.

was a contemporary of Stirling's at Balliol, and no doubt also came under John Keill's influence. Bradley later set new standards of high precision in astronomical observation, and made a number of key discoveries. He succeeded Halley as Astronomer Royal in 1742.[45]

English politics were conducted more on party lines after the Restoration than before, and the party labels 'Whig' and 'Tory' came into use. The Whigs were inclined to favour the underprivileged, the Dissenters, and Low Church opinions, whereas the Tories stood for the interests of the landowners, and High Anglican churchmanship. The University of Oxford was mostly Tory throughout the half-century we have under scrutiny in this chapter, and within it Balliol was pretty consistently of that complexion.[46] Its Tory reputation, indeed, was a significant factor behind the steady improvement in its financial security during the early eighteenth century, because it encouraged a steady stream of Fellow-Commoners and Noblemen-Commoners. Most of them were drawn from the Tory country gentry, and confidence in the political soundness of a Balliol education outweighed the College's lack of grandeur. But for this, many of that class would have taken themselves and their money elsewhere.

There was Whig pressure in the later years of Charles II to have the King's brother James excluded from the line of succession to the throne, because he was a Papist. During a crisis on this issue in 1681, Charles took the extraordinary step of summoning Parliament to Oxford. The Whig peers, led by the Earl of Shaftesbury, petitioned against this inconvenient and far from impartial location, but could not budge the King. Shaftesbury therefore set about securing accommodation, using the good offices of his friend John Locke. Balliol's sympathies were not at all with the Whigs, but the College was too hard up to let such good business pass it by. Most of the Whig peers stayed and messed in Balliol. When they departed, at the end of the session, Shaftesbury and fourteen of his noble colleagues presented a massive gilt bowl and cover, by way of thanks and payment.[47] The Whigs failed, and James of course did inherit the throne in 1685, but

---

[45] A. Chapman, 'Pure Research and Practical Teaching: The Astronomical Career of James Bradley, 1693–1762', *Notes and Records of the Royal Society of London*, xlviii (1993), 205.

[46] The consistency of the College's Tory leanings would appear to be contradicted by John Baron's alleged reputation as a firm Whig. In fact his politics are not easy to nail down from the many references to him. Tory Thomas Hearne's obituary summary suggests that Baron was one too, who moderated his views in his later years: '. . . a man who might have left a good character behind him, had it not been for some very foolish things in the Latter part of his Life, on purpose to gain Favour with the Trimmers': *Hearne's Collections* (hereinafter cited as Hearne, pub. *Oxf. Hist. Soc.*), vii. 319.

[47] The gift weighed 167 oz. 10 dwt.; it has been remade more than once. The largest piece derived from it which remains is an elegant water-jug bearing the names of the donors; like that mentioned in ch. 11 n. 57, it is in daily use in the Senior Common Room.

he did not last long, because he united the main political forces in the country against him. In 1688 he fled, and was replaced by his Protestant daughter, Mary, and her husband, William of Orange. The Tories were not entirely happy about this turn of events, but mostly concurred with it, as a compromise between their devotion to traditional monarchy and their hatred of popery. But for a few of the Tories it was more than their consciences could bear to shift their loyalty formally from James to William and Mary. Those who refused to take an Oath of Allegiance— the first 'Nonjurors'—became ineligible for places such as college fellowships. The majority of college heads were able to certify, in 1691, that all their Fellows had complied. But the Master of Balliol had to admit that Theophilus Downes, William Bishop, and John Hughes had not. Hughes was certified to be 'afflicted with a deep and dangerous melancholy', and the King was willing to indulge him, but Downes and Bishop were peremptorily ejected.[48] The Nonjurors ranged in attitude from those who sullenly but passively declined to conform, to those 'Jacobites' who actively supported the claims of James and his descendants to the throne. Balliol was generally believed to be a rallying point for Jacobite agitation, although extreme sentiments only came into the open at times of special tension. The accession of Elector George of Hanover as King George I of Great Britain in 1714 was generally very unpopular in Oxford. Although he was the next Protestant in line, there were many others with a better genealogical claim. An official attempt to celebrate his birthday on 28 May 1715 was a flop, as the Jacobite diarist Thomas Hearne records:[49]

This being the Duke of Brunswick, commonly called King George's Birth-day, some of the Bells were jambled in Oxford, by the care of some of the Whiggish, Fanatical Crew; but as I did not observe the Day in the least my self, so it was little taken notice of (unless by way of ridicule) by other honest People, who are for K. James IIId. who is the undoubted King of these Kingdoms, and 'tis heartily wish'd by them that he may be restored.

The next day there was serious disorder, with people running about the streets shouting 'King James the third, the true King!', 'No usurper!' A riotous outbreak was feared on the following 10 June, because this was the birthday of 'King James the third' (i.e. the 'Old Pretender'). Hearne and his 'honest' (i.e. Jacobite) Balliol friends withdrew to avoid the trouble, and made their protest in private:[50]

For my own part I walk'd out of Town to Foxcomb with honest Will. Fullerton and Mr Sterling, and Mr Eccles all three non-Juring Civilians of Balliol Coll. and with honest Mr John Leake formerly of Hart-Hall and Rich. Clements (son to old Harry Clements the Bookseller) he being a Cavalier.

[48] Historical Manuscripts Commission, *Report on the Manuscripts of the late Allan George Finch*, iii, ed. F. Bickley, 1957, p. 282.

[49] Hearne, v. 61.   [50] Hearne, v. 65.

On 18 August there was another disturbance, when a recruiting officer was mobbed and abused in Broad Street by a crowd of Balliol men shouting 'Down with the Roundheads'.[51] Incidents like this continued at intervals for several years, often involving Balliol men, but tempers eventually cooled and by 1719 the College seems to have steadied itself on moderate Tory lines. Had this not happened, the Duke of Chandos would certainly have been deterred from entering his son (Carnarvon) at Balliol. As it was, when Carnarvon came up, the Duke was able to write to the young man's Tutor in all confidence that his instructions would be carried out. He was to be given a 'thorough knowledge of the excellency of our Ecclesiastical Constitution'. Nothing was to be allowed 'in his way which may lead him to think amiss of our happy Establishment in State', and it was hoped that he would emerge as a 'Strict Churchman, and a Sincere Friend to our present settlement'.

The making of parties and interest permeated the whole of society in eighteenth-century England, from national and ecclesiastical government right down to minor and even domestic appointments. As an illustrative example, let us consider Hearne's account of the Pembroke Mastership election of 1710. This is not a spectacular irrelevancy, because there was an abortive attempt to couple it with the appointment of a new Cook at Balliol:[52]

The two Candidates were Mr Colwell Brickenden & Mr Will. Hunt ... Both of them have the reputation of being honest men ... but ... Mr Brickenden is an illiterate person, Mr Hunt is a man of learning; Mr Brickenden is a boon Companion, or, as, some style it, a Sot, Mr Hunt is a man of Sobriety and Discretion ... Mr Hunt had infallibly carried it had it not been for the defection of one Mr Mouldin, who ... had several times solemnly promised to serve Mr Hunt when a Vacancy of the Headship of Pembroke-Coll should happen, and it was upon this Consideration that the Master of Balliol College (of which Coll. Mr Hunt has an ingenious Brother Fellow) made a First Kinsman of his Cook of that College. Mr Mouldin gratefully acknowledged his Favour and promis'd ... that nothing should draw him from giving his Vote for Mr Hunt. But when the time of tryal came ... whether upon Prospect of the Rectory of St Aldates (which belongs to Pembroke Coll ...) or for the sake of a wife ... he went over to Mr Brickenden's Party, and ... most shamefully and scandalously broke his word, and deserted his friends when 'twas exspected he should have done a kindness ...

Note that the attack is not directed at what the people involved were trying to do, but at the fact that one of them had broken the rules. Similar machinations can be detected in all the Balliol appointments made in the early eighteenth century into which we are allowed an intimate look. Scholarships were especially open to allocation on what now seem shady

---

[51] Hearne, v. 99. [52] Hearne, ii. 344.

grounds, because they were at the disposal of individual Fellows, who were, naturally enough, inclined to favour their families and home areas. When a Fellow had a Scholarship free with no pre-empting call on it, a casual encounter might suffice—Milles notes meeting a man in a tavern for the first time one evening in February 1700/1, and disposing of his Scholarship to the same man's son two days later. Fellowships were determined with rather more ceremony. There was an examination, but this was probably often a mere ritual, with the votes being solicited privately in advance. Milles again provides our example, the election of Reginald Jones in 1702:

> *12 Nov.* . . . Jones came to desire my vote for a Fellowship.
>
> *28 Nov.* In the morning the Candidates for a fellowship disputed, and in the afternoon were examin'd in Greek and Latin Authors . . .
>
> *29 Nov.* . . . after prayers proceeded to Election, & chose in Sr. Jones.
>
> *30 Nov.* . . . at night Sr. Jones made the usual Treat and I sat up till one a Clock playing at cards. *Miserere Mei Deus.*

Similarly, when he hoped for a turn as Bursar, also in 1702, he 'waited on the Master to desire his vote for . . . being Bursar, which he granted'. But the kind of influence which relatively ordinary dons could bring to bear by working on private friendships, and using jobs for remote cousins as sweeteners, was nothing compared to the power a magnate like the Duke of Chandos could wield. By his liberality to John Baron and Joseph Hunt, he created obligations to be called in when there was a chance of installing some protégé or relative in the College. At least one Fellow owed his election to 'Dr Hunt's vote, which was obtained purely at his Grace's request'. This was Brydges Thomas, in 1720; he was a distant relative of the Duke. During the following year Chandos used his interest to oblige Lord Harcourt, who had been asked to approach him by the father of Thomas Coxe, a Scholar coming up for a Fellowship. A letter from the Duke explaining the situation, stressing the excellent reputation of the candidate's father, and asking for Hunt's friendship on Coxe's behalf, produced the desired result. Hunt was soon repaid, for on hearing that Baron was ill, the Duke wrote to say that he would use his influence to secure for Hunt the support of an uncommitted Fellow, if there should be a Mastership vacancy: 'I will use my interest with the Bp. of London to engage Mr Bree in yours.' Shortly afterwards, as expected, Baron died and Hunt succeeded him.[53] The Duke wrote to send his congratulations, and to say that he was pleased to have played a part, but then immediately

---

[53] According to Hearne, the election was unanimous and popular: when Hunt returned from waiting on the Visitor in London to be confirmed in office, he was met on the road and escorted into Oxford by 'near 400 horsemen (several of w^*ch* were Scholars)': Hearne, vii. 329, 333.

indicated that he hoped the son of a friend would find favour at the next Fellowship election. Perhaps this request was met,[54] but in any case fate soon gave the College a grander opportunity to oblige the Duke. When the office of Visitor fell vacant by the death of the Bishop of London in 1723, the honour was conferred not on another Bishop but on the Honourable and Reverend Henry Brydges, the Duke's brother.[55]

Joseph Hunt's Mastership was short. He had married a 'brisk, buxome' wife twenty years his junior shortly after his election, but he left her a widow within four years. 'It had been more prudent in him, and more for his health, had he abstain'd from matrimony,' thought Hearne.[56] Before Hunt was even in his grave,[57] there was a move afoot to offer the Mastership to Henry Brydges. On hearing this, the Duke wrote straight away to their nephew Theophilus Leigh, Fellow of Corpus Christi. He urged him to get to work on his Balliol contacts, 'that no time may be lost in making Interest'. This was rather premature, as Henry Brydges himself seems to have been cool about the proposal—even before he had received a tactful but pointed letter from four of the Fellows, one of whom (William Best) was himself a candidate for the Mastership. They put it to Brydges that the post ought to be beneath the Visitor's dignity. One of them also wrote privately to say that he did not think the invitation to Brydges had been 'intended as any real compliment to our worthy Visitor, but only to disappoint Mr Best'. To the exasperation of his brother the Duke, Brydges could not be induced to stand. The Duke moved swiftly to make interest for Theophilus Leigh instead. Early in May 1726, six of the Fellows successfully petitioned Brydges as Visitor for his 'consent, in the election of a Master for Baliol College, to chuse a person who is not of the College'.[58] His approval removed a possible objection to Leigh, and set the stage for one of the most convoluted and notorious elections ever held in Oxford.

[54] The Fellow concerned was probably Charles Godwyn.

[55] Henry Brydges, Archdeacon of Rochester, was elected Visitor in 1723. He died on 9 May 1728: see *The List of the Queen's Scholars ... of Westminster ...*, collected by J. Welch, 1852, p. 217.

[56] Hearne, ix. 102.

[57] Joseph, son of Stephen and Margery Hunt, was baptized at Kingsclere, Hampshire, on 6 March 1679. He married (16 Feb. 1722) Sophia, a natural daughter of the Duke of Buckingham by Mrs Herbert, and had a son Edmund born on 15 Dec. 1723, baptized at St Mary Magdalen, Oxford, 9 Jan. 1723, who survived to be admitted to Balliol 5 Mar. 1741. Hunt died at Astrop Wells on 14 March 1725, and was buried in the church of King's Sutton, Northants. He was said to have been a good-natured, plump, and lusty man. (Hearne, viii. 50, 146, and 166; ix. 102 and 103.)

[58] See Chapter 13 for a full account of this election and its documentation.

13
The Mastership of Theophilus Leigh

RECEIVED opinion would have us believe that the election of Theophilus Leigh was scandalous, corrupt, and nepotistic. Perhaps. A phenomenal volume of documentation survives,[1] but the evidence is equivocal enough to rule out any unqualified conclusion.

The candidates were William Best and Theophilus Leigh.[2] Best, a Fellow since 1716 and a well-known Tutor, had been Joseph Hunt's right-hand man, and often his Vicegerent during the ill health of his last year.[3] According to a number of Hunt's friends, including his brother, Best would have been the late Master's nominee. Leigh, in contrast, had only social, political, and family ties with the College (see Fig. 5);[4] Thomas Hearne reports but one previous appearance by him in the Balliol sphere, as Lord Canarvon's proxy at the baptism of the Master's son in 1723/4.[5] Since the College had not freely elected an outsider to the Mastership for more than a century, Leigh entered the contest with tradition against him.[6]

---

[1] The correspondence of the Visitor and others is in the Archives, mostly at D.3.18–20; sworn statements relating to the affair run to over 400 foolscap sides (D.3.19b). Thomas Hearne's account (*Hearne's Collections*, hereafter cited as Hearne, pub. *Oxf. Hist. Soc.*, ix. 131, 206, 285, 287, 289) must be read with his Tory position in mind. James Brydges' Letter Books (Stowe Collection, The Huntington Library, San Marino, California) contain several relevant references. See also the material indicated in n. 4 below.

[2] The name of former Fellow John Wills was also considered. Wills might have commanded a clear majority, but news of his death was received before a serious campaign had been started: see Hearne, ix. 106, D.3.18b (5), and allusions in D.3.19b. According to Hearne (ix. 131), Senior Fellow Joseph Sanford was a candidate at an early stage; this is not corroborated, although it is known that he had opposed Hunt for the Mastership in the previous election (D.3.19b, fo. 228).

[3] On the life and character of William Best, see W. Best, *The Merit and Reward of a Good Intention*, ed. with an introduction by P. Spalding, privately printed, Darien, Georgia, 1968.

[4] The principal sources for the life and character of Theophilus Leigh are (*a*) the correspondence of the Leigh family of Adlestrop, together with Mrs Gwen Beachcroft's unpublished work thereon (deposited in the Bodleian Library; see especially MS Dep. c. 577.); (*b*) MS 403; and (*c*) material indicated in n. 1 above.

[5] Hearne, viii. 166.

[6] Only one other Master (Sir David Lindsay Kcir) of the last three hundred years was, like Leigh, without a previous connection with the College when elected.

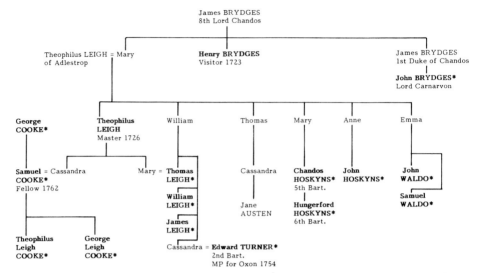

Fig. 5. Some eighteenth-century Brydges and Leigh connections with Balliol. An asterisk indicates admission to Balliol as an undergraduate; only links of interest in the Balliol context are shown, so the families are incomplete.

By mid April 1726 the voters were marshalled into two parties of equal strength.

For Best: William Lux, William Best, Thomas Rich, Thomas Wilson, Brydges Thomas, Thomas Walker.
For Leigh: Joseph Sanford, John Jones, Thomas Loveday, Thomas Coxe, Charles Godwyn, Humphrey Quick.

The Duke of Chandos felt entitled to insist that Thomas, whose own election he had fixed, should change sides. On 24 March 1725/6 he wrote imperiously to Thomas's father:[7]

Dr Hunt, the Master of Baliol Colledge in Oxford, being dead, my nephew Leigh stands Candidate for the Honour of succeeding him in that Capacity. He has already acquired a very considerable Interest, and has reason to believe that if your son can be prevailed to vote for him, there will be no difficulty in carrying the Election. I must therefore desire you'l be so obliging as to write to your son in pressing terms; and even to use your authority in demanding this of him, in favour of my friend. For as Mr Leighs success seems to depend very much upon

---

[7] Quoted, by kind permission of the Huntington Library (San Marino, California), from James Brydges' Letter Book (ST 57), which is in their Stowe Collection. The Duke also wrote to Brydges Thomas himself on the same day.

the part your son takes, I shall think it discurteous if my Nephew owes his disappointment to a Gentleman whom I put upon that Establishment.

Leigh reported to his uncle Henry Brydges (the Visitor) that he had backed up this pressure with a personal visit, to no avail. But he seemed to accept that Thomas's promise to Best was binding, and did not complain unduly about it, or at attempts to nobble two of his own supporters.[8]

I have been some time in Herefordshire with Mr Thomas's father. He shew'd me a very pressing letter from the Duke to him in my Behalf; he wrote to his son to come to him, I sent man and horses, but to no purpose. I believe by the help of Mr Brydges and his son of Tiberton I could have brought the father with me to Oxford; but whether he doubted his interest with his son, or, after the young man had laid himself under such engagements he thought he ought not to apply warmly, or that his son could not recede with Honour, he seeming to be disinclined, I desired him not to give himself any further trouble. I assured him that I canvas'd only upon supposition that his son might disengage himself, and save his Honour; I thought his Duty and Gratitude were obligations previous to that rash promise, and tho' not by salvo secured, yet strongly implyed. I told him if they could not think as I did, it would be a crime in the Father to make any attempt upon the Son, and in the Son to comply. As the case now rests, the Weaker Six remain with me; I think they will be very firm, notwithstanding Mr Pye of Faringdon hath just removed his son from Mr Jones my friend, and placed him under Mr Best; notwithstanding Ld. Bathurst (who came to College on Saturday to promote Mr Bests Interest) hath signified that his son shall be remov'd from Mr Godden[9] unless he shall think proper to desert my Interest . . .

Leigh's 'Weaker Six' were a statutable minority, because it was laid down that if two candidates proved equipollent, then the most junior Fellow's vote was to be transferred. Quick was the most junior, so Best's party was all set for victory.

Sanford, the Senior Fellow, put the official notice convening the election on the outer door of the Chapel[10] on 30 April 1726. On 12 May, with Lux as next senior duty-bound to assist him, he was ready to receive votes in the Chapel. Lux was a non-resident eccentric, who had been brought up from the country by Best's supporters. Unfortunately Lux's behaviour on the day was very disconcerting. He was led in dazed, wearing his dressing-gown, and did not seem to be able to cope with his task as scrutineer. Best and his men insisted on remaining in the Chapel to see fair play in the voting for themselves. This was contrary to immemorial custom,

---

[8] D.3.18b (10).

[9] i.e. Charles Godwyn. The threat appears to have been carried out, because in September 1726 Hearne (ix. 187) mentions Henry Layng of Balliol as Tutor to young Bathurst.

[10] The outer Chapel door was the traditional place for all important notices. Lists of candidates for graduation are still posted there.

which required the Fellows to attend and vote one by one, leaving afterwards. Sanford refused to proceed in the face of this irregularity, whereupon the Best faction withdrew, after holding an election among themselves and declaring themselves victors. When they had gone, Sanford engaged Jones, as next willing senior after Lux, to assist him in a further scrutiny. The remaining Fellows then voted in accordance with the customary procedure, and elected Leigh. The College was thus split down the middle, each half claiming to have the true and duly elected Master. The situation could only be resolved by the Visitor. He moved slowly, with caution and sagacity.

Best's side argued that the custom of private and secret voting in the Chapel was not an inflexible constraint. The Visitor himself, they pointed out, had been elected at a meeting convened for the purpose by the Master in his Lodgings, because he had 'taken physick and was fearfull of venturing out'. Several other instances were cited to show that the College was free to use its discretion in matters not explicitly covered by the Statutes. Their case was voluminous, but weak, lacking examples of elections which had involved real decisions by voting. A second line of attack was aimed at Quick. By some oversight he had failed to take the Oath of Allegiance, and it was maintained that his Fellowship was therefore void, and his vote worthless. Leigh's team entered fully into the spirit of the thing. Adherence to ancient custom was strongly defended. Was it in order for Best to vote for himself? Was Lux *compos mentis*? If not, was his vote valid? And so on. After much deliberation and minute argument on these and other points, Leigh's election was eventually confirmed on 13 March 1726/7, by the Visitor sitting with two assessors.[11]

The office of Master of Balliol was not a very prestigious one, and the emoluments he received directly from the College were modest. His combined stipend, allowances, dividend,[12] accommodation, and services were probably worth between £100 and £150 p.a. But there were hidden advantages. As we have already heard, the Master stood to make quite substantial sums out of Fellow-Commoners, although in fact Theophilus Leigh does not appear to have been as grasping or lucky as his two immediate predecessors in this respect. The Master's income was greatly augmented by the concession that he was allowed to hold one of the College livings, and indeed to have first refusal of any that fell vacant.

---

[11] Hearne, ix. 285, 287, and 289.

[12] The dividend was determined by taking the apparent surplus for the year, as shown by the second half-yearly account, and dividing it into fourteen equal shares (two for the Master and one for each Fellow) and a fifteenth share (usually slightly less than a Fellow's share) including the odd shillings and pence for Domus. In 1726 a Fellow's share was worth £31.

Besides numerous preferments of modest value, the College had several (e.g. Fillingham, Tendring, Duloe, and Huntspill[13]) of sufficient worth to enable the holder to pay a curate or vicar, and still be left with a considerable sum in hand. Taking this into account, the Mastership was probably worth about £300 p.a.[14] It cost Leigh about a year's income in legal fees to secure the position,[15] but it was a good investment. He was to enjoy its fruits for nearly sixty years. A comfortable income with light duties, it was as good a situation as a Tory cleric could hope for with the Whigs dominant. In later life he fished for Crown preferment,[16] but by then his politics had become Whiggish against a rising tide of Toryism. As well as financial security, the Mastership gave the freedom to abandon celibacy. Following Joseph Hunt's example, Leigh began negotiating a marriage settlement soon after his election: he married Ann Bee of Beckley in 1728. He initiated his incumbency with a firm hand, adopting a stricter attitude than had been customary on residence and the discharge of official duties. On 21 October 1728, it was resolved that College officers should be obliged to reside fully for at least a month in each term, and that a higher standard of attention to duty was to be expected.[17] The problem of absenteeism may have been brought to a head by the behaviour of Thomas Walker, one of the Chaplain Fellows. He had become the subject of much critical comment for frequent absence without leave, and for 'declining to take pupils and never acting as Chaplain when present in College'.[18] The probable reason for his absences became clear early in 1729, when strong rumours were circulated that he had been courting, and even that he had recently married, although he showed no sign of resigning his Fellowship. The Statutes had nothing to say about the marriage of Fellows or of the Master, although long-standing practice seemed to establish rather clearly that the Master alone was permitted a

---

[13] The advowson of the Rectory of Huntspill was purchased for £1,200 in 1724: £800 of the cost was contributed by Nicholas Docton, who had no previous connection with the College. By a special Act of Parliament in 1778 the Master was deprived of his general claim to College livings, and assigned a portion of the Huntspill rectory income not exceeding £300 p.a. This annuity was still being paid by the Diocese of Bath and Wells as recently as 1986, when the College decided to waive its right to it indefinitely, provided the money was diverted to Huntspill Church Building Fund. The 1724 correspondence is in the Second Latin Register, fos. 54–9; see also C.15.19 and C.17.31. The Revd Dr J. S. MacArthur (1893–1970), one of the College's most munificent benefactors of recent years, was the Rector of Huntspill 1955–70.

[14] This was the value the Duke put on the Mastership in a letter to Henry Brydges on 19 March 1725/6 (James Brydges' Letter Books).

[15] Some of the bills survive; the total was at least £278; see D.3.19 (15).

[16] See Bodleian MS Dep. *c.* 577, fos. 26, 59.

[17] Second Latin Register, fo. 76.

[18] D.3.23a (3).

wife. Leigh obtained a ruling to this effect from the new Visitor, Sir John Dolben,[19] on 14 April 1729:[20]

I cannott but think that by the nature of the thing, it should not be allowable for Fellows or Scholars to marry, & continue on the Foundation. For no founder could ever have it in his heart to fill his College with women and children (to mention no other inconveniences) which such an allowance might, and must probably do. It is not the custom of any other learned society, that I know of, to permitt it, and the practice of our predecessors in Baliol, in vacating Fellowships and Scholarships on such occasions sufficiently shows that they had the same sense of this matter. Wherefore I am of opinion that a legal proof of any Fellow or Scholar of Baliol's being married is a warrantable ground to declare such persons' Fellowship or Scholarship to be vacant ...

You tell me, Sir *that by the Statute you have no other right to marry than a Fellow; but that precedents and custom are on your side*; by which you seem to expect my thoughts on this question also, tho' you do not say so. I confess I think your case very different from that of the Fellows. There is but one Master, but many Fellows; and since, where local Statutes are silent, custom and reason are our only guides. Since the former of these is manifestly for you, and the latter not against you, I am of opinion that the Master of Baliol may marry, consistently with his Headship.

Walker, however, had been one of the defeated party in 1726, and Best seized the opportunity to stir up trouble, writing to the Visitor to say that 'the Fellows desire to be heard in behalf of the Privilege they presume they have to marry'. It is difficult to believe that Best really thought anything could come of this mischievous proposition. The Visitor nevertheless proceeded with perfect correctness, and carefully considered written arguments for and against. Leigh pointed out, on 23 June 1729,[21] that Walker's resignation would not only be consistent with custom but also opportune, as providing a solution to a separate problem which was exercising him and many of his colleagues. This concerned the future of John Jones, one of Leigh's supporters in 1726, whose Blundell Fellowship was due to expire. Blundell Fellowships could be held for ten years only, and Jones had already had nine. It had occurred to Jones's friends that if Walker were to resign, Jones might succeed him as Chaplain on a Foundation Fellowship, and thereby be kept on the strength, because such Fellowships could be held indefinitely. He was, Leigh told the Visitor, 'one of great use to us, especially in the Quality of Tutor', and his retention was supported by 'a general Inclination, founded, I dare say, upon a True Zeal for the good of the College'. The Visitor ruled against Best, Walker

---

[19] The Revd Sir John Dolben, Bt. (1684–1756) was elected Visitor in 1728. His portrait hangs in Hall.

[20] D.3.23a (1).   [21] D.3.23a (3).

resigned, and Jones took his place, but the principal source of aggravation was already on his way out anyway. Leigh closed his case to the Visitor by saying 'Mr Best is just enter'd upon his year of grace,[22] being instituted into the Church of St. Lawrence Jewry. We live, I thank God, in a friendly and peaceable way ...'

Jones's sidestep from a Blundell place on to the ancient Foundation was not a unique manœuvre. Humphrey Quick resigned his Blundell Fellowship on 23 November 1728, only to be elected to an ordinary Fellowship at the annual election six days later. The effect of such moves was to increase the Devon bias, because all the Blundell Fellowship vacancies were naturally taken by Tivertonian Scholars. The use of ancient Foundation places in this way only became controversial if there was another claimant, as happened in 1732. In that year, Blundell Fellow John Land was appointed to a vacant Chaplaincy Fellowship, just as Jones had been a few years before. But this time there was another member of the College, Gerard Andrewes, who wanted the place. He protested to the Visitor, claiming that Land was ineligible because of his Blundell Fellowship, and that he, Andrewes, 'was the only Candidate that appeared at the said Election, and that notwithstanding no statutable objection was made to him, he was rejected ...'.[23] Dolben dismissed the appeal, but with great reluctance:[24]

Whereas there is no Statute broken, no infringement of former Decrees or Injunctions, there can be no ground to relieve Mr Andrewes or to vacate the Election already made. But as far as appears to me this practice is not right, and cannot but be attended with ill consequences.

'That a private Engraffment should swallow up an Ancient Foundation was *prima facie* a shocking consideration', he thought.[25] This was only a slight exaggeration. At the end of 1733, seven out of the twelve Fellows were from Devon. Although Leigh rejected the charge that Balliol was in danger of becoming a 'County College'[26] the Devonian contingent was more or less dominant for the rest of the century.

The Visitor was left in relative peace for nearly twenty years after the Andrewes affair, but his arbitration was needed again in 1751, this time over caution money. A new scale had been fixed in 1733 for the amounts

---

[22] Fellows were allowed a 'year of grace', during which they continued to receive College emoluments, on presentation to a living sufficient to oblige them to vacate their Fellowships.

[23] D.3.49.

[24] D.3.23a (7).

[25] D.3.23a (9). *Engraffment*: an addition, a graft.

[26] D.3.46.

which were to be deposited as financial guarantees on admission:[27] £15 for a Fellow-Commoner, down to £5 for a Servitor. The deposit was usually reclaimed on going out of residence. Now the electors for the University seats in Parliament were all those of MA standing whose names were still on the books of their respective Colleges. There was a three-cornered contest for the Oxford seat in January 1750/1. This was a time of great confusion of party, and in addition to traditional Whig and Tory candidates, Sir Edward Turner stood for the 'New Interest'. Turner was a Balliol man, a College benefactor, and Leigh's brother-in-law. Leigh was by this time well on the way to shaking off his early Tory allegiance, and was very active on Turner's behalf. He was dismayed to discover that 'opposition, very unusually, very unnaturally, very violently, began within and sett out from our own walls; against a Gentleman who had been of most Exemplary Behaviour, and a very considerable Benefactor to us'.[28] Observing that much of the opposition came from non-resident members who had withdrawn their caution money, he saw in this a reason and means to disenfranchise them. He refrained from action at the time because of his family connection with Turner[29]—a most un-eighteenth-century consideration—but resolved to correct the situation in the following year, seeking the Visitor's approval for striking off the books the names of any members who did not within a reasonable time renew their caution money. This provoked turmoil. George Drake, a Fellow since 1736, was the senior objector in a group of four Fellows. He had been Dean eight times, and Bursar twice, and was an active teaching Fellow.[30] The Master labelled him a 'most zealous, artfull, and dangerous man'[31] (one of the very few hard-hitting remarks to be found in his letters) and blamed the objection on 'a Restless spirit, disrelishing subordination and Government; and which Spirit, it is thought, will then most likely Triumph, when assisted by Incursions of Rustick forces, long disus'd to Regulations . . .'.[32]

The Visitor again proceeded with caution, and eventually persuaded Leigh to compromise on a new regulation allowing non-residents to stay

---

[27] Second Latin Register, fo. 83.   [28] Northamptonshire Record Office, D(F)87a & b.

[29] Turner was defeated in the 1750/1 contest for the University seat, but was elected for the County of Oxfordshire in 1754.

[30] He was frequently a College Lecturer, in several years covering four subjects at once. A Lectureship in metaphysics, of which he was the first and usual holder, was begun in 1743, at the expense of the Lectureship in poetry; it does not appear after his death in 1752. In his autobiographical notes, John Douglas (1721–1807) says under 1738 that his 'Tutor was Mr George Drake, whom I shall always have an affectionate Rememberance of as I profitted much by his superintending my Studies': British Library Egerton MS 2181, fo. 6.

[31] Northamptonshire Record Office, D(F)87a & b.

[32] Northamptonshire Record Office, D(F)82.

on the books for half the caution money taken from residents. This, Dolben thought, was 'a laudable piece of condescension in the Master' and he regretted that the objectors still seemed unwilling to give an inch, lecturing them in forceful style:[33]

... The best cause that is, Gentlemen, may be pushed to a faulty Extreme; and as you seem to be jealous of your Liberties, so, on the other hand, it is not fitting that the Master, whom you acknowledge to be a principal and vital part of your Society, shou'd be made a Cypher of in his College ...

The dispute dragged on, mainly because Sanford and Godwyn, the two senior residents, obstinately refused to take sides. It was not until four years later that a new regulation along the lines of Leigh's compromise was approved. Even then the matter was not closed, for in 1759[34] we find Sir William Bunbury,[35] Dolben's successor as Visitor, dealing with appeals from members whose names had been removed from the books, for failing to comply with the new arrangement. Bunbury's reply was that everyone who was or might be affected should be given ample warning, and only struck off if they still failed to conform. This, he hoped, all parties would 'embrace voluntarily', rather than 'submit to as directed by Visitatorial Authority'. The whole affair aroused passion quite disproportionate to the amounts of money involved, and had momentum enough to run on for nearly a decade only because of the political motives of the participants. But the successive Visitors, whose misfortune it was to have all this squabbling thrust upon them, emerge with credit: they both exercised their authority with patient and impartial wisdom.

Theophilus Leigh's politics moderated towards the middle of the century, but the College was at the centre of spasmodic Jacobite outbursts even after the '45. On the evening of 23 February 1747/8, a boisterous group of Balliol men and their guests emerged from College ('where they had that day met at an entertainment') and marched down the Turl, shouting 'God bless King James!' and 'other treasonable and seditious expressions' as they drew close to Winter's coffee-house, which was near the High Street. There they disturbed one Richard Blacow, who was sitting 'in company with several Gentlemen of the University, and an Officer in his Regimental Habit'. Blacow, a young MA, overcome with righteous indignation, rushed out and followed them down the High Street and into St Mary Hall lane. They stopped and stood shouting in front of Oriel. When Blacow approached them, he was assaulted, and had

---

[33] Second Latin Register, fo. 104A.

[34] Bunbury's letter of 4 Dec. 1759 is stuck in the Second Latin Register at fo. 109ᵛ.

[35] The Revd Sir William Bunbury, Bt. (*c.* 1710–64), was elected Visitor in 1755 following the resignation of Sir John Dolben, who seems to have been instrumental in his successor's appointment (D.3.23b).

to take refuge inside Oriel. The crowd became a mob, and the disturbance a riot. Even more explicit treason was proclaimed: 'Damn King George and all his assistants!' The riot continued for some time, only breaking up when one of the Proctors appeared on the scene. The ringleaders were Charles Luxmore BA, and Robert Whitmore, both of Balliol, together with James Dawes of St Mary Hall.[36] Blacow reported the affair to the Vice-Chancellor, who 'said he was sorry for what had happened; but that nothing could prevent young fellows getting in liquor: but that they should be severely punished'. The severe penalty he had in mind, it transpired, was only an imposition and 'putting off their degrees for one year'. Blacow expostulated with the Vice-Chancellor in vain several times during the next few days, but the affair soon attracted national publicity. Luxmore, Whitmore, and Dawes were charged with treason on Blacow's information, and tried in the Court of the King's Bench. Luxmore was acquitted, but Whitmore and Dawes were sentenced to a fine, two years in prison, to find securities for their good behaviour for seven years, and to be paraded round Westminster Hall with papers on their foreheads stating their crime and sentence.[37]

Perhaps Balliol's lingering Jacobite inclinations had something to do with its Scottish connections. The Scots on Snell or Warner Exhibitions (both, usually) were not welcomed at all warmly into the College under Leigh. The atmosphere was soured by litigation over the financial arrangements, and the College lost no opportunity of diverting Exhibition moneys to College purposes. The Exhibitioners, for their part, regarded the College as fraudulent. Paradoxically, considering this unhappy state of affairs, the three most notable alumni of the period were all Scots. Adam Smith, the great political economist, is the most famous. He wrote to his guardian shortly after taking up his Snell Exhibition in 1740:[38]

I am indeed affraid that my expences at college must necessarily amount to a much greater sum this year than at any time hereafter, because of the extraordinary and most extravagant fees we are obliged to pay the College and University on our admittance. It will be his own fault if anyone should endanger his health at Oxford by excessive study, our only business here being to go to prayers twice a day, and to lectures twice a week.

On the other hand, the second of our distinguished Scots, John Douglas, a Snell contemporary of Smith's who was later Bishop of

---

[36] St Mary Hall was closely associated with Balliol at this time. Its Principal, William King (1685–1763; Balliol 1701: *DNB*), was the University's leading Jacobite.

[37] *Gentleman's Mag.* xxv (1755), p. 168; G. B. Hill, *Dr Johnson, his Friends and his Critics*, 1878, p. 68; New College Archives 7813, 8741–3. The Vice-Chancellor at the time of this affair was John Purnell, Warden of New College.

[38] *The Correspondence of Adam Smith*, ed. E. C. Mossner and I. S. Ross, 1977, no. 1.

Salisbury, had a more appreciative view of the academic climate.[39] A generation later, the third of this group, Matthew Baillie,[40] who was to become Physician to George III, wrote that he held his Tutor Richard Prosser in 'very great esteem', although it appears from his letters[41] that the studious way in which he spent his time (almost exclusively on classics) was largely self-directed.

Of the English Balliol men of the time, Henry Bathurst (Lord Chancellor 1771–8) is the first to come to mind because his portrait is the largest in Hall, but he was not a particularly distinguished figure. Similarly, James West was one of the lesser Presidents of the Royal Society (1768–72). Perhaps the most lasting achievements were those of John Hutchins (1698–1773), the great Dorset antiquarian and historian, and Thomas Knight (1759–1838),[42] the celebrated horticulturalist. In the eighteenth century, for the first time in the College's history, we also have American alumni to consider. At least seven were admitted:[43] one of them was William Henry Drayton, who came to Balliol from South Carolina via Westminster School in 1761; he went back to South Carolina to become a prominent agitator and revolutionary leader there.[44] In March 1776, he was elected Chief Justice of the State of South Carolina, and on 23 April of that year—two months before the Declaration of Independence—in his charge to the Grand Jury, after a tirade of vigorous legal and historical argument in justification, he pronounced

that George the third, King of Great Britain, has abdicated the government ... that is, HE HAS NO AUTHORITY OVER US, AND WE OWE NO OBEDIENCE TO HIM ...

He was elected to Congress in 1778, but he died aged only thirty-seven in the following year, or he would have left more of a mark.[44]

[39] See n. 30 above. John Douglas was appointed to a Snell Exhibition in 1745.

[40] Matthew Baillie (1761–1823) was appointed to a Snell Exhibition in 1779: his portrait hangs in the Library. See the *DNB*, etc., A. E. Rodin, *The Influence of Matthew Baillie's Morbid Anatomy*, Springfield, Illinois, 1973, and F. Crainz, *The Life and Works of Matthew Baillie*, Italy, 1995.

[41] In the Library of the Royal College of Surgeons of England.

[42] See the *DNB*, and N. B. Bagenal, 'Thomas Andrew Knight 1759–1838', *J. Royal Horticultural Soc.* 63 (1938), 319.

[43] The seven, and the dates of their admission, were: James Trent (s. William, of Philadelphia), 1717/18; Charles Hill (son of Charles, of Charlestown, South Carolina), 1735/6; William [Henry] Drayton and his younger brother Charles (sons of John, of St Andrews, South Carolina), 1761; Phillip Grymes (son of Phillip, of Virginia), 1764; Lewis Burwell (son of Lewis, of Virginia), 1765; and Arthur Mabson (son of Arthur, of Long Island), 1779.

[44] W. M. Dabney and M. Dargan, *William Henry Drayton & the American Revolution*, Albuquerque, 1962. I owe this reference to M. A. McDonnell: for further information on early Balliol Americans collected by him, see MISC 198.

During Leigh's Mastership there was a fundamental change in the way tutorial arrangements were made. At the beginning of the century, the Master seems often to have acted as a broker establishing contact between the incoming new members, or their fathers, and Fellows willing to take them on as pupils. But the matter remained essentially one of private contract. It was independent of the College and its officials. Sometimes the Master would be nominal Tutor, appointing a junior colleague 'Sub Tutor'. By about 1770 this had evolved into a system in which the appointment of Tutors had become the Master's prerogative and duty. In 1772, for example, James Cochrane stated, in the course of a dispute over his Snell stipend and tuition charges,[45] '... if a Tutor was not appointed for me, ... it was owing to the Master's Negligence, whose Province it confessedly is'. The payments, however, were transactions between the immediate parties, and nothing to do with the College. Cochrane again confirms this, by remarking that he was being sued, following Charles Godwyn's death, 'on account of a small sum supposed due to him for Tutorage'. The sum would have been small, because it was Godwyn's practice to excuse advanced students like Cochrane from some exercises, and to remit the fees pro rata. Godwyn was a learned, dutiful, and reasonable Tutor who, like Drake earlier and Prosser later, earned the respect of his pupils. But there were negligent, incompetent, and avaricious Tutors as well. Cochrane was a rebel, and perhaps his invective ran away with him, but his attacks on John Cooke, Richard Heighway, and Samuel Love were not adequately refuted, and were supported by his Snell colleague Andrew Greenfield. Cooke and Heighway drew the most direct criticism. They were accused of giving no instruction to one student for a whole year, despite his express requests to be taught, and of taking four guineas more annually for neglecting their duty than Godwyn had expected for performing his. For the lectures they did give, their competence was derided:

Let us see then how you are qualified to teach in the least and easiest of Lectureships. Your Province is Latin, your Book at present Cicero *de Natura Deorum*. Have your Studies ever directed you to a proper Disquisition of the Theology and Mythology of the Antients? Have you any Notion of the different Systems of their Metaphysical and Philosophical Principles? Can you speak with Fluency, or even without it, on the Method of conducting the Work, and of the striking Beauties of the Style? Have you any Knowledge of the historical and fabulous Points referred to by the illustrious Roman? Or of the various Books and national Customs to which he alludes?—Do you dignify with the Name of a Lecture, your sitting silently in a Chair, and in hearing the Undergraduates

---

[45] There is a collection of the printed material circulated by, in support of, and against James Cochrane bound into one volume in the College Library.

construe, sometimes right and sometimes wrong, and render an English Word for a Latin Word as faithfully as you can do? If this be the Case, can there be a more base Prostitution of such a Lecture, and may not the Understanding and Taste be equally improved by reading over the Dictionary? Indeed, what are all the public Lectures of Baliol which are read? In Geometry for Instance. Have they advanced farther than the 7th Proposition of the 1st book of Euclid through the Whole of this Long Term? To finish a Book of Euclid even in the Course of many Years, is a Phaenomenon almost unknown in Baliol. Yet if Mr Love will compare what he does with what he ought to do, as directed by the College Statutes, he will find his Deficiency astonishing.

Love's defence was limp: he was a stand-in Lecturer, he said; he had begun the course late in the term; there were only two lectures a week; the twenty or thirty who attended (all undergraduates were supposed to) included beginners whose presence dictated a slow pace; a public execution had drawn the audience away from one of the lectures. On the other hand, he was able also to say that 'in cases of deficiency and absence ... I have endeavoured that those in either situation should not be left behind, by giving them a private lecture in my room'. Love's 'private lecture' in his room on the topics covered at the 'public lectures' in Hall may be seen as part of the integration of the work of Lecturers (the College's responsibility) and Tutors (a private matter) which was beginning. A further step in that direction is evident in the accounts, which show that from about this time some Tutors had help in collecting their fees from the College, which collected arrears on their behalf through battels: in the Final Accounts for 1781, for example, there is a payment of £5, 'Tutori Prosser e Battellis Soc. com. Troyte. 1780'.[46]

Charles Godwyn[47] was a regular correspondent of John Hutchins. Most of the letters[48] are concerned with literary or antiquarian matters, but several of 1766–9 are about a pupil Godwyn owed to Hutchins.

I am greatly obliged to you, and to the lady who proposes to place her son under my care. I am concerned that the young gentleman has a tender state of health, and that there will be occasion for his keeping a horse. It is a dangerous kind of a remedy. But, if it be necessary, it must be complied with. We reckon fourscore pounds a year a proper allowance for a Commoner, and two hundred the allowance

---

[46] *Soc. Com.* = Fellow-Commoner. The payments were somewhat variable, but were usually £5 p.a. for a Fellow-Commoner, and £2 for an ordinary Commoner. No payments by Servitors appear, but there are several by Scholars.

[47] On the life and character of Charles Godwyn, see J. Nichols, *Literary Anecdotes of the Eighteenth Century*, viii, 1814, p. 224. For his benefaction to the Bodleian Library, see I. Philip, *The Bodleian Library in the Seventeenth and Eighteenth Centuries*, 1983, p. 101. For verses on his death, see *The Reading Mercury and Oxford Gazette*, 14 May 1770.

[48] Extracts from many of Godwyn's letters to Hutchins are printed in Nichols, op. cit.; the originals are in Bodleian MS Top. Gen. d. 2.

of a Gentleman-Commoner. The yearly expence of keeping a horse is to me twenty pounds. It will probably occasion a greater expence to a young gentleman; but all this will depend greatly upon the young gentleman's discretion, and that discretion will be put to a greater trial in case he be a Gentleman-Commoner. I therefore agree with you in advising that he be entered a Commoner. When we have had some experience of his conduct, I shall know what to say further upon that subject. It may perhaps be likewise of some advantage, if the money intended for his allowance shall pass through my hands. I will take care to provide a handsome apartment for him, and will beg the favour of you to give me about two months notice, that I may take an opportunity of securing one that will be agreeable to him.

The young man was Thomas Barker. Godwyn was able to offer him a wainscoted room on the first floor of his own staircase, with a garret bedchamber above it, at a rent of £10 p.a.;[49] his colleague Joseph Sanford was the 'landlord'.[50] Barker was admitted a Commoner in 1768, and Godwyn seems to have been an attentive Tutor, reporting back later that he was doing well and making 'a very proper use of his horse'. As Godwyn's earlier letter shows, he also kept a horse himself,[51] but his main diversions from teaching work were his own studies. He never published anything—through 'singular and unaffected modesty', according to Hutchins—and gave instructions in his will for his writings to be destroyed, but he was respected as a considerable scholar by his contemporaries. This is borne out by the valuable library and coin collection which he left to the University, together with the bulk of his fortune. He died in College on 23 April 1770, having been a Fellow for nearly fifty years. Remarkably, he was nevertheless denied the dignity of being Senior Fellow, because his close friend and senior colleague Joseph Sanford survived him.[52] Sanford was a resident Fellow 1714–74, the longest run in the history of the College. His life was, like Godwyn's, a contradiction of the popular

---

[49] In addition to the rent payable, the incoming tenant would be charged 'thirds' of £14 for furnishings, which was regarded as cheap.

[50] The earlier custom, which allowed Fellows to sublet rooms allocated to them, had by this time evolved into a system in which each Fellowship had certain rooms assigned to it which were regarded as a practically inalienable part of the Fellowship, and the corresponding rents part of its emoluments.

[51] There were stables by the back gate, but these were probably for the Master's household. It was unusual for Fellows to keep their own horses—they usually speak of horse 'hire' in their letters and accounts—and if they did, they probably kept them in the town. As late as the 1890s, two Fellows with private means (J. L. Strachan Davidson and Sir John Conroy) kept their own horses.

[52] On the life and character of Joseph Sanford, see *Gentleman's Mag.* 86 (1816), 212. Exeter College Library, where his portrait hangs (it was overlooked by Mrs R. L. Poole in her catalogue of 1925), has a catalogue of his books written in his hand. There is a memorial to him in St Mary Magdalen Church, high on the wall to the right of the Altar in the south aisle.

image of eighteenth-century dons as dissolute idlers. He was a less active Tutor than Godwyn, but enjoyed a similar reputation as a powerful scholar and is said to have assisted Benjamin Kennicott in his work on the Hebrew Bible. He was among the Bodleian's most regular readers, and a great bibliophile: he left his books to Exeter College.[53]

The architectural legacy of Leigh's predecessors was a hotchpotch of old and new buildings. The grandiose unified design for completely rebuilding the College which the *Oxford Almanac* published in 1742 was anonymous, and the background to it is obscure. Leigh was probably behind the scheme, as the principal backer for the first phase was Sir Edward Turner, his brother-in-law. He gave £300 towards the cost of executing the new design for the block between Trinity and the main gate, and the Leigh arms were placed under the cornice at the Trinity end. This work was carried out between 1738 and 1743 by the Townesends.[54] Unfortunately money, enthusiasm, or both, ran out. The rest of the scheme was set aside, and the urge to build did not return until 1762, when Sanford and Godwyn became aware that Hutchins's Dorset friend and neighbour Henry Fisher intended to be a Benefactor.[55] Fisher, an ex-Fellow of Jacobite opinions, was the incumbent of the College living of Bere Regis. Delicate negotiations, in which Hutchins was instrumental, eventually resulted in a promise from Fisher that he would give £3,000 for a new building. Henry Keene designed and supervised the construction of the two staircases (now numbered X and XI) which are known as the Fisher Building, in 1769–70.[56] The finishing touch was the enigmatic inscription below the central first-floor window: 'Verbum non amplius Fisher.' The tag is from Horace. Its literal translation is 'A word no more Fisher', but there is a tradition that it is a word puzzle which remains undeciphered.[57]

The enrolment of the University fell sharply towards the middle of the eighteenth century, and Balliol shrank more than most colleges. The

---

[53] It is curious that neither Sanford nor Godwyn followed the example of their friend George Coningesby, and left their books and collections to Balliol. Coningesby was in his younger days a Jacobite. He found a sympathetic home as a senior Commoner in Balliol, in 1739. When he died in 1768, he left his large library to Sanford and Godwyn in trust for the College, together with ample funds for cataloguing, etc. (his will was proved in the PCC); he also gave 18 important manuscripts.

[54] H. M. Colvin, *Unbuilt Oxford*, 1983, p. 105.

[55] Henry Fisher was elected to a Blundell Fellowship in 1707; he was instituted at Bere Regis in 1725, and died 20 June 1773 aged 90. His will was proved in the PCC: he made a legacy to the College of £100, having made his main benefaction in his lifetime.

[56] P. Howell, 'The Fisher Buildings at Balliol', *Balliol College Record*, 1981, p. 31.

[57] There was a small brass memorial to Henry Fisher on the north wall of Bere Regis church until about 1980, when it was stolen. A skull and an hour-glass were depicted, and it bore the same puzzling inscription as the Fisher Building

11. Richard Prosser, Fellow 1773–93.

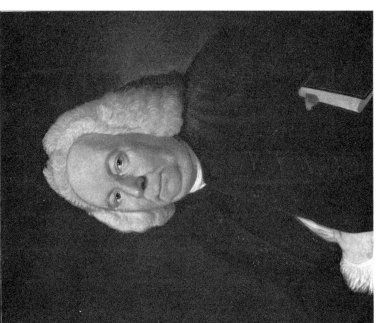

10. Joseph Sanford, Fellow 1714–74.

proportion of Fellow-Commoners admitted diminished steadily,[58] sapping the College's financial strength at a time when it was engaged in expensive litigation, especially over the Snell Trust. The Fellowship dividend did not suffer, but this was a result of the rather artificial way in which it was computed.[59] All expenses had to be met from current income, as there were practically no realizable assets or contingency funds. Although there were a few individuals swimming against the current, the academic ardour of the College cooled as well, as in the University generally. There was a decade or so of respite from this decline towards the end of Leigh's Mastership, largely due to the support he received from Richard Prosser, Fellow 1773–93.[60] With some difficulty, intellectual ability was restored as an important criterion in Fellowship elections. In 1779 a defeated candidate, Henry Edwards Davis, appealed to the Visitor.[61] He already had a substantial, if controversial, publication to his credit,[62] but he had been passed over for a much less accomplished candidate. The papers in the case suggest that Davis's main deficiency in the eyes of the majority was lack of tact, and of due deference to his seniors. Leigh and Prosser supported him, declaring that he had 'conducted himself, ever, in a moral and scholarlike manner', and the Visitor ordered his admission to the disputed Fellowship. Five years later there was another quarrel over an election contest between Charles Wood, an undergraduate Domus Scholar, and John Parsons, a Wadham BA.[63] The minority (comprising Leigh, Prosser, John Barnes, and John Matthew) were for Parsons, and they appealed against Wood's election on the grounds that he was of greatly inferior ability. The Visitor quibbled over both elections, and would allow neither, but Parsons was sufficiently encouraged to try again the following year, when there were two vacancies, and both the earlier contenders were elected. Parsons and other outsiders who got in during this period were not the first to do so, but they were probably the first elected on merit against internal competition—the few previous instances[64] were, in all

[58] The number of Fellow-Commoners in residence reached a peak of about 20 around 1720. It fell steadily through the eighteenth century, in both relative and absolute terms. The last two were admitted in 1796. The category was revived so that there would be a unique distinction to confer on Robert Wilberforce (1887–1990; Balliol 1908) to mark his 100th birthday.

[59] G. Beachcroft, 'Balliol College Accounts in the Eighteenth Century', in J. [M.] Prest (ed.), *Balliol Studies*, 1982.

[60] On the life and character of Richard Prosser, see J. [H.] Jones, in *Balliol College Record*, 1980, p. 58, and material collected subsequently in MISC 5.13. His portrait hangs in Hall.

[61] D.3.50–4.

[62] H. E. Davis, *An Examination of the Fifteenth and Sixteenth Chapters of Mr Gibbon's History . . .* , 1778.   [63] D.3.56–61.

[64] e.g. Samuel Reynolds of Exeter and Corpus Christi Colleges (father of Sir Joshua) was elected a Fellow of Balliol in 1705.

probability, unopposed. These affairs, and another of similar flavour not long after Leigh's death,[65] were important steps towards making the Balliol Fellowships genuinely open, and dependent solely on academic merit: Leigh and Prosser were always on the side of that tendency. The tone of the place was raised in other ways as well, so that on 12 February 1784 Leigh was able to write '... we are making great improvements in College; I am glad to foresee, by Michaelmas Term, at least by Cath. Tide, Strict Residence required; College ... [discipline?] and Lectures well observed ... I have great satisfaction in our promising Tutors.'[66] Prosser, 'much worn out by long and close attention to Pupils', was soon to step down as Tutor, but Leigh was glad to have found 'a most promising successor in Mr Matthew'.[67]

Theophilus Leigh had a bad press at the hands of political opponents in his lifetime. He was inclined to pomposity, with a taste for overdone jokes (especially puns), and some of his public activities had an element of farce. The mock lament published during the County electioneering of 1753 provides an example of the kind of barbed ridicule he attracted.[68]

> He had read of a Dervis, who nimbly could shoot
> His Soul with a Word into Body of Brute;
> This Art with Impatience he labour'd to find,
> It kill'd his Repose and distracted his Mind;
> 'Till at last, with hard Plodding and Study unsound,
> This wonderful Secret was happily found.
> But eager an Art so surprizing to try,
> He fix'd on an Ass, that by Chance trotted by.
> The Word was pronounc'd, the Soul instantly fled,
> And down dropt the Carcas of T— L— dead:
> The Soul, from its pitiful Mansion releast,
> Grew pleas'd with a Dwelling so much to it's taste:
> Before, while imprisoned, 'twas tortured, in vain,
> To work on a Pimping, all-fool-scheming Brain;
> In political Books doom'd for ever to pore,
> And remain (O! surprising!) as wise as before:
> But now, in a Trice of it's Punishments eas'd,
> Might saunter or bray or be dull as it pleas'd:
> Despis'd it may be and abus'd, but no more
> Than it patiently suffer'd in T— L— before:
> So prudent for once, rather chose to reside
> With innocent Dulness than Folly and Pride....

[65] D.3.66–71.   [66] Bodleian MS Dep. c. 577, fo. 134.

[67] Bodleian MS Dep. c. 577, fo. 136.

[68] J. Freinshemius (pseud.), *Threnodia, or an Elegy on the unexpected and unlamented Death of the M— of B—*, 1753. Kindly pointed out by Dr R. H. Lonsdale.

When assaulted by Death, who's commission'd to strike
The Tory, the Whig and the Trimmer alike,
With a Sigh and a Groan he was heard to invoke
His best belov'd Goddess of Dulness, and spoke:
'O, Goddess! thou Foe to the Learned and Wise,
Thou, who mad'st me a M———, a J–st—e, a V—;
Who with most tender Care o'er my Infancy hung,
And form'd every sentence, that dropp'd from my Tongue;
Whose Hand, with a Parent's Affection, hath spread
O'er the Mind of thy Offspring thy Mantle of lead;
Hath stamped thy own Mark on whatever I writ,
And gave me immortal Aversions to Wit;
As thy Influence always my Intellects blest,
O, hear and comply with this single Request:
Transform me when dead, and bid fair-flying Fame
To give me (what, living, I want) a good Name!'

Historians since, scandalized by the way he was elected, have also been hard on him, tending to blame him for the doldrums into which the College slid in his time. But his opponents do not emerge from critical scrutiny very well either, and what happened to the College was also the University's fate. His letters, which are mainly concerned with family affairs and politics, survive in abundance to show him in a more favourable light as a kindly man given to gossip, and suggest that he was sensitive in the former, and shrewd in the latter. Original scholarship would seem to have played little part in his life, but there is no hint to be found of spite, corruption, or folly. Nor was he inactive in promoting the academic work of the College. He achieved little, but the Fellows were a ponderous and conservative influence, dominated by the Devon interest most of the time. In his old age, with backing and stimulus from Prosser, he was an enthusiastic supporter of attempts to supplant some of the College's laxer practices with a better regulated and more studious regime. During his ninety-first and last year, he took a full part in College business, especially the Fellowship election, 'because he thought the future Election of his friend Mr Prosser depended on it'.[69] He died in College on 3 January 1785.[70] In the event, Prosser was not chosen as Master, and there was a relapse, but Leigh had, with his assistance, sown the seeds of reform.

[69] Bodleian MS Dep. c. 577, fo. 137.
[70] He was buried on 10 Jan. 1785 at Adlestrop (which was also his birthplace, 28 Oct. 1693), near his wife (Anne, daughter of Edward Bee of Beckley; she died 5 Oct. 1766) in the railed enclosure by the south outer wall of the church chancel, as he had instructed in his will (PCC). There is a memorial tablet on the north inner wall of the chancel which gives his tenure of the Mastership as 56 years: it was actually nearly 59 years.

14

From Obscurity to Pre-eminence 1785–1854

BALLIOL came near to total collapse in the closing years of the eighteenth century. Numbers had fallen much more sharply in mid century than in the University as a whole, and lost ground had not been regained. The buildings were in extreme disrepair and the College was in debt. A Fellowship had been sequestered (in modern jargon, a post had been frozen) since 1775, and the dividend which would have been paid to its holder had been used for corporate—'Domus'—purposes, but after the interest on outstanding loans had been paid this had sufficed for little more than essential repairs and alterations.[1] In 1800 there was still a net debt (see Fig. 6) and there were only four admissions in that year. The resident body shrank to about half a dozen Fellows, with three or four BA members, and twenty-five or so undergraduates, including a single Servitor working his way.[2]

Academic activity sank to a minimal level, and the teaching became perfunctory and mechanical. People were concerned more with dress and social life than with study and reflection. Robert Southey came into residence in 1793, after expulsion from Westminster for publishing a rebellious protest against excessive flogging, in a school magazine called *The Flagellant*. He had been rejected by Christ Church as a probable trouble-maker, and he expected to meet with 'pedantry, prejudice, and aristocracy'. In matters of behaviour, recreation, and reading, he went his own way. He declined to have his hair dressed and powdered by the College Barber. He learned to row (though this would have been for leisurely boating rather than vigorous exercise), he walked prodigious distances, he kept to the company of a small circle of friends, and he read widely. He also began to write, often rising at five in the morning to do

[1] James Wyatt supervised extensive repairs and alterations in 1791–4; James Pears was the builder. The Kitchens, Buttery, etc., and the screens passage, were moved from the south end of the Hall (now the main wing of the Library) to the north end. The ornate entrance arch of the screens passage was moved to the opening of the Chapel passage. The Hall and Library roofs, previously steep and without any parapets, were reconstructed to be relatively flat, and crenellated parapets were added. A proposal for rebuilding the Broad Street front at a cost of over £2,500 was also submitted by Wyatt at this time, but not carried out.

[2] The last Servitor was admitted in 1810.

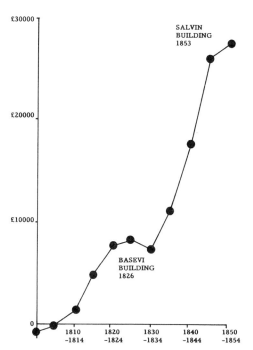

Fig. 6. The financial position of the College, 1800–1854. Five-year averages of the balance of debts, cash, and credit at the end of the financial year, expressed in pounds at the 1800 value.

so, completing 'Joan of Arc' whilst still an undergraduate. An independent attitude was encouraged by his Tutor, Thomas How, who once said to him 'Mr Southey, you won't learn anything from my lectures, sir; so if you have any studies of your own, you had better pursue them.' Just as Southey was an unusual undergraduate, so How was an atypical Fellow. He once astonished and pleased his pupil 'by declaiming against the war [with France], praising America, and asserting the right of every country to model its own form of government'. It is unlikely that many of Southey's Balliol acquaintances shared his radical views, or equalled him in imagination, but he met a kindred spirit in Balliol through one of them in the summer of 1794. Samuel Taylor Coleridge, on a walking tour, called at the College to see his friend Robert Allen, who introduced him to Southey. They hit it off immediately, and Coleridge stayed for two or three weeks, during which they were constantly together thrashing out an idea for the foundation of a new society. A party of well-educated, liberal-minded, married gentlemen was to emigrate to America, or some other virgin territory. There they would establish an egalitarian self-ruling colony, with all the fundamental freedoms and all property in common. Basic needs would only require each man to labour a couple of hours a day, they computed: the rest of the time would be spent in reading, discussion, and educating the children. 'Pantisocracy', as they called it, was not an idle dream to them. It was a serious plan, which they apparently intended to carry through. They got as far as recruiting adventurers to go with them, but there were some serious defects, including the right of individuals to opt out, and the whole thing eventually came to nothing. Southey's rooms, where this abortive scheme was drafted, were close to the old back gate and the privies ('Temple of Cloacina'), roughly where the Junior Common Room now is.[3]

The stage was nevertheless set for improvement. As we have seen in the last chapter, several outsiders had been elected to Fellowships in the 1780s, despite the claims of internal candidates, largely as a result of the influence of Richard Prosser. One of these was John Parsons. The son of Isaac Parsons, butler of Corpus Christi College, he attended Magdalen College School and then Wadham, whence he was elected a Fellow of Balliol in 1785. Accounts of him do not mention any scholarly works, but in fact he was responsible for the preliminary work on the preparation of an Oxford edition of Strabo. Association with this was not exactly something to advertise, as it contained many errors which had been seized and enlarged upon by the *Edinburgh Review*, in one of its scornful attacks on Oxford scholarship and education. As a young Fellow he was also a regular anonymous contributor to the *Monthly Review*, until its political position became more inconsistent with his own (which was Tory through and through) than he could stand. He was probably the main work-horse of the administrative efficiency which was established during John Davey's Mastership (1785–98): from this period, minutes of College Meetings were recorded in detail and in English, businesslike accounts were kept, and the College started regularly to use the services of banks. Of Davey himself, the only Blundell Fellow ever elected Master, not much is known. A bachelor suspected of 'Romanising tendencies', he was vicar of Bledlow in Buckinghamshire. He deprecated strongly the growing tendency of the College to throw elections to Fellowships open, instead of conferring them on existing Domus Scholars. This was contrary to College interests, he vainly argued, commenting 'there is no encouragement for a Parent to send his son to Balliol, as the preferments within the House are so constantly bestowed on Foreigners'. He does not seem to have had any scholarly activities of his own, or to have taken much interest in the academic side of College life. On the other hand, he was a painstaking, efficient administrator, and must be allowed to share with Leigh, Prosser,

---

[3] For Southey at Balliol see: J. Simmons, *Southey*, 1945; *The Life and Correspondence of the late Robert Southey*, ed. C. C. Southey, 1849; and also *New Letters of Robert Southey*, ed. K. Curry, 1965.

and Parsons a small part of the honour due to them for enabling recovery to begin.[4]

Parsons was elected Master in 1798. He was 'distinguished for great vigour of intellect and soundness of judgment, which had received every improvement from useful studies, and consistent and indefatigable attention to business'.[5] Although frequently incapacitated for weeks on end by gout, he was a dominant figure in the University during his Mastership. One of the prime movers behind the Honours Examination Statute of 1800 (which initiated the development of the modern examination system), he also tightened up the academic arrangements in his own College. The Library was refurbished and reorganized, with the imposition of tight discipline, and increased fees. Collections on the Christ Church model were introduced for all undergraduates:

Robert Finch to Dr R. Roberts of St Paul's School, 3 April 1802
... It is customary and indeed obligatory in our college to analyze every author, whom we read, in the same nature as the collections at X[t]: church. I think this is a good exercise, since it facilitates the retention of striking events in the memory, and reduces the matter of a book to a skeleton, as it were ...

W. S. Hamilton to his mother, 2 April 1808
... I have been so busy with Collections, which are public examinations, at the end of each term, before the master and public lecturers ...

These examinations, which were largely, if not entirely, oral, have evolved on one hand into the informal College written examinations which are still known as 'Collections', and on the other into the interviews which undergraduates have with the Master and their Tutors ('Handshaking') at the end of term. Parsons was not a liberal reformer, however: he was a Tory disciplinarian, primarily interested in bolstering the Protestant establishment. It may seem paradoxical to a modern reader that an unshakeable Tory should have been behind what appears now as a reforming movement, but it must be remembered that in the thinking of the time laxity, liberality, and originality in matters of religion and scholarship were associated with revolution. A tightening-up of 'academical discipline' was a defence of the established order of things. This approach had a mixed reception, and Balliol men were slow to show interest in the

---

[4] His views on open elections are in D.3.68; for his 'Romanising tendencies', see G. C. Brodrick, *Memories and Impressions*, 1900, p. 77, and J. Wickham Legg, *English Church Life*, 1914, p. 362. His will was proved in 1798 (PCC); he asked to be buried in Bledlow churchyard, in a frugal manner.

[5] From an appreciation of Parsons written by Richard Jenkyns at the end of John Parsons's Memorandum Book. See also the *DNB*, etc. The Chapel memorial to him was saved when the Chapel was rebuilt, and is now in the Antechapel. His widow was buried in the Chapel beside him in 1827. His portrait hangs in Hall.

13. Shute Barrington, Visitor 1805–26.

12. John Davey, Master 1785–98. In 1792 Robert Southey called on 'Dr Davey, of Balliol College Head' to be admitted. He described the experience shortly afterwards in a rhyming letter to T. D. Lamb, reporting on Davey that

> Dear Tom, his wig
> Was not so big
> As many Doctors wore,
> And so I may
> Presume to say
> His wisdom is the more.

Honours examination. There was a substantial faction comprising, to judge from their correspondence,[6] cultivated and widely read men, who resented any attempts to impose a regimented system of lectures and examinations, which they thought 'an insult upon sense and learning'. The main teaching mode was College lectures: the surviving accounts condemn them as tedious recitations of closely defined and prescribed material, which interfered with any plans a man might have for wider reading. Hamilton was the hardest critic, writing to his mother in 1807:[7]

... I am so plagued by these foolish lectures of the College Tutors that I have little time to do anything else—Aristotle today, ditto tomorrow; and I believe that if the ideas furnished by Aristotle to these numbskulls were taken away, it would be doubtful whether there remained a single notion. I am quite tired of such uniformity of study ...

There is a glimpse of what sounds like a modern tutorial in a letter written by Robert Finch to his father in 1802: '... I find Mr Rogers a pleasant tutor and well-inform'd scholar. Sometimes an interview takes place between me and himself in which we not only read, but criticise and descant upon the author before us ...'; but Finch's father reacted as if this were a novelty, and no further allusions to tutorial teaching are found until much later.

Men living in College in the first decade of the nineteenth century had very spacious accommodation—Finch had a large sitting-room and four smaller rooms[8]—and, with numbers well below capacity, some members had the use of more than one set. Small though it was, the College was split into cliques. Social activity took place almost exclusively in private apartments. There was no Junior Common Room—it seems that there was an attempt to get one started around 1805, but it fell foul of Parsons, who objected to anything having its own rules and independence operating within his sphere.[9] Finch found 'noisy parties, trifling chit-chat and Bacchanalian orgies' not to his taste, and regretted that although the 'public discipline' of the College was satisfactory, there were 'private irregularities ... as in all societies of young men', because it was 'impossible for the eyes of a master to pry into the domestic habits of all those who are under

[6] See especially the correspondence of Robert Finch (admitted to Balliol 1802) with his contemporaries: Bodleian MSS Finch.

[7] J. Veitch, *Memoir of Sir William Hamilton, Bart.*, 1896, p. 30.

[8] Bodleian MS Finch e. 40, fo. 150.

[9] H. W. C. Davis, *A History of Balliol College*, revised by R. H. C. Davis and R. [W.] Hunt, 1963, p. 170; see also Bodleian MS Finch d. 6, fo. 230.

his authority'.[10] Another of Hamilton's letters to his mother has left us a sketch of the daily routine:[11]

... No boots are allowed to be worn here, or trousers or pantaloons. In the morning we wear white cotton stockings, and before dinner regularly dress in silk stockings, etc. After dinner we go to one another's rooms and drink some wine, then go to chapel at half-past five, and walk, or sail on the river, after that. In the morning we go to chapel at seven o'clock, breakfast at nine, fag all the forenoon, and dine at half-past three ...

Richard Jenkyns, a fervent adherent to the Parsons line, was elected to a Fellowship in 1803. He was soon the principal College Tutor. Jenkyns had been a Scholar of the College, and as such had enjoyed a relatively smooth progression to a Fellowship. The 1507 Statutes which were still in force left the Fellowships on the ancient Foundation free of regional or other restrictions, but gave existing Scholars a *ceteris paribus* advantage. The extent to which this advantage could be stretched was still a fiercely disputed issue, despite recent precedents for the election of outsiders— including, as we have already seen, the case of Parsons himself. The election of William Vaux of Christ Church, in 1806, provoked two appeals to the Visitor which focused the arguments. The appeals were lodged by three Scholars who had been passed over, and two dissident Fellows. The principal basis of both appeals was that three eligible Scholars with adequate qualifications had offered themselves, and that according to the Statutes one of them ought to have been preferred to an outsider. Parsons, advised by Prosser behind the scenes, made a vigorous reply: he insisted that Vaux was clearly the best candidate, citing his performance in the new Public Examination as evidence. He also argued that the *ceteris paribus* preference for Scholars needed to be applied with caution because they were appointed without competition, each Fellow having the private patronage of a Scholarship. The Visitor was Shute Barrington, Bishop of Durham.[12] By exercising in his favour its unique privilege of electing its own Visitor in 1805, the College had given the last word in its affairs to an ardent Tory, who could be expected to support Parsons. Barrington rejected the appeals and rebuked the instigators so firmly that all sub-sequent elections (except to the two closed Fellowships on the Blundell Foundation) were conducted on a completely open basis, without a murmur from anybody. Barrington held office until his death in 1826, by which time the College was completely controlled by men who had been elected in open competition. Balliol names first appeared in the class lists of 1808, and the earliest Firsts were obtained in 1810. An intermittent

---

[10] Bodleian MS Finch e. 40, fos. 152 and 147ᵛ.
[11] Veitch, op. cit., p. 30.   [12] See the *DNB*, etc.

trickle continued for the remainder of Parsons's rule. He was appointed Dean of Bristol in 1810, and Bishop of Peterborough in 1813, and after this was often absent. His Vicegerent was generally Jenkyns, whose influence therefore grew, extending from 1816 even to the control of admissions.

Noel Ellison and Charles Ogilvie were elected Fellows in 1816. Like Charles Girdlestone, who followed in 1818, they were First Class Honours men. Tradition gives this trio the credit for the marked improvement in the fortunes of the College which began at about this time, and soon led to a waiting-list for admissions. Ogilvie, who was the most influential, and served longest, was a vigorous and outspoken man who later described himself as 'an attached and zealous member of the Church of England as by Law established'. He was for many years a correspondent of, and seems to have been much influenced by, Hannah More, the religious writer, who was 'much pleased' with Ogilvie's 'account of the good discipline and studious character of the College'. 'Genial, joyous, graceful Ellison', a Corpus Christi contemporary and intimate friend of John Keble, was also rigidly High Church: once, whilst Rector of Huntspill, he refused to bury a Methodist child until episcopal pressure had been applied. Girdlestone was of a more liberal inclination.

The first twenty years of the nineteenth century also saw a return to solvency (see Fig. 3). Without this recovery the College would have been held back later by inability to build new accommodation for increased admissions. Rising revenue from the ancient estates in Northumberland, beneath which coal-mining developments were taking place, was responsible. The principal beneficiaries were the Master and Fellows, because the procedure was that the income remaining after various fixed allocations of funds and expenses was divided into fifteen shares, one for each Fellow, two for the Master, and only one for Domus. But Domus was absorbing the dividend of the unfilled Fellowship, as well as its own share, and in 1802 Master and Fellows resolved[13] to increase the Domus share of all Northumberland profits in excess of £700, from the normal one-fifteenth to one-third. By 1816 all the debts were cleared, the College's realizable wealth was growing at a healthy rate, and it was neither desirable on academic grounds, nor financially justifiable, for any Fellowship to continue vacant.

Parsons died of 'suppressed gout' in March 1819 and was buried with elaborate funeral pomp in the Chapel. After some hesitation and backstage activity, Jenkyns was elected to succeed him. A small and sometimes ridiculously pompous man—'The little Master'—accounts of him are

---

[13] English Register, 12 June 1802.

dominated by affectionately related but ludicrous anecdotes.[14] Benjamin Jowett's reminiscences of Jenkyns around 1840 (written about 1888) are of particular interest:[15]

In attempting to portray the Balliol of fifty years ago I must not forget the figure of the old Master, who was very different from any of the Fellows, and was held in considerable awe by them. He was a gentleman of the old school, in whom were represented old manners, old traditions, old prejudices, a Tory and a Churchman, high and dry, without much literature, but having a good deal of character. ... 'His young men', as he termed them, speaking in an accent which we all remember, were never tired of mimicking his voice, drawing his portrait, and inventing stories about what he said and did. ... His sermon on the 'Sin that doth so easily beset us', by which, as he said in emphatic and almost acrid tones, he meant 'the habit of contracting debts', will never be forgotten by those who heard it. ... The ridiculousness of the effect was heightened by his old-fashioned pronunciation of certain words, such as 'rayther', 'wounded' (which he pronounced like 'wow' in 'bow-wow'). He was a considerable actor, and would put on severe looks to terrify Freshmen, but he was really kind-hearted and indulgent to them. He was in a natural state of war with the Fellows and Scholars on the Close Foundation [i.e. the Blundell Foundation]; and many ludicrous stories were told of his behaviour towards them, of his dislike of smoking, and of his enmity to dogs. Some excellent things were undoubtedly said by him, but so fertile was the genius of undergraduates that, as in some early histories, it is impossible to separate accurately what is mythical from what is true in the accounts of him. One evening he suddenly appeared in Hall to strike terror into a riotous party, and found that the Master's health had been proposed and that an undergraduate was already on his legs returning thanks in his name. He was compared by John Carr[16] to a famous old mulberry tree[17] in the garden, well-known to all Balliol men; while of another mulberry tree newly planted, Carr said, 'And that is Tait'.[18] He was short of stature and very neat in his appearance; the deficiency of height was more than compensated by a superfluity of magisterial or ecclesiastical dignity. He was much respected, and his great services to the College have always been

---

[14] An amusing selection is gathered together in J. Morris, *The Oxford Book of Oxford*, 1978, p. 213.

[15] Appendix D in W. Ward, *William George Ward and the Oxford Movement*, 1889.

[16] John Carr, Fellow 1819–38, died 1861.

[17] This old mulberry-tree is still alive at the time of writing, but it has been a propped-up wreck as long as anyone can remember (and probably since 1898: Sir John Conroy to E. J. Palmer, 17 Aug. 1898, Conroy Papers). See the photograph on p. 317. It is in the Garden Quadrangle by the wall of the Fellows' Garden. There is a tradition that it was planted by Elizabeth I, but it is more likely that it was grown from one of the seeds distributed by James I as part of his abortive campaign to establish an English silk industry. There are two other mulberry-trees in the Quadrangle (one planted by HM Queen Mary in 1921 and one planted by HRH Princess Margaret in 1950), as well as two more in the Fellows' Garden.

[18] A. C. Tait, of whom more later. The tree to which he was compared is one of the pair in the Fellows' Garden.

acknowledged. But even now, at the distance of more than a generation, it is impossible to think of him without some humorous or ludicrous association arising in the mind.

Jenkyns was no great scholar, but made no pretensions in that direction, writing nothing for publication except obituary notices for the *Gentleman's Magazine*. A shrewd organizer and good judge of men, he had an inflexible view of what was right, and usually got his way, in part perhaps as a result of his attitude to meetings. In the private memo book which he used during his Vice-Chancellorship (1824–8), he exhorted himself: 'NB— Never come unprepared to a Meeting—but by previous enquiry and conversation gain a competent knowledge of the business to be discussed, and form an opinion—and a decided one too, upon the same . . .'

One of the earliest problems of Jenkyn's reign came from the will of Thomas How, who had made a bequest to establish two closed Exhibitions at Balliol for his kin or the sons of Somerset and Devonshire clergymen. The bequest was declined because it was restrictive: it was later accepted by Exeter College. The region which would have been favoured by this arrangement was the home ground of the closed Blundell Foundation, which had at times created an overwhelming inbred Devonshire party in the College. It had come to be seen, perhaps unfairly, as a parasitic burden. Jenkyns maintained a consistently obstructive policy towards it, regarding it with near paranoid suspicion. He once denounced it to the Visitor as follows:

The Blundell composition, or rather the Foundation resting upon it, as it ever has been, will continue to be, the very bane of our Society. Extreme poverty, I suspect, compelled our Predecessors to make so improvident a bargain . . . My principle, as that of my respected Predecessor, always has been, to deal strict justice, but to give no advantage (as was formerly the case with an overpowering party in the College from Devonshire) to the Blundell Foundation. They must in justice have their pound of flesh—but not an ounce more.

In 1825, for example, the progression of the Blundell Scholar Edward Kitson to a Fellowship was obstructed, albeit only temporarily.

From the English Register, 29 Nov. 1825
In the examination . . . Mr Kitson appeared from habitual neglect so grossly deficient in the literary qualifications required by the Statutes of the College (the force and authority of which the framers of the Blundell composition expressly recognise) that the Society did not feel themselves justified in proceeding to an election; since the admission to a fellowship of a Candidate under Mr Kitson's circumstances seemed to them, in their consciences adverse at once to the letter and spirit of their institution.

Although the College was powerless to change the way the Blundell places were filled, it had complete freedom of action so far as the Domus

Scholarship places were concerned, because they were without geo-
graphical or other restrictions. All that was necessary was for the Fellows
to surrender their rights of nominating individually, which they agreed
to do in May 1827. In future the Scholarships (which were doubled in
value at the same time) were to be filled by 'a general competition of
candidates, whether members of the College or not'. The examination was
to be similar to that for Fellowships, but set at an appropriately lower
level; there was to be only one examination a year, which the Master
was to give 'greater importance and notoriety' by advertisement. The
first three Open Scholars were elected, after examination at length, on
29 November 1827.[19]

From the Latin Register, 29 Nov. 1827
... Eodem die electi sunt in Scholares Domus, ex antiqua fundatione, Petrus
Samuel Henricus Payne, Edwardus Hartopp Grove et Edwardus D'Oyley
Barwell; quippe qui Magistro et Sociis, jure suo singulos Scholares nominandi
decedentibus (vid. Reg. Angl. Martii 1, 1828) post Examinationem habitam, prae
cunctis Candidatis sese commendaverint ...

Two of the three came from Shrewsbury, and correspondence about the
examination survives in the papers of Samuel Butler, the great headmaster.

Grove's father to Samuel Butler

Kings Arms Inn
Oxford
Nov 29 1827
My dear Sir,
   This has been a day of bustle and anxiety but I am unwilling to bring it to a
close without transmitting to you the result of the late Examination at Balliol
which, after four days of what has generally been considered hard work, has
placed Payne, Grove and Barwell as the successful Candidates for the vacant
Scholarships of Balliol, ... I trust you will have an honest pride and a heartfelt
pleasure in finding two of your own Pupils at the head of the list, and not the
less so when you know that they were placed in competition with Ten or Eleven
Candidates, and some three of four Members of the University ...

The arrangements were an immediate success, attracting a succession of
outstanding men. Shortly after the 1833 examination, Payne, by now a

---

[19] The date given in previous accounts is usually 1828 or 1834. This is because of
confusion created at the time. The decision taken in May 1827 was not minuted until a
resolution to record it was taken at a College Meeting in March 1828. The decision to
seek a change of Statutes incorporating the new arrangements was delayed until 1834. It
appears that although there was no doubt that what was being done was right, there was
uncertainty about its legality, because it was at variance with long-standing Statute
and practice. That the first examination and elections actually took place in 1827 is
unambiguously documented.

Fellow of the College, reported to Butler:

P. S. H. Payne to Samuel Butler, 1 Dec. 1833
... I have been for the last week engaged, as one of the fellows, in the examination for our Balliol Scholarships. There were 30 candidates, and it was a competition only second in point of severity to that for the Ireland. Most of the public schools sent in some of their best men ...

It was usual for the examination to begin with a call on the Master.

A. P. Stanley to his sister Mary, 27 Nov. 1833
... We went on Saturday to the Head of Balliol to present our certificates, etc.—we were all shown in to the drawing room—and then brought up one by one to him—something like a dentist's operation—I had been cautioned to make as beautiful a bow as I possibly could, as he is very ceremonious ...

This was followed by a week of written examinations involving translations and composition in Latin, Greek, and English, and also papers in Divinity and Mathematics. In some respects accounts in memoirs and letters make it sound like a modern examination, although a week including two consecutive days of eight hours' writing would be regarded as punitive now. The week's effort came rapidly to a dramatic climax:

A. P. Stanley to his sister, 29 Nov. 1833
We all assembled in the Hall and had to wait one hour—the room getting fuller and fuller of the Rugby Oxonians crowding in from various parts to hear the result. At last the Dean appeared in his white robes and moved up to the head of the table. He first began a long preamble—that they were well satisfied with all—that those who were disappointed were many in proportion to those who were successful, etc., etc.,—all this time everyone was listening in the most intense eagerness—and I almost bit my lips off—till 'the successful candidates are Mr Stanley'—I gave a great jump—and there was a half shout among the Rugby men—(the next was Lonsdale from Eton). The Dean then took me into the Chapel, where was the Master and all the Fellows in white robes. And there I swore that I would not dissipate the property, reveal the secrets, or disobey the Statutes of the College—I was then made to kneel on the steps and admitted to the rank of Scholar and Exhibitioner of Balliol College, nomine Patris, Filii et Spiritus—I then wrote my name in a book and so was finished—I am to be matriculated today.

The examination week—always the last in November—was a very busy time for the Fellows. Non-residents returned to Oxford if they possibly could, and all present took part in the examination and elections. The new regulations were a great success from the very start, attracting large numbers of strong candidates. The cream of them were no doubt drawn by one of the few available opportunities to demonstrate their prowess; the rest simply hoped to do well enough to earn the offer of a Commoner place. Commoner places were at the sole disposal of the Master, who

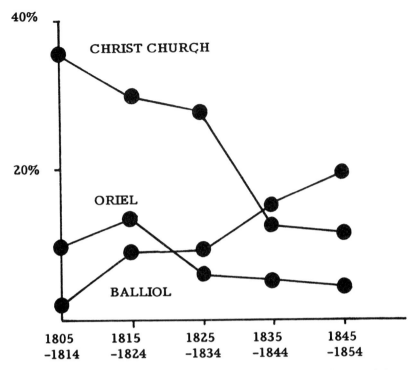

Fig. 7. Numbers of Firsts obtained, as percentages of the total number awarded, 1805–1854. Ten-year averages.

chose to fill many of them with competent runners-up in the Scholarship examination, which thus became in effect a competitive general admissions examination. Balliol was the first college to have such a system. A new residential block had been built by George Basevi in 1826, 'In consequence of the deficiency of Rooms to satisfy the very numerous and pressing applications for admission', but the College was soon over-subscribed again. During the thirties and forties Jenkyns had a regular stream of ingratiating letters about admission. As the disposal of Commoner places was at the discretion of the Master alone, even a senior Fellow could not be confident of getting a protégé in 'except under the circumstance of his appearing to advantage in a scholarship examination'. In 1834, Robert Peel failed in an approach on behalf of a friend's son, and several peers and bishops were also gently rebuffed. By the mid thirties, Balliol was generally recognized as the leading college: its Open Scholarships and Fellowships were the greatest distinctions in the University a young man could aspire to, and it was dominant in the Honour Schools, having risen as Oriel and Christ Church declined (see Fig. 7). Up to about 1830, the increasing stature of the College was largely the work of a small core of active Fellows. The new system enabled Balliol to draw into itself a much larger number of outstanding individuals, not only renewing its own strength but gradually expanding and diversifying its influence. Of the forty or so Scholars elected in the first twenty years of open examinations, about a quarter died young or made no special mark, but the rest all distinguished themselves in one way or another. Eleven of them became Fellows of Balliol, including A. C. Tait, J. G. Lonsdale, W. C. Lake, Benjamin Jowett, James Riddell, and H. J. S. Smith. A like number took Fellowships at other colleges. Half a dozen became prominent public-school headmasters, and several rose to distinction in the law, among them Lord Chief Justice Coleridge. Others eventually emerged as ecclesiastical leaders, like Archbishop Tait. Two held senior ministerial positions and were elevated to the peerage (Lords Cardwell and Iddesleigh); two were notable poets (Matthew Arnold and A. H. Clough). The other members of the College in the same period—admitted as Commoners in the wake of those awarded Scholarships, or as Fellows from other Colleges—were no less remarkable for the range and distinction of their careers, and by 1850 the 'Balliol System' had proved itself—not only in its own academic terms but also by the criteria of the real world beyond the College gates.

In 1834 the Scholarship scheme, 'having been found productive of the best results', was 'with a view of enforcing its perpetual observance' formally embodied in the Statutes after confirmation by the Visitor. It was the unanimous view of those who saw its effects at first hand that this reform was the making of Victorian Balliol. To whom is the credit due? H. W. C. Davis tells us that Jenkyns merely concurred, 'not because he expected any good from the change, but because the tutors were unanimous on the other side',[20] and oft-repeated tradition singles out Ogilvie as the key figure. Ogilvie certainly played a large part in the affair, but he was very much the Master's man, and it seems hardly plausible to suggest that Jenkyns, who was at this time ruling all departments of the College with an iron hand, acquiesced weakly in a radical change he was dubious about. There is no hint of this in the immediate documents. In any case it is quite clear that the Master's influence on the execution of the new scheme was considerable. He was effectively Tutor for Admissions, and handled all the correspondence. He also had two votes in the elections. On one occasion he got his way when in a two-against-three minority: the doubling of his vote made it three all and the tie was broken by the statutory obligation of the most junior Fellow (who was of the original majority) to change sides. It is pleasing to note that Jenkyns's man had a

[20] Davis, op. cit., p. 184.

distinguished career,[21] whereas the choice of the majority slipped into untraceable obscurity.

Another novel notion which took root in the 1820s was the award of prizes for excellence in academic competition:

From the English Register, 20 Dec. 1822
It was agreed to present a set of Books to Mr Bazalgette by way of testifying our sense of the distinction lately obtained by him at his Examination in the Schools, and of his uniformly meritorious conduct during his residence in College.

The award of a prize for a First was routine thereafter. In the will he made in 1827, George Powell established a prize for an English Essay competition.[22] Richard Prosser's will of 1828, setting up six Exhibitions with the stated purpose of encouraging the 'Intellectual Improvement of the Undergraduates of Balliol College, combined with general good conduct', can be seen as part of the same trend. The selection procedure for the Prosser Exhibitions was also a new departure: it was entirely in the hands of a board consisting of the Master, the Senior Dean, the Senior Tutor, and the Mathematical Lecturer, i.e. the key academically active people, rather than the full Governing Body comprising the Master and all the Fellows, which always included several who took no part in the educational work of the College.

The University generally took its exercise in the form of casual open-air activities—long walks, boating excursions, and so on. Organized competitive sport began to appear around 1820, in step with the increasingly competitive attitude in academic matters. Boxing was briefly popular: participants included Manning, the future cardinal. When Jenkyns was Vice-Chancellor, he became very concerned about this and wrote to the Chancellor on the subject:[23]

... our young men with so many and alluring pursuits to divert their attention from their Academic Studies, have of late manifested a more than becoming taste for pugilistic exercises. Pains indeed have been taken to check this taste, on account of the low and abandoned company, and the gambling practices to which it almost necessarily leads. ...

[21] Alexander Grant (admitted to Balliol 1844), later Principal of Edinburgh University: see the *DNB*, etc.

[22] Elected as an *extraneus* from Brasenose in 1786, he resided in College until his death in 1830. His was the last burial in the Chapel; his memorial stone was saved when the Chapel was rebuilt, and is now in the Antechapel. A recluse who took few pupils, he had some kind of observatory at the top of the front gate-tower above his rooms (Bodleian MS Finch e. 40, fo. 150). He left his astronomical books to the Radcliffe Observatory. He appears as 'Daniel Barton' in J. G. Lockhart's novel *Reginald Dalton*, 1849. Essay prizes named after him are still awarded.

[23] MS Jenkyns VIA. 22.

He was also very much opposed to horse-racing,[24] and his attitude to such amusements made him a very unpopular Vice-Chancellor with under-graduates, who at Commemoration in 1825 received his entrance into the Sheldonian with a 'prolonged storm of hisses and hootings'.[25] The earliest definite allusion to Balliol rowing is in 1823, when there was a 'boat match between the Rowers of Balliol and Christ Church, which was won by the former, after a well-contested race'.[26] This was part of the general festivities of Commemoration week, and there is no indication of the kind of boat involved, but Balliol was certainly one of the four colleges competing in an eight in the summer races of 1825. Two Balliol men rowed for Oxford in the first University Boat Race at Henley in 1829, in a boat lent by Balliol for the occasion. To begin with, Jenkyns was no more enthusiastic about rowing than he was about other sports, and he thought to prevent J. J. Toogood from representing the University, by insisting that he should attend a midday logic lecture on the day of the race. But at fourteen and a half stone Toogood was not easily intimidated by a Master half his size, and the race was in the evening anyway, so after the lecture he was rushed to Henley in time to take up his position at number five, and do his bit for Oxford's victory. Jenkyns remained suspicious of rowing for some years, but was eventually won round,[27] and it soon became a central part of College life.[28]

The leading Tutors in the late 1820s were Ogilvie, J. T. Round, and George Moberly. They were assisted by J. M. Chapman and Frederick Oakeley. The job of the College Tutor was the delivery of College lectures to classes, rather than tutorial teaching, and those who wanted more intimate assistance made their own arrangements with a 'Private Tutor' or 'Coach', although in 1836 and 1837 one of the most senior Fellows (John Carr) 'occasionally looked over the weekly Essay, dividing the work with the Master'. Nor it seems, was there much informal social contact between Tutors and undergraduates. Round retired from Oxford in 1831, and Ogilvie, who had at one time been 'generally designated in public opinion as the future Master of Balliol', dropped out of the teaching in 1830, resigning in 1834, despite Keble's lament[29] that Oxford would become 'a very sink of Whiggery' without him. Moberly vacated his Fellowship by marriage, also in 1834, but remained as a married Tutor of the College for nearly a year, before leaving to be Headmaster of

---

[24] Reminiscences of E. D. Wickham, in *Our Memories, Shadows of Old Oxford,* ed. H. Daniel, 1893.

[25] MS 408 (typescript), fo. 29.

[26] *The Oxford University and City Herald,* 14 June 1823.

[27] Davis, op. cit., p. 185.   [28] Detailed Boat Club records survive from 1837.

[29] Bodleian MS. Eng. Lett. d. 124, fo. 24.

Winchester. Tutorial appointments were the Master's prerogative, and Jenkyns invited A. C. Tait to fill Moberly's place.

Jenkyns to Tait, 26 August 1835
You probably are aware that the event of Moberly's honourable appointment at Winchester will deprive Balliol of his valuable services, & subject me to the necessity of endeavouring to supply his place in the tuition. I cannot but feel *extreme* anxiety on this point—the credit, the character, which the College has for many years past happily maintained, so mainly depend on the talents, learning & (what is equally if not more important) the *habitual* & *constant diligence* of the Tutors in continuing our system of discipline and education, that I am naturally desirous of securing, if possible, the assistance of one who has himself been brought up under it. My anxiety is however in some measure relieved by the hope that *your* engagements will allow you to give the College the benefit of your knowledge and experience; & I now hasten to express this hope that if you accede to my wishes, you may have ample opportunity to make such arrangements as may enable you to enter upon your official duties at the end of the present Vacation . . .

Tait was the dominant Tutor for the next seven years together with, for most of the time, Robert Scott. W. G. Ward[30] was Mathematical Lecturer; J. G. Lonsdale and E. C. Woollcombe came in the early forties. An important development during this period was the agreement, probably at the instigation of Scott, that 'The use of the books in the Library should under certain conditions & the vigilant attention of Tutors, be allowed to the Undergraduates of the College'. This was a magnanimous sharing of what had previously been reserved strictly for Fellows, and was consistent with the marked easing of the formality of the relationships between teachers and taught which also took place.

From W. C. Lake's reminiscences of Tait
He gave me at once that impression of strength and spirit which I always associated with him through life. I soon became almost, or quite, his earliest College pupil; and felt at once his genuine kindness and interest in his pupils. In those days at Oxford—I know not how it is now—intimacies between tutors and pupils ripened rapidly. I was his companion on a short tour in Belgium and Germany in 1837, and again in 1839, and during my last undergraduate year in 1838 was constantly with him . . .

Tait was at the centre of an increased earnestness among the Tutors about the teaching arrangements and methods, and when he resigned he was concerned that the efficient machine he had established should not be jeopardized.

---

[30] Ward, op. cit.

Tait to Jenkyns, 29 July 1842

I was yesterday elected Headmaster of Rugby. It therefore becomes my duty, with very mixed feelings to resign into your hands the Tutorship which I have now held for seven years ... It is satisfactory to think, that, in going away thus suddenly, I leave two colleagues in the Tutorship behind me, who have your full confidence, and of whose zeal and ability for their work there can be no question. Of Woollcombe, with whom I am the most intimate, I must speak in the very highest terms. I never knew anyone more really alive to the importance of the duties which devolve on him as Tutor, taking a more deep interest in the welfare both of his pupils and of the College generally or who would be more ready to make any sacrifice for his duty. Of the Scholarship and ability of both Woollcombe & Lonsdale, we, who remember their examination, must always have the highest opinion: and of the admirable disposition and conciliatory manners of both, as their colleague, I must speak most highly ... I should not feel that I was doing right, if I did not urge you to continue to them your entire confidence: and, if it is necessary to look out for some fresh assistance for them, I rejoice to think, that in Lake and Jowett, you have two such eminent scholars, and two men of such sterling goodness of character, who, being both old Scholars of the House, so fully understand the system, by which now for so many years the College has flourished ... I feel sure that they possess that tact and sound judgement, and full appreciation of the goodness of the system, under which they have been educated, the want of which, I cannot but fear, would make Wall but ill-suited for any office in the Tuition ... Respecting Wall most highly as I do, I still feel that he is a stranger to the merits of what I may call the Balliol System. This, with the peculiarities of manner which you must yourself have observed, and the deficiency in scholarship which struck us all at his examination, would disqualify him, I cannot but think, for the office of Tutor ...

The remark about Wall's examination is particularly revealing. He had been elected a Chaplain Fellow in 1839. There was little competition in such elections, as candidates had already to have been ordained priest, and they took place casually, on occurrence of a vacancy, rather than as regular, well-publicized events like the ordinary Open Fellowships. Indeed, there had been two previous cases of also-rans in Open Fellowship competitions being elected Chaplain Fellows (Cheese in 1810 and Oakeley in 1827). Jenkyns agreed with Tait about Wall, who seems to have been a tiresome and litigious man. Although Wall was older than Lake and Jowett, they were preferred to him. Temple joined them as Mathematical Lecturer in the same year, and the tutorial method of teaching took the lead from about this time.

The academic development of the College between 1830 and 1845 took place against a background of political and religious controversies, many of which were centred on the Balliol Common Room. The grip of the firmly conventional Protestant Tories on the College had begun to weaken in the late twenties, with the election of men like F. W. Newman and

Oakeley. Oakeley surprised Jenkyns by voting for Robert Peel (and by implication for Catholic Emancipation) in 1834, and relations between them became uneasy. Divergence from the old ways suddenly burgeoned, and Jenkyns found himself with Fellows who were either edging towards Roman Catholicism with the Tractarians, or moving in the opposite direction with Thomas Arnold. The Tractarian movement, in which Oakeley and Ward were prominent, was profoundly disturbing to Jenkyns, and he struggled to check its advances in Balliol.

From Oakeley's reminiscences, c. 1836
The Master began to deal blows against the obnoxious doctrines on the right hand and on the left—some of them effectual, but more of them impotent ... The criticism of the weekly themes gave the Master many opportunities of dealing his anathemas against the new school; but his most powerful weapon was the terminal examination at collections. He had certain trial passages of the New Testament which he employed as the criteria of the religious tenets of an undergraduate suspected of 'Puseyism'. One of those most frequently produced was that in which the errors of the Pharisees are exposed. When a man had completed his translation of some such passage, the Master would proceed as follows: 'Now, tell me, Mr —, of all the various religious sects and parties which exist among us, which would you say corresponds the most with the Pharisees of the Gospel.' If the examinee was not fully up to the import of the question, he would perhaps answer, 'The Puritans, sir'. This was a safe reply, and in quieter times would have been the best for the purpose; but just then a more powerful antipathy even than the dread of Puritanism was uppermost in the academical mind; and he who wished to receive the Master's highest commendation would always answer, 'The Roman Catholics, sir' ... The fellows, of course, were less tractable subjects of the anti-Tractarian head of the college than the undergraduates. They had their status in the Society, and their rights, which justified them in making a stand against any vexatious or unconstitutional opposition whenever such was seriously contemplated; but matters did not as a fact, ever proceed to extremities, and stopped short in 'brushes' or 'scenes', which partook rather of the ludicrous than the serious.

The controversies in the Senior Common Room were very tangled, with the relatively liberal Tait opposed to Ward, and Scott pulling with inordinate conservatism against them both. In 1838 these differences intruded into Fellowship elections. In the summer of that year A. P. Stanley, a rising liberal star, asked whether he would be an acceptable candidate for the forthcoming Fellowship election, was discouraged, and therefore offered himself to University College, which elected him. Tait fought hard to avoid the loss of a good man, but the right wing had their way. Jenkyns said that he regretted losing Stanley, but made no positive move in his favour; he was probably relieved that the others had in effect blackballed him.

Scott was disturbed not only by the prospect of elections producing Fellows with dangerous views, but also by the established practice of electing Fellows who, having no intention of proceeding to ordination, anticipated resignation before the Statutes obliged them to do so. In 1837, he petitioned the Visitor for clarification, asking whether all Fellowship candidates should be required to enter into an undertaking to take orders. In taking this line, he was completely alone. Jenkyns, although accepting the sincerity of Scott's motives, professed his 'own entire freedom from doubt' on the matter and successfully defended the practice as being not only statutable but in the interests of the College.

Within my own experience of 38 years, several Persons have been elected to Fellowships who at the time of their Election were professedly studying Law— some of them afterwards took orders; while others, pursuing their original intention, retained their Fellowships only till such time as the Statutes Ch-32 (*De promotione ad sacerdotium*) required them to be ordained—viz. four years after taking the M.A. degree. They have then, on account of their non-compliance with the Statutable injunctions been obliged to resign their Fellowships. Your Grace [Archbishop Howley, the Visitor] will permit me to say that under these circumstances, when no such limitation as the Appellant (Mr Scott) could expect, is enjoined by the Statutes, it would be neither wise, nor just, to impose any restriction on a mode of Election, which from its very freedom has for many years contributed to the interests and credit of the College. The inevitable results would be to impair the competition by excluding Candidates of high character for talents and attainments—nor would it be fair to require of young men, at a period of life when their views and opinions are scarcely formed, any declaration of their future intention or any pledge of their entering upon a Profession which they may afterward perhaps wish to relinquish . . .

Ward's lead in the march to Rome became a progressively greater embarrassment to Jenkyns and some of the Fellows. He was a plump untidy man of charismatic personality, powerful intellect, extrovert manners, and occasional eccentricity. When he was examined for an Open Fellowship in 1834, 'he rather startled his competitors by stretching himself on the floor of the Master's dining room and going to sleep for an hour before he began his essay'.[31] A lover of music, especially opera, he entertained Jowett with songs from 'Don Giovanni' one summer evening in 1839, as they walked down the Iffley Road in the twilight on their way back from hearing Newman preach at Littlemore.[32] He was much loved by his brother Fellows, including those with whom he was in disagreement, and by his pupils, over whom he exercised great influence. In 1841 Tait, urged on by Woollcombe and Scott, persuaded Jenkyns to ask Ward to give up

[31] Reminiscences of W. C. Lake, Appendix C in Ward, op. cit.
[32] Appendix D in Ward, op. cit.

his Mathematical and Logic Lectureships on the grounds that he was contaminating his pupils with deviant doctrine. Jenkyns readily agreed— 'For what heresy may not be insinuated in the form of a syllogism?', he is supposed to have said[33]—but while he was still considering how to grasp the nettle, Ward cheerfully took the initiative and resigned his Lectureships without being asked.

There were other intense religiously rooted disagreements as well—a ludicrous dispute in 1843 about extravagant rebuilding proposals with religious implications, for example.[34] The steady dilapidation of the main buildings, which had taken place since the repairs and alterations carried out by Wyatt fifty years before, had reached a critical point, and Basevi was called in again. There were frequent meetings during 1842 at which his proposals—the most ambitious of which was to rebuild the Broad Street front as sets of rooms, with an imposing new Master's House roughly where the back gate now is—were discussed, and fund-raising had been begun. Nearly £4000 had been promised by the end of the year, a third of it from Jenkyns and his relatives alone. Basevi attended in person several times, and modified his designs again and again in attempts to meet the Fellows, who had been cool from the start, but his ideas were finally rejected. Jenkyns had supported Basevi throughout, and had also made the mistake of allowing him to think that the rebuilding was essentially a matter between the two of them, so he lost face considerably by this decision, but he nevertheless accepted it, and welcomed Oakeley's offer to obtain an opinion from his 'friend Mr [A. W. N.] P[ugin], so well known for his pre-eminent skill in Gothic Architecture'. Word of this soon got round and there was adverse comment outside the College about the proposed employment of an architect who, not being content with conversion to Rome, had turned viciously upon the Protestant establishment, in a pamphlet attacking the Martyrs' Memorial and its subscribers. Jenkyns (a contributor himself) began to get cold feet at this point, and although Pugin was in the end officially invited to submit designs, it was agreed as a compromise that even if his designs proved acceptable, the building should be done under someone else's direction. A few days later the Master gave in completely to good Protestant opinion, and at a special College Meeting in the Chapel, solemnly declared that he would refuse to affix the College seal to any document employing Pugin. The resident Fellows would not swallow this unconstitutional veto, and told the Master so in a formal memorial, submitted through the

---

[33] Appendix D in Ward, op. cit.

[34] For a full account of this affair see J. [H.] Jones, 'The Civil War of 1843', *Balliol College Record*, 1978, p. 60, and L. B. Litvack, 'The Balliol That Might Have Been: Pugin's Crushing Oxford Defeat', *J. Soc. Architectural Historians*, 45 (1986), 358.

proper channel of Oakeley, the Senior Fellow, who tried to be a neutral intermediary. Pugin came to Oxford as Ward's guest, took measurements, and returned to London for a fortnight of manic activity, during which he produced detailed designs for a rebuilt Balliol in grand Gothic style. Before he had finished, however, Jenkyns had taken an altogether more practical step and 'all of the name Jenkyns withdrew their promised subscriptions'. The Fellows admitted defeat, and at a stormy College meeting on 4 April 1843—remembered many years later as one of the first occasions when Jowett made his presence strongly felt—the rebuilding plans were set aside indefinitely, and it was decided to carry out only minimal repairs, sufficient to prevent actual collapse of the Master's House.

Ward stirred things up again in June 1844 with the publication of his book *The Ideal of a Christian Church Considered in Comparison with Existing Practice*. In this he argued at great length in favour of reforms which would have amounted to reconciliation with Rome. His style was deliberately provocative, as in his remark 'Three years have passed since I said plainly that in subscribing the Articles I renounce no Roman doctrine; yet I retain my fellowship which I hold on the tenure of subscription, and have received no ecclesiastical censure in any shape.' Jenkyns was very disturbed by the book, and concerned about Ward's effect on the College. To stop undergraduates being tainted by further contact with Ward, Jenkyns resolved to refuse permission for long-vacation residence. Lake counselled otherwise, arguing that the men themselves felt that Ward's influence was 'with them a mere chimera'.

Lake to Jenkyns, 1 July 1844
I am induced to take the liberty of writing to you by a letter which I received last night from Woollcombe, & I am sure that in your eyes I shall need no other apology than the interest in our joint college, and your own kind & frequent encouragement to speak with openness to you on all that concerns it, will supply. I confess I am very much alarmed and grieved to hear that in consequences of the pain occasioned to you by Ward's book & your dread of its influence you wish not to allow our men to continue in Oxford, & I would venture very very respectfully to submit you some reasons which make me think that while no danger can possibly be apprehended for the men by their staying, their removal may be most injurious to us in the eyes of any who shall hear of it ... I assure you that not only has Ward (to my entire belief) scrupulously abstained from any attempt to influence our undergraduates, but that we are keenly alive to the importance of his not even coming into contact with them, in such a way as might lead to intimate acquaintance. Nay more, I do not believe that since I have been a tutor Ward has through any means formed *the slightest acquaintance* with any undergraduate, and I have more than once particularly avoided asking him

14. The Chapel, about 1825.

15. Pugin's design for a new Chapel, 1843.

to meet them, when I should otherwise have wished for his company. And this because I am most anxious to avoid the least occasion for a charge of proselytism … And thus, during the vacation, sure as I feel that Ward would abstain, (as a matter of fact I imagine he will be absent for much of the first part of the time) I may add that you might trust us more implicitly for not bringing the men into his society. And they are not likely to wish it: for as a party they are perhaps some of the most 'Anti Puseyite' members of the most 'Anti Puseyite' college in Oxford …

During the long vacation of 1844, Jenkyns studied the book in detail. He decided to prevent Ward deputizing for Oakeley in Chapel, and even went to the lengths of creating a scene at the beginning of Michaelmas Term in order to stop Ward exercising his traditional right, as Senior Fellow present, of reading the Epistle.

At about the same time, the Hebdomadal Board appointed a Committee of six, including Jenkyns, to report on Ward's book and advise the University on a course of action. The eventual upshot of this initiative was a meeting of Convocation on 13 February 1845 at which it was agreed by 777 votes to 391 that Ward's book was 'utterly inconsistent with the Articles of Religion of the Church of England, and with the Declaration in respect of those articles made and subscribed by William George Ward previously and in order of his being admitted to the degrees of BA and MA'. This censure was followed by a further motion, passed by a much smaller majority—569 against 511—depriving Ward of his degrees. Jenkyns was no doubt very gratified, as he had solicited support for Ward's censure and degradation widely among former Fellows and pupils. He immediately consulted privately with his own lawyers and drafted a long case for the opinion of counsel as to 'whether the Master of Balliol would be justified in declaring Mr Ward's fellowship, *ipso facto degradationis*, vacant', but the question was never tested, as Ward vacated his Fellowship by marriage on 31 March 1845—he had been secretly engaged throughout. Ward and Oakeley both joined the Roman Catholic Church a few months later.

Despite this succession of crises, the College held together, and the Master and Fellows stayed on warm personal terms with each other, co-operating well in matters concerning the welfare of the young men. The fact that Balliol was able to come through the turmoil of the Oxford Movement with its reputation still rising sets it in marked contrast with Oriel, which tore itself apart and accelerated its decline.

About 1840 Jenkyns began to yearn for ecclesiastical dignity. It was not that he sought financial rewards—his circumstances were 'such as not to render the want of preferment a matter of pecuniary inconvenience'— but rather that he wanted a position which would eventually 'afford a comfortable & honourable retirement'. He persuaded his cousin, Henry Hobhouse, to suggest his name to Robert Peel when the Deanery of Wells (which was a Crown appointment) fell vacant in 1845. Peel made soundings about Jenkyns with the Dean of Christ Church (Thomas Gaisford, Jenkyns's brother-in-law) and then offered him the position. More than fifty letters of congratulation from members of the College survive. F. D. Foster's contains typical sentiments:

Tidings have reached us this morning of your appointment to the Deanery of Wells, & I must avail myself of the first Post to offer you our hearty congratulations on your promotion to so honourable a position—which, however, you seem richly to have merited, by the firm & decided stand you have made against the spread of Romish principles & practices. You were the first to act against Tractarianism; by suspending a Jesuitical Tutor, clever & useful though he were, as a mathematical teacher, & you preferred continuing to live in your Master's Lodge without its requisite alterations, rather than be indebted for them to the aid of the Roman Catholic Pugin . . .

Many of the congratulatory letters seem to assume that Jenkyns was being pensioned off, but it turned out that he was to have another nine years. There was nothing in the Law or the Statutes to prevent him being Master of Balliol and Dean of Wells at the same time, and it appears that his resignation of the Mastership from Balliol was not considered. Although public opinion was in general moving against pluralities, and legislation to abolish this particular from of plurality was on the way, there was no adverse comment. He had dispensation from his residence obligations which allowed him to be absent from Oxford when decanal business called, but he usually managed to stay up for most of University term-time. At any rate, he missed only one College Meeting between his appointment to Wells and his death, despite also attending 151 out of 168 Wells Chapter Meetings.[35] He tried to retain his control of the College while spending about two-thirds of his time at Wells, and being much engaged there by the aftermath of ecclesiastical reform, theological controversy, and extensive building work on the Cathedral—to which he subscribed generously himself.

The atmosphere in Oxford was much calmer after 1845, following the secession to Rome of Newman and his followers. In a much-quoted chapter of his recollections, Cox tells us that the 'controversy had worn out', 'speculative theology gave way to speculation in railroad shares', and 'instead of High Church, Low Church and Broad Church they talked of high embankments, the broad gauge and low dividends'.[36] Certainly

---

[35] P. Barrett, *Barchester: English Cathedral Life in the Nineteenth Century*, 1993, p. 79.
[36] G. V. Cox, *Recollections of Oxford*, 1868, p. 338.

C11.   The Front Quadrangle, about 1820.

C12.   Richard Jenkyns, Master 1819–54.

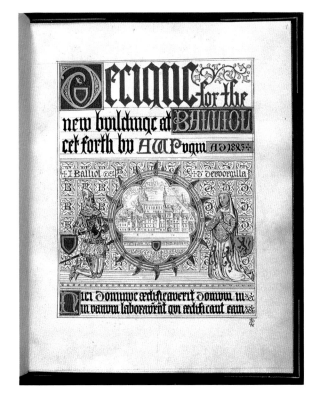

C13. The binding and title page of A. W. N. Pugin's proposals for rebuilding the College, 1843.

C14. The Chapel, rebuilt (1856–7) by William Butterfield, October 1986.

C15.   Inside the Chapel, about 1820.

C16. Inside the Chapel, October 1986.

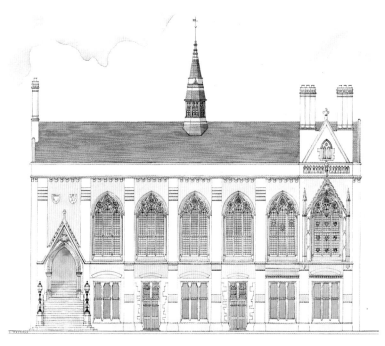

C17.   The Hall as it was in 1880.

C18.   The Hall, April 1985.

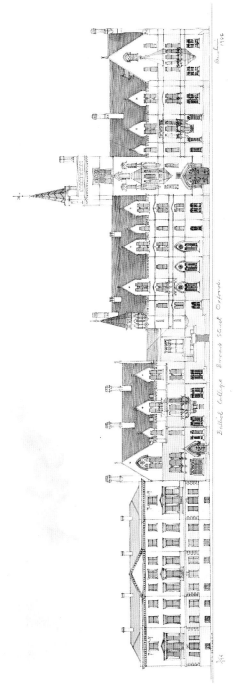

Balliol College, Broad Street, Oxford

C19.   The Broad Street front.

C21. A. L. Smith, Master 1916–24.

C20. J. L. Strachan Davidson, Master 1907–16.

we hear no more of *odium theologicum* in Balliol, and the impression given by the College Register is one of a relapse into a preoccupation with practical matters to do with estates and livings. This impression is misleading. Several Fellows, but Jowett especially, were becoming deeply involved in the beginnings of a serious University Reform movement, although the main thrust of this movement was directed at the University, and at other colleges. The Royal Commission, which was appointed in 1850, included Tait, and had Stanley as Secretary. Jenkyns's reply on its first approach to Balliol was that he held himself responsible only to the Visitor. He had defended this position before, in 1837, when an abortive attempt to launch a Commission had been made in Parliament. It was not that he feared what a Commission might say. What worried him was the erosion of the College's independence which might follow, if it was once admitted that the State had any right to pry into the affairs of a corporation which had been 'founded and endowed solely by the munificence of private individuals'. The College had been subject only to its own Statutes, and the authority of its Visitor, for nearly six hundred years. Under the 'salutary influence of such Visitatorial power', the College had faithfully and, it was hoped, 'successfully laboured to promote the cause of sound Religion and useful learning'. It did not shrink from the 'strictest examination' of its 'own lawful Visitor', but deprecated any 'extraneous interference which would supersede the provision wisely made by the Founders themselves for regulating the object of their bounty'. He stuck to this line—as did most other Heads of Houses—and Balliol made no official answers to the Commission's questions. By this time, however, Jenkyns's dominance over his Governing Body was diminishing. He was now nearly seventy, and absent at Wells much of the time, whereas the Fellows into whose hands the actual running of the College fell—Woollcombe, Jowett, Lake, and Henry Wall—were young, very experienced in academic politics, and full of self-confidence. Jowett, Lake, and Wall felt able to tell the Commission that, although they could not assist in their capacities as College officers, they would, as individuals, be glad to help and make available the College books and information which they happened to have in their possession. When the Commission reported in 1852, it had little to say that was critical of the College, and indeed used it as an example to support the case it made for the general abolition of closed Scholarships and Fellowships:

From the report of the Royal Commission, 1852
   Balliol, which now enjoys so high a reputation, was at the beginning of the present century regarded as one of the worst Colleges in Oxford. Its Fellowships and Scholarships, which were long bestowed as matters of personal favour, were,

we believe, first thrown open to public competition by the exertions of its late, and its present Head . . .

The decree was, indeed, in itself wise and liberal, and having been carried into execution wisely and liberally, it has brought honour to Balliol and the University . . .

It is the most distinguishing characteristic of this Foundation that it is most peculiarly free from all restrictions which might prevent the election of the best candidates to its Headship, Fellowships, Scholarships, and even to its Visitorship. The result of this has been that Balliol, which is one of the smallest Colleges in Oxford, as regards its Foundation, is certainly at present the most distinguished . . .

The chief internal business of the College during Jenkyns's last years was a rebuilding programme. The Hall was enlarged, new kitchens were built, and a row of dilapidated buildings near the back gate was demolished, to make way for a plain and functional new block (now Staircases XVI and XVII).[37] Jenkyns was responsible for the choice of the architect: he engaged Anthony Salvin, who was also working on Wells Cathedral. Jenkyns died in the Master's Lodgings on 6 March 1854, a few months after completion of the new buildings.[38] 'He found Balliol a close college among the least distinguished collegiate bodies at Oxford—he left it almost entirely open, and confessedly the foremost of all.'[39]

[37] There is a manuscript account (by Richard Jenkyns) of this building programme inserted at the end of the English Register 1794–1875. The new block was primarily residential, but also included a lecture-room (now the Russell Room), and, in the cellars of what is now Staircase XVI, a laboratory (of which more later).

[38] He was buried in Wells Cathedral, where his most prominent monument is the quire pulpit. There was an elaborate obstructive tomb in St Katharine's Chapel there which has now been replaced by an inscribed floor slab. He married Troth Grove, daughter of Grey Jermyn Grove; St Thomas's church, Wells, was built at her expense in his memory. In College the Chapel was rebuilt as his principal memorial. He had no children. He was a benefactor, establishing Exhibitions by his will (MS Jenkyns VIA.27). His portrait hangs in Hall; separate portraits of him and his wife hang in the Master's Lodgings.

[39] *The Times*, 7 March 1854.

17. Robert Scott, Master 1854–70.

16. Benjamin Jowett as a young Tutor, about 1850.

15

On the Crest of a Wave: Jowett's Balliol

BENJAMIN JOWETT was only thirty-six when Jenkyns died, and he looked even younger, but he had already been a Fellow for fifteen years. A lot of travel, experience, teaching, and reading had been crammed into these years. He had learned German and sharpened his mind on the modern philosophy of Hegel[1] and Kant. In religion, neither the Evangelicals nor the Tractarians had attracted him. He was moving towards a more liberal interpretation of Christianity. In the University reform movement he was a leader, and his voice commanded attention in the Cabinet. A heroically industrious Tutor, he kept an ever-open door. His students worshipped him, despite the disconcerting long silences for which he was notorious, and his impatience with small talk and ill-considered remarks, which often led to a devastating snub. The College's debt to him was administrative as well as tutorial, for he had taken his turn in various offices with credit, notably as Bursar, and had played a large part in seeing the Salvin Building project through. He was thus an obvious candidate for the Mastership, though at first he affected not to think so himself,[2] and it soon transpired that he had strong support. It came predominantly from the younger Fellows, all of whom had been taught by him. On the other hand, he had the reputation of being a sulky and prickly man when things did not go entirely his way, and some of those who sympathized with his views were reluctant to put him in charge. And there were a few for whom he was just too radical and unorthodox.

Robert Scott, then Rector of South Luffenham, but nevertheless in close touch with academic affairs, was the only other serious contender, although Frederick Temple (a radical reformer like Jowett, but perhaps personally more attractive to some) was also considered in the preliminary stages.[3]

---

[1] Jowett was much influenced by Hegel; late in his life he wrote 'Though not a Hegelian I think I have gained more from Hegel than from any other philosopher' (Abbott and Campbell, op. cit., ii. 250). He was largely responsible for introducing Hegel's thought into England, and the 'adapted Hegelianism' (Abbott and Campbell, op. cit., ii. 249) of his pupils T. H. Green and Edward Caird was the origin of the British school of Absolute Idealism (see A. M. Quinton, 'Absolute Idealism', in A. [J. P.] Kenny (ed.), *Rationalism, Empiricism and Idealism*, 1986).

[2] R. Duckworth, *A Memoir of Rev. James Lonsdale*, 1893, p. 45.

[3] W. Tuckwell, *Reminiscences of Oxford*, 1907, p. 202; K. Lake, *Memorials of William Charles Lake*, 1901, p. 65.

Jowett's official biographers say that Scott was brought up from the country by the forces of reaction only in order to keep Jowett out, but this is to underrate him. Jointly with H. G. Liddell, he had produced a monumental work of scholarship—the standard Greek–English lexicon (first edition 1843)—and as long before as 1845, Jenkyns had thought of him as the next Master.[4] Scott had also been a respected Balliol Tutor in his time (1835–40), and had a following of well-disposed ex-pupils. Indeed, Jowett himself had been taught by Scott, and his personal relations with his old mentor were still warm. But Scott was not a liberal man. He could always be relied upon to obstruct any measure threatening the slightest erosion of the Established Church's position and privileges. His theology was uniformly orthodox, and he was opposed to any easing of the disabilities of Jews, Catholics, and Nonconformists. Of University reform, he wrote in 1852 that he would have suppressed the Commission if it had been in his power to do so.[5] The consistency with which he took the right-wing stance was almost matched by the regularity with which he found himself on the losing side, but he was always the gentleman, both in attack and defeat, and he never lost his dignity.

The electors were, in order of seniority:

Woollcombe, E. C. Oriel 1833. Fellow of Balliol 1838–80. A gentle and conscientious man, but an ineffective Tutor; held conservative views close to Scott's; despised by Jowett.[6]

Lonsdale, J. G. Balliol 1833. Fellow of Balliol 1838–64, but non-resident most of the time. Sympathetic to the Oxford Movement; of a retiring disposition; respected by Jowett.[7]

Lake, W. C. Balliol 1834. Fellow of Balliol 1838–59. A liberal in some respects but orthodox in theology; unpopular (nicknames 'Serpent', and 'Puddle'—sometimes corrupted to 'Piddle'). Later Dean of Durham.[8]

Jowett, Benjamin.

Wall, Henry. St Alban Hall 1828. Fellow of Balliol 1839–71. Conservative; pedantic and litigious; disliked and distrusted by Jowett.[9]

Riddell, James. Balliol 1840. Fellow of Balliol 1845–66. One of Jowett's most successful early pupils, but a moderate conservative.[10]

[4] Jenkyns to Henry Hobhouse, 7 May 1845, quoted in J. M. Prest, 'Robert Scott and Benjamin Jowett', *Balliol College Record*, Supplement, 1966.

[5] Scott to W. E. Gladstone, 1852, quoted in Prest, op. cit.

[6] J. W. Burgon, *Lives of Twelve Good Men*, i, 1889, p. xvii; F. W. Farrer's reminiscences, Jowett Papers E; Jowett to Florence Nightingale, 14 Oct. 1866 (*Dear Miss Nightingale. A Selection of Benjamin Jowett's Letters to Florence Nightingale 1860–1893*, ed. [E.] V. Quinn and J. [M.] Prest, 1987, p. 108).

[7] Duckworth, op. cit.; *DNB*.

[8] Lake, op. cit.; Tuckwell, op. cit., p. 205; *DNB*.

[9] Tuckwell, op. cit., p. 203; Jowett to Florence Nightingale, 14 Oct. 1866 (see n. 6).

[10] Burgon, op. cit., p. xv; *DNB*.

Palmer, Edwin. Balliol 1841. Fellow of Balliol 1845–67. An admirer of Jowett's, but of a High Church family. Later Archdeacon of Oxford.[11]

Salter, W. C. Blundell Scholar, Balliol 1842. Fellow of Balliol 1848–61.

Walrond, Theodore. Balliol 1842. Fellow of Balliol 1850–7. Later Civil Service Commissioner.

Smith, H. J. S. Balliol 1844. Fellow of Balliol 1850–74. Liberal reformer; one of Jowett's consistent allies; later Keeper of the University Museum.[12]

Owen, D. M. Blundell Scholar, Balliol 1847. Fellow of Balliol 1852–66.

The accounts we have of the decision-making process and voting are discreetly vague and not perfectly consistent, but it is clear that Woollcombe, Lake, and Wall were firmly for Scott. Less obviously, Lonsdale is also likely to have preferred Scott. Smith and Walrond would have been strongly behind Jowett; it is probable that Salter and Owen were too. The election would then have depended on Riddell and Palmer, neither of whom was clearly of one party or the other. In the event both must have decided to support Scott, giving him the six votes he needed for election. According to both Lake and W. Tuckwell, Riddell transferred his vote from Jowett to Scott at the last moment, somewhat unexpectedly. Without this change of heart, Jowett would have been the victor: he was an elector himself, and only needed the votes of five others.[13]

Soon after Scott's election, Parliament enacted that 'from and after the first day of Michaelmas Term 1854 it shall not be necessary for any person upon matriculating in the University of Oxford, to make or subscribe any Declaration, or to take any Oath'. Thinking to frustrate this so far as Balliol was concerned, Scott proposed to a College Meeting that in future anyone being admitted to the College at any level

... shall at the time of his admission make and subscribe the following Declaration in the presence of the Master and Fellows;–viz

'I, A. B., do declare that I am a member of the Church of England'

Without any official explanation or remark at time of signing.

[11] Abbott and Campbell (op. cit., i. 229) speak of two votes on which Jowett had counted, but did not obtain, one of which 'may have been influenced by family associations'; this is probably a veiled allusion to Palmer, whose brothers Roundell Palmer (1812–95) and William Palmer (1811–79) were well known for their High Church views (see the *DNB*).

[12] *DNB*; there is a memoir (with personal recollections by, among others, Jowett) in J. W. L. Glaisher, *The Collected Mathematical Papers of Henry John Stephen Smith MA FRS*, i, 1894.

[13] For accounts of the election, see Abbott and Campbell, op. cit., i. 228; Lake, op. cit., p. 65; Tuckwell, op. cit., p. 202. Lake only identifies the voter who changed sides as 'a distinguished scholar and friend of Mr Jowett', but this fits Riddell's reputation well, and Tuckwell actually names him. According to Abbott and Campbell (op. cit., i. 229) he was talked over 'on theological grounds by a disciple of Dr Pusey'.

This was considered at five full College Meetings within the space of less than a fortnight.[14] Regulations for the declaration were finally passed on 15 November, but Scott had to use his second casting vote. Jowett was aghast. 'Is it legal? is it statutable? is it right?' he wrote to A. C. Tait.[15] 'It is a gross thing to attempt to keep out Presbyterians.' An appeal was made to the Visitor, although it was 'an awkward thing for a Bishop to do justice to Dissenters'. Perhaps it was uncomfortable for him, but Bishop John Jackson of Lincoln did not flinch from his duty. He wrote early in 1855 to annul the resolution.

Jowett brought out a two-volume work on St Paul in 1855. Although mild enough by modern standards, it started a controversy, which was aggravated by his appointment to the Regius Professorship of Greek. This chair was in the gift of the Prime Minister, and the nomination was probably in part a recognition of Jowett's services to the Government, in connection with Civil Service and Oxford University reform. Trouble-makers like Charles P. Golightly protested to the Vice-Chancellor, and to Scott, that it was outrageous that an exponent of heretical views (especially on the doctrine of the Atonement) should hold an official University post, and be a Tutor in Balliol. The Vice-Chancellor called Jowett in to subscribe to the Thirty-nine Articles, and began to harangue him, only to be cut short by his immediate submission. Scott for his part behaved rather well, taking no action over the demand that Jowett should be removed as a Tutor, and evading an invitation to contradict him from the pulpit of St Mary's. It was shortly after this that Jowett withdrew from the social side of College life, hardly attending Hall or Common Room. He even absented himself from most of the College's discussions of the proposals being made for reform of the College's Statutes.[16] We do not know why he went into retreat in this way, but one must presume he was embittered by the treatment he had received—from his colleagues over the Mastership, from theological nit-pickers over his book on St Paul, and from the University and Christ Church authorities over his emoluments as Regius Professor of Greek, which were maintained at a derisory level for many years because of his views, in contrast to the relatively generous treatment of the other Regius Professors. Some of this period of withdrawal he used to write a contribution to the notorious *Essays and Reviews* (1860) on 'The Interpret-ation of Scripture'. This was a masterpiece of cool argument for the use

---

[14] College Meeting Minutes, 3, 6, 9, 14, and 15 Nov. 1854.

[15] Jowett to A. C. Tait, 10 Nov. 1854, printed in Prest, op. cit.

[16] The Minutes of the many special College Meetings on the Statutes 1855–7 were not recorded in the English Register as usual, but in two separate volumes which are in the Archives, kept with other material concerning the Statutes: 'Meetings on the Statutes' (6i) and 'Meetings on the Statutes (continued)' (6ii).

of reason in the interpretation of Scripture, which should be approached 'without *a priori* notions about its nature and origin'; it was 'to be interpreted like other books, with attention to the character of its authors, and the prevailing state of civilisation and knowledge, with allowance for peculiarities of style and language, and modes of thought and figures of speech'. Jowett's essay, inevitably an assault on many traditional beliefs derived from a literal interpretation of the Bible, exacerbated the theological controversy which already surrounded him, and he was regarded with deep suspicion by the Church of England for the rest of his life, although he did not produce any more theological books.

The reforms which followed in the wake of the Royal Commission were manifold. They really belong to the history of the University rather than that of any individual college, so we shall say little about their details or lesser provisions. The most significant changes for Balliol were as follows:[17]

1. Abolition of the general obligation on Fellows to take Holy Orders, except that there were always to be a few who were clerics.
2. Abolition of all oaths, except that Fellows on admission were to promise to be 'true and faithful' to the College, 'to observe its Statutes and bye-laws', and to 'promote its interests and studies'.[18]
3. Removal of the *ceteris paribus* advantage of Scholars in Fellowship elections, and also the bastardy disqualification.
4. Permission for a limited number of Fellows to marry.
5. The introduction of a provision 'to elect distinguished persons to Honorary Fellowships'.[19]
6. Abolition of the Blundell Fellowships.
7. Extensive reorganization of the Scholarships and Exhibitions.

There were also changes elsewhere in the University which were of consequence for Balliol. Chief among these was the abolition of the regional affiliations, and other restrictions, which had hitherto been imposed on many Fellowships. The number of academic openings available on an unrestricted and competitive basis was thereby greatly

---

[17] *Ordinances concerning Balliol College made in pursuance of the Act, 17 and 18 Victoria*, chapter 81, 1863.

[18] The promise Fellows are still required to make on admission uses the same words.

[19] The first Honorary Fellow appears to have been Robert Browning the poet (1867); he had no previous formal connection with the College but was well known to Jowett. In the early days the College used Honorary Fellowships to bring distinguished people into the College (e.g. William Stubbs the historian, 1876), but the convention was quickly established that only distinguished ex-members were eligible. For lists of Honorary Fellows 1867–1989, see *Balliol College Register*, 5th edn., ed. J. [H.] Jones and S. Viney, 1983, p. 559, and 6th edn., ed. J. [H.] Jones and C. Willbery, 1993, p. 568.

enhanced. Balliol men were prominent among those who took advantage of the new situation, leading to an expansion of Jowett's power base in the University, by the 'colonization', as his biographers put it, of other colleges.

Two months after Jenkyns's death, the College agreed 'that the Master apply to Mr Butterfield to ascertain whether he can undertake the Restoration of the College Chapel as a Memorial of the late Master'. Despite minority opposition (which included Jowett) the project snowballed: 'restoration' soon became 'rebuilding' and then 'construction of the New Chapel'. The demolition of the old Chapel was begun in Easter week 1856, and the new one was finished by October 1857: its lines and general plan are remarkably similar to the Pugin designs which had been rejected in 1843. At the same time, Butterfield laid out anew the grounds to the north, and created the present Fellows' Garden.[20] The new Chapel was consecrated by Tait, at this time Bishop of London, on 15 October 1857, and there was a special dinner to celebrate. Jowett could not decently stay away, but he did not take his place at High Table, sitting instead with undergraduates in the body of the Hall. In his speech Tait said of him: 'I was his Tutor in the old days: he was much more worthy to teach me.' There was a pause and then Jowett rose from where he sat and said 'Any one who labours amongst the young men will reap his reward in an affection far beyond his deserts.'[21]

The minutes of College Meetings 1855–65 are remarkable for their procedural rigidity. On matters of substance it was usually impossible to achieve consensus by discussion. Practically everything had to be decided by voting on formal motions. Nowadays the College only actually votes on questions which are too trivial to fuss over in any other way, or which have been thrashed out very thoroughly without attainment of broad agreement—happily not often the case. The difference is that Robert Scott's Balliol was sharply and almost equally divided into parties—High Church and reactionary, versus Broad Church and progressive. Scott had the upper hand when first elected, but only just, and with Lonsdale not usually in residence, he did not always get his way. We cannot tell what the real issues were when he proposed unsuccessfully in 1858 'That no Undergraduate be allowed to travel by Railway [in term-time] without the Master's leave'—probably to do with inhibiting access to London

---

[20] There is a detailed account (with references to the original material) of the design and construction of the Chapel, and of the rearrangement of the gardens, in *VCH*, Oxfordshire, iii. 91. The new Chapel was inspected by Queen Victoria and Prince Albert on 12 Dec. 1860 (*Diary of C. P. Ilbert*, photocopy in Balliol Library); this is the only known visit to the College of a reigning British Monarch.

[21] Abbott and Campbell, op. cit., i. 247.

flesh-pots on his side, and reluctance to increase his authority one tiny bit on the other. This was not an isolated instance. He was given a spectacular rebuff early in 1859, when a Committee (himself, Wall, Jowett, and Smith), appointed to consider the creation of new Domus Exhibitions, reported 'that the [Domus] income would allow two Exhibitions of the value of £60, tenable for four years'. Jowett dissented, and immediately gave notice of a motion to establish eight such Exhibitions, which was agreed at the next Stated General Meeting. Probably even more painful to Scott was a lost rearguard action five years later, against excusing Nonconformists from Chapel.

Scott's position weakened as the turnover of the Fellowship worked in favour of the opposition. By the mid sixties Jowett was the real leader, and the way was clear for liberal initiatives. Various plans which had been long in his mind now began to take practical shape. The degree to which religious observation and academic work were enforced was reduced, moral pressure and persuasion replacing rules and regulations. College lectures, instead of being imposed, were left open to the free choice of the students, provided they attended a certain number. The divinity teaching was remodelled, Jowett taking some of it on himself. On week-days, compulsory Chapel was replaced by a roll-call, held before the service began, so that a disinclination to Chapel could not be an excuse for late rising. A scheme was launched for extending the benefits of the University to poorer students. In a letter to a friend, Jowett wrote in October 1866:[22]

I found that my scheme of University Extension was very favourably received. I want men (1) to live in Lodgings which we are to build and furnish and let at a rent of £10 a year: (2) to be allowed to attend College lectures free: (3) to have small Exhibitions of £25 a year given away by examination . . . I reckon that paying £10 a year for rent, and having nothing to pay for instruction, they could live for the academical year of twenty-four weeks on £50 a year, or deducting the Exhibition, for £25 a year ... At present not a tenth or twentieth part of the ability of the country comes to the University. This scheme is intended to draw from a new class ...

Shortly after this was written, the principle was accepted by the College, and it was resolved:

That the College undertake gratuitously the instruction and superintendence of a certain number of students (not at first to exceed 20 in all) who would otherwise be unable to meet the expenses of a University Education; such students not to

---

[22] Abbott and Campbell, op. cit., i. 377. The 'friend' was Florence Nightingale.

reside or battel in College, and to pay no College fees except a fee of £1 on admission.

Furthermore, the Hebdomadal Council was asked to bring forward a new Statute enabling such 'out-students' to live in town lodgings instead of halls. Ancient Statutes which required undergraduates to reside within the walls of a college or recognized hall were still in force. But the Balliol reformers were too impatient to wait on Council's deliberations. No time was lost in organizing out-accommodation within the prevailing regulations, and on 1 May 1867 a Committee comprising Jowett, Smith and T. H. Green was authorized to rent 26 St Giles for use as 'Balliol Hall',[23] where the out-student Exhibitioners would live under Green's supervision. Green had only been a Fellow since 1861, but he was already well known as a philosophy teacher and social reformer; he was a layman. The scheme attracted a lot of attention outside the College, and it was reported in Parliament on 5 June 1867 by Jowett's friend Robert Lowe (1811–92; first Viscount Sherbrooke, 1880) that 'To their great honour the Tutors of Balliol had resolved that, if poor students were allowed to become members of the College without being obliged to live within the walls, they would give to all such students the benefit of their tuition— the best in the University of Oxford—making no charge whatever for it'. A year later it was agreed by the College 'That with the object of extending the advantages of the University to a class of persons which now has a difficulty in obtaining them, 24 exhibitions of £40 a year each, tenable for four years, be given, 6 in each year', and a committee consisting of the Master, Jowett, Smith, W. L. Newman, and Green was appointed to recommend details to this end. A further provision was that 'these Exhibitioners be allowed to become members of any other College, or unattached students'. At this stage Jowett's 'small scheme of University Extension' becomes something of general importance for the development of the University, involving the modification of long-established requirements for college or hall residence, and the setting up of machinery for non-collegiate students.

There was some resistance, but these fundamental adjustments began quite quickly, so that in the summer of 1869 Jowett was able to tell his mother:[24]

... They have been making great changes in the University, which will, I think, be for the advantage of Balliol College. Students are now to be allowed to lodge

---

[23] 26 St Giles is described as 'Balliol Hall' in Oxford directories 1869–99 but not in 1867 or after 1899. It was south of the junction of St Giles Street with Keble Road, opposite St Giles graveyard.

[24] Abbott and Campbell, op. cit., i. 432.

out, which will enable them to come to Balliol, instead of going to other Colleges. If we had a little more money we could absorb the University ...

The various measures aimed at attracting students from the whole population, instead of just the upper classes, were to some extent successful. There was one embarrassing gaffe. Balliol and Worcester College collaborated in a scheme to award some Exhibitions based on performance in the Oxford Local Examinations, and advertised to the effect that they would offer them to 'those among the Senior Candidates who shall obtain the highest places'. The only other stipulation was that certificates of good conduct would be required. In 1873 the best marks were obtained by A. M. A. H. Rogers (1856–1937), but her initials concealed femininity, and the College had to retreat hastily, making her a present of books. Annie Rogers was a pioneer of education for women in Oxford. When she retired, Balliol gave a dinner in her honour.[25]

Even as late as 1868, it was still possible for Scott, and his diminishing minority, to obstruct a measure which contravened custom or Statute enough to justify an appeal to the Visitor. This was so, for example, when it was resolved 'That the College shall have a veto on the appointment of Tutors'. The nomination of Tutors was by immemorial practice in the hands of the Master, not merely in his capacity as principal executive officer but as a matter at his sole discretion. The Visitor upheld Scott's appeal, and disallowed the resolution of the majority. But this did not happen on any other issues of great significance, and on 20 October 1868 Jowett wrote to his mother again:[26]

... Oxford, or rather Balliol, is much pleasanter than formerly. I have no longer any trouble in carrying out my views, from the Fellows; and I believe that we shall succeed in making it a really great place of education. One thing gives me great pleasure; that our new building is really beautiful—the best thing that has been done in Oxford in this way. An old lady has given us about £15,000 towards the completion of it ...

The generous old lady was Hannah Brackenbury.[27] Jowett implies in this letter, and his biographers reinforce the impression, that the Scholarships she endowed and the buildings she largely paid for were, like so much else in Balliol in this era, creatures of his vision and energy. This is not so, and is unfair to Scott, for he handled the negotiations with Miss Brackenbury. The rebuilding of the south and east ranges of the College, from the Master's Lodgings round to the Chapel, seems to have been very

---

[25] See College Meeting Minutes, 16 Feb. 1869 and 11 Oct. 1873. For Annie Rogers, see the *DNB*, and V. Brittain, *The Women at Oxford*, 1960, p. 18.

[26] Abbott and Campbell, op. cit., i. 380.

[27] For an account of Hannah Brackenbury, see the *New DNB*, in the press.

much Scott's project from start to finish. Jowett and his party contributed little beyond suggestions of detail, and they humiliated Scott by meanly holding expenditure on the Lodgings down to an absolute minimum, a curb about which he made no public complaint. Hannah Brackenbury was a wealthy spinster with no living close relatives, who believed that she was the 'last lineal descendant of Perse Brackenbury of Sellabye, near Barnard Castle, who married *c.* 1086 a daughter of Hugh Ballyeul, progenitor of John Balliol'. Her wealth was derived from her brother James, a Manchester solicitor, who had made a fortune out of the Lancashire and Yorkshire Railway. She had also had another brother, Ralph, a doctor, and she conceived the idea of perpetuating the family name by doing something for the professions to which her brothers had belonged. In April 1865 she approached Scott, through an intermediary, to propose the creation of some Scholarships at Balliol, picking Balliol because of the supposed ancient connection of her family with the Founder's. Scott persuaded her that her purpose could best be achieved by funding 'Brackenbury Scholarships' in history and natural science. In 1866 he hinted that the Broad Street buildings were very dilapidated, and although she was initially not very interested, she was eventually coaxed into paying for reconstruction, partly because she liked the idea that her Scholars would be living in the rooms which she had provided. Alfred Waterhouse was commissioned to produce designs. He borrowed Pugin's drawings of 1843 whilst he was working on the project,[28] and incorporated some features of them into his own plans, so Pugin's efforts were not after all entirely wasted. Waterhouse's designs were accepted, after minor modification, and executed under his supervision. The demolition of the old buildings began in April 1867; the new Master's Lodgings and Brackenbury Buildings were soon completed. They comprise residential accommodation (now Staircases I–VII), a Porter's Lodge (which formerly had a flat attached for the Head Porter), and a Lecture Room (now the Bursary). Scott's diplomacy and Hannah Brackenbury's generosity are commemorated in the stonework: his arms are prominent by the door of the Master's Lodgings,[29] while hers appear over the main gate, and in several other places on Staircases III–VII.[30]

In October 1869 Jowett and Gladstone were house guests together at Camperdown House, Dundee. They spent many long hours in discussion together. Irish political problems were one of the chief topics of

[28] Waterhouse to Scott, 7 July and 9 Nov. 1866 (D.21.77).

[29] To the right of the front door, beneath the large first-floor window.

[30] The correspondence about the Brackenbury benefaction and buildings is in the Archives: see especially D.16.1–7 and D.21.77. Whether she was entitled to the arms is very doubtful.

conversation. It was probably this encounter which prompted Gladstone to think of favouring Jowett in some way. Jowett's friend Robert Lowe (then Chancellor of the Exchequer) was asked to make tactful enquiries. The Prime Minister probably had in mind some Crown appointment for Jowett himself, but his reply was that he did not intend to leave Oxford, so the only thing which could be done for him was 'to make Scott a Dean or a Bishop'. Within six months Scott was Dean of Rochester, and on 7 September 1870 Jowett was elected Master of Balliol unopposed.[31]

Scott accepted the Rochester appointment gracefully, although he must have known that it was a kick upstairs. Some of his later remarks seem to reveal a lingering bitterness. Although he no longer had any *locus standi*, in 1871 he was consulted by the Visitor about proposed new Statutes,[32] the main novelty of which was to reduce the number of clerical Fellows. The Visitor was inclined to resist,[33] but Scott counselled concurrence. He did not think there was much to be gained from insisting on any particular number of clerical Fellows, not 'so long as a College is wholly in the hands of a party whose leanings are dead the other way'. In any case, if the proposals were obstructed, this would lead, he wrote, to 'contrivances for evading the Visitor's decision in such ways as, *I know*, a practically unanimous College can'. Some asperity also comes through in the comment he made at the same time on a proposal (which soon fell by the wayside) to make the Mastership tenable for no more than twenty years:

The proposal to superannuate the Master absolutely after twenty years service seems to me simply monstrous: but it is very characteristic of its author. Disinterested, it undoubtedly is; since Jowett proposes to place himself under it. Yet I suspect that the gentle pressure of friends will not be wanting to induce *him* to retain his rights.

Scott left a good memory in Rochester, where he is reckoned among the more notable of its Deans, presiding over a vigorous Chapter and seeing through an extensive programme of restoration.[34]

---

[31] Abbott and Campbell, op. cit., i. 409; Prest, op. cit. In 1845 Richard Jenkyns had been able to accept a deanery without resigning the Mastership. But the Pluralities Act of 1850 (13 & 14 Vict. c. 98) explicitly prohibited the tenure of any deanery by a college head, except in the case of Christ Church. Scott had therefore to resign the Mastership in order to become Dean of Rochester.   [32] The correspondence is in MBP 23.

[33] The Visitor was John Jackson, elected as Bishop of Lincoln in 1853, but by this time Bishop of London (*DNB*). He was the last churchman, and also the last non-member of the College, to be appointed Visitor. Since his death in 1885, the College has always chosen a distinguished Balliol lawyer or statesman.

[34] He died in his deanery on 2 Dec. 1887, and was buried in Rochester Cathedral Cemetery. In the Cathedral itself, the west side of the medieval screen which separates the quire from the nave was reworked as his memorial, and his son and daughters gave the brass communion rail which is still in use.

Jowett took immediate advantage of his new position to reshape College life in several ways which were not especially remarkable individually, but which, taken together, amounted to a major change. The elaborate Latin versicles and responses, which had hitherto been recited alternately by one of the Scholars and the Fellows as a grace after their dinner, were abolished.[35] This custom had often meant that the Scholar on duty was kept hanging about long after the rest of the undergraduates had gone. The head cook had died, giving an opportunity for a shake-up in the kitchens. Jowett thought this 'an important matter' because he was 'very desirous that we should have a good reputation for eating and drinking'. Henry Wall was Bursar at the time. His accounts and papers are all exquisitely neat, giving every appearance of efficient management, but Jowett did not get on at all well with him, and was probably relieved that he agreed to take the Huntspill living at this juncture. One of Jowett's first thoughts after becoming Master was to find a 'Bursar or man of business for the College', and although Wall was asked to continue in office for the time being, he was relieved of responsibility for the Buttery, Kitchen, stores, and furniture. Jowett took virtually all the practical domestic aspects of the Bursar's job into his immediate control. Even the details of a new system for laundry had his personal attention.

Also early in his Mastership, the abolition of compulsory Chapel was completed, by the extension of the roll-call option to Sundays, as well as weekdays; the length and formality of weekday services were reduced; and the Catechetical Lectures (established by the will of Dr Richard Busby, who died in 1695) were terminated, the proceeds of the fund being used for a theology prize (with the approval of the Charity Commissioners). When Scott heard of this last reform, he wrote from his Deanery to tell the Visitor how much he deplored it.[36] 'I have very little doubt', he said, 'that in the hands of the present Body, there is danger that it may turn out to be an inducement & stimulus to "free handling" of Holy Scripture—the only thing that some people understand by Theology.' But although he knew in his heart that he was wasting his time, he did not entirely give up hope that a time would come, 'if it please God, when the Governing Body may not be banded together against all dogmatic teaching'.

Consistently with its liberality in matters of Christian religion, Balliol was also quick to take in Jewish students following the passing of the University Tests Act of 1871, which abolished restrictions which had prevented them from taking degrees. In 1882, a survey[37] showed that there were twenty-three Jewish students in the University; nine of them were at Balliol and no other college had more than two.

---

[35] The grace is printed in Abbott and Campbell, op. cit., ii. 21. See also F.12.22^{a-c}.

[36] MBP 23. [37] D. M. Lewis, *The Jews of Oxford*, 1992. p. 100.

The College was now in a period of steady numerical expansion, and the pressure on accommodation was again keenly felt. Hall could not contain the whole College at once; in 1870 it was necessary to restrict the entertainment of guests, and for some time an overflow dinner was served in one of the Lecture Rooms. In February 1871 the four remaining sets of three rooms were subdivided into six sets of two rooms. At about the same time, enquiries were initiated with a view to the purchase of Mr Frederick Morrell's nearby house and garden,[38] and notice to quit was served on the OU Rifle Corps, who had since 1860 rented the old stables for use as an armoury. The site of the stables, which were where Staircase XX now is, was wanted for a new residential wing. Waterhouse was asked to draw up plans for a block of sixteen rooms there in February 1873, but practical considerations limited its capacity to eight rooms. Authority to go ahead was given in Trinity Term, and was followed, at the beginning of Michaelmas Term, by the appointment of a committee to report 'on the desirableness of building a new Hall and additional rooms'. By the end of the term it had been agreed in principle that this was indeed desirable, and subscriptions were solicited from old members. Jowett was an indefatigable and very successful fund-raiser. He regarded mere circulars as of little use, and wrote in addition enormous numbers of personal letters. Waterhouse was again the architect. As well as the Hall and additional rooms, the new complex on the northern edge of the College included a new Common Room, Lecture Rooms, and, below and behind the Hall (where the Music Room now is), a Chemical Laboratory. The new buildings were opened at a banquet on 16 January 1877, to which as many old members as possible were invited.

The new Chemical Laboratory, which was relatively spacious, is a typical imaginative Jowett touch. A small laboratory had been set up in the cellars of the Salvin Building in 1853; it is now part of the Lindsay Bar. Some College physical science teaching had been done there in the 1850s by Henry Smith. When B. C. Brodie[39] was elected to the Aldrichian Professorship of Chemistry in 1855, he was allowed to carry out research and give instruction in the Balliol Laboratory until the University Museum was completed in 1860. This first College Laboratory seems then to have fallen into disuse, probably because it was more convenient for the few

---

[38] The purchase (1873, after negotiation 1872–3) of this property moved the entire northern boundary of the College site about 40 feet to the north: H. E. Salter, *Oxford Balliol Deeds*, 1913, p. 81; A.3.82, A.3.85, and A.3.142.

[39] On Benjamin Collins Brodie the younger, Bt. (1817–80; Balliol 1834), see the *DNB*, etc., and *The Atomic Debates*, ed. W. H. Brock, 1967. Brodie, an atheist and radical reformer, was a contemporary and close friend of Jowett's; it is remarkable that Scott tolerated him on the premises.

Balliol men taking science to be farmed out to the University Museum. But the demand increased, and Jowett probably also thought it would be better to bring the teaching of Balliol scientists back under College control, so on 21 March 1874 it was resolved that 'the Architect be authorised to introduce a Laboratory into his plans [for the Hall]'. Although Jowett was largely ignorant of science, he well understood its importance, and the College's commitment to it increased greatly under him. Shortly after the new Laboratory came into use (in co-operation with Trinity), Jowett persuaded the ninth Duke of Bedford to endow a Lecturership in Physical Sciences. The first Bedford Lecturer was H. B. Dixon; in 1886 he became the first experimental scientist to hold a Balliol Fellowship.[40]

The appearance of science in the curriculum was by no means the only change which took place in the second half of the nineteenth century. When Jowett began his academic career in the 1840s, all undergraduates in the University did either classics (*literae humaniores*) or mathematics or both. By the end of his life, a much wider variety of degree subjects was available for the student to choose from.[41] Of the Balliol men admitted between 1886 and 1889, for example, about two-thirds took a Final Honour School (the rest mostly took Pass Degrees, left after Classics Moderations, or were ICS Probationers). The subjects they took were distributed roughly as follows:

Literae Humaniores	40%
Modern History	25%
Jurisprudence	15%
Natural Science	10%
Mathematics	5%
Oriental Studies, Theology, etc.	5%

Classics was clearly still the principal discipline—even more so than the above figures show, in fact, because many men took Classics Moderations and then changed subject—but its position was being steadily eroded.

Before the end of his first term Jowett had re-established an Undergraduates' Library. The initial funds for this came from Lord Francis Hervey, who returned his Scholarship emoluments to the College. At first the books provided as the Undergraduates' Library were simply made available to students in one of the Lecture Rooms. But before long the

[40] For a full account of the Balliol–Trinity Laboratories and the development of science in the College, see T. [W. M.] Smith, 'The Balliol Trinity Laboratories', in J. [M.] Prest (ed.), *Balliol Studies*, 1982.

[41] An excellent guide to the curriculum in this period, covering all the Final Honour Schools then established, is given in A. M. M. Stedman (ed.), *Oxford: its Life and Schools*, 1887.

old Hall, no longer required for its original use, was free for conversion into a reading-room. The books of the Undergraduates' Library were moved into it, together with books from the main College Library selected as being of use to undergraduates. New Library Rules were drawn up, and a Library Committee was established. Jowett was so pleased with the new arrangements that he had a door made to give direct access into the Library from the Master's Lodgings. It was necessary for some junior assistant Librarians to be engaged, and Jowett used this need as a device to bring poor, but promising, lads into the higher education system by seeing that they were prepared for a University course, along with their Library work. One such was Frank Fletcher, who progressed from the Library to become Jowett's secretary in 1886, taking his degree in 1890. Matthew Knight was a similar case, although he never took a degree. He was the son of Jowett's butler. Jowett educated him, and employed him as a personal assistant at the same time. He became a considerable scholar in his own right, and would probably have made a mark independently of his master, had he not died soon after the great man himself; as Jowett acknowledged freely, his translations of Plato's Dialogues owed much to Knight, who made many 'valuable suggestions' and prepared draft translations of some parts.

Before Jowett became Master, amateur dramatics were frowned upon. The earliest evidence of any acting in College is a programme for 'Balliol College Private Theatricals', which took place in the rooms of Edmond Warre (later Head Master of Eton) on 9 December 1857.[42] The names of the actors in the programme of farce appear to be fictitious. Readings of Shakespeare were presumably more respectable, and there was an active society for this purpose in 1867–8, if not earlier. The institution of a Shakespeare Prize early in Jowett's Mastership was probably a mark of approval and encouragement. But the first public performance of a play in Balliol did not take place until 3 June 1880, when the *Agamemnon* of Aeschylus was put on in the College Hall.[43] The cast, styled 'Philothespians', included only a few Balliol men, but Jowett agreed to the performance with alacrity (the more so perhaps because several other University magnates had snubbed the producers) and attended it himself, bringing Robert Browning as his guest. His enthusiasm for acting in the University came out again strongly a little after this, when as Vice-Chancellor (1882–6) he actively encouraged the foundation of the OUDS. Similarly, he took bold and generous initiatives to get music established

---

[42] A. Mackinnon, *The Oxford Amateurs*, 1910, illustration facing p. 3.
[43] Oscar Wilde was involved in this production: R. Ellmann, *Oscar Wilde*, 1987, p. 101. Wilde had several close friends in Balliol: S. Leslie, *Memoir of John Edward Courtenay Bodley*, 1930, pp. 17–27.

in College life. John Farmer was the key figure in this. Farmer had received his musical training in Germany between 1849 and 1852. After an unsuccessful start in his family's lace-making business, and, according to family tradition, a spell as a circus bandmaster, he had been appointed to teach music at Harrow in 1864. He was an energetic and passionately musical man who cared little for convention. At Harrow he had made music very popular, and it had become a vital factor in the social cohesion and ethos of the school. This Jowett became aware of through visiting Harrow, and he set out to recruit Farmer to do the same for Balliol. Farmer was appointed Organist and Director of Music in 1885. A few years before this, he had remarked when dining with Jowett that the Hall gallery would be a good place for an organ, and when he took up his appointment Jowett provided the Hall with a 'Father' Willis organ at a cost of £2,000 out of his own pocket. With enthusiastic encouragement from Jowett, Farmer started the Balliol Concerts on Sunday evenings. The first was held on 18 October 1885. The concerts were the first secular concerts to be given in England on Sundays, and Jowett was attacked as a Sabbath-breaker, but the innovation was soon forgiven, and the tradition, consolidated by Farmer's successor Ernest Walker[44] (Director of Music 1900–25), has gone from strength to strength.[45] Chapel music was boosted too, by the complete reconstruction of the Harrison organ, again entirely at Jowett's expense. Farmer also arranged weekly informal singsongs in Hall, and produced a Balliol Songbook[46] for these occasions. Unlike the Concerts, they did not long outlive their founder, but something of their spirit lives on at meetings of the College's Victorian Society.

Jowett also fostered the sporting side of undergraduate life, which grew in his lifetime from insignificance to be enormously important, as the Victorian admiration of muscular Christianity, and devotion to team games, worked its way up from the public schools into the University. With the passage of the years Jowett sympathized more and more, and in the late eighties some six or seven acres in Holywell were bought from Merton, for use as a playing-field. He contributed to the purchase himself, and raised subscriptions from others, writing systematically to one or two old members every day. Any want of sympathy which he encountered did not deflect him from his purpose, and he found that persistence paid, as his letters to one old member show:[47]

August 1889 ... Will you kindly read the enclosed circular? It relates to a matter

---

[44] On Walker (1870–1949), see the *DNB* and M. Deneke, *Ernest Walker*, 1951.

[45] [R.] A. Burns and R. [J.] Wilson, *The Balliol Concerts: A Centenary History*, n.d. [1985].

[46] *Balliol Songs*, ed. J. Farmer, privately printed, 1888. On Farmer (1835–1901), see the *DNB*, and MISC 217.   [47] Abbott and Campbell, op. cit., ii. 371.

in which I am deeply interested, and which I believe to be very important to the College. We have done what we can for ourselves ...

12 August 1889 ... You have sent me rather a severe lecture instead of a liberal subscription: will you not, as an old friend, add the latter to the former?

Later ... I was very much touched by your kind letter and gift ... The old members of the College have been very generous to us ...

In the matter of the field, as with the Hall and other schemes, Jowett came to appreciate well the value to the College of a strong corporate spirit linking old members to, and involving them with, the College of the moment. His correspondence gave sustenance to this spirit, but it was fostered in other ways too, especially by the regular 'Gaudies' which he began about 1877, possibly following on the great success of the gathering held when the Hall was opened.

He did not allow his exertions in the interests of better facilities and a richer life for Balliol students to interfere with his efforts to make the advantages of higher education more generally accessible. Soon after his elevation to the Mastership, it was resolved (11 October 1873, adjourned meeting) 'That the College take measures, either alone or in conjunction with other Colleges, towards the establishment of Lectures in one of the large Towns', and that it was willing to find £200 p.a. to this end. A movement had begun towards creating a local college or university at Bristol. Jowett wrote to the people involved, and informed them that help might be forthcoming from his own College, and probably one other. After some negotiations, Balliol and New College made a definite promise to support a college at Bristol with £300 p.a. for at least five years, with certain stipulations, including the conditions that women, and working adults on a part-time or evening basis, should be able to benefit. Jowett also spoke on at least two public occasions staged to whip up support for what has become the University of Bristol, and in 1877 he was instrumental in the appointment of its first Principal (Alfred Marshall, 1842–1924, Fellow of Balliol 1883–5, a distinguished economist).[48]

For many years Jowett had been interested in the selection and preparation of men for the Indian Civil Service (ICS). He was a member of Macaulay's Committee which reported on this subject in 1854, and was to a large extent responsible for the way the ICS was subsequently opened to university men. In 1875 the College announced that it was willing to accept up to ten ICS Probationers, and Arnold Toynbee was appointed to be their Tutor. In 1879, for example, more than half the ICS Probationers in the country were studying at Balliol. Logically enough, Indian

[48] On the origins and early days of University College, Bristol, see J. W. Sherborne, *University College, Bristol 1876–1907*, 1977.

students were encouraged as well. Of the 49 Indians who matriculated in the University during Jowett's Mastership, 22 came to Balliol, 16 to other colleges, and the rest were non-collegiate. There were a number of admissions from other oriental countries in the late nineteenth century as well—only a few, but a remarkable few, such as Tomotsune Iwakura (Balliol 1873; son of the Prime Minister of Japan); Mochiaki Hachisuka (Balliol 1873; Japanese Minister of Education 1896); Nasr-ul-Mulk (Balliol 1879; Prime Minister of Persia 1909; Regent 1910–14); Prince Kitiyakara Varalaksna of Siam (Balliol 1889; son of King Chulalongkorn); Prince Svasti Sobhana of Siam (Balliol 1883; son of King Mongcut); Mohammed Mahmoud (Balliol 1897; Prime Minister of Egypt 1928). Some 16 per cent of all Balliol men entering the University between 1874 and 1914 spent a substantial part of their working lives in India, compared to (e.g.) 4 and 6 per cent for Keble and St John's respectively. Jowett fostered Indian studies in the University too, and was actively involved in the foundation · of the Indian Institute. On top of all this, three of his pupils (Lansdowne,- Milner, Curzon) were successive Viceroys of India, 1888–1905. It is clear that Jowett was a major influence in the government and development of India, without ever seeing it or having any official responsibility to do with it. His early concern about Indian affairs may have been prompted by the fact that two of his brothers had served and died in the subcontinent; later his enthusiasm probably became self-sustaining, but must have been stimulated by his correspondence with Florence Nightingale, with whom the interest was shared.[49]

As well as looking after the ICS Probationers, Toynbee, who was very much one of T. H. Green's disciples, was active in social and educational work among the London poor. Jowett approved of this, but took no direct part in it. In much the same way he spoke from time to time in favour of the education of women and encouraged Green and his wife in their campaigning, but did not get directly involved in the movement himself. Toynbee died, aged only thirty-one, in 1883 (Toynbee Hall in Whitechapel was set up in his memory[50]), and Green also died young at forty-six in 1882: their idealism and practical achievements laid the foundations of the concerned social awareness, and constructive left-wing political attitudes, for which the College became famous.

There was a further round of University reform in the late seventies in which Jowett was again prominent. The main results of the Commission

---

[49] On Balliol, Jowett, and India, see R. Symonds, *Oxford and Empire*, 1986, and *Record of the Establishment of the Indian Institute*, 1897, Oxford (compiled for subscribers to the Indian Institute Fund).

[50] A. Briggs and A. Macartney, *Toynbee Hall—The First Hundred Years*, 1984.

were to do with the use of money, and professors versus tutors: Jowett
was on the anti-professorial side, and was lukewarm on the endowment
of research. As things turned out, the reformed Statutes of 1881 had little
direct impact on the collegiate and tutorial system. But they were of
importance to the Fellowship, because of a further reduction in the
obligation of the College to have clerical Fellows, and an increase in the
scope for marriage. These and other changes such as the creation of
pension rights were important steps towards making college teaching
posts into professional career appointments.[51] The unendowed private
halls were to a large extent suppressed by the Commissioners, mostly by
merging them with the colleges with which they were associated. But one
of them—New Inn Hall—was not closely linked with any college. Jowett
set out to obtain it for Balliol, with the intention of using it to house the
ICS Probationers. The Chancellor, in whose discretion the matter lay,
agreed, and in 1881 the Commissioners made a Statute for the union of
Balliol and New Inn Hall, to be effective when H. H. Cornish, the incumbent Principal, vacated his position. Cornish died in 1887. It proved
impracticable to use the old Hall buildings, which were near the Bonn
Square end of New Inn Hall Street, on the west side, and they were sold
in 1899.[52] At one stage, the relocation of New Inn Hall as a Balliol annexe
in Holywell was considered,[53] but when this scheme foundered Jowett
decided that it would be better to make most of the land which was
available in that area into a playing-field. New Inn Hall was thus never re-
established, its assets and members being quietly absorbed by Balliol: New
Inn Hall Street, some silver, and a few Butlers' books, are all that remain
to remind us of an academic hall which had flourished since medieval
times. The plan to hive off the ICS Probationers into a separate annexe
came to nothing too. Instead they gradually became more fully integrated
with the rest of the College, and although they were numerically strong
until well into the twentieth century, they stood out as a class less and less.

The Mastership did not stop the flow of Jowett's writing or even
interfere very much with his closeness to the undergraduate community.
He rarely passed a day in term-time without seeing two or three of them
socially—often at breakfast or on walks—and he kept up tutorial contact
as much as he could, taking essays from several undergraduates a week.
He established regular meetings of the Tutors, which he always attended,

---

[51] On the emergence of the academic profession in Oxford, see A. J. Engel, *From
Clergyman to Don*, 1983.
[52] There is extensive documentation about the annexation of New Inn Hall in the
Archives: see especially A.6.
[53] Abbott and Campbell, op. cit., ii. 344; *Recollections of Thomas Graham Jackson*, ed. B. H.
Jackson, 1950, p. 198.

going through the whole College list, and satisfying himself about the work of every man. And during vacations he continued, as before, to invite some of his men to stay with him. He was completely uninhibited in the rebukes and exhortations he delivered, often in pithy direct terms which brooked no evasion or discussion. He took special trouble with 'unsteady' young men, who seemed to be going wrong; with the rich and titled, whom he sought to influence to use their positions and inheritances for good (he was accused of snobbery because of this); and with the financially disadvantaged, to whom he privately made numerous gifts out of his own pocket, just as he had himself been helped by an initially anonymous friend, when he was an impoverished student. He had the power of influencing young men to a degree little short of the supernatural, and he wielded it for half a century, turning out a dedicated élite. By the end of Queen Victoria's life, they dominated many departments of the imperial establishment, and left few professions without Balliol men among their leaders. This did not endear Jowett and his pupils to those outside the charmed circle, but it was a fact. This can be seen in the printed Registers, and it would be tedious to give here the names of all Jowett's worthies.[54] The statesmen are perhaps the most striking group—Lansdowne, Asquith, Curzon, Grey, Milner, Samuel, and Amery—but there are also an archbishop (Lang), and many permanent under-secretaries in the Civil Service, together with diplomats, law lords (including Lord Loreburn, Lord Chancellor), distinguished academics, headmasters, poets (Gerard Manley Hopkins, Swinburne), and so on. However, it is salutary to be reminded that this almost overwhelming conventional distinction was leavened by a few who are remarkable for more unusual reasons: A. G. Vernon Harcourt[55] (pioneer of chemical kinetics; possibly the White Knight of *Alice in Wonderland*); J. A. Symonds[56] (man of letters; pederast and blackmailer); C. H. Hinton[57] (mathematician interested in four-dimensional space; tried for bigamy; invented an automatic baseball pitcher for practice—powered by charges of gunpowder, it delivered balls with such ferocity that players were afraid of it); E. G. Fraser-Luckie[58] (long-distance racing cyclist; discovered a 509-ounce nugget in the British Guiana goldrush; married a daughter of the President of Peru; made an immense fortune out of sugar, but lost it in 1929); and H. D. Rawnsley (founder of the National Trust).

[54] See, in addition to the printed College Registers, H. [B.] Hartley, *Balliol Men*, 1963.

[55] J. Shorter, 'A. G. Vernon Harcourt', *J. Chem. Educ.*, 57 (1980), 411; M. C. King, 'The Course of Chemical Change: the Life and Times of Augustus Vernon Harcourt (1834–1919)', *Ambix*, 39 (1984), 16, and references therein cited.

[56] P. Grosskurth, *The Memoirs of John Addington Symonds*, 1984.

[57] D. MacHale, *George Boole. His Life and Work*, 1985, p. 259.

[58] C. A. H. Villiers, *Edgar Fraser Luckie*, 1986.

In Hilary Term 1881, a broadsheet entitled 'The Masque of B–ll—l'
was circulated. It consisted of forty 'Balliol Rhymes' about members of
the College. The best known of these jingles is about Jowett:

> First come I. My name is J–W–TT,
> There's no knowledge but I know it.
> I am Master of this College.
> What I don't know isn't knowledge.

Tennyson is supposed to have said of this, 'Very unfair. Jowett never set
up to be omniscient.' Unfair it certainly seems, as is the fact that this little
jingle, characterizing him as a pompous know-all, has survived to be so
well known.[59]

A great deal has been written about Jowett, some of it hagiographic
and some of it scholarly, but a really satisfactory biography is lacking.
Writing one would be an enormous challenge, for he was a complex and
many-faceted man, who interacted with most of the leading figures of
Victorian Britain, by no means all of them from Balliol: Gladstone,
Browning, Florence Nightingale, Tennyson, for example. In Florence
Nightingale he found a far-sighted spirit with a determination to get
things done which was not unlike his own, and she was his most consistent
correspondent—they exchanged many hundreds of letters between 1860
and his death in 1893.[60] He had ideas on theology, the Church,[61] home
and imperial politics, education at all levels,[62] literature, philosophy,
administration, and government. Only in scientific and technical matters
was he at a loss, but he was wise enough to appreciate this, and even here
he always seemed to be able to grasp what mattered and what did not. He
was not at all a dreaming idealist, but a man who got things done. His
schemes were imaginative and often radical, but their objectives were
always attainable. If, as he did a few times, he encountered immovable
obstacles, he would recognize the fact and apply his energies to something
else. When he was Vice-Chancellor, for example, he had grand plans for
changing the local geography of Oxford by means of engineering works
designed to alter the drainage of the Thames Valley, in order to reduce
flooding and make the environment more healthy. But the authorities

---

[59] *The Balliol Rhymes*, ed. W. G. Hiscock, printed for the editor, Oxford, 1955.

[60] Jowett's letters to Florence Nightingale are in the College Library, and a selection has
been edited for publication: Quinn and Prest, op. cit.

[61] On Jowett's theology and relations with the Church of England, see P. [B.] Hinchliff,
chapter 6 in J. [M.] Prest (ed.), *Balliol Studies*, 1982, and id., *Benjamin Jowett and the Christian
Religion*, 1987.

[62] See especially J. M. Prest, 'Jowett's Correspondence on Education with Earl Russell
in 1867', *Balliol College Record*, Supplement, 1965, and *Letters of Benjamin Jowett MA*, ed. E.
Abbott and L. Campbell, 1899, Section II.

18. Benjamin Jowett as Master, about 1880.

concerned could not agree and little was achieved—perhaps Jowett's biggest failure, but not one where he wasted much effort in a pointless further campaign. We have alluded to the pithy remarks and long silences for which he was renowned. Anecdotes about him are many, as are the aphorisms with which he is credited. Some are doubtless apocryphal, and he himself pronounced many to be pure invention. A haphazard selection is given below:

Be a reformer. Don't be found out. [To a Head Master of Eton.]
Never explain. Never apologize. [To a Viceroy of India.]
One man is as good as another until he has written a book.
The best rest is change of work.
On all great subjects much remains to be said.
Nowhere probably is there more true feeling, and nowhere worse taste, than in a churchyard.

He was undoubtedly the greatest Master the College has had in modern times, if not the most human, and none before or since has had such standing or influence. He recorded his conception of the duties of his office in a private memorandum book about 1875.[63]

The Head of a College

The Head of a College should be identified with the interests of the College. The life of the College is his life. His money is the money of the College. He is married to the College and has a duty to support his family.

He should put forward the undergraduates, suggest thoughts and plans to the Fellows, create a common spirit. He should be absolutely above personality. He should inspire a feeling of duty in the whole College. He should know how to 'put pressure' upon everybody.

He died on 1 October 1893,[64] having met his own specifications in every respect.

---

[63] Abbott and Campbell, *Life and Letters*, 78.

[64] He was buried in St Sepulchre's Cemetery on 6 Oct. 1893, near the gate. Seven of his eight pallbearers were Balliol men who had become heads of other colleges. His will is printed in Abbott and Campbell, *Life and Letters*, ii. 476: after personal bequests, he made the College his residuary legatee, and he also left it the copyright in all his works.

16

Effortless Superiority 1893–1914

THERE was strong feeling among some influential old members that J. L. Strachan Davidson should be Jowett's successor. He had been a Tutor and Dean for many years. In these offices he had earned widespread love and respect, so he seemed the natural choice for Master. His claim was pressed by Evelyn Abbott and Sir John Conroy, both of them Fellows, and they probably had the majority of Balliol men behind them, anxious for the preservation of tribal unity.

H. Craik[1] *to Conroy, 16 Oct. 1893*
I have thought much—without any right to do so—on the critical choice which lies before the Fellows. I have also spoken to several Oxford men: and everywhere I have found the strong bias and tendency of feeling to be in favour of the choice of Strachan Davidson. Frequently there is expressed some doubt as to whether health would allow it: but if this difficulty is got over, I have found uniform agreement as to their personal choice ... It is of immense importance, if good men are to stay in Oxford, that the prominent posts shd. fall to those who have given their lives to Oxford. Take one of yourselves, identified with Balliol at each point in his career—the product of her teaching and training—and you cannot better prove that confidence in your own resources which will command the confidence of England. No one will venture for a moment to say that Strachan Davidson is not the equal of any, the superior of most, of the Heads of Colleges in Oxford at this moment as regards intellect, character and attainment. If he is not widely known, the reason simply is that he has devoted himself to the College and sunk his identity in her ...

P. Lyttleton Gell[2] *to Conroy, 27 Oct. 1893*
... The fact is that you are all so humble minded that I think you do not realize how attached old Balliol men are to their Fellows, and how deeply they appreciate their devotion to the College. It would be an enormous—and at this juncture a dangerous breach in the general 'connexion' of Balliol and in the feeling toward it, if old Balliol men came up to find at the Master's Lodge a Pharaoh who knew them not ...

---

[1] H. Craik (1846–1927), Balliol 1865; *DNB*.
[2] P. Lyttleton Gell, Balliol 1871.

But among the Fellows the majority, led by A. L. Smith, thought that an old-fashioned conservative, of no special academic distinction, would not be able to maintain the momentum gained by the College under Jowett: they wanted a liberal intellectual figure-head. Their candidate was Edward Caird, a sometime Snell Exhibitioner who had been Professor of Moral Philosophy at Glasgow since leaving Oxford in 1866, after being a Fellow of Merton. Caird baulked at the prospect of being Master with strong opposition, and hesitated. Balliol needed him, he was told. Without him it was 'in danger of losing its power of leadership and liberal initiative' and would be 'swept by inertia into a groove of gentlemanliness and mediocrity'. He still hesitated, and only when Strachan Davidson himself urged him to do so did he accept:

... the generosity of Mr Strachan Davidson, and the kind messages I have received from other Fellows of the College, have removed my main outward difficulty, and at the same time have enabled me to feel that, in accepting the office of Master, I can be sure not only of the support, but also of the sympathy, of all with whom I shall have to act. I hope you have judged rightly in calling me to such a position. He would be rash man, who would undertake to follow the great man and great teacher whom we have lost, without many doubts and fears. I can only promise that whatever powers I have in me will be now to serve the great College that has chosen me, and to keep it true to the spirit which it has inherited from Jowett and Green, from Henry Smith and Lewis Nettleship ...

Strachan Davidson made his magnanimous support for Caird public by speaking warmly in his favour in Hall a few days later, and the two of them worked in close and friendly co-operation throughout Caird's Mastership, with the administrative burdens falling increasingly on Strachan Davidson's shoulders as Caird's health failed. Strachan Davidson had his reward: he was elected Master unanimously within a few days when Caird resigned in 1907.[3]

The College's self-confidence and sense of corporate identity were never stronger than at this time. At a dinner in 1908, the Prime Minister, H. H. Asquith, said that Balliol men were distinguished from lesser souls by their 'tranquil consciousness of effortless superiority'.[4] The phrase has

---

[3] For a full account of Caird's election, with references etc., see J. [H.] Jones, 'A Contested Mastership. The Election of Jowett's Successor', *Balliol College Record*, 1977, p. 49, where long extracts from many of the relevant documents are also given. Caird resigned in 1907 and died on 1 Nov. 1908. He was buried near Jowett in St Sepulchre's Cemetery, close to the gate.

[4] The dinner was given by Balliol men in Parliament to celebrate Asquith's appointment as Prime Minister. It was held on 22 July 1908, and his remark was reported in *The Times* on the following day. For a survey of the men he had in mind, see H. [B.] Hartley, *Balliol Men*, 1963. Dorothy Sayers's character Lord Peter Wimsey was supposed to have been at

dogged subsequent generations. It was not really conceit: they *knew* they were superior. They had only to look to Parliament, the Church, the Civil Service, and the Empire to see Balliol cabinet ministers, archbishops, permanent under-secretaries, and viceroys. The evidence that Balliol men were indeed some kind of master race was everywhere. The chorus of Hilaire Belloc's song 'To the Balliol Men still in Africa' may make those bred up with modern inhibitions and modesty cringe with embarrassment, but it captures well how they felt about their College:

> Balliol made me, Balliol fed me,
> Whatever I had she gave me again:
> And the best of Balliol loved and led me.
> God be with you, Balliol men.

Nor were these feelings confined to members of the College, for the perception of outsiders looking in was often the same. John Buchan (Brasenose), for example, speaking of the closing years of the century:[5]

The Balliol generation of my time was, I think, the most remarkable in Oxford, only to be paralleled by the brilliant group, containing Charles Lister and the Grenfells, which flourished on the eve of the War. It was distinguished both for its scholars and its athletes, but it made no parade of its distinction, carrying its honours lightly as if they fell to it in the ordinary process of nature. It delighted unpedantically in things of the mind, but it had an engaging youthfulness, too, and was not above high-jinks and escapades.

On how Balliol men came to be so successful, both in collecting distinctions and prizes in the University and in their subsequent careers, there were and will remain several opinions. Some thought it was the influence and teaching of a great Master backed up by able and devoted Tutors. There are many contemporary allusions to the 'Secret of Balliol' and the 'Balliol System' to be found, but in fact there never was any thought-out policy or considered and deliberate approach to the educational process. Indeed, the diversity of types and activities is a feature of the College at this time which draws comment from those who saw and experienced it. The unvarying themes in Jowett's exhortations to his pupils are to do with working hard, not wasting opportunities or talents, persevering in the face of difficulty, and so on. There is nothing very original or specially inspiring about such precepts, but what was remarkable was the extent to which they were taken to heart. The superiority was not effortless at all. This, perhaps, is part of the explanation for the College's pre-eminence. Davis was inclined to attribute it more to great men teaching that dogma

Balliol in the era of effortless superiority: she uses the word 'Balliolity' for it (e.g. D. L. Sayers, *Murder Must Advertise*, 1933, reissued 1971, p. 11).

[5] J. Buchan, *Memory Hold-the-Door*, 1940, p. 52.

19. Edward Caird, Master 1893–1907.

should be rejected and that 'within the limits prescribed by faith, reason is the only trustworthy guide'. This teaching, he thought, was 'the origin of a mental attitude which was at first acknowledged by friends and enemies as peculiar to Balliol but now tends more and more to be characteristic of Oxford men at large'.[6] Hastings Rashdall, reviewing Davis, thought this too high-flown and favoured a more down-to-earth opinion.[7]

Few non-Balliol men will be able to accept without qualification Mr Davis's somewhat transcendental view of 'Modern Balliol', and will be disposed to attribute the undoubted, and of late years unapproached success, of Balliol men in academical competitions and in after life rather to the fact that, owing to its being the first college to open the bulk of its scholarships to general competition, it has enjoyed the pick of the schools, than to the exceptional virtues of a supposed 'Balliol System'.

It was certainly a select society. In 1900 80 per cent were English, and one in four of these was an Etonian. Scots made up half of the rest. The number from overseas was rising, but was still under 10 per cent. It was soon to be boosted by the addition of Rhodes Scholars, who favoured Balliol from the outset, despite Balliol's prominent role in the opposition to Cecil Rhodes's honorary degree in 1899. 'In an ideal College, as in an ideal world, all men would be brothers', but there were cliques, although the 'Dons, bravely aiming at the impossible, did their best to discountenance them'. The most evident in every way were the Etonians, who included some of the most brilliant and wild Balliol men ever admitted. Aubrey Herbert was an extreme example. Although his eyesight was very bad, his roof-climbing feats were notorious. He was in continuous trouble with the Proctors, and was eventually rusticated by the College. But he got a First all the same; the adventurous life he had subsequently in Parliament, war, and Eastern Europe has all the flavour of the imagination of John Buchan, who used him as a model for 'Greenmantle'. Herbert was a famously riotous member of the Annandale Club, ostensibly a debating, but in fact a dining, club. Predominantly Etonian, it was a perennial problem. On the night of an 'Anna' dinner, the College was liable to be taken over and havoc wrought. But if they destroyed large quantities of College crockery in ritual 'waterfalls' down the Hall steps, they would at least pay up without complaint the next morning. The authorities were remarkably tolerant, and so were the other members—

---

[6] H. W. C. Davis, *Balliol College*, 1899, p, 197.

[7] Hastings Rashdall (1858–1924: see the *DNB*, etc.) was, among other things, a distinguished historian of the medieval universities. He was Chaplain of Balliol 1894–5, although this does not appear in the printed College Registers. His review of Davis is in *English Hist. Review*, 16 (1901), 195.

none more so than 'Moonface' Norman Campbell, a retiring and abstemi-
ous man. It was part of the traditional high spirits after dinner, before
the 'waterfalls' began, for the diners to climb the stairs to Moonface's
room, where he would be at his books, and there to kneel in mock
worship before him 'O Moonface ...' After a selfless life of teaching at
Trinity College, Kandy, Campbell returned to fight, and was killed in the
trenches, like many of his tormentors.[8]

The 'Gordouli' belongs to this epoch. One evening, after a dinner in
College, probably in 1896, a certain Bobby Johnson of New College, who
was a guest, remarked that a Trinity man with the imposing name Arthur
Mario Agricola Collier Galletti di Cadilhac (nicknamed Gordouli, after a
popular brand of Egyptian cigarettes) had a face like a ham. It must have
been a good dinner, because the party was so amused by this pinnacle of
wit that they rushed out into the quad to chant at Trinity:

> Gordoo-ley,
> He's got a face like a ham,
> Bobby Johnson says so,
> And he ought to know.

This shout over the wall quickly became a regular post-prandial activity.
Before long it had been set to music of sorts. Trinity devised various
replies, including:

> Balliol, Balliol,
> They can't r-o-w,
> Joe Legge says so,
> And he ought to know.

Joe Legge was a rowing parson who used to coach the Trinity Eight. As
the years passed the exchanges became, on Trinity's part, racist ('Bloody
Basutos' was among their responses), and on Balliol's part simply abusive,
with the addition of several more verses. The Gordouli, in its extended
and unprintable form, is still sung on appropriate occasions.[9] Its insults
are usually ignored by Trinity, but the tiresome tradition of nocturnal
raids in both directions probably sprang from it.[10] Bobby Johnson had a

---

[8] The quotations and anecdotes in this paragraph are taken from L. E. Jones, *An
Edwardian Youth*, 1956. On Aubrey Herbert, see also Buchan, op. cit., and M. FitzHerbert,
The Man who was Greenmantle, 1983.

[9] G. N. Knight, 'The Quest for Gordouli', *Balliol College Record*, 1969, p. 35; 'A Gordouli
Fragment', ibid., 1974, p. 39.

[10] For example, during the present author's time as an undergraduate: Balliol provided
Trinity JCR with a complete carpet of turf one night, and Trinity, on another occasion,
managed to paint the word 'Belial' large and clear on Balliol Hall roof. For a detailed
account of the Trinity–Balliol feud, with sources, see C. Hopkins and B. Ward-Perkins in
Trinity College Oxford Report, 1989–90 and 1990–91. More recently, in 1994 H. Lime and
Sons, Auctioneers, Balliol, advertised a Trinity College Closing Down Sale, but there were
no bids: MISC 195.

lot to answer for.

The Honourable Charles Lister was one of the most abandoned members of the Etonian set. He finally went too far for the College authorities in 1908, and was rusticated for the absurd offence of making the Dean of Trinity dance around a bonfire with him after a party. His departure was marked with an elaborate mock funeral, and the epitaph 'I wist not, brethren, that he was the High Priest' was cut into a stone by the entrance of his staircase. But this same Lister was also an active practical Socialist, who took a First. On one occasion he organized support for a strike by women employed at the Clarendon Press. When he was sent away he spent the time working at an East End Mission.[11] For Fabian Socialism was as marked a feature of Edwardian Balliol as its Annandale excesses. Caird was a supporter, but A. L. Smith was the movement's most energetic prophet in the College. William Beveridge, one of the leading architects of the British Welfare State, was at Balliol 1897–1902: his interest in social problems was inspired then.[12] Smith was a strong exponent of the ideas of Jowett, Green, Arnold Toynbee, and others, about University Extension, and was an active participant in the Workers' Educational Association (WEA). Through him the College admitted Joseph Owen, a married man aged twenty-four, who had left full-time schooling when only eleven years old to work in a cotton-mill. His talents were spotted at an Oldham Extension Course, and he was brought to Oxford in 1894 to be coached for University admission, which then involved compulsory Latin and Greek. In 1895 he won a Brackenbury Scholarship, and then went on to a First and a Fellowship at Pembroke College, before taking up his permanent career as an Inspector of Schools. His success probably influenced attitudes to extra-mural education and working-class students as much as any of the Balliol campaigners did. When the work of the WEA expanded to include Summer Schools, it was natural for them to turn to Balliol, despite a rather grumpy attitude on the part of Strachan Davidson, and Smith gave them his time and energy unstintingly. The first Balliol Summer School was held in the Long Vacation of 1910. It ran for two months, and was attended by nearly a hundred students. In the following year twice as many attended, and a tradition was soon established which was to survive the War.[13] Smith was not content to limit

---

Sons, Auctioneers, Balliol, advertised a Trinity College Closing Down Sale, but there were no bids: MISC 195.

[11] L. E. Jones, op. cit., p. 56; C. Bailey, in Lord Ribblesdale, *Charles Lister . . .* , 1917, p. 244. On the mock funeral and the oration by Patrick Shaw-Stewart, see also *End of an Era. Letters and Journals of Sir Alan Lascelles 1887–1920*, ed. D. Hart-Davis, 1986, p. 45.

[12] J. Harris, *William Beveridge*, 1977.

[13] H. P. Smith, 'A Note on the Contribution of Balliol to the Making of the Tradition of Extra-Mural Education', unpublished typescript, in the College Library; L. Goldman, *Dons and Workers. Oxford and Adult Education since 1950*, 1995.

the application of his ideas about social problems and practical Christianity to the vacations, and schemes which involved only a few dons, but sought also to inspire the undergraduates. Early in Michaelmas Term 1906, he arranged a series of meetings in Hall on the application of religious principles to ordinary life. The first two meetings, which were well attended, considered social problems, and brought out a widespread feeling that the College should not merely debate the issues, but should do something. Smith seized the opportunity, and suggested that a committee should be set up to consider what might be done. Before the end of the term a report was ready. It made two main recommendations. The first related to what was then known as Ruskin Hall: it was proposed that a close liaison between Ruskin and Balliol should be developed, in the interests of better understanding between the different social classes from which they were drawn. The second, and major, proposal was that the College should start a Boys' Club in an Oxford slum. During the first fortnight of the following term, suitable premises were secured in St Ebbe's, financial support for the first three years was guaranteed, and a system of management and participation by undergraduates was approved. The Club opened on 7 February 1907. It was immediately over-subscribed by local lads, mostly in the fourteen to fifteen age-group. Muscular Christianity was the underlying theme. Most of the Club's activities were vigorous games and sport, especially soccer and boxing. Every evening session was the responsibility of one of the undergraduate members of the Club Committee, who took it in turns to organize things and lead the prayers which were a regular part of the programme. In vacations, camp holidays, with an emphasis on open-air activities, were arranged, and supervised by student leaders. The Club ran very successfully on these lines for more than sixty years, until the redevelopment of the St Ebbe's area swept it away.[14]

In Michaelmas Term 1899 the College undergraduate roll stood at about 165. There were also a few graduates doing advanced work or research, and a number of ICS Probationers. The undergraduates included 28 Scholars and 26 Exhibitioners. The awards were made following an examination in November, which was held in conjunction with Christ

---

[14] C. Bailey, *A Short History of the Balliol Boys' Club 1907–1950*, 1950: revised and reprinted for private circulation by Martin Slade for the Balliol Boys' Club Association in 1995, as C. Bailey and J. Roughley, *A History of the Balliol Boys' Club 1907–1971*. After the First World War, the Club was given new premises in memory of T. E. K. Rae, a prominent supporter and organizer, who was killed in 1915. When the St Ebbe's area was redeveloped (about 1970), Keith Rae House was sold and the Club was wound up, but the proceeds of the sale were invested by the Keith Rae Trust, and are still used for the support of youth clubs.

Church and Trinity.[15] Commoners could also obtain admission if they did well enough in this competition, but there was another entrance examination for them only which was held three times a year. Scholarships were worth £80 p.a. (Exhibitions £70 p.a.) and covered about half an average man's total expenses, which were in the range of £40–50 a term. The distribution of subjects studied by the undergraduates was heavily biased in favour of classics and history: Literae Humaniores 36; Classics Moderations 49; Modern History 41; Law 11; Mathematics 10; Natural Science 17. There were only twelve Fellows, nine of whom took a regular part in the teaching of undergraduates, but the Senior Common Room also had four Lecturers not on the Foundation, as well as a Chaplain and a Director of Music.[16] The leading Tutors of the period were Strachan Davidson, A. L. Smith, F. F. Urquhart, Sir John Conroy, Evelyn Abbott, H. B. Hartley, A. W. Pickard-Cambridge, E. J. Palmer, Cyril Bailey, H. W. C. Davis, and A. D. Lindsay. Caird was a somewhat remote Master, who made little impact on the undergraduates, but the Tutors spent practically all their time with them, teaching prodigiously long hours by modern standards, and students were encouraged to invade the private lives of the Tutors in the evenings and vacations. Urquhart in particular was legendary. He was universally known as 'Sligger'.[17] A widely read and successful history Tutor, he made no direct contribution of his own to historical scholarship. He did not regard that as his calling. His purpose was the education, in the most general sense of the word, of the young men—and not only his own history pupils. For the greater part of his time he lived on the first floor, over the back gate. The great bay window of his main room faces the Protestant Martyrs' Memorial, a curious outlook for a devout Roman Catholic—he was the first to hold a Balliol Fellowship since the Reformation.

Here of an evening about 10.30, when work was done, you would find some six to ten undergraduates talking, sometimes in groups, sometimes in common. Now

---

[15] The details of the arrangements for the Scholarship examination changed quite often in the period. There was a lot of bickering between the colleges on the subject, because of jealousies over the capture of the best candidates.

[16] The statistics quoted here, and much of the other detail given in this chapter about College life at the time, are derived from a collection of 'Official Papers and Miscellaneous Information' which was put together for an exhibition or conference of some kind in 1900 (MISC 1). L. E. Jones (op. cit.) and Ernest Barker (in *Father of the Man*, n.d., *c.* 1948) give especially vivid autobiographical accounts of Balliol in their time (1904–8 and 1893–8 respectively).

[17] The nickname was probably derived by corrupting 'Sleek one' to 'Sleeker' and thence to 'Sligger' (C. Bailey, *Francis Fortescue Urquhart*, 1936, p. 25). Several of the other Fellows had bizarre nicknames: 'Smuggins' = 'A. L.' = A. L. Smith; 'Fluffy' = H. W. C. Davis; 'Picker' = A. W. Pickard-Cambridge.

20. **Senior Common Room Dinner for the Visitor, about 1899.** *Back row, left to right:* E. Jenks (Lecturer in Law); E. Walker (Assistant Organist); E. Abbott (Fellow and Tutor in Classics; in his wheelchair); H. W. C. Davis (Lecturer in Modern History); F. L. Armitage (Modern Languages); J. W. Russell (Lecturer in Mathematics); A. W. Pickard-Cambridge (Fellow and Tutor in Classics). *Middle Row:* J. A. Smith (Fellow and Tutor in Philosophy); John Farmer (Organist); Sir William Markby (Fellow and Tutor to the ICS Probationers; Senior Bursar); E. Caird (Master); Viscount Peel (Visitor); J. L. Strachan Davidson (Fellow and Tutor in Classics; Dean); A. L. Smith (Fellow and Tutor in Modern History); G. U. Pope (Chaplain; University Lecturer in Tamil and Telugu); Sir John Conroy (Fellow and Tutor in Natural Science). *Sitting on the ground:* F. F. Urquhart (Fellow and Tutor in Modern History; Junior Dean); E. J. Palmer (Fellow and Tutor in Theology; Chaplain); D. H. Nagel (Fellow of Trinity; Demonstrator in Natural Science).

and then there might arise a discussion on some question of art, or politics, or behaviour—never a long argument, for Sligger disliked it and would cut it short by an abrupt transition to another subject. Frequently the talk was mere undergraduate gossip or pure nonsense—for this was the hour of relaxation for everyone. It was rarely brilliant, and some may have found it at times dull or insipid. But always there was an atmosphere of natural and easy enjoyment. . . . Towards midnight the 'out-College' men would have to go, and one by one the Balliol men would drop off to bed, but as likely as not one intimate friend would stay behind, and it would be well into the small hours before Sligger got to bed.[18]

Through the regular use of his rooms in this way, practically on a daily basis, he came to influence a vast number of men drawn from all disciplines and even other colleges. In the Long Vacations he took reading parties to his Chalet near Saint-Gervais, in the French Alps.[19] He was a cultivated, gentle, and tolerant man who never said or did anything especially remarkable, but he had a great talent for subtle social catalysis, and he was the hub of Balliol life for many years. It is unlikely that any other don has ever known and earned the affection of so many undergraduates.

Urquhart, Strachan Davidson, and Conroy were lifelong bachelors with no great passion for original work, or interest in University affairs. Living in College, with modest private means, they had little to distract them from whole-hearted devotion to their pupils. A. L. Smith was married, but his was a special case. Towards the end of his life, Jowett had conceived the idea of building a grand Tutor's House in Holywell. This was at first envisaged as the initial phase of the scheme to rebuild New Inn Hall as a Balliol annexe, but Jowett was unable to carry the scheme through because the College was against him.[20] Instead he arranged to install Smith and his growing family in the house, encouraging him to expand his practice of taking in young men to be coached for the entrance examination.[21] The Smiths moved into their new home—the King's

[18] Bailey, *Urquhart*, p. 47.

[19] The first Chalet reading party was in 1891. They continued with Urquhart as *Patron* annually for forty years, except during the War (see Bailey, *Urquhart*, for details, including the names of the participants 1891–1931). He died in 1934, but arrangements were made to continue the tradition, and reading parties still go to the Chalet. A related venture in the fifties, providing a peaceful vacation retreat and work-inducing environment at The Mount, Churchill, Oxon., enjoyed only limited success and never got onto a permanent footing (see *Balliol College Record* in the period, especially 1954 p. 11 and 1959 p. 6).

[20] E. Abbott and L. Campbell, *The Life and Letters of Benjamin Jowett*, ii. 1897, p. 344; *Recollections of Thomas Graham Jackson*, ed. B. H. Jackson, 1950, p. 198. Jackson's drawing of the whole scheme, comprising the King's Mound essentially as it was built, and a grand collegiate building where Nos. 5 and 7 Mansfield Road now stand, is on display in the King's Mound.

[21] Numerous references to Smith's pre-Balliol pupils can be found in [M. F. Smith], *A. L. Smith* . . ., 1928.

Mound, by T. G. Jackson—the day after Jowett's death. Their family life became closely integrated with that of the College through the pupils they had who became Balliol men, their hospitality, and Smith's active participation in College sport. They had two sons who entered the College, and five of their seven daughters married Balliol men.[22] The general feeling among the senior Fellows, however, was that a Tutor should be celibate, and live in, if he was to do his job properly. When, as happened with increasing frequency after about 1900, a young Tutor announced that he proposed to 'commit matrimony', he could expect a cool reception from his elders. Neville Talbot's election in 1909 was in effect made conditional on his remaining a resident bachelor: Tutorial Fellows elected whilst still single were obliged to vacate, if they married in the first seven years, and Talbot was told that he would not be able to rely on automatic re-election. There was a statutory requirement for four unmarried men engaged in the educational work of the College to live within the walls, a stipulation which was becoming difficult to meet. In 1913, the Governing Body considered the possibility of changing the letter of the Statute to enable its spirit to be met by accommodating married Tutors on the site. A Committee of four senior Fellows was appointed. They reported that 'if the alteration in the Statutes is made, and if it becomes necessary for a married Fellow to reside in College, it would be much better to have a house in College for a married Fellow, than to make him reside in term in bachelor quarters' and added that 'even apart from such necessity, the Committee think it would be a great gain to the life of the College to have another Fellow resident within the walls'. Their proposal was that most of Staircase XII should be reconstructed, and given a door to the street. An ample house, sufficient for the comfort of a family with children was envisaged, but the plan seems to have been forgotten for good when war broke out.[23]

Research was, like matrimony, also an increasing lure, seducing the younger Fellows from full-time work and intimacy with undergraduates. On the science side, the Laboratories needed more space. None was available in Balliol, so there was expansion into Trinity, a jointly controlled and housed complex being established in 1897. This was primarily to meet the pressures of rising student numbers in science, but it was accompanied by growth in the amount of chemical research carried out. A research community began to evolve. It became the practice for the more committed chemists to stay up a year or two after taking Schools, to do some research and help with the laboratory demonstrating work. Hartley was the leader

[22] At least nine of A. L. Smith's grandchildren, and four of his great-grandchildren, have also been admitted to the College. Furthermore, the marriages of his descendants link them to other well-known Balliol families (Cairns, Davin, Hartley, Hodgkin).

[23] College Meeting Minutes, 17 June and 9 October 1913; MBP 48.

in this, his small group maintaining a modest flow of papers on the physico-chemical properties of solutions from 1906 onwards. The use of College resources for the support of research was somewhat controversial,[24] but it slowly increased in both direct and indirect ways. The modern luxury of sabbatical leave, for example, first appears regularly in the Minutes of this period.[25] But the first explicit approval of research by Tutors had to be forced out of the College. In 1910 H. W. C. Davis (Fellow and Tutor in History, elected 1902) made it clear that he was thinking of resigning, in order to have more time for his own work. A special College Meeting was called to consider how his loss might be averted, and it was agreed that it was 'most desirable that Davis' whole time should not be taken up with tuition, but that, both in his interests and those of the College, time should be given to him both for his research work and his writing, as work itself directly beneficial to the College, and conducive to its reputation as a place of advanced study'. It was decided that, without reduction in stipend, his undergraduate teaching load should be reduced to twenty hours a week and also that he should be allowed to live out if he wanted to. It was enough: Davis stayed for another eleven years.

Asquith linked his famous remark about effortless superiority to reservations about the increasing size of the College. Strachan Davidson was also concerned that the Balliol élite might be diluted if numbers were allowed to rise any more. But the times, and most of the Fellows, were against him. In 1906 E. P. Warren's building (now Staircase XXI) by the back gate enabled more students to be housed.[26] It also had the great novelty of baths in its basement, and tin baths in private rooms (usually with cold water) became a rigour of the past. Warren was employed again in 1912–13, for the construction of the present Staircase XV. This commission emerged from protracted discussions during 1909–11, as a result of which the College almost decided to build Bursary offices and residential accommodation on the east side of the Garden Quadrangle.[27]

---

[24] MBP 7.

[25] It was resolved (7 Nov. 1872) that Tutors and Lecturers should be allowed a 'year of grace' for writing or study, on two-thirds emoluments, every fourth year, but it is not clear whether the privilege in this form was ever used.

[26] For correspondence about Warren's Building of 1906, see MBP 33(1). Warren also built, at the same time, a Lecture Room on a small piece of land which stuck out from the College's northern boundary. Strachan Davidson bought this piece of land (part of the garden of the property then known as 1 St Giles) for the purpose and gave it to the College (see A.3.87). The Lecture Room was demolished when the present Staircase XXII was built. The remainder of 1 St Giles was bought in 1989, but was immediately leased back to the vendors for 25 years: see A.3.157–160.

[27] There has been intermittent discussion about building on the east side of the Garden Quad ever since (e.g. in 1949: MBP 48).

This was put aside on 11 March 1912, and it was resolved instead 'that a three-storeyed building be erected in the Basevi style between the present Basevi and Salvin Buildings, to provide accommodation for 15 undergraduates, and a Junior Common Room on the ground floor: and that the present Junior Common Room[28] be converted into a Fellow's set'. Hartley was the driving force for this project, which was opposed by Strachan Davidson for the same conservative reasons as before, reinforced by the fallacious notion that the gap between the buildings was necessary for the free circulation of fresh air. The new staircase displaced the old latrines—'Lady Periam's'—and the new ones were built on the far side of the quad, where their shell remains, converted into storage space for the gardeners.[29]

Warren's new staircases were functional rather than decorative, although his main façades (1906 outwards, 1913 inwards) are quite pleasing. The aesthetics of the buildings, both inside and out, were very much on the College's mind at this time. In 1910, Paul Waterhouse redesigned and panelled the interior of the Hall, no doubt improving the atmosphere within, but altogether spoiling the external appearance of his father's work, as the panelling made it necessary to block up the lower part of the windows.[30] Any controversy this might have aroused at the time was soon dwarfed. Everyone agreed that the east window Butterfield had designed for his new Chapel in 1858 was hideous, and at the summer Gaudy of 1911 it was announced that it was to be replaced with ancient glass saved from the old Chapel. Walter Morrison, one of the most senior old members present, suggested that the College should be bolder, demolish Butterfield's 'rasher of bacon monstrosity', and build a replica of the sixteenth-century Chapel it had supplanted. He promised £20,000 for the purpose. Strachan Davidson hurriedly called a College Meeting in the vacation. Morrison's offer was accepted. T. G. Jackson was consulted, and he began

---

[28] On the evidence of the Furniture Inventory Books, the JCR was on the Library Staircase from soon after the College resolution of 17 Jan. 1890, in which assent was given 'to the wish of the Undergraduates to have a Junior Common Room on the condition, suggested by themselves, that no wine, beer or spirituous liquors be allowed in it'. See also the unpublished autobiography of Cyril Bailey (Balliol Library, 81 e 10/8), p. 56.

[29] Hartley outlined the circumstances attending the construction of Staircase XV (which he supervised) in H. W. C. Davis, *A History of Balliol College*, revised by R. H. C. Davis and R. [W.] Hunt, 1963, pp. 233–4.

[30] Voluminous papers survive concerning the 1910 work in the Hall by Paul Waterhouse: MBP 29(5 and 6) and MBP 33(5). The Benefactor was Robert Younger, later (as Lord Blanesburgh) Visitor. The work was done by H. H. Martyn and Co. of Cheltenham (on whom see J. Whitaker, *The Best: a History of H. H. Martyn & Co.: Carvers in Wood, Stone and Marble*, 1985).

To
the Master
& Fellows of
Balliol College
this Plate is dedicated
with their special
permission
by the
Artist

S.t Giles'
Street

Here is the
Church of
S.t Mary
Magdalen

New to Trinity
College

Broad Street

21. Balliol in 1911, by Edmund H. New.

to consider the proposition, but things soon went embarrassingly wrong. It transpired that old members generally had become attached to Butterfield's Chapel, and in any case those old enough to remember its predecessor were very few in number. The proposal to knock down a sound building was attacked as a scandalous waste of money, and six of the Fellows, led by A. L. Smith, decided that they ought to retract, setting out their reasons in a memorial to the Master:

The conversations of some of us with old members of the College, and other Oxford men, have brought home to us more and more clearly a considerable feeling of opposition to the proposal. Although of course some of those present at the Gaudy in July associated the religious life of the College with the former Chapel, the associations of the great majority of living Balliol men are with the present Chapel.... We believe that in consideration of the tradition of Balliol policy, of what Balliol stands for in our own minds and in the eyes of the world, it would be economically wrong for us to sanction the expenditure of so large a sum on this object. The whole tendency of the modern development of Oxford, in which Balliol has taken and is taking a leading part, is towards efficiency and economy; the aim in the mind of a large part of modern Oxford is to open the University as widely as possible to all who see fit to come, and to prevent the expenditure of money on objects which are not vital to such development. We do not of course underrate the moral and spiritual value of a beautiful place of religious worship, nor do we forget that this large sum would be the outcome of a munificent benefaction, but we do feel strongly that, when great practical objects are needing all possible assistance and Balliol is looked on to lead the way, as far as it can, in such extensions and developments, it would not be consistent with our responsibility to accept so large a gift for a purpose which is, under the circumstances, a spiritual luxury.

The College then took the unusual, possibly unique, step of writing to all the Honorary Fellows and numerous other distinguished old members to seek their views and advice. The replies gave practically unanimous counsel against Morrison's plan. Most admitted disliking Butterfield's Chapel as a piece of architecture but had affection for it all the same, and thought that replacing it would be an extravagance which would bring discredit on the College. Only one, Lord Francis Hervey, was positive about the merits of the Chapel as it was: 'A boon! A boon! Spare your Chapel—it is a building of great beauty. I am grieved to hear that it is almost doomed; that gold has permeated the hearts and minds of some of those who should be the protectors of this innocent and chaste poem in stone.' In the face of such an overwhelming body of opinion the College could only withdraw, and it became Strachan Davidson's painful duty to put the £20,000 back into the donor's hands. Morrison did not hide his irritation, and gave the money to the University for the support of

Egyptology and the augmentation of professorial pensions; the College proceeded with its original plans for the windows.[31]

The lives of the undergraduates were very closely regulated. Unless they attended Morning Chapel, they had to present themselves in academical dress before 8.00 a.m. under the gateway, where the Porter marked them off, under the watchful eye of the Dean. Attendance in Chapel at least once on Sundays was compulsory, unless a man's parents or guardians objected; under Jowett, attendance at the early morning roll-call had been an acceptable alternative to Chapel, even on Sundays. Leave of absence from Oxford during term was only given for special reasons. Anyone returning to College late in the evening was booked in by the Porter, and reported next day to the Dean. Out-residents did not escape this control: they could only live in approved lodgings, and the keeper of the lodgings was required to report all absences and returns after 10.00 p.m. to the College Porter. It does not seem to have been found necessary to spell out any other disciplinary rules except 'Music Hours' (2–5 p.m. and 7–10 p.m. only). Bounds were mostly set by custom, and the Dean's word was law. Disciplinary resolutions of College Meetings appear occasionally in the Minute Book, standing out from all other business because they alone were still recorded in Latin. This curious and deliberate anachronism is not explained. Perhaps it was to conceal the peccadilloes of the young gentlemen from the Bursary clerks, who had access to the Minutes. Fines, gating (confinement to the College premises), and occasionally impositions, were the penalties for minor infringements, which were dealt with by the Dean. More serious matters went to a College Meeting; the most common outcome was a period of rustication. Students were expected to dine in Hall most days, but could sign off occasionally. Breakfast and lunch were normally taken in private rooms, the servants running a delivery service from the kitchen, except that breakfast was served in Hall on Sundays—a practice introduced in 1894, in order to discourage extravagant private breakfast-parties. In 1900, 105 of the 165 undergraduates lived in. The rooms were fully furnished and lit by electricity from 1896, but any water which was needed had to be carried in, coal fires were the only form of heating, and there were no lavatories or bathrooms near by. Most men would have had a sitting-room, and a small adjoining bedroom; they were looked after by the staircase 'scout' (manservant). There was a Junior Common Room (JCR), but it had nothing like the centrally important position in College life of today's JCR. Membership was not compulsory, and it was little more than a place

---

[31] The correspondence with T. G. Jackson, Walter Morrison, the Honorary Fellows, *et al.* about the 1911 proposal to rebuild the Chapel is in the Archives: D.10.16.

for tea and newspapers. JCR Minutes survive from 1903, when an attempt to reorganize and instil some life into it seems to have been made, but they are exclusively concerned with domestic trivia. Literary and debating societies, on the other hand, were vigorous. The most important were the Dervorguilla (founded 1871), the Brackenbury (1877), and the Arnold (1889)—all were debating societies, and their programmes all ranged over similar political, social, and humorous territory. The Musical Society also flourished, usually offering five concerts a term, with special performances during Eights Week. Eights Week, in the summer term, was when the inter-college boat races were held. Rowing was practically a religion to the greater part of the University, and Eights Week also provided an excuse for balls and general junketing. The College Boat Club had been firmly established since about 1840, and rowing was the dominant sport in 1900, as it still is. Other sports—tennis, soccer, rugby, cricket, hockey— were not played much on an organized College basis until about 1860– 80, but from that time became increasingly popular.[32] Until 1889 there was no College field, and teams played in scattered locations, without a settled base. This Jowett began to remedy in 1889 and 1891, when two adjacent pieces of land in Holywell were bought from Merton, which then owned almost the whole of the parish. The original field was to the north of Love Lane, which no longer exists, but which then ran in a straight line from the present Eastman House to the point where Savile and Mansfield Roads now intersect. When Jowett died in 1893, it was thought appropriate to commemorate him by continuing the colonization of Holywell which he had begun, and extending the field southwards. This meant closing Love Lane, lopping off the northern ends of the gardens of several houses in Holywell Street, and driving a new road through from St Cross Road (then called Church Street) to Mansfield Road, replacing Love Lane, but further south. The negotiations with Merton and others for this complex arrangement were carried out by Strachan Davidson and Conroy. The necessary work was carried out in stages, as the leases of the houses affected permitted. The present layout of The Master's Field, bounded by Jowett Walk to the south, was completed in 1898.[33]

[32] A. L. Smith was a great friend to all kinds of College sport from 1879 onwards. All the sports clubs in College combined to form a single strong administrative and financial organ through his initiative in 1880: student sport and recreation is still run through the 'Amalgamated Clubs'.

[33] More detail of the piecemeal way The Master's Field was acquired is given by J. H. Jones, in 'The Development of Holywell between 1700–1900', *Top. Oxon*, 22 (1978), 9. It was clearly the intention that the field should be known as *The* Master's [i.e. Jowett's] Field. The road is correctly called 'Jowett Walk', not 'Jowett's Walk': it did not exist until

Women hardly entered the lives of undergraduates at all. Ernest Barker (Balliol 1893) recalled:[34]

We knew nothing, in those days, of the women students in Oxford. They were few; and they were still in purdah ... I recall only one or two women students at the lectures which I attended (women then rarely read classics); and I remember the chaperones (one with clicking needles, which flew as the lecturer talked) better than the students whom they guarded.

The memories of L. E. Jones (Balliol 1904) were similar:[35]

... We had no truck with girls in our courts and quadrangles, and would certainly have regarded their daily and casual invasion of these sanctuaries as an interruption and a bore. Let them come, less as fellow-creatures than as a distant species, lightly touched by mystery, to Eights Week or to Commemoration Balls, but never to disturb our brave masculine preoccupations! And when they did come, our relations with them were strangely formal and mannered. We waltzed with them at the Balls and they were in our arms, but for the thoughts and words we exchanged with them it was still the age of the square dance and the minuet.

A woman in a private College room would have been quite unthinkable, and when Barker needed nursing through influenza some trouble was taken to find a male nurse to look after him. Women had been allowed to attend formal science lectures in College since 1884, in limited numbers and subject to chaperones—but individual lecturers seem to have been allowed to decide on this for themselves; Sir John Conroy would not allow them to attend his laboratory practical classes, apparently because he thought things might get out of hand if they were allowed to move about informally.[36] Jowett's activities had brought numerous remarkable women into his circle (most notably Florence Nightingale) and he had been instrumental in helping one of them through the University. This was Cornelia Sorabji,[37] Oxford's first Indian woman student. She was determined to qualify as a lawyer and practise on behalf of women in purdah, who were at an enormous disadvantage because they were unable to consult male lawyers. Jowett arranged for her to attend lectures in All Souls and in Balliol, took her under his wing, and was largely responsible for getting a special decree passed so that she could take the BCL exam-

after his death, and a walk along its route in his lifetime would have been an assault course through the back gardens and over the fences of Holywell.

[34] Barker, op. cit., p. 78.   [35] L. E. Jones, op. cit., p. 162.
[36] College Meeting Minutes, 25 Oct. 1884; Conroy Papers, Sir John Conroy to Mrs Johnson (Secretary, Association for the Education of Women), 1893, Letter Book II, fo. 160.
[37] On Cornelia Sorabji (1866–1954), see the DNB and R. Symonds, Oxford and Empire, 1986, p. 258.

ination in 1892. But in the cause of women's education generally, Jowett was cautious. In 1886 he gave some support to the Association for the Education of Women, by delivering lectures on Boswell and Johnson for it in the College Hall, but he was inclined to think that 'the average woman cannot with advantage to herself work as much intellectually as the average man', and that for most women a little genteel study was what was needed, rather than intensive work and competitive examinations.[38] A more positive attitude came in with Caird (perhaps a result of his being Scottish, for coeducation had advanced further in Scotland than in England), and one of the first resolutions of his Mastership was an unqualified College resolution enabling members of the Association for the Education of Women to attend College lectures.[39] He joined the Association on coming into residence as Master, and was its President for the last decade of his life. An outspoken advocate of degrees for women, he was for many years Vice-President of the Council of Somerville College, and was also Chairman of the Oxford Home Students Committee, which controlled the women students in Oxford who were not members of colleges.[40] When he resigned, Balliol was left without a leading representative in the movement for women's education in Oxford. A. L. Smith, and after him A. D. Lindsay, were sympathetic, but their reforming energies were directed more towards the improvement of working-class opportunities. It was sixty years before the College again had a leader who was a real torchbearer for women.

[38] On Jowett's attitude to education for women, see Abbott and Campbell, op. cit. ii. 157.   [39] College Meeting Minutes, 12 Jan. 1894.
[40] H. Jones and J. H. Muirhead, *The Life and Philosophy of Edward Caird*, 1921, p. 150.

17
The Great War

THE Hanover Club was a select University Society, spawned by the 1911 crisis in Anglo-German relations. Its object was 'to promote the cause of good feeling between Germany and England by giving Englishmen and Germans in the University opportunities of meeting, and discussing topics of interest and importance to both nations'. Balliol men, especially Walter Monckton, Philip Guedalla, and Count Felix von Schwerin, were very prominent in it, and its Minute Book has found its way into the College Archives. Aspects of the threat of war were debated, generally with pessimistic and sadly accurate prophetic conclusions. On 5 December 1911 Guedalla gave a 'brilliant paper' on the 'Probable Course of the next European War', declaring 'that the next great European war would be fought out between England and France on the one side, and Germany on the other'. The following February, a motion 'That under the present situation of European politics a rapprochement between England and Germany is an unrealistic ideal' was carried by seven votes to six. But the Hanover Club was a small one, and its life was short. In the early months of 1914 a more carefree attitude prevailed, as the Minute Book of the Brackenbury Society shows:

27 January 1914
In public business, Mr R. H. Thornton moved 'That this House deprecates the present custom of wearing Grey Bags which obtains in this University'. His speech travelled, with a blend of lightness and authority, from the chromatic to the monastic sides of the question, from the College to the Greater World. The Secretary represented, by contrast, a still and small voice: he spoke of the trousers of the British Workman. Mr Macmillan then rose to his feet and spoke of compromise: a plea for the wearing of grey flannel coats. At this point the house remembered an important appointment, and fled like dromedaries in a field of maize.

8 March 1914
In Public Business, Mr G. Elton moved 'that this House condemns the Publication of "Oxford Poetry".' Mr Elton's speech moved gracefully from Motor Busses to Chops and Worcester Sauce, and included a violent attack on the Secretary. The President, opposing the motion, made some relevant remarks about thumb-prints and paper-cutters. Mr M. Wrong gave a sympathetic study of Napoleon. Mr

F. W. Ogilvie shocked the house with a horrible double entendre, and in the ensuing uproar the Secretary was inaudible. Mr V. A. L. Mallet gave a fitting conclusion to the debate by quoting from the unpublished verses of a spiritual housemaid. Members laughed immoderately, and forgot to divide on the motion.

Trinity Term 1914 was an idyllic one, with perfect weather. 'All that summer we punted on the river, bathed, sat in the quad, dined and argued with our friends, debated in the Union, danced at the Commemoration Balls,' remembered Harold Macmillan.[1] Nothing was further from their minds than war, and when Macmillan heard the newspaper-boy's cry 'Murder of Archduke' on 29 June, it did not immediately strike him as significant. Even when war came a few weeks later, it was expected to be over by Christmas. The chance of glory and adventure was too good to miss, and there was a rush to take part before the fun was all over.

Many former members of the College had in their time joined the University Officers' Training Corps; some belonged to the Territorial Army; a few were professional soldiers in the Regular Army. They were the first to go. John Manners, a natural member of the Eton and Balliol set, had joined the Grenadier Guards when he went down in 1913. He was killed in action on 1 September 1914, the first Balliol man to die. Robert Gibson, Fellow and Tutor in Philosophy since 1911, and Acting Domestic Bursar of only a few weeks standing, was mobilized on the first day of the War, and in France before the beginning of Michaelmas Term. He is the only Fellow whose name is on the War Memorial in the Chapel Passage, but all except a handful of the most senior spent the War on military service or work for the Government. The College had two Chaplains in 1914, N. S. Talbot and H. H. Gibbon.[2] Both immediately joined up and served as Army Chaplains in Europe for the duration. Gibbon was a Sandhurst man, who had been invalided out of the Bengal Lancers in 1888. He took to the cloth, and was already a prominent Oxford Evangelical when he was appointed Balliol Chaplain in 1902. He was awarded the OBE, and twice mentioned in dispatches for his wartime service. Talbot was a great giant of a man, an active and much loved Junior Dean. He had distinguished himself in the Boer War before being ordained, and repeated the performance in a different way in the Great War, with an MC and three mentions in dispatches. Science Tutor H. B. Hartley also had a remarkable military career, as Chemical Adviser to the

[1] H. Macmillan, *Winds of Change 1914–1939*, 1966, p. 45. See also the diary of Alfred Balmforth (Balliol 1911, killed at Ypres, 1917) for the Term: MISC 224.

[2] Talbot was Fellow and Chaplain 1909–14, Chaplain again 1919–20, then Bishop of Pretoria 1920–33. Gibbon was Chaplain 1902–27 (Fellow 1913). Further details can be found in the College Registers: on Gibbon, see also G. I. F. Thomson, *The Oxford Pastorate*, 1946.

3rd Army 1915–17, and ultimately became Brigadier-General directing the Chemical Warfare Department of the Ministry of Munitions.

More than nine hundred members of the College went on active service. Nearly two hundred were killed and another two hundred were wounded. G. N. Walford and J. A. Liddell were awarded the VC posthumously; Adrian Carton de Wiart was honoured in the same way,[3] but despite being wounded eight times, he survived to command a division in the Second World War.[4] More than a hundred earned the MC, a dozen of them with Bar. Other decorations included the DSO twenty-four times, the Croix de Guerre several times, and the Iron Cross (First Class) twice. The average mortality for the Balliol men who fought was 22 per cent, double the national rate, and was highest for the youngest. All but thirty-four of the Balliol men who served did so as officers, most of them in the infantry, and it was the young infantry subalterns who generally fared worst, with an average life expectancy, in the horror of the Western Front, which was reckoned in weeks rather than months.[5]

Most of those who died were known only to their families, the College, and God, but several had begun to make names for themselves, and a few were already well known before the war. Raymond Asquith,[6] the Prime Minister's son and an archetypal effortlessly superior Balliol man, was killed in the Battle of the Somme. His death was a poignant sequel to that of Friedrich von Bethman Hollweg (Balliol 1908; killed in action 1915), whose father had been the German Chancellor in 1914. Charles Lister,[7] the poets Julian Grenfell[8] and Patrick Shaw-Stewart,[9] and F. S. Kelly[10] the musician, were cast in the same Eton and Balliol mould as Asquith: all

[3] Five Balliol men have been awarded the VC. A. V. Batten-Pooll, VC, was admitted in 1922; Robert Blair (Balliol 1851) was awarded the VC for an exploit during the Indian Mutiny in 1857. There was almost a distinguished sixth VC: the minutes of the College Meeting of 9 December 1919 record the admission of B. C. Freyberg, VC (later Lord Freyberg, died 1963), but the War Office would not release him, and he never came into residence (information from D. M. Davin, 1985).

[4] A. Carton de Wiart, *Happy Odyssey*, 1950.

[5] Details of the war service of members of the College can be found in the College Registers. Obituaries and photographs of almost all who died are collected together in the 'Balliol College War Memorial Book' (2 vols.), 1924. Neither the War Memorial Book nor the War Memorial in the Chapel Passage is quite complete for the British dead, and German dead do not appear at all: see J. M. Winter, 'Balliol's Lost Generation', *Balliol College Record*, 1975, p. 22, where a statistical analysis is also given.

[6] J. Jolliffe, *Raymond Asquith: Life and Letters*, 1980.

[7] Lord Ribblesdale, *Charles Lister. Letters and Recollections,* 1917.

[8] N. Mosley, *Julian Grenfell. His life and the times of his death 1888–1915*, 1976. See also the *DNB*.

[9] R. Knox, *Patrick Shaw-Stewart*, 1920.

[10] F. S. Kelly (1881–1916; *DNB*) was also the greatest sculler of his time. He won the Diamond Sculls at Henley in 1902, 1903, and 1905 (taking 23 seconds off the record).

22. **The Rugby XV, 1912–13.** *Back Row, left to right:* R. W. H. Mellor; J. H. Lowden (killed 1916); J. D. O. Coates; H. B. Stokes; W. Ker (killed 1916). *Middle row:* N. F. Smith; C. R. Cook; S. J. H. van den Bergh (killed 1917); F. Whittle; W. H. Shepardson. *Sitting on the ground:* W. R. F. Wyley (killed 1916); A. L. Jenkins (killed 1917); J. L. Brown (killed 1918); unidentified; one man missing.

perished. Ronald Poulton[11] was a hero of a slightly different kind. Capped in the English Rugby XV seventeen times between 1909 and 1914, and captain of the team in 1914, he was shot dead one night, while out with a working party in the trenches near Ploegsteert in 1915.

What were their feelings? Julian Grenfell loved war, which was the climax of his life. He revelled in it all, even the excitement of the personal kill, as if it were an entertainment. In October 1914 he wrote to his mother, 'I *adore* war. It is like a big picnic without the objectlessness of a picnic. I've never been so well or so happy.' Three weeks later he described the lone excursion across no man's land to kill a sniper, which won him the DSO:[12]

... So I crawled on again very slowly to the parapet of their trench. It was very exciting. I was not *sure* that there might have been someone there—or a little further along the trench. I peered through their loophole, and saw nobody in the trench. Then the German behind put his head up again. He was laughing and talking. I saw his teeth glisten against my foresight, and I pulled the trigger very steady. He just gave a grunt and crumpled up.

In his Game Book, immediately after a note of '105 partridges' shot in the previous October, he entered the exploit 'November 16th: 1 Pomeranian'. His best-known poem, 'Into Battle', written just before his death in 1915, is a hymn of celebration for life and the fighting man. Eric Lubbock's letters show a more boyish kind of pleasure in adventure, this time in the air:[13]

... Our fight was a splendid one, as both of us were turning and twisting like corkscrews. I was sometimes perpendicularly upwards and sometimes on vertical banks, and then the dive as I chased him down over the trenches was wonderful. My machine however has got to go away for repairs so I shall never see her again, and she was a topping machine ...

When he was recommended for the MC, that was 'topping' too, but when he had killed an opponent, he remarked 'It's an awful thing this war'. He was killed himself, in a dogfight over Ypres in 1917. Others were more thoughtful, like S. H. Hewett, Secretary of the Brackenbury Society in 1914, writing to Urquhart from France two years on:[14]

---

[11] E. B. Poulton, *The Life of Ronald Poulton*, 1919. He is buried near where he fell, but the oak cross which was erected on his grave in 1917 is now fixed against the east wall of Holywell Cemetery.

[12] Mosley, op. cit., p. 242.

[13] Alice Avebury, *Eric Fox Pitt Lubbock*, 1918, p. 182.

[14] S. H. Hewett, *A Scholar's Letters from the Front*, 1918, p. 51.

... One gets hardened to much of the grimness and crudity of things out here, but not so easily to the pathos, the 'lacrimae'. To miss a rifle-grenade by a few yards, or to see one of the best men in one's platoon with his face smashed in, is a horror, or at least a shock to which one may get used: but the feeling of spring in a quiet orchard and repose behind the line—a few days of peace between a monotony and routine of trench-work—have far more power to make one *think* ...

He was lost in the chaos of the Somme soon afterwards. Of course the evidence for the attitudes of the slain is biased. The College War Memorial Book is moving reading, but its fulsome obituary prose is often unconvincing, and the letters of the fallen which were picked for publication are likely to have been selected to illustrate and emphasize their gaiety, courage, piety, and stoicism rather than any feelings of fear, disgust, or resentment they might have had. Even after making due allowance for this, however, the most determined cynic cannot deny that the picture which remains is one of largely uncomplaining and willing sacrifice.

At least one member of the College well qualified to do so raised his voice in public protest. R. H. Tawney, a Scholar of 1899 who had enlisted in the ranks and refused a commission, was badly wounded in action at Fricourt during the summer of 1916, and sent home to recuperate. He was disgusted by the glorified popular image of the carnage which had been established by the newspapers, and published a bitter attack in the following October.[15]

There has been invented a kind of conventional soldier, whose emotions and ideas are those which you find it most easy to assimilate with your coffee and marmalade. And this 'Tommy' is a creature at once ridiculous and disgusting. He is represented as ... finding 'sport' in killing other men, as 'hunting Germans out of dug-outs as a terrier hunts rats' ...

We regard these men who have sat opposite us in the mud as victims of the same catastrophe as ourselves, as our comrades in misery ... we are depicted as merry assassins, rejoicing in the opportunity of a 'scrap' in which we know that more than half our friends will be maimed or killed ... taking a profitless part in a game played by monkeys and organised by lunatics ... in the letters of the rank and file who have spent a winter in the trenches, you will not find war described as 'sport'. It is a load that they carry with aching bones, hating it, ... hoping dimly that by shouldering it now, they will save others from it in the future ...

Tawney recovered from his wound. He was elected to a Balliol Fellowship in 1918.

---

[15] 'Some Reflections of a Soldier', first published in *The Nation*, Oct. 1916; reprinted in R. H. Tawney, *The Attack and Other Papers*, 1953. Four other members were imprisoned for objecting to the War: S. H. Hobhouse (S. Hobhouse, *Forty Years ...*, 1951; *The History of the University of Oxford*, viii, ed. B. Harrison, p. 17); C. H. Haessler and M. L. Rowntree (*Balliol College Register*, 2nd. edn., ed. I. Elliott, 1934); and R. P. Dutt (*DNB*).

Harold Macmillan was also one of the survivors. He came up in 1912, and got a First in Mods in 1914. After some delays he was commissioned into the King's Royal Rifle Corps in November 1915, instead of returning to his work for Greats. Because his battalion was not immediately employed abroad, he became impatient, and through family and Oxford connections wangled an exchange into the Grenadier Guards in March 1915. By September 1916 he had fought at Loos, at Ypres, and on the Somme; he had been wounded, engaged in hand-to-hand combat, and suffered the loss of many friends. No doubt his experience was typical, but it is difficult to believe that many were quite as detached as he was about his last severe wound. He was immobilized in a shell-hole between the lines during the Somme advance of 15 September 1916. He had his Greek *Prometheus* in his pocket, and, whilst he was waiting to be picked up, occasionally feigning death as German soldiers ran by, he made use of it: 'It was a play I knew very well, and seemed not inappropriate to my position. So, as there seemed nothing better to do, I read it intermittently.'[16]

Over half the men who had been expected to keep Michaelmas Term 1914 were caught up in the War, and the number of undergraduates in residence fell sharply from 200 to 90. It fell again in each of the following two terms and remained at about 40 until the Armistice in 1918. The few who did reside were either foreign nationals, or unfit for service, or getting in a few months at University before reaching military age. Of the handful who completed their degrees during the war years, Aldous Huxley is the best known. Poor eyesight kept him out of the Army. In the main, he was taught out of College, although he saw a fair amount of Urquhart. The arrangements for his tuition did not work very well, but his private reading, and his attachment to Lady Ottoline Morrell's court at Garsington, gave him ample intellectual stimulation. 'Crowned with the artificial roses of academic distinction', he went down with a First in 1916.[17]

Although its membership was greatly depleted, the College was not empty. In the autumn of 1914, in fact, there were probably more men living on the premises than at any other time before or since. Three companies, numbering four hundred men, of Kitchener's Army and the Territorials, were quartered in College. From January 1915 to February 1916, eleven groups of subalterns, five hundred men in all, passed through on short training courses. The subalterns were followed by officer cadets: ten companies of a couple of hundred each, one after the other between March 1916 and December 1918. The College assumed the character of a barracks, and the Garden Quad became a drill square. The few remaining dons might easily have resented this military take-over, but they saw it as the College's contribution to the war effort and welcomed the cadets,

[16] Macmillan, op. cit., p. 88.   [17] *Letters of Aldous Huxley*, ed. G. Smith, 1969, p. 112.

taking an active interest in their work and amusements. The cadets for their part took on the role of war-substitute undergraduates with enthusiasm, and at the end of 1917 the Master was able to write of his pleasure that

... the various companies identify themselves with the Colleges in which they are quartered, so that to hear 'well rowed Balliol' greeting a victorious Four of Australian oarsmen, or to hear the tumultuous partisanship expressed on the Master's field in a Balliol v. Trinity match, sounds quite like old times.

Some two thousand men, a quarter of them either Anzacs or Canadians, enjoyed four months' temporary membership of the College in this way. Picked as officer material after service in the ranks, they found Balliol a pleasant respite from the relentless slaughter which probably claimed several hundred of them when they went back with their commissions.[18]

For the small body of undergraduates in residence, life was inevitably rather different from that of the pre-war years, quite apart from the overwhelming presence of the Army. Numerous petty cost-cutting and labour-saving measures were necessary. At the first full College Meeting of the War, for example, it was resolved 'that for the present only cold baths be supplied, and that the times and tariff be left to the Junior Bursar', and the occasional luxury of meals being served in private rooms was abolished. At the same time it was agreed that the concerts which had been arranged should take place, but that the programmes should be scrutinized 'in order to secure that the music shall be such as is suitable to a time of national danger and mourning'; no encores were to be allowed. In October 1915 formal concerts were suspended altogether, but it was decided that 'Dr Walker should be at liberty to organize informal music for members of the University and officers attending the courses of instruction of the Officers Training Corps'. Permission was renewed for the following term, and the tradition of music on Sunday evenings was maintained throughout the War. College societies were in abeyance, and sport was at a greatly reduced level. For all the fit undergraduates except those of neutral nationality, much time and energy which might otherwise have been spent on the river or the Master's Field was applied to military training. The tutorial system operated as usual, the small number of Tutors who were available taking on a tremendous work load. Despite all the difficulties, the Master was able to write hopefully in 1917 that there was 'every reason to think that the traditions of the College are being

---

[18] The principal sources of information for this paragraph are the Master's Christmas Letters of 1917 and 1918 and 'The Souvenir', a record of the residence of A Coy., No. 6 Officers' Cadet Battalion in the College 10 Nov. 1917–26 Feb. 1918, printed for the editor (H. Wardale-Greenwood), 1918.

maintained, and that there will be a revival of its full activities when the War is over'.[19]

Hardly any disciplinary incidents were recorded. 'Rags' were not unknown,[20] but the young bloods whose horseplay had been a problem before the war were almost all fighting overseas. One of the few entries in the College Minutes concerning conduct is a resolution of May 1915 'That in view of his services to the country during the War, the resolution of June 22nd 1912 concerning Mr E. W. Horner be rescinded'. Horner, an old member of 1906–10 vintage, had put himself beyond the pale by causing a gross disturbance along with some Etonian cronies. There had been 'a great bear-fight' in the Quad, and 'all the furniture in one man's rooms was thrown out of the window'.[21] He had been banned from College indefinitely. His restoration to favour spared the College severe embarrassment, as he was shortly afterwards reported wounded in France. He eventually recovered and returned to active service, dying of wounds received in action at the First Battle of Cambrai. The War Memorial Book says of him 'At times he could be exasperating; but he also had, to a marked degree . . . an infinite capacity for being forgiven.'

The College had begun to acquire a somewhat exaggerated cosmopolitan reputation around the turn of the century. In the years before the War, especially after the Rhodes Scholarship scheme was established (1903), there was always a modest number of overseas undergraduates about. The sudden reduction in the number of native-born students in 1914 made the foreigners relatively prominent. There were of course no longer any Germans, but their loss was offset by the fact that Belgian refugees were taken in. Furthermore there was pressure for some of the spare places to be allocated to Indian candidates. Before the War, the College had quietly operated an informal restrictive quota system for Indian students without attracting adverse comment. In 1909, it was minuted 'That this College is strongly of the opinion that it is inadvisable that the total number of Indian Students at the University should be considerably increased, but is prepared, under that condition, to take its fair share of the number'. This position came under heavy fire from the Under-Secretary for India early in 1915:[22]

. . . Your suggestion of a proper 'proportion' of Indian Students in a College is at least capable of being presented in the form that the Indian Students are an undesirable and indigestible element in a College, to be tolerated in a strictly limited dose . . .

[19] The Master's Christmas Letter, 1917.
[20] R. Niven, 'Balliol in 1916–17', *Balliol College Record*, 1984, p. 26.
[21] *Pages from a Family Journal 1888–1915*, privately printed for Eton College, 1916, p. 272.
[22] College Meeting Minutes, 16 March 1915.

The College's reply was cool. They wanted to be helpful, but would not budge on the principle:[23]

... But we wish it to be understood that we intend to adhere to the limit upon the number of oriental students whom we will receive at any one time, upon which we decided some years ago after a careful consideration of the whole problem.

We believe it to be essential to the interest alike of the University in general and of the Indian students themselves that they should not be gathered in too large numbers in any one college: all colleges should take their share, and if each takes a few Orientals, there will be more prospect of a real assimilation of such students in the life of the University. The same considerations have been applied by us to other classes of men who differ from the prevalent type of English Public School boys, and we carefully limit in the same way the numbers of Colonial, American, French and other foreign students in proportion to the total numbers of the College. Our experience shows that if any considerable number of men of one special type are brought together in one college, they tend to keep together and form a small community by themselves apart from the general life of the place.

There was great concern at the beginning of the War about its impact on College finances. Fee and rental income slumped, and there was a substantial new building which looked likely to remain unoccupied. Firm measures were taken. The Master and Fellows imposed a 25 per cent reduction in pay on themselves, and undergraduates in lodgings were required to move back into College. Stricter regulations about the prompt payment of battels were introduced. Difficult circumstances did not, however, inhibit largesse to individuals who were in the forces or in difficulty because of the War. Domestic staff who enlisted were promised the difference between military pay and College wages, as well as being guaranteed a job to come back to. Although Fellowship emoluments were reduced, Fellows absent on war service were still paid—according to their circumstances, but generously. Belgian refugees were allotted rooms on the understanding that they were not expected to pay until they were in a position to do so. As it turned out, the situation was not as black as it seemed, because solvency was preserved by the Army's use of College facilities.

Ezra Hancock, a legendary paragon of a Head Porter, died on 29 November 1914. Under-Porter from 1878, he had been appointed Head Porter by Jowett in 1891. A kind-hearted man of unfailing memory and tact, he was universally well loved and respected, and Ronald Knox's verses about him were widely praised.[24]

[23] College Meeting Minutes, 16 March 1915.

[24] J. W. Mackail, *James Leigh Strachan-Davidson*, 1925, p. 116; L. E. Jones, *An Edwardian Youth*, 1956, p. 9.

23. Ezra Hancock, Head Porter 1891–1914.

The ready hand, the deferential speech
    We knew and loved, the eye with welcome lit—
Was Peter's self more cognizant of each,
    More stern to exclude, more gracious to admit?

'Ask Hancock' was our only common creed
    In Balliol, and although we left your care,
We knew that threshold held a friend indeed;
    Our first impression, our last memory there;

Till that grim Guest, whose coming all men wait,
    Not with belated reveller's blustering din,
But knocking gently, called you to the Gate:
    And you stepped back, and smiling let him in.

Strachan Davidson, worn down by the College's problems and distress over its losses, died suddenly on 28 March 1916.[25] The Fellows in Oxford almost immediately asked A. L. Smith to succeed him. On 4 April, Hartley wrote from France to say that he had heard the news.[26]

... I have always hoped someday to see you Master, little thinking that you would come not to carry on a tradition, but almost to re-establish it ... I don't worry much about Balliol after the war, it seems so distant; I am sure there will be a Balliol, different in some ways to the old one, but in others I trust as near to it as possible. I rejoice that you will be there to command us and to keep the continuity of the College tradition as nobody but you can do. It will be a great work of reconstruction ...

Reconstruction was the catchword of the moment, and Smith sprang on his new platform to assert himself more strongly in the debate. He was already well known for his support of the Workers' Educational Association, but he now had an influential position and he lost no opportunity of pressing his view that national reconstruction could only be achieved by reform and extension of education at all levels. He spoke publicly on the subject all over the country, and was instrumental in co-ordinating the WEA pressure which led ultimately to the Education Act of 1918. This Act, which he described as 'the outcome of the Conference held in the JCR in June 1916',[27] raised the minimum school-leaving age to fourteen and promised the provision of state education to eighteen. In 1917 the Government Reconstruction Committee, which later gave way to the Ministry of Reconstruction, appointed a committee to report on adult education. Smith was its chairman, and Tawney was a member too. Most of its meetings were held in Balliol, and it is 'THE MASTER OF

[25] He is buried in Holywell Cemetery, quite near the entrance, a few feet to the right of the path. The place is marked with a tall Celtic cross inscribed on its base.

[26] Strachan Davidson Papers 30.

[27] The Master's Christmas Letter, 1917.

BALLIOL', not A. L. Smith, who is listed as Chairman.[28] His articles and public addresses at this time are credited in the same way. He brought back to the office of Master that special authority and influence in Government which Jowett had commanded for it. In his message to the College at the end of the War, he quoted from the report of his Adult Education Committee:

Only by rising to the height of our enlarged vision of social duty can we do justice to the spirit generated in our people by the long effort of common aspiration and common suffering. To allow this spirit to die away unused would be a waste compared to which the material waste of the war would be a little thing; it would be a national sin, unpardonable in the eyes of our posterity. We stand at the bar of history for judgement, and we shall be judged by the use we make of this unique opportunity.

[28] Final Report, Adult Education Committee, Ministry of Reconstruction, 1919.

18

Balliol Between the Wars

As soon as men began to be released from the Army, the War Office made special arrangements for returning students. On 9 January 1919 the last contingent of 150 officer cadets left the College. A week later about the same number of undergraduates took their places. By the end of term there were 160 men in residence, of whom 113 had been in the Army. In Trinity Term the number rose to 233, 188 of them ex-servicemen. A few old hands who had matriculated before the War returned to give College life some continuity. About 150 new members admitted since 1914 had not been able to matriculate: 28 of them had been killed, but over three-quarters of the survivors appeared by the end of the first post-war academic year. Before the War the number of undergraduates in the College had rarely exceeded 200, so there was some overcrowding, and resources were strained. In February 1919 it was resolved to establish a 'Colony' for the accommodation of undergraduates at 21 Beaumont Street, and a little later a 'Holywell Colony' was settled at a similar outpost in Holywell.

Even before the War had ended, discussions had begun about the form the College's memorial to its fallen should take. The results were predictable enough: an appeal to increase the endowment, expand the Fellowship, and improve the Chapel; a Memorial listing the names, in the Chapel Passage, and a corresponding book of collected biographies. Members willingly subscribed in remembrance of sacrificed friends, and there was a special camaraderie among the survivors of the fighting.[1] But of the War itself, those who had fought wanted no military reminder. In December 1919 the College accepted a *Minenwerfer* from the War Office as a trophy, and put it in the Fellows' Garden. It was not welcome: it had to go. One night, although it weighed almost half a ton, it was manhandled on to Lady Periam's roof and then, with the Junior Dean actively assisting, heaved over the wall into Trinity, where it devastated a cucumber frame.[2]

[1] A dining club—the '1919 Club'—was formed from the Balliol generation of 1919–20, most of whom had served in the Army. They dined regularly in College for more than sixty years, and only called a halt in 1986, when the survivors decided to make the annual dinner their last.

[2] R. Massey, *When I was Young*, Toronto, 1976, p. 230. See also the account in *The Balliol–Trinity Frontier TT 1919–TT 1931. A Study in Social History*, compiled by T. F. Higham, 1932 (unpublished typescript, Trinity Archive, Higham Papers).

There was still a feeling about that many were 'deterred from coming to the University by the idea that large expenditure is necessary'[3]—an echo of Jowett. Some reduction in the cost of living would be necessary if poorer men were to be attracted to the place. Towards the end of 1918, as the College began to reassemble, measures to increase domestic efficiency and bring costs down were introduced. But in general the life-style of the community returned rapidly to more or less normal (i.e. pre-war) ways. Within a year of the Armistice, the major sports clubs and College institutions, such as the Boys' Club, were on their feet again. There was no Commemoration Ball in 1919, but there was a ten-shilling dance in Hall instead. No undergraduate was to have more than £1 a week credit in the Stores (Bath Olivers 1s. 7d. a tin, Cooper's marmalade 8d. a pot, best whisky 4s. 10d. a bottle) and Buttery, but a limited number of people a day were to be allowed to give luncheon parties in their rooms. Restraint, but not exactly asceticism.

A. L. Smith's Mastership had a momentum of its own by 1920, which was not affected by the erratic health of his last years. He had a major operation in 1921 and died in 1924.[4] He is the easiest of all the College's Masters to warm to, saving of course those still alive. Dr Johnson warns that the author of a lapidary inscription is not on oath, but Smith's tablet in the Chapel rings unusually true.[5]

Let Balliol men remember the name of Arthur Lionel Smith MA, Scholar, Fellow and Master, who for more than fifty years gave himself wholly to this House. He was a man of keen mind, eager spirit and invincible hope; he fired the minds of his pupils with the love of history, and spurred them to a strenuous life; holding no class of men alien, he welcomed students from overseas to the College gladly, and strove to extend the teaching of the University beyond its walls to the workers of England. He fostered with the care of a father the work and play of Balliol Men, followed the fortunes of his friends with constant affection, and bound colleagues and pupils to him in love. He died on the 12th of April 1924, in the 74th year of his life.

He left no obvious successor. Urquhart was Senior Fellow, and had several times acted as Vicegerent very successfully. He commanded enormous respect and was asked to be a candidate, but he declined because he felt he was not the man for the job. He was probably right. As a social

---

[3] Memorandum of Expenses, January 1919: D.3.196. The total cost of living in College was estimated at £140–160 p.a., including £25 p.a. tuition fee and excluding only books, clothes, recreation, and travel. See also the Stores Price Lists: D.3.199.

[4] He is buried in Holywell Cemetery, near the gate, on the left of the path.

[5] His record of universal tolerance is not, however, without stain: in 1920, under pressure from Lord Curzon, he would not allow Andrew Rothstein (Balliol 1916) back into residence because of his communism. (Andrew Rothstein, correspondence with the author, 1994.)

24. A. R. Wheeler posing for F. F. Urquhart beside a captured *Minenwerfer* in the Fellows' Garden, Michaelmas Term 1919. Behind to the right is the Cottage (otherwise Staircase XXIII) which was demolished to make way for the Bernard Sunley Building (Senior Common Room, opened 1966).

stimulant he was unparalleled, and he was a major influence on all who attended his salon or visited his Chalet. But there was an adverse view of him and his presumed homosexuality. His popularity was not universal. Sligger was a sensitive, deeply religious, rather monkish man, without the dynamism for the Mastership. The three Fellows next in seniority to him were all more suitable material: A. W. Pickard-Cambridge, H. B. (General) Hartley, and Cyril Bailey. H. W. C. Davis, by this time Professor of History at Manchester, was also fancied by some.[6] It was generally expected that one of these would be chosen, so old members and the University at large were a little startled by the election of A. D. Lindsay. The votes of the younger Fellows must have been decisive. Their action was construed as a deliberate political statement, because Lindsay was a member of the Independent Labour Party: the first Labour Government was in power. For an active Labour supporter to be the head of an Oxford college was rather shocking. Lindsay, of University College in the first place, had been a Fellow 1906–22, and since then Professor of Moral Philosophy at Glasgow (as Caird had been 1866–93; the chair was Adam Smith's 1752–63). He was a convinced Christian in the Scottish Calvinist tradition, whose philosophical and social thought was interwoven with his faith. He was passionately committed to democracy, education for the working class, and the world's underdogs. The debauches of the Annandale Club and its like, which had been such a feature of the pre-war Balliol, had given him a powerful distaste for the idle rich, although his revulsion was tinged with a certain admiration for the intellectual brilliance of the same set. He was rarely afflicted with doubts about his views, and when normal procedures threatened to obstruct him he was not above underhand means to get his way. A majority against him when he was in the chair, for example, might be declared an impasse calling for deliberation in another, more favourable, forum. He was a very strong-willed Vice-Chancellor (1935–8), pushing through schemes for new science departments, and for the absorption of Lord Nuffield's benefactions by the University. Nuffield College was established along lines mapped out by Lindsay; its foundation was clouded by the resentment Nuffield felt because he thought he had been bullied by Lindsay, and cheated out of the College devoted to engineering which he had really wanted.

Shortly after Lindsay's election as Master was settled, Pickard-Cambridge wrote to him clearing the air:[7]

... what you are sure to hear sooner or later from others and what I would rather tell you myself—that during a great part of our discussions I did not think this

[6] J. R. H. Weaver, *Henry William Carless Davis ...*, 1933, p. 48. See also the *DNB*.
[7] D. Scott, *A. D. Lindsay*, 1971, p. 104.

25. A. D. Lindsay, Master 1924–49.

was the best choice, not for any reason really personal, nor because I did not think you would make a good Master, but because I feared (and still fear!) that the part you have taken in political affairs might, at least for some time, have an unfavourable effect on our sources of recruitment, at a time which in certain ways is rather critical . . .

The prediction that Lindsay would be politically active was well founded, but this did the College no harm. In 1926, during the General Strike, he gently discouraged undergraduates from volunteering to help break it, galvanizing them to campaign for reconciliation instead.[8] When Mahatma Gandhi was in England in 1931, he was most solicitously entertained for two weekends in the Master's Lodgings.[9] Most important of all, in the Oxford by-election of 1938, Lindsay stood for Parliament against Quintin Hogg on an anti-appeasement ticket: he was not elected, but he greatly reduced the Conservative majority. The voting figures were: Hogg 12,797; Lindsay, 12,363. It was a hard-hitting campaign, with slogans such as 'Hitler wants Hogg'. Lindsay's supporters included Harold Macmillan and Edward Heath.

Gandhi's visits to Oxford in 1931 were meant to be rest periods punctuating a hectic programme of political discussions in London, but he did not retreat into seclusion. On the contrary, he spent most of his time at Balliol in discussion. He made a very deep impression on the Lindsays, and Mrs Lindsay kept in touch with him afterwards, even when he was in prison. One of his letters to her from jail is now in the Library,[10] through the kind gift of her daughter. Its message is a moving piece of simple uninhibited saintliness, a unique item from the College's post-bag:

Dear Sister,

Thanks for your sweet letter. Yes, it would be tragic, if God was accessible only to the learned—my feeling coincides with your washerwoman's. There was once

---

[8] A group of them went to London, borrowed a working capital of £500 and an office off the Strand, and there compiled, produced, and distributed a conciliatory newspaper they called *The British Independent*. The prime mover was W. F. Oakeshott, but many others were involved, notably J. R. Hicks. According to P. Mason (*A Shaft of Sunlight*, 1978, p. 63) there were five issues, with a final circulation of 20,000, but copies of only two survive (No. 1, 11 May 1926, and No. 2, 12 May 1926: British Library Newspaper Library; Nuffield College Library; Library of the University of Keele Lindsay Papers, ref. L164). In a letter to the author in 1995, Dr Mason recalled 'the assumption common in the period to the sons of Balliol, that the affairs of the nation could not go forward without guidance from us'. For correspondence etc. about this enterprise see MISC 208.

[9] Scott, op. cit., p. 212. Gandhi stayed in the large ground-floor bedroom in the Master's Lodgings which now serves as an office for the Senior Tutor and Tutor for Admissions. He signed the Master's guest-room book on 26 Oct. and 8 Nov.

[10] This letter (which is also printed in Scott, op. cit., p. 218) was written from Yoravda Central Prison (Poona), 5 Oct. 1932.

a scientific expedition in search of God. The scientists are reported to have come to India and to have found God not in the homes of Brahmins, nor in the palaces of kings, but they found him in a hut of an untouchable. Hence my cry to God to admit me to the untouchable fold. After fifty years trial He found me worthy to be so admitted. And I rejoice over the event. My love to all of you, in which Mahadev joins.

Yours

M K Gandhi

Lindsay's appointment to the Mastership might have cost the College a very special member. In the summer of 1920, a Norwegian schoolmaster made discreet enquiries about the possibility of two of his pupils being admitted. Smith replied as follows:

As to your second case, which I understand is to be kept quite private and confidential at present, I have only communicated it to a few of my colleagues, to get their consent.

We feel of course that it is a compliment to be invited to help in the education of one who will have in his hands so much of the future welfare of a whole nation. At the same time, we should in his own interest, as well as in accordance with our own principles, expect evidence that he would be up to our standard in intellectual capacity, that is, be fit to 'read for Honours',—which means that he would aim above the minimum required for a mere Pass Degree. More than half the students now in Oxford, and all of those admitted to our College, 'read for Honours' in this sense.

We should also like to be assured that he wishes to mix on quite equal terms with other men, as the Prince of Wales did at Magdalen College, spending, as he said, two very happy years there in this manner.

The subject of this letter was Crown Prince Olav of Norway. Three years later King Haakon was still minded to send his son to Balliol, 'I. Because it was chosen by the Prince's old schoolmaster. II. Because of B's reputation as a working college. III. Because there must be a very definite understanding that the Prince is being sent to an English University to work.' However, around Christmas 1923, the Prince of Wales 'stood up for his College' and tried to persuade King Haakon that Prince Olav would be better off at Magdalen. The King had been told that Balliol was 'one of the best, if not the best', but he took further counsel in January 1924. This only confirmed his original inclination, although he admitted a slight fear about Balliol that 'perhaps the boys got very socialistic ideas there'. His advisers seem to have hesitated again when Lindsay was elected, but the King was not alarmed: '. . . it does not look as if he is trying to enforce his personal point of view on the young people under his charge, so I do not see any reason why I should change my mind on sending my son to his college.' This was the last word on the matter.[11] The Prince, later HM King Olav V, resided 1924–6, and put on record the high regard he came to have for Lindsay.[12]

The number of junior members in residence peaked at 275 in 1920, and then settled around 240 as Lindsay's Mastership began, a net increase of about 25 per cent on the average pre-war figure. It rose jerkily to about 265 over the next fifteen years. In December 1924, 140 men were accommodated in College in 138 sets, compared to 232 people in single rooms now. Space was created for a few more souls by E. P. Warren in 1926, with the construction of Dicey Staircase—so called not because it is precarious, but in honour of the distinguished lawyer A. V. Dicey (Balliol 1854), and not really a staircase at all but actually a corridor running along the top of the Bristol–Basevi block. The JCR, which was to blossom as a centre of College life from this point, was enlarged at the same time by allowing it to expand into what is now the television-room at the foot of Staircase XIV. The financial burden of these works was carried in part by an anonymous undergraduate Benefactor. He was later identified as W. A. Coolidge.[13] But the Dicey scheme was not enough to meet the College's need for more accommodation. In 1927 an approach was made to Merton with a view to acquiring more property in the Holywell area. The houses and gardens between Jowett Walk and Holywell Street were considered first, but Merton was unwilling to sell. When this was reported to a College Meeting on 14 December 1927, 'the Estates Bursar was instructed to ascertain whether Merton would negotiate for the disposal of Holywell Manor House'. This proved a much more fruitful initiative. In 1929 the College was able to purchase, 'for the erection of a building to be used as *Aedes Annexae*', the freehold of most of the Manor site, with a 99-year lease of the ancient Manor House itself, all for a consideration of £12,000 and a nominal rent of £10 p.a. The purpose of this rather complicated arrangement was to satisfy Merton's understandable reluctance to part entirely with the focal point of a manor they had held for more than six hundred years.

The history of the Manor House in the two centuries before it passed into Balliol's hands is rather indistinctly defined, but not without colour. In the mid and late eighteenth century it was divided into three tenements.

---

[11] King Haakon's letters are in the Archives, together with the other correspondence and papers about his son's admission and studies: D.23.42 and D.23.42a (both closed for the time being). See also MISC 110.

[12] Scott, op. cit., Foreword.

[13] W. A. Coolidge (Balliol 1924) has since been a major Benefactor in other ways, notably in creating the Coolidge Atlantic Crossing Trust, which enables several undergraduate members to travel extensively in the USA every summer.

The central one served as a workhouse. To the north-east was a covered arena for cock-fighting which belonged to a tavern known as 'The Cockpit';[14] to the south, between the house and the church, there was a spring and 'Cold Bath'. The workhouse is not heard of again after about 1800, but the 'Cold Bath' was popular well into the nineteenth century, frequented, for example, by John Henry Newman around 1825.[15] It was large enough for several people to swim about in at the same time, and had dressing-rooms at the east and west ends. By the time the cockpit (a polygonal building with a conical roof, constructed before 1675) was demolished in 1842, it was already derelict, although the associated inn was still in business under the new sign of 'The Robin Hood'. The Oxford Female Penitentiary Society, founded in 1832 to help retired prostitutes and other fallen women, had a base in the Manor House from about 1860, and it is starkly labelled 'Female Penitentiary' on early Ordnance Survey maps. This institution, which would have been more kindly described as a home for unfortunate girls, was run by an Anglican Sisterhood,[16] under whom this use of the Manor continued until 1929. The Sisters were no doubt partly dependent on donations, but supported themselves and their charges, to some extent, by operating a laundry service.[17] They also persuaded themselves that the source of the former 'Cold Bath' was the original Holy Well of Holywell,[18] and restored it as the centre-piece of the little chapel they built over it: its site is now a garden, and only the chapel walls remain.[19]

George Kennedy (Balliol 1901) was engaged as architect for the Holywell project, and given the rather difficult brief of producing a plan which would accommodate about forty members, on an irregular

---

[14] The construction of a new dining room at Holywell Manor in 1992–3 led to the discovery of the wall of a circular structure (cut through by a later well shaft) which was identified as the fighting stage of the cockpit: see *The Oxford Archaeological Unit Newsletter*, December 1992, and MISC 207.

[15] *The Letters and Diaries of John Henry Newman*, ed. I. Ker and T. Gornall, ii, 197, p. 161.

[16] The Community of St John the Baptist of Clewer; there were about half a dozen Sisters.

[17] MBP 240 contains an invoice of 1921 from 'The Manor House, Holywell' for washing Buttery table-linen: cheques were to be payable to 'The Sister Superior'. A 1928 ground-floor plan (in MBP 327) shows that a considerable part of the premises was given over to the laundry business.

[18] There were in fact several wells in the vicinity which are candidates for this identification: all dried up when the drainage of the vicinity was radically altered, by engineering works connected with the opening of Holywell Cemetery.

[19] For further information about the history of Holywell Manor, see (*a*) V. H. G. [V. H. Galbraith], *A Memorandum of Holywell Manor*, 1937, (*b*) *VCH*, Oxfordshire, iv, and (*c*) Mrs Bryan Stapleton, *A History of the Post-Reformation Catholic Missions in Oxfordshire*, 1906, pp. 211–22.

triangular site, without destruction of the ancient Manor House. He considered leaving it standing free as a separate entity, but concluded that this would make it an 'archaeological incubus'. The proposal he produced in 1931 involved demolition of practically everything on the site except the old house itself, which was to be incorporated into a larger complex of connected buildings. Once agreed, the plan was swiftly executed, despite the fact that insufficient funds had been raised, in order to take advantage of the low building costs prevailing at the time. This boldness met with general approval from old members, who eventually subscribed the entire cost of about £50,000. The new annexe was ready to be opened by Lord Blanesburgh at the beginning of Michaelmas Term 1932. There was accommodation for 37 students, each of whom had a bedroom and sitting-room; two sets were also provided for Fellows, one of them to be a resident warden, known as the *Praefectus*. The first was J. S. Fulton. No dinner was served there, but breakfast was, and tea in a JCR. Lunch could also be provided in rooms on request. The whole enterprise was staffed by a man and wife as porter and housekeeper, a cook, a bathman, four ladies giving room service, a JCR helper, and a couple of boys. There were no male 'scouts', in striking contrast to the old College. Charges were such that the cost of living there was about the same as in College itself. There was central heating, running water in each set, and bathrooms on all floors. In these respects the Manor was well in advance of the Broad Street site. In 1930, plumbing had yet to be installed in most parts of the College. Although fitful modernization was under way, water had to be carried to some rooms as late as 1951. Lavatories and baths were not conveniently distributed either, but were mostly concentrated in the Garden Quad and in the basement of Staircase XX respectively. The residents of today are spared the rigours of these arrangements, although several staircases are still waiting for central heating. Whilst he was reluctant to accept that Holywell Manor was luxurious, the Domestic Bursar admitted in 1934 that 'the amenities to life are certainly considerably greater than what one is accustomed to in the ancient College Buildings'. At any rate, there was no difficulty at all in filling the Manor up, mostly from men who would otherwise have lived in the town—i.e. usually third- and fourth-year students. The picture of relative luxury is confirmed by an undergraduate's report to his mother in 1935:[20]

Holywell Manor gets full marks! My sitting-room and bedroom are both very

---

[20] Pat Moss, *Canadian and English Letters 1924–1936*, 1940, p. 362. T. P. Moss died whilst still up on 15 May 1936, in very mysterious circumstances which have never been satisfactorily explained: see P. McIntyre, in the *Oxford Mail*, 20 June 1986. See also the *Oxford Mail*, 16 Feb. and 16 Mar. 1971.

comfortable indeed, and the really satisfying thing is that the place is well thought out, and not full of irritating little stupidities like wrongly placed lights. It is certainly very nice having running water in one's bedroom. Also having breakfast brought in instead of going into hall for it is a welcome luxury, and the whole place, being quite new, is clean and not as dingy and drab as the rooms in College. It was only built four or five years ago, I believe, and is very attractive outside as well as in—neo-Georgian, in yellowish-gray stone, with a charming little garden quad at the back built round on three sides.

Great care was taken over the original furnishings of the Manor and the layout of the garden, for which old members and other benefactors were encouraged to give unusual plants and shrubs. All this went very smoothly, but there was difficulty over the decoration of the JCR ante-room. Gilbert Spencer was approached about painting murals there, with the legend of the College's foundation as their theme. But for reasons which are now concealed—expense or cold feet at an adventurous design, one suspects— it was decided not to proceed. Kennedy made an impassioned plea for reconsideration. He felt that the constraints within which he had been obliged to work had involved a sacrifice of dignity and coherence. Externally he had tried to 'put the building on easy terms with its site and to connect its future with the fortunes of the garden and the trees planted in relation to it', trusting that it would 'acquire in the course of time a certain human and disarming quality in its appearance'. Internally, on the other hand, he was much less confident. The murals were essential to give some colour and character to what might otherwise have given a mean, inarticulate, anonymous, non-committal impression'. He carried the College with him; Spencer's murals were unveiled on 18 March 1936.[21]

The Holywell Manor scheme would certainly have foundered without the support of the Master, but on this occasion the leadership and ideas came mainly from Kenneth Bell. Bell was a History Tutor, superficially the antithesis of his colleague Urquhart, with whom he was supposed by undergraduates to be permanently at odds. An ex-Army, back-slapping, hearty, beer-drinking man of action is what he was perceived by some of them to be,[22] although the fact that after an upheaval in his private life

---

[21] Material relating to the acquisition, extension, and early days of Holywell Manor is in the Formal Archives (see especially A.5), and with Departmental Records under Holywell Manor; see also MBP 327 and MISC 4 (which includes some photographs taken during the building work). On the murals, which were executed 1934–6, see G. Spencer, *Memoirs of a Painter*, 1974; the idea for the theme must have been derived from those painted by C. E. Fremantle on Staircase II (1st floor, then occupied by R. A. B. Mynors; now numbered II.5 and occupied by the author) about 1929.

[22] At least this was how Graham Greene (*A Sort of Life*, 1971) and Anthony Powell (*Infants of the Spring*, 1976) saw him.

he took holy orders and became a parish priest suggests there was more to him than this. Bell's pivotal role in the Manor business arose because he was Secretary of the Balliol Society, which he had initiated in 1926. The stated purpose of the Society was to strengthen the ties between old members and the College, particularly in the first place by producing a revised College Register, but also by improving and enlarging the annual *Balliol College Record*, organizing dinners, and so on. As Bell was to show, the Balliol Society also provided a potent means for raising funds, and for involving old members in what the College was doing in Holywell.

The Dicey scheme and Holywell Manor were not the only building projects of the period. In 1924 Warren designed, and had built for the College, Nos. 5 and 7 Mansfield Road, bringing the number of houses available for married Fellows around The Master's Field to seven. The following year, the alteration of the interior of the Chapel was begun.[23] Butterfield's intricate designs on the walls were obliterated, the floor was paved with a simple pattern of black and white marble, and the east end was panelled in walnut. This was done under the supervision of Walter Tapper. He was probably assisted by his son Michael, who also designed the ornate silver-gilt altar[24] which was made as a War Memorial in 1927, and who supervised the execution of the second phase of his late father's plans for the Chapel ten years later. In 1937 further panelling, including a new organ case, was put up, and new seating was installed, all at the expense of the Visitor, Lord Blanesburgh.[25] Fortunately, the seventeenth-century pulpit from the old Chapel was still in existence,[26] so it was restored to its former position.[27] Of the furnishings and fittings there today, only the altar rails (made in memory of Cyril Bailey in 1960) have been added since the Tappers' scheme for the transformation of the Victorian interior was completed. Externally Butterfield's hand will show

[23] See *Balliol College Record*, 1925, p. 17.

[24] [D. W. Jackson], 'The Chapel Altar', *Balliol College Record*, 1980, p. 76.

[25] See *Balliol College Record*, 1937, p. 5.

[26] It is not clear where the old pulpit was between 1854 and 1937. Photographs of Butterfield's interior taken about 1890–1900 show no pulpit at either end of the Chapel (PHOT 11). It was resolved, without recorded explanation, on 10 Oct. 1890, that the pulpit should be removed from Chapel. The present pulpit is shown on the left, near the altar, in a drawing of the interior of the old Chapel of about 1820 (the drawing hangs in the Old Common Room; copy in PHOT 11).

[27] The restoration of the ancient front gates to the College in 1926 was similarly symbolic. They had been sold for firewood in the previous century, but had survived, and come into the hands of an antique dealer, from whom two Balliol men bought them for the College. They now hang in the Library Passage: *Balliol College Record* 1926, p. 3.

as long as his Chapel stands, but inside only the roof paintwork over the east end bears his stamp.[28]

What undergraduate life was like in the thirties is well conveyed by the recollections of K. C. Bowen (Balliol 1937):[29]

I had £200 p.a.[30] in scholarships, almost as much as a starting professional salary. My family had very limited means and I was even able to help with some of the cost of keeping me in vacations. I never had to worry about how to make ends meet, but I was, in any case, not extravagant, by nature and background.

I spent money on domestic items, like cups and saucers (3 *d.* or 6 *d.* from Woolworths); on clothes, Balliol blazer, ties, scarf, sports shirts and so on; and on books. Typically, I paid only pence for most books, haunting the second-hand shops, although even new books were hideously cheap in comparison with today. Accounts could be opened in shops without identification being asked for—we just stated name and college. Settlement was never pressed very hard, and a term's account could run on until the next lot of money arrived. The 'young gentlemen' were trusted to a degree which is part of a bygone age.

There were no domestic chores. Laundries were cheap and the scouts sent things out and checked them back in, shirts, collars, bedclothes, the lot. Meals were mainly taken in Hall, except for tea in the JCR (crumpets, cucumber sandwiches, toasted teacakes and suchlike). When lectures allowed, I might have coffee in town in the mornings and, as an occasional afternoon extravagance, a Devon Tea (11 *d.*!) at the Cadena in the Cornmarket—with an orchestra playing. I seldom ate an evening meal out of College: if I had to go elsewhere, I would make up with tea and cakes in my room.

Most afternoons were given to exercise: soccer, hockey, squash, and tennis were my main games (I still use the same tennis racquet, 37 *s.* 6 *d.* Blue Flash, bought in 1937 from Shepherd and Woodward—made to last) ... Even through morning lectures, I was not inactive, cycling madly between colleges, for the students all came to the lecturer in his or her own college (I had little feeling of University—I was at Balliol, not Oxford—there were colleges, all different, with different ways of life and different excellences). My bike, a good one, cost 2 *s.* 6 *d.* and I gave it to the College bike-man when I went down. I also biked out to sports grounds, sometimes an energetic way of preparing for a hard game and sometimes a weary way of returning.

I went often to films, repertory cinema at the Scala in particular, and to the film society there on Sundays. I rarely missed the New Theatre's pre-London runs: if one queued early enough, it cost 6 *d.*, or 1 *s.* for closer seats in the gallery.

---

[28] Some small pieces of movable furniture which are still in the sanctuary may be to Butterfield's design. The pews were sent partly to Duloe, and partly to Burbage, for use in the College churches there. the rest of the woodwork was put into the cellar beneath the Old Common Room, where most of it remains.

[29] These unpublished recollections, kindly written at the present author's request, are now in the College Archives.

[30] Compare n. 3, above.

Scouts were among the most important people in the College, philosophers and friends who addressed us as 'Sir', told us off when stupidity overrode intelligence, sold useful things like gowns and teapots, and kept our rooms tidy and serviced. Nelson was my first scout, in XXI–3, a rather dark but nice room—and, luxury, a separate bedroom.[31] I am glad he became Head Scout, he was a splendid counsellor. It was the custom to give 2 s. 6 d. at the end of each term and similar small sums for special service, but even his ordinary service was special and he always seemed to be available in a crisis. He laid fires and kept them going while I was out, if the weather was cold, and he brought piping hot water every morning—for there was no running water in the rooms and no bathrooms except for the communal baths. These, usefully, were just below, with the one-armed Cornell presiding, always with the glowing stub of a cigarette in the corner of his mouth. He too was a philosopher. I once complained of a missing pane of glass at street pavement level. Cornell said: 'If a man passes and looks in, it doesn't matter; if a lady passes and doesn't look in, it doesn't matter; and if she does, sir, she's no lady, so it still doesn't matter.'

A great deal of time was spent talking, of here and eternity. We would gather in someone's room in an evening and might go on for many hours; although my habit was to go to bed about 10pm—I worked hard and played hard—I often stayed later. I remember once that we broke up at 6am and I walked in the Parks before breakfast and then just about survived the next day. My friends were chemists, historians, classicists, PPE and English students—mathematicians were, on the whole, classmates with whom I was friendly. The others were the ones I learnt from in those evening sessions or on daytime walks—all sorts of topics, invariably ending with religion.

Life was, I suppose, both spartan and regulated, by modern standards. In our first terms, at least, we were to be in College after 9pm several days a week, and never out after midnight without special permission. I remember running back many times after enjoying drinks and discussions in other colleges. And, of course, pubs were out of bounds, and gowns had to be worn or carried after 9pm. Even in College there were logistic problems: with only the dons' private lavatories on the staircases, and chamber pots having restricted capacity, frequent visits were paid to Lady Periam (now deceased). Rain or shine, most people had to brave the elements for relief, as for baths. In my second year, luxury intervened. I had a large room in Holywell Manor ...

Disciplinary regulation was still firm, although it was beginning to relax in some respects. The College Rules of 1919 stated that undergraduates were expected to attend Chapel at least once on Sundays, unless they had leave from the Master—but the requirement is not repeated in any subsequent edition. Attendance at roll-call, on the other hand, was nomin-

---

[31] Before, and immediately after, the First World War everyone had a 'set' of rooms (i.e. a study–sitting-room and a bedroom), but by the late thirties quite a lot of the accommodation had been rearranged for use as bed-sitters.

ally required right up to the Second World War, except for graduates of other universities and mature students. Late return or overnight absence was treated as a very serious matter, and considerable ingenuity was employed in frustrating the authorities.

... Absence from rooms in College at night was normally covered by arranging for a friend to untidy the bedclothes, and urinate in the chamber pot, the night before; thereby giving the impression that the owner had risen early, and (when the scout called him with a jug of hot water) was already up and abroad. Alternatively, it was possible to climb into College before dawn, though by that method Balliol was a College not particularly easy of access ...[32]

An accomplice, and the fire-escape rope-ladders provided on some of the upper floors, made things easier, as F. E. von Stumm (Balliol 1933) recalls:[33]

... Now after 50 years I must confess that on a warm June night I helped [my cousin] climb out of his window overlooking Broad Street in full evening dress to attend a dance somewhere in town. We had found a rope ladder in a cupboard outside his room. In the morning he woke me up sleeping in his bed by pulling a string which was attached to my leg and I let down the rope ladder again. Happy youth ...

Sport flourished, but never dominated the College. There were triumphs both for teams[34] and individuals,[35] and corporate pride was taken in them without any undue fuss. This was partly because the College had so much else to be proud of—distinguished alumni by the score, academic prowess (in 1928 a record was set with 27 Firsts out of some 65 candidates, i.e. nearly 40 per cent[36]), success in Union elections,[37] and so on. But a liberal attitude left everyone free to go his own way within reasonable limits,

[32] Powell, op. cit., p. 157. Although it was difficult to climb into Balliol at night there were ways—from the roof of a hansom cab driven on to the pavement, for example (Massey, op. cit., p. 227). In the early sixties there was a route up a drain-pipe, and along a ledge into a bathroom window on Staircase XIII, until a serious accident prompted the College to allow unrestricted access through the gate.

[33] Unpublished, as n. 29, above.

[34] Head of the River in Torpids 1928 and 1929; Inter-Collegiate Rugby Cup 1930 and 1933.

[35] Nine Rowing Blues and sixteen Rugby Football Blues between 1920 and 1939; the Nawab of Pataudi (Balliol 1927) scored 238 not out against Cambridge in 1931, a record which still stands.

[36] In the same year the next most successful college got 12 Firsts.

[37] Twenty-three Balliol men were elected President of the Union between 1918 and 1940 (i.e. more than one in three presidents were from Balliol).

with no pressure to conform or take part in extra-curricular activities which did not appeal to personal taste. For the same reason, there was a wide variety of active societies—some twenty of them, ranging from the long-standing and serious to the ephemeral and frivolous. The Musical Society, which had already become a College institution, held its thousandth concert on Sunday, 28 November 1937, with Edward Heath conducting the choir.[38] This Jowett would have applauded. Acting, on the other hand, was embraced by the authorities of the twenties rather cautiously. Thus, on 7 November 1923, it was agreed to give leave for a play to be performed in College only if a list of actors was submitted and subject to veto. It was laid down that nobody would be allowed to act in the play if they were also performing with the OUDS. This cool attitude did not deter Raymond Massey (Balliol 1919) from laying the foundations of a distinguished career on stage and screen. By 1926 the Governing Body had softened, and permission was given for 'certain members of the College to arrange to tour in the South of England acting the "Hippolytus"'. This was in fact the third tour of 'The Balliol Players'. A troupe of Balliol men would put on a play—usually a Greek classic—after the end of Trinity Term at a series of public schools and country houses. One of the participants has freely admitted that

... for most of those who took part the tour meant an excuse for a pleasant fortnight travelling gently round the west and south of England, sleeping in the open, usually well fortified by evenings at various pubs which had met us before, and made allowances. It was, of course, necessary for a small group of enthusiasts to make sure there was a play cast and rehearsed when the time came for the tour to begin, but for most of the company the play was an amusing incidental, I should say, rather than the main objective.

To judge from the programmes which survive in the Archives, this somewhat understates the standards set, but it was a light-hearted tradition, more important for its *esprit de corps* than its contribution to dramatic art.[39]

Balliol's histrionic talents were also employed in one of the most successful undergraduate hoaxes ever perpetrated, in 1922. Notices were distributed to everyone of importance in Oxford inviting them to a lecture entitled 'Freud and the New Psychology' which was to be given by

---

[38] [R.] A. Burns and R. [J.] Wilson, *The Balliol Concerts: A Centenary History*, n.d. [1986].

[39] There is a good collection of material relating to the Balliol Players in the Archives: everything used here is in this collection. A history of the first ten years was privately printed in 1933: T. G. Usborne and M. S. Whitehouse (eds.), *The Balliol Players 1923–1932*. See also P. Mason *A Shaft of Sunlight*, 1978, pp. 58–61. The tradition survived the War, and remained vigorous until about 1965, but then degenerated. Complaints about the script, delivery and off-stage behaviour became an embarrassment, and the Dean had reluctantly to deliver the *coup de grâce* at a College Meeting held on 15 Nov. 1978.

Professor Emil Busch in the Town Hall on 15 March. A large audience turned up on the day. The lecturer looked the part—black morning coat, stiff wing-collar, dark bow-tie, luxuriant moustache. His discourse was mostly about 'Co-aesthesia'.

My honoured master Freud has overlooked this factor ... Co-aesthesia is to a large extent the cause of sexuality. Co-aesthesia fragments the personality. Co-aesthesia also knits it together ... It is the all-denying microcosm, the inner consciousness of communal being, ladies and gentlemen ...

Afterwards there was a lively discussion, and full reports appeared in the papers. It was all pseudo-scientific rubbish. The hoaxer was George Edinger (Balliol 1919), who later had a distinguished career as a cosmopolitan journalist.[40]

The Fellowship more than doubled in size (from 14 to 30) between the wars, although the student body expanded by only 10 per cent (from 240 to 265, ignoring the post-war bulge). This meant there was a wider subject-coverage among the Fellows, and enabled the amount of farming out to be reduced. It also added greatly to the distinction of an already distinguished body. Roy Ridley, possibly the model for Dorothy Sayer's Lord Peter Wimsey,[41] was the first Fellow in English, elected in 1920. C. N. Hinshelwood, Nobel laureate in Chemistry, was also elected in that year. J. W. Nicholson appears on the list in 1921. He became a great worry to his colleagues, and was eventually certified insane, spending the last twenty-five years of his life in institutional obscurity. His name has been practically forgotten because of this misfortune, but it now seems that his early work was one of the main influences on the development of Niels Bohr's atomic theory.[42] The Fellows appointed in the twenties also included great names in historical and classical scholarship like V. H. Galbraith and R. A. B. Mynors, both of whom took senior academic posts outside the College after service as Tutors. Charles Morris, Humphrey Sumner, and J. S. Fulton did likewise. Balliol Tutors had left College teaching before to become University Professors—T. H. Green, H. W. C. Davis, and A. W. Pickard-Cambridge, for example. These cases could have been due to individual temperament or special circumstances. But now opinion was moving towards the acceptance of research, and the advancement of knowledge, rather than teaching, as the primary function of a university, and men who would remain by conviction and self-dedication College Tutors all their working days, like Urquhart, were becoming fewer. A. B.

[40] C. Day Lewis and C. Fenby, *Anatomy of Oxford*, 1938, p. 261; see also MISC 74.
[41] B. Reynolds (ed.), *The Letters of Dorothy L. Sayers*, 1995, p. 79 and p. 80 n. 21.
[42] R. McCormmach, 'The Atomic Theory of John William Nicholson', *Archive for History of Exact Sciences*, iii (1966), 160. See also MBP 49.

Rodger (Tutor in Modern History 1923–61; Dean 1933–52), Theo Tylor (Tutor in Law 1926–67; Estates Bursar 1947–67), and Russell Meiggs (Tutor in Ancient History 1939–70; Praefectus of Holywell Manor 1945–69) were among the last of the breed. The balance of the Governing Body was also given more weight on the research side in this period, by the introduction of Junior Research Fellowships, and by the attachment of three important new chairs. There were only two Professor-Fellows in 1919: A. A. Macdonell, Boden Professor of Sanskrit, and T. R. Merton, *ad hominem* Professor of Spectroscopy. To these were added, as *ex-officio* Fellows, in 1926 the Professor of Pharmacology (first incumbent J. A. Gunn, 1917–37), in 1930 the George Eastman Visiting Professor (first incumbent J. L. Lowes, 1930–1), and in 1937 the Nuffield Professor of Surgery (first incumbent H. W. B. Cairns, 1937–52). All these connections have brought kudos to the College, but the George Eastman Professorship stands out. It has had an unequalled succession of stars, including several Nobel laureates. One of them, indeed, was awarded two Nobel prizes— Linus Pauling, for Chemistry and Peace.[43]

The change in attitudes towards research and new subjects is well illustrated by the development of the Balliol–Trinity Laboratories. Before the War, these had been primarily teaching laboratories, with an annual research output under Hartley's direction of two or three papers. After the War this quickly rose to about 15 p.a., and Hinshelwood became the leading light. The nature and calibre of the work changed too, from precise but relatively routine physico-chemical measurements to fundamental explorations of chemical kinetics and photochemistry. Over 300 original papers appeared between 1919 and 1939, and the Laboratories became the University Department of Physical Chemistry in all but name, in recognition of which the College arms are displayed on the façade of the present Departmental building in the University Science Area.[44]

The administration of the College was changed quickly after the War. Previously everything had been done by the Master and Fellows, working with practically no assistance. But limited bureaucracy began to set in about 1920. From 1924, the Minutes of College Meetings were typed up by someone from the slowly expanding, but still very small, secretariat, instead of being written in longhand by a Fellow; the post of College Secretary was also created in that year. The office of Domestic Bursar had been established in 1920, with a job description very much like today's.

[43] It was while he was in Oxford as George Eastman Professor and Fellow of the College that he discovered the α-helix: L. Pauling, *Protein Science*, ii (1993), 1060.
[44] T. [W. M.] Smith, 'The Balliol Trinity Laboratories', in J. [M.] Prest (ed.), *Balliol Studies*, 1982. See also K. J. Laidler, 'Chemical Kinetics and the Oxford College Laboratories', *Archive for History of Exact Sciences*, xxxviii (1988), 197.

The first Domestic Bursar was the monocled Colonel Duke.[45] He was a resourceful and energetic professional soldier, whose previous experience of University life was limited to a brief period as a Cambridge under-graduate, but his Army career had involved him in supply, accountancy, and large-scale organizational problems. The College was cautious at first, and supervised him with a small committee, but he soon showed his capabilities and was given a free hand. He was made a Fellow in 1929. When he retired from office in 1939, the College took the then remarkable step of appointing Miss Annie Bradbury to succeed him—chosen from a short list of four women, with a clear and stated prejudice in favour of a woman in the post.[46] She was never made a Fellow, but in other respects enjoyed the same status as her male immediate predecessors had done, and has a good claim to be regarded as the first woman member of the College. Shortly before Colonel Duke arrived on the scene, it was decided to attempt to fill all available College rooms for fourteen vacation weeks of every year with 'members of approved conferences and societies and other approved visitors'.[47] Duke was able to implement this policy very effectively. Thus was the 'conference industry', which has become a vital part of the College's life and economy, born.[48] One of the first Balliol conferences was arranged by the Industrial Welfare Society on 17–20 September 1920;[49] now known as the Industrial Society, the same organ-ization has been coming back ever since. The running of the College's external affairs also underwent radical change in this period. The estates from which most of the endowment income was derived were too widely scattered for administrative efficiency, and in 1920 it was resolved to redevelop the Long Benton estate, take advice about Ufton, Woodstock, and Wootton, and seek permission to dispose of a farm at Stamfordham.[50] All were eventually sold, and the College now holds none of the agricultural land with which it was endowed in its early days; it has mostly been turned into paper wealth in the City of London. The real estate currently

---

[45] See College Meeting Minutes, 1920, and MBP 197.

[46] See College Meeting Minutes, 21 April 1939. She attended College Meetings (without a vote) from 1941; she retired in 1956.

[47] College Meeting Minutes, 16 March 1920.

[48] According to P. Sturges, writing in *The Oxford Times*, 20 April 1984, Balliol was the first college to engage in conference business. The decision to do so seems to have been based partly on financial considerations, and partly on concern for the welfare of the domestic staff. Until this time it was usual for most of the scouts to be laid off in the long vacation. Many of them found seasonal work in seaside hotels, but in some cases the system caused hardship. The introduction of a conference programme gave them uninterrupted employment.

[49] Information kindly provided in 1984 by M. Hyde, Secretary of the Industrial Society.

[50] College Meeting Minutes, 7 Oct. 1920.

owned is all urban property. Paradoxically, at the same time as the College was beginning to think about reducing its holdings of land, it greatly increased its ecclesiastical patronage, by accepting, in 1919, Lady Lucas's gift of the advowsons of Harrold, Blunham, Clophill, and Flitton with Pulloxhill (all in Bedfordshire) and Aston Flamville with Burbage (Leicestershire).[51] But the report of the committee which was sent to inspect the Bedfordshire parishes reveals an altogether different attitude to patronage from that which had obtained a hundred years earlier:[52]

It is evident that the patronage recently accepted by the College of these Lucas Livings presents an important problem. The College, having no axe of its own to grind in the matter, can do great good by selecting the right kind of incumbents, can exercise a very healthy and stimulating supervision by occasional visits, can give much greater encouragement to deserving incumbents, and can bring to bear greater weight and influence in the parishes than any individual patron. On the other hand, the College has no pecuniary interest whatever in these parishes or in this district except the alternate presentation to St Mary's, Bedford. The College would not like the patronage to be exercised at all in favour of Balliol men as such, but only according to absolute fitness between the different applicants. It is impossible for us to escape a considerable expenditure of time in considering applications and testimonials, and in interviewing applicants, etc, a certain expenditure of money in the visitations which ought to be made from time to time by members of the Patronage Committee and others; and there is also the inevitable obligation, moral if not strictly legal, which will tend to impose burdens on the College in the way of subscriptions, etc, to various good works in the seven parishes (five in Bedfordshire and two in Leicestershire) in which the presentation to the livings has been transferred to the College under the Lucas bequest. An ideal thing would have been that, along with the devolution of the patronage to the College, there should have gone the assignment of a regular sustentation fund for subscriptions, contributions to buildings, etc; but it would be very difficult just now to make such a suggestion to the present donor of the patronage, and it would have been very ungracious to refuse a trust offered to us by our old member the late Lord Lucas, and confirmed by his sister, the present Lady Lucas.

The careers of the men who were admitted to the College between 1918 and 1939 are all set out in the printed Registers. It would therefore be superfluous to linger much on the subject. Suffice it to say that their achievements are as diverse and worthwhile as those of their predecessors. The pages of *Who's Who* are thick with them—diplomats, professors, captains of industry, educators, senior civil servants, judges, men of letters, etc. But just a few have risen above that worthy level to become leaders with influence over millions. One such was Shogi Rabbani (Shogi Effendi),

---

[51] The advowsons of Fordham and Great Horkesley in Essex were similarly acquired in 1921. [52] MBP 221.

who was recalled from Balliol to Haifa in 1921, to be revered first
Guardian of the Baha'i Faith. Another surprising product of a nursery
which had so recently been better known for its Christian dignitaries is
Israel Brodie (Balliol 1916; Chief Rabbi of the United Hebrew Congregation of the British Commonwealth 1948–65). Of Heads of State,
HM King Olav V of Norway was, as Crown Prince, at Balliol 1924–6;
Dr Richard von Weizsäcker, President of the Federal Republic of
Germany, was briefly associated with the College in 1937. Only one Balliol
man of the period became Prime Minister (Edward Heath, President of
the JCR 1938, Prime Minister 1970–4), but his successors as President of
the JCR in 1939 and 1940 (Denis Healey and Roy Jenkins) might easily
have emulated him. Both of them made it as far as the Exchequer, but
no further.

Soon after Hitler seized power in 1933, the distinguished Jewish bio-
chemist Hans Krebs was peremptorily ejected from the Medical Faculty
of Freiberg University.[53] Word of this quickly reached Balliol, and on
17 May it was agreed, unknown to Krebs, that the possibility of securing
his services should be investigated. A month later he left Germany and
travelled to Oxford, where he saw the Master, who later wrote making a
definite offer. Unfortunately, Lindsay handled the meeting badly, and
unintentionally gave him the quite false impression that nobody was
particularly keen to have him, so Krebs went to Cambridge, and thus
denied the College association with another Hinshelwood. But there were
other distinguished Jewish refugee scholars adrift. On 19 June, the College
decided to assist at least one. Although it was wary about accepting lasting
responsibilities, Albrecht Mendelssohn Bartholdy was promised help in
the autumn of 1933: his chair of international law at Hamburg had been
abolished, in order to get rid of him. He replied to Lindsay, an old friend,
with passionate thanks: '. . . with things being what they are here and
today, it is a message from another world to get such a letter.' The
following year, with help raised from several trusts and benefactors, the
College elected him to a Fellowship.[54] In 1938 some ten or a dozen
displaced German and Austrian scholars were given a temporary home
and financial assistance for a few weeks or months, while permanent
places were being found for them in Britain and America.[55] They were

[53] H. Krebs, *Reminiscences and Reflections*, 1981.

[54] See A. Mendelssohn Bartholdy's personal file. Rudolph Olden, a distinguished anti-
Nazi writer, was a similar case, admitted as a senior associate in 1937; despite his
exceptionally sound political credentials, he was interned early in the War and then
pressurized into emigrating to the USA; he was drowned in September 1940, along with
77 young British evacuees and many others, when the *City of Benares* was torpedoed in
mid-Atlantic (M. Finetti, *Die Zeit*, 21 Sept. 1990).

[55] See College Meeting Minutes, 18 July and 5 Dec. 1938.

senior established people, but young Jews were also fleeing from Germany. One such was Walter Lewy-Lingen, a nineteen-year-old Berliner who obtained a short-term UK visa late in 1938. Balliol admitted him to read chemistry, and obtained an extension of his permit. He joined the Army in 1940—now with the more English-sounding name Landon—and died of wounds after the Battle of Arnhem in 1944.[56] There was another young German from Balliol who died in 1944, and earned a place of honour for his name on the College War Memorial, but he was an Aryan aristocrat: Adam von Trott zu Solz (Balliol 1931).[57] He was executed for his part in the abortive conspiracy to assassinate Hitler on 20 July 1944.

In November 1937 the College discussed air-raid precautions, and in the following May turned its mind to such matters as the safe storage of its treasures in the event of war. By June 1939, contingency plans were well advanced, and the Minutes seem to expect the worst, although the College Dance, and the special Gaudy for Cyril Bailey's retirement,[58] went ahead as planned. Three months later, as the lights began to go out all over Europe, the Office of Works requisitioned most of the College[59] for use by the Royal Institute of International Affairs,[60] and the Balliol men in residence were exiled to accommodation arranged in Trinity.

[56] See W. Landon's personal file.

[57] G. MacDonogh, *A Good German. Adam von Trott zu Solz*, 1989. The listing of German names (especially that of Claus von Bohlen und Halbach, Luftwaffe, Iron Cross, killed in action Jan. 1940, the first reported Balliol fatality of the War) on the War Memorial was opposed by a strident minority of old members in 1947 (MBP 53).

[58] Bailey had been deeply disappointed at not being elected Master in 1924, but he became an equally revered figure in Balliol anyway; he also served on the Council of Lady Margaret Hall 1915–53 (Chairman 1921–39); see the *DNB* and his unpublished autobiography (Balliol Library, 81 e 10/8). Although he retired in 1939, he returned to help out as Lecturer in Classics in 1940.

[59] Several other college buildings were similarly requisitioned at this time: e.g. those of St Hugh's became a hospital, and its people took over Holywell Manor for the duration (P. Griffin, ed., *St Hugh's. One Hundred Years of Womens' Education in Oxford*, 1986). As it turned out that Chatham House did not in fact need all the available rooms, Balliol's exile only lasted a year, and a sort of College life resumed on home territory in 1940, with A. G. Ogston as resident Dean and ARP supremo (see A. G. Ogston, 'Reminiscences 1911–1988', unpublished typescript, copy in, *inter alia*, Balliol Library).

[60] Alias Chatham House (Director of Studies: A. J. Toynbee), whose staff were transferred to Balliol on 2 Sept. 1939 as the Foreign Research and Press Service (FRPS), from which the Foreign Office Research Department (FORD) evolved. The main function of this organization, which remained in place until mid-1943, was to prepare reports, mostly based on newspaper gleanings, on events in enemy-controlled and neutral countries; it occupied the Library and the greater part of the west side of the Garden Quad; many Balliol people were involved as well as Toynbee, including R. P. Bell (Scandinavian Section) and B. H. Sumner (Russian Section). This information was kindly provided by R. P. Bell, and also by the Department of Research and Analysis of the Foreign and Commonwealth Office (successor to FRPS and FORD), for whom R. A. Longmire has compiled a history, including an account of its origins.

Epilogue

EARLY in 1943, it was decided that the intelligence work being done by Chatham House in Balliol should be reorganized and relocated. The War Office had designs on the requisitioned accommodation which would be released by this move, but Lindsay wanted to put one of his own projects[1] into action on home ground. Churchill squashed the War Office to prevent a squabble.[2]

Prime Minister to Secretary of State for War and
Minister of Works

25 Apr 43

I am informed that arrangements had been made for weekly and week-end courses to be given in Balliol College, Oxford, for Dominion and American troops, where the university atmosphere would be particularly valuable in giving these troops from overseas a further insight into English life and history. I understand that this proposal is in jeopardy because the War Office are proposing to take over Balliol College for a senior officers' course.

I am sure that Balliol College would be of more value in the former rôle, and I can hardly believe that no alternative accommodation for the War Office could be found. Let me have a report on some of the alternatives.

Most of the College was derequisitioned on 9 August 1943, and the first Short Leave Course began on the same day.[3] The Courses each ran for about a week, comprising lectures on aspects of English life and culture, discussions, and social events. Some seventy or eighty servicemen, mostly American and Canadian, but with a sprinkling of British and other nationalities, attended each Course. There were only short breaks between Courses, and several thousand people had passed through the College in this way when the programme ended in October 1945.[4] The drive and

---

[1] Lindsay was very active in promoting democratic ideals during the war, especially through educational schemes for the armed forces: see D. Scott, *A. D. Lindsay: A Biography*, Oxford, 1971, chapter 15.

[2] W. S. Churchill, *The Second World War. Volume IV, The Hinge of Fate*, 1951, p. 851.

[3] College Meeting Minutes, 8 Oct. 1943. The Joint Recruiting Board remained on Staircase II, and the Institute of Statistics continued to occupy Staircases V–VII, the Front Lecture Room (now the Bursary), and the Lower Library, until 1946.

[4] As the bureaucratic aspects of the Courses had nothing to do with Balliol itself, there are no systematic records in the Archives. In particular, very few names of the participants are known to the College. See, however, Scott, op. cit., MISC 46, and MISC 98.10 (which includes lists of names for the Courses which began 24 July 1944, 31 July 1944, and 26

26. Short Leave Course participants relaxing in the Garden Quad, 1944 or 1945. The grassy bank in the foreground is part of the surroundings of a fire brigade water reservoir. Two such 'static water tanks' were set up as part of the College's air-raid precautions; the other can also be seen, just in front of the buildings to the left of the Hall, which were demolished in 1966. Both reservoirs were removed after the war, and the lawns were re-levelled.

finance came from the Westminster Fund,[5] a private trust for the promotion of Anglo-American understanding, of which Lindsay was a trustee; local administration was in the hands of a Committee chaired by him, with Giles Alington of University College as co-ordinator. Two Balliol dons were regularly involved as lecturers: M. R. Ridley and J. N. Bryson. Every effort was made to make those attending feel that they were welcome, and that they had joined the College in a small way, as indeed the certificates they were given on departure implied. In 1946, Lindsay was awarded the Medal of Freedom with Bronze Palm[6] 'for exceptional achievement which aided the United States in the prosecution of the war against the enemy in Continental Europe, as Chairman of the University Committee for Leave Courses at Balliol College', in which capacity his 'tireless energy' had made 'an essential contribution to the success of the war effort' by giving 'young officers and enlisted men' a 'cultural and intellectual background' and 'physical and spiritual recreation'—in plainer language, for boosting morale.

Part of the Master's Field was requisitioned by the Ministry of Works in late 1943. The College 'did not feel it proper to make any objections', but it was resolved to press for a swift release of the land when normal conditions prevailed again, because the whole Field would be needed for sport when there was a full complement of undergraduates. The Government promised that the area required by the 'Admiralty project for building hutments' would be 'given up within six months after the termination of hostilities with Germany'.[7] The huts, which were on the south side of the Field, were needed to provide temporary working accommodation for an expanding organization known as the ISTD (Inter Services Topographical Department). The ISTD was formed early in the war, and based at the School of Geography. Its task was to prepare topographical intelligence summaries for use by military commanders and planners, especially in relation to landing operations. W. S. Watt, Classics Fellow, was attached to the ISTD from 1941, as a civilian editor employed by the Admiralty Naval Intelligence Division (NID); he was commended for the clarity and value of the report he assembled for the North African

February 1945, with copies of other ephemera to do with the Courses). M. R. Hardwick (Balliol 1945) attended the Course which began 24 July 1944: it was his first contact with the College. There is an excellent set of Ministry of Information photographs with informative captions in the Imperial War Museum, reference D19108–D19152.

[5] The Westminster Fund's other main activity was the support of the Churchill Club at Ashburnham House, Westminster School.
[6] The documentation is with the Lindsay Papers in the Library of the University of Keele, reference L223.
[7] College Meeting Minutes, 14 Jan. and 21 April 1944.

landings of late 1942, Operation Torch. By 1944, so many people were engaged in ISTD work that the space available in the School of Geography (and Manchester College on the other side of the road, which was also used) was not enough, hence the huts on the Master's Field.[8] In 1946, the possibility of upgrading the huts vacated by the ISTD, to enable fifty undergraduates of the demobilization bulge to be housed in them, was costed. A plan involving sharing these temporary facilities with New College and Brasenose was discussed,[9] but before the beginning of Michaelmas Term the huts were taken over by squatters.[10] The squatters were still there over six months later, and the City Corporation was pressed by the Ministry of Health (which thought the huts 'in excellent physical condition', and was willing to authorize expenditure on improvement) to negotiate with the College for a ten-year lease, using the threat of extending the requisition period by five years anyway if the College would not agree.[11] The College submitted to this blackmail, and granted a lease at a rent of £120 p.a. until September 1957;[12] the Corporation agreed to maintain the huts in a decent state and ensure that they were occupied by 'respectable and responsible tenants only', and to return the site to the College in good order when it was vacated. Towards the end of the lease, the City Housing Committee asked for an extension until 1960, but this was refused, and the area was cleared and returfed by the City at the end of 1957.[13]

Of the Fellows given leave for war work or military service, some, including several of those near the top of the seniority list,[14] never came back. Two successive Senior Fellows[15] resigned during the war for personal reasons which would now be thought irrelevant. And four more long-standing Tutorial Fellows moved on to distinguished posts elsewhere soon after the War ended.[16] By 1948, all but two—Rodger and Tylor—

---

[8] Information kindly provided by Mrs P. Woodward, Administrator of the School of Geography (MISC 107) and W. S. Watt (MISC 108.e).

[9] College Meeting Minutes, 13 Feb. (Report of the Domestic Committee) and 27 May 1946.

[10] College Meeting Minutes, 11 Oct. 1946.

[11] College Meeting Minutes, 14 July 1947.

[12] College Meeting Minutes, 8 Dec. 1947. The lease agreement is the Archives (A.3.148); it has a plan annexed showing twelve huts on a site running along the whole of Jowett Walk, from the School of Geography to the gates of the Master's Field, and extending 108 feet into the Field.

[13] College Meeting Minutes, 7 Oct. and 12 Dec. 1955, 11 Nov. and 9 Dec. 1957.

[14] C. R. Morris, B. H. Sumner and R. A. B. Mynors.

[15] K. N. Bell and M. R. Ridley; the spirit in which they resigned—that is to say, whether they jumped or were pushed—does not show in the formal record.

[16] J. S. Fulton, D. J. Allan, W. M. Allen, and J. H. C. Whitehead.

of the Fellows elected before Hitler came to power had gone. They had younger colleagues remaining on the strength from the later thirties[17] who were, like them, to be powerful influences in the life of the College for another fifteen years or more, but there had to be a substantial infusion of new blood. In 1944 there was a discussion about the procedure for selecting Fellows. By degrees during the previous hundred years, there had been erosion of the severe and open process for the examination of Fellowship candidates, on which the College's modern vigour had been founded. The Statutes prescribed that the Master should nominate Fellows for election by the Governing Body, and it seems that things had generally been done very informally.[18] There had no doubt usually been considerable consultation between the Master and the Fellows before nominations were made, and it is difficult to see that any harm was done, unless a high proportion of gremial Tutors is deemed a bad thing in itself.[19] But in future, 'when the College had decided that an election is desirable', a Committee was to be set up, comprising 'one or more of the Tutorial Fellows in the subject concerned, together with one or more Tutorial Fellows (ordinarily one senior and one junior) in other subjects, with the Master as Chairman'. The Committee was to make a recommendation to the College after 'surveying the field and investigating the qualifications' of the candidates; vacancies were normally to be advertised, and if the Committee felt otherwise the College was to be given an explanation.[20] The Statutes were not changed, however, and the Master's prerogative was preserved by a technicality. When W. A. Waters was elected, the decisive minute[21] was 'After full discussion it was agreed that if at the next Stated General Meeting the Master nominates Dr W. A. Waters the Master and Fellows will accept the nomination and elect Dr Waters.' The background politics are not recorded, but Lindsay sounded almost apologetic about this important decision—which, on paper at least,

[17] R. P. Bell, R. W. Southern, A. G. Ogston, J. E. C. Hill, and Russell Meiggs.

[18] W. S. Watt (Balliol 1933), for example, was simply called in by the Master in January 1937 just before he took Schools and asked if he would like to succeed Cyril Bailey; he was elected in 1938 after brief service as a Lecturer in Glasgow (W. S. Watt to the author, 29 January 1992).

[19] Even if a biased selection system did operate, it must be admitted that the Balliol men who were elected in this period were both able and committed. Probably the high proportion of Balliol-bred Fellows elected before the war has more to do with their homing instinct than prejudice; even after nearly half a century of advertised and above-board elections, we find in the *Balliol College Record* for 1994 that of 55 Fellows, 19 had been student members. If we look only at the Tutorial Fellows with tenure, the proportion is even higher: 15 out of 32.

[20] College Meeting Minutes, 17 June 1944.

[21] College Meeting Minutes, 12 November 1944.

diminished the Master's power significantly—when he reported it to old members two years later,[22] although by then the new rules had been put to the test more than half a dozen times. All five of the new Official Fellows elected 1944–5 were strangers to the College.[23]

What may well have been the first attempts at a quantitative comparison of academic performance between Oxford colleges were made by W. S. Watt in 1949 and 1950.[24] The annual 'Norrington Table', although it employs (it is claimed) more subtle computations of excellence, has its origins in Watt's analyses. The Norrington Tables have appeared in the national press annually since 1964, and while it became the done thing in the Senior Common Rooms of the University to affect indifference to what they claimed to demonstrate, the Tables were as avidly studied by dons as they were by potential applicants for admission and their advisers.[25] The bases of the comparisons have changed over the years, which makes long-term comparisons problematic. But it is possible to make some convincingly sweeping statements: that in the period 1956–91 a higher percentage of Balliol candidates obtained Firsts than the percentage averaged over the whole University in every year except 1988, and even in that year Balliol's score was a mere whisker below the average;[26] and that by Norrington's criteria Balliol was the most consistently successful of all the colleges during 1964–86.[27] It is pleasing to add as a finishing touch to this Epilogue that in 1995 the College came top of the Table.[28]

Norrington's Table is an incomplete indicator of a college's academic performance, because it tells only of undergraduate achievements. In Balliol's case, undergraduates now make up less than two-thirds of the resident membership. Although the success of the graduate students is not so easily quantified, they have in recent years been outstanding in numbers of higher degrees, University Prizes, and Research Fellowships obtained.

Sport has been an important part of Balliol life since the Second World War, especially during the fifties, but has had little to do with the shaping

[22] *Balliol College Record*, 1946, p. 3.

[23] W. A. Waters, E. T. Williams, F. L. M. Willis-Bund, J. P. Corbett, and Thomas Balogh.

[24] *Balliol College Record*, 1949, p. 17, and 1950, p. 6.

[25] See A. J. P. Kenny on the subject, writing as Master, *Balliol College Record*, 1985, p. 9, and 1988, pp. 13–15.

[26] Data produced for the Annual Academic Report 1990/1 by K. C. Hannabuss: Tutorial Board Paper TP91/25.

[27] The *Encyclopaedia of Oxford* (ed. C. Hibbert and A. Hibbert), 1988, entry for *Norrington Table*.

[28] *The Times* Norrington Table of 17 July 1995 actually placed Balliol third, but it was wrongly computed: 34 Balliol people got Firsts, not 33 as reported.

of the College's ethos since the mid-sixties. Nobody has been admitted for prowess on the playing field or the river since Keir's time; nor has indifference or ineptitude at games been held against anybody. It has not been possible for many years to label Balliol 'sporty'. Paradoxically, as the College's sense of identity with its teams and crews has diminished, and the profiles of élitist sportsmen have become lower, the average amount of time spent at exercise by students has increased, and the range of sports they engage in has widened. The 1st VIII and the 1st XV have no special prominence now, and the Gordouli Boat Club no longer advertise themselves with distinctive scarves or commit postprandial outrages, swinging in and out of decanal approval. The competitive and institutional spirit has largely evaporated, making it easier for the ordinary reasonably fit but not particularly athletic member to participate for the simplest and best of reasons: fun and relaxation. In the fifties when the College was Head of the River—as it was three times—the ensuing Bump Supper was a binge for everyone, but nowadays more than half the College would wonder what all the fuss was about.

We might expect to find some relationship between the College's consistently successful academic record and admissions policy. In 1945 this was set out as follows:

for scholarships and exhibitions we judge—granted the usual formal testimonial to character—solely by intellectual performance and promise. But this is not so with our selection of commoners. The number of candidates for admission has lately been so much in excess of our vacancies that our entrance examination has become pretty savagely competitive, but in determining the results of the competition we take into consideration, and very serious consideration, other factors besides comparative marks on paper work ... we would far rather have a boy here who is likely to cut some ice, and so far as one can forecast, some more after he goes down, even if he only gets a decent third, than a boy who drifts blamelessly through his three years, gets some kind of middle second, and leaves without having made any mark here and apparently having no prospect of making a mark anywhere else later ...[29]

Fifty years on, the Tutor for Admissions would get brickbats from all directions for such heresy, but he was obviously not alone in attaching great importance to non-academic qualities. *The Master's Letter* in the annual *Balliol College Record* of the fifties and early sixties, for example, recites sporting achievements with an enthusiasm which sometimes seems to value them quite as much as Firsts and University Prizes. In 1949, old members were told 'The College continues to admit a number of men as

---

[29] Paper by M. R. R[idley], then Tutor for Admissions, dated 1 Feb. 1945, attached with the meeting's approval to College Meeting Minutes, 17 Feb. 1945.

Commoners on their showing in the Scholarship Examinations, but still admits many Commoners by the old-fashioned gate, despite the larger numbers attempting to storm it.'[30] And a year later it is reported that 'Nearly 30 [a little less than 10%] sons of old members were in residence'.[31] In 1986, the Junior Common Room professed unease on the subject of family connections, and the Master wrote to the President:[32]

20 February 1986

Dear President

You asked me to put on paper the College's policy regarding the admission of candidates who have family connections with the College. I am happy to do so, but I think it would be more helpful if I set my reply in the general context of non-academic criteria for admission to the College.

It is the College's policy that academic criteria should be paramount in determining admission to Balliol: we should aim to admit those among the candidates who are best qualified to pursue with profit the courses for which they have applied. Promise as well as performance should be taken into account in determining the academic potentiality of a candidate; but no candidate should be admitted in preference to a candidate who is better qualified academically. This would be unfair to the candidate passed over; it is also no service to the candidate chosen. Nobody admitted to Balliol should ever be able to think that they were accepted on non-academic grounds in favour of better candidates.

There are, however, cases where it is not possible to decide between candidates on the basis of purely academic criteria. In these cases there is no unfairness in allowing non-academic criteria to have weight in the decision. Such considerations include the College's desire to achieve a good balance between the sexes; our aim to secure an intake from a wide variety of schools; the potentiality of a candidate to contribute to extra curricular activities; and the existence of a family connection with the College. The weight to be given to any or all of these factors will naturally differ from time to time and from candidate to candidate.

In order to ensure that I was not misrepresenting College policy I read a draft of this letter to my colleagues at Tutorial Board and they have approved its content.

Yours sincerely

Anthony Kenny

There was much discussion following this letter, and it was agreed[33] that in future the College Office should no longer draw the attention of

---

[30] *Balliol College Record*, 1949. The old-fashioned gate, i.e. admission following an interview without much formality, was still open in 1960–1, when the present author entered thereby, having applied to the College on alphabetical grounds.

[31] *Balliol College Record*, 1950.

[32] MISC 108.f.

[33] Tutorial Board Minute TB86/125Y.

Fellows to the family connections of admissions candidates. In the following year, however, fifteen children of old members were admitted (i.e. about 10 per cent), one of them[34] a representative of a veritable Balliol dynasty, able to claim blood relationship to at least twenty men in the College before him. The proportion of members with a family connection of some sort varies erratically from year to year, but now averages 5–15 per cent; it was only slightly greater a century ago. But the bias now is introduced by the candidates themselves wanting to follow in family footsteps. Anyway, the very notion that there has been at any time in the recent past, or could have been, a clear College policy on admissions is dashed by the fact that the decisions in individual cases have for many years been taken by the appropriate small groups of subject Tutors.

Student admission and Fellowship election procedures determine the composition of a college, and therefore its character; Mastership elections *a fortiori*. In his review of the 1963 revised edition of Davis's *A History of Balliol College*, G. E. Aylmer asked the rhetorical question 'Indeed, do Masters really matter so very much anyway: do they make a great difference, or are they merely a chronological convenience for college historians?'[35] They matter as individuals much less than they did. Since the Second World War, the power of the Master has been reduced bit by bit, and diluted by the expansion of the Fellowship, which has never lacked forceful characters. But although the Master is now a constitutional monarch, he is still the most influential member of the Governing Body, as a simple consequence of being its Chairman, and the wider world tends to see him in the role of ship's captain. So Masters are indeed important. Mastership elections are of special interest, because they stimulate discussions of very broad issues of policy. Furthermore, they are titillating to a degree unequalled by most other College business, with glimpses of intrigue, party formation, and backbiting.

Lindsay was invited to enter the House of Lords during the war, but did not accept until October 1945, when a Labour Government was in power. He put his resignation into the College's hands, but was asked to wait and see how much his peerage would interfere with his obligations to Balliol.[36] He for his part felt that he should see the College back on its feet. Although he was politically active, he was never given Government office. But he was increasingly involved in educational affairs, especially the foundation of the University of Keele. He remained as Master until 1949, when he was in any event required by Statute to retire, moving on

---

[34] P. Z. Fremantle.

[35] G. E. Aylmer (Master of St Peter's College 1978–91), *Balliol College Record*, 1964, p. 11.

[36] College Meeting Minutes, 7 Nov. 1945.

to be the first Principal of Keele.[37] In his valedictory *Master's Letter*,[38] he reflected at length on class and the College since Jowett:

If you consider you will surely see that the things we are proud of here, intense care for distinction and values, a life of the kind of leisure and free conversation among equals which helps to cultivate the things of the spirit, and a wide and generous toleration, are on the whole aristocratic virtues. They flower most easily at any rate in an aristocratic atmosphere. Jowett took young men of that England and of that class and purged them, I think, of aristocratic vices—indolence, arrogance and selfishness. He prepared the aristocracy of England to play a real and living part in a democracy ... I think that is what Jowett did, and I think the society into which I was introduced in 1906, even its most conservative members, had been touched by the spirit of what Jowett did. But Balliol at the beginning of the twentieth century, as I first knew it, was anything but a classless society. There were the Balliol aristocrats whose special seat was Staircase XIV. They were the people, I am sure, who gave rise to Asquith's remark about 'the tranquil consciousness of effortless superiority.' ... They were very able, the pick of the great public schools, and they seemed to be able to do everything with equal ease ... They were brilliant and personally charming, and I was very fond of most of them; but they were most of them insolent, and only condescendingly aware that there were other sets in the College besides their own. They seemed to me, coming from outside, to be accorded a strange impunity. That was all a long time ago, and the College was gradually transformed into something like a classless society.[39]

One of Lindsay's young dons, Christopher Hill—who displayed a photograph of Lindsay prominently in his study when he was Master himself— found pathos in Lindsay's last *Master's Letter*; Keele was not classless either, but it was more nearly so than Balliol and Oxford, and perhaps Lindsay was happier there.[40]

The College started to consider the Mastership succession in October

[37] W. B. Gallie, *A New University. A. D. Lindsay and the Keele Experiment*, 1960.

[38] *Balliol College Record*, 1949, p. 1.

[39] If Lindsay meant that there was little class-consciousness within the College he was perhaps near the truth, although there was still such consciousness in the early sixties; mercifully, none shows in the nineties. But in origin, the members of the College have been drawn predominantly from the privileged levels of society throughout modern times, and are so still. Of the 461 undergraduate admissions with sole UK nationality in the academic years 1986–90, approximately 55% came from fee-paying schools and only 45% from the state sector; but about 80% of all the 16–18-year-old school students in England and Wales in the same period were attending state schools. Again, in 1995 there were 342 UK undergraduates in residence: of these 200 were on a means-tested basis not entitled to a personal LEA grant (residual parental income over about £30,000 p.a.), and only 42 were entitled to a maximum personal grant (residual parental income less than about £15,000 p.a.).

[40] *DNB*, 1950–60, entry for *A. D. Lindsay* (by J. E. C. Hill).

1947. As this was nearly two years before Lindsay's statutory retirement, and the Statutes did not then allow election before a vacancy, they were changed to make it possible to do so six months ahead of the anticipated vacancy.[41] At the same time, the Fellows began to talk about possible candidates. The two who soon emerged were R. A. B. Mynors (then Professor of Latin at Cambridge) and his Balliol contemporary Robert Birley (then an educational adviser in occupied Germany). So far as there is any meaning in such classifications, Mynors was the candidate of the right and of most old members; Birley, the candidate of the left, was thought to have Lindsay's support. A straw vote towards the end of 1947 gave Mynors 14 votes to Birley's 13, so the College looked around for a candidate who might command more support. Sir David Lindsay Keir (then Vice-Chancellor of Queen's University, Belfast) was suggested in the summer of 1948, and he was dined in College on 29 October of that year.[42] But a straw vote then gave Mynors 13 to Keir's 14. Birley was still nominally a candidate, but shortly afterwards, to the surprise and dis-pleasure of the Fellows of Balliol, he was appointed Head Master of Eton. To put an end to the uncertainty, W. S. Watt, Keeper of the Minutes, collected signatures from Keir's 14 supporters pledging themselves to him, and on 1 February 1949, at a special College Meeting, held first in the Old Common Room and then in the Chapel, Keir had a majority of one.[43] The decision made, all present then combined to make a formally unanimous election. Some aspects of the procedure followed in 1949 are very ancient (see pp. 18 and 42 above), but in its drawn-out consultations, the invitation to an outsider candidate, the dining of candidates, and final unanimity, it broke new ground and was to be the pattern for all Mastership elections since.

Keir was the first Master since Theophilus Leigh who had not been any sort of member of the College before election, and, like Leigh, has left a memory which is somewhere between lukewarm and adverse behind him. He cared too much about his own perquisites and dignity, some erstwhile colleagues have said; those who were students under him will

---

[41] College Meeting Minutes, 10 Oct. 1947.

[42] At about the same time, the Visitor (Lord Samuel) asked Vincent Massey, who was later Governor-General of Canada, if he would consider being Master. Massey declined, but seems to have been under the impression that the job was his for the asking. V. Massey, *What's Past is Prologue*, Toronto, 1963, p. 449.

[43] Most of the information in this paragraph was kindly provided by W. S. Watt and Sir Edgar Williams in 1990–2: see MISC 108.c and MISC 108.e. The drama had some associated comedy; well before the formalities in Chapel, two undergraduates (J. R. Lucas and D. G. Craig) hid in the organ-loft, hoping to overhear the election (and expecting Mynors to be the winner), but they were discovered and ejected by the Head Porter (Cyril King) as the Fellows were filing in: see MISC 108.h.

27. Sir David Lindsay Keir, Master 1949–65.

remember that a dark suit, gown, and ritual humility were obligatory for a magisterial audience. Before the War, he had combined his donnish life as a Fellow, Estates Bursar, and Dean of University College with scholarly work on English constitutional history, but he gave himself entirely to educational administration and public service from 1939 onwards. He did a good job holding the fort at Queen's University, Belfast through the War, and helped that institution to get on its feet afterwards, earning himself a knighthood. This was his apogee. As Master of Balliol, he was active on various Committees concerned with health services at home and higher education abroad, especially in former colonies, but he was never in the public eye like Lindsay. He was not an imaginative or forward-looking man, but a stolid traditionalist. Only in being rather straight-laced did he emulate his immediate predecessor. In 1953, although the Fellows wanted to elect E. H. Carr (a very distinguished senior academic, but an historian with a Marxist view, living in a state of adultery, albeit stable and respectable) to a Fellowship, Keir refused to nominate him for more than a Lecturership.[44] And there were disagreements later over broad and fundamental issues. He accepted the growth of graduate studies reluctantly, and saw in coeducation only a threat to the old ways: in his farewell message to the College,[45] he recorded publicly his dissent from the proposal to set up a Balliol–St Anne's Graduate Institution.

Christopher Hill, who succeeded to the Mastership in 1965,[46] was in complete contrast to Keir in almost every respect. He had been a Scholar of the College, and then, after a brief spell away, Fellow and Tutor in Modern History for some thirty years. A prolific Marxist interpreter of the seventeenth century, he had visited Russia in the thirties, and had been a member of the Communist Party; although he had washed his hands of the Party after the brutal suppression of the 1956 Hungarian Uprising,[47] he was most emphatically a man of the left. Even if his

---

[44] This was the last occasion when the Master was able to obstruct the Fellows in a matter of any substance. See E. H. Carr's personal dossier; College Meeting Minutes, 25 May and 22 June 1953.

[45] *Balliol College Record*, 1965.

[46] It was public knowledge that R. P. Bell was the other principal contender. It would not be decent to enter into a discussion of the details for this and more recent Mastership elections: but the present author has laid down in the Archives (sealed for the time being) as much material as he has been able to gather together. See: MISC 108.b (Hill's election); D.3.203–5 (Kenny's election); D.24.10 and 13 (Blumberg's election); and D.24.24 and 25 (Lucas's election).

[47] The British Communist Party was not left without prominent Balliol men, however; Andrew Rothstein (Balliol 1916, Hero of the JCR 1987, died 1994) and R. P. Dutt (Balliol 1914, died 1974), both 1920 foundation members, continued in their Stalinism until they died. See F. Becket, *Enemy Within. The Rise and Fall of the British Communist Party*, 1995.

28. J. E. C. Hill, Master 1965–78.

election was not a reaction to Keir, many of the steps taken soon afterwards plainly were. The Statutes were changed to deprive the Master of the ability to obstruct the wishes of the Fellows in elections, several other prerogatives were taken away from him (with Hill's 'hearty approval'[48]) and vested in Committees, the office of Vice-Master was invented, and E. H. Carr was elected to an Honorary Fellowship. The election of an ex-Communist to the Mastership attracted some wry comment, but no more than that. Old members mostly welcomed the appointment, knowing full well that he was a distinguished scholar, that his politics were not doctrinaire, and that he upheld such fundamentals as the tutorial system. Perhaps it helped that he had played for the College in the XV which had won Rugby Cuppers in 1933. Although many grumbled because he did not live in the Master's Lodgings, this was a groundless complaint. Some ten extra rooms became available for student occupation because of this break with tradition. In any case, Christopher Hill and his wife Bridget become far better known to most junior members through their relaxed and frequent entertaining than the kindly but more formal Sir David and Lady Lindsay Keir had ever been. In his relations with the Fellows too, there was only one serious clash, when, at a College Meeting, he lost his patience over some problem or other and threatened to resign unless he got his way. But even some of those who were with him on the issue (whatever it was—the corporate memory is clear about the crisis but woolly about exactly what caused it) were offended by this tactic, and after a hastily convened meeting of Fellows in Rhodes House, he was told that if he ever tried that ploy again his resignation would be accepted. But in general he was patient with students who were sometimes exasperating, and with colleagues who were not invariably helpful. He steered the College through the difficult years of student unrest (P. G. H. Sandars gave wise counsel as Senior Tutor in that unsettled period), and he helped it to make up its mind about admitting women. On that issue, he had the satisfaction of swearing in Carol Clark as the first woman Fellow, and of seeing through the decision to admit women as students, but the date set for their arrival was just too late for him to be able to welcome them himself.

In the election of Hill's successor, it was apparent at an early stage that Anthony Kenny was the front runner, but there was some hesitation over his age. It would, according to Statute, have given him twenty-one years

---

[48] *Balliol College Record*, 1978, p. 9. Furthermore, Hill gave up the Master's right of allocating two Commoner places at his sole discretion (which had been the origin of a lot of ill feeling: see A. B. Rodger to W. S. Watt, 26 Dec. 1960, MISC 98.8), his *ex officio* chairmanship of all College Committees, and his exclusive use of the area still known as the Master's Garden—all privileges Keir had elicited from the College early in his reign.

C22. The Garden Quad in Wartime, by R. Eurich, about 1945.

C23. From left to right: A. E. (Bert) Blagrove, porter and sage; Sir Ashley Ponsonby, Bart. (Balliol 1939), Lord Lieutenant; and the Master (A. J. P. Kenny, 1978–89). In Hall, after Mr Blagrove's investiture with the BEM, 1983.

C24. A view from a helium balloon over the Master's Field, looking towards Holywell Manor (left of St Cross Church), with the Dellal Building (left) and Martin Building (right) in the foreground, 1992.

C25. Holywell Manor, photographed by Chris Honeywell, 1993.

C26. A group of graduate students in Holywell Manor garden on their matriculation day, 18 October 1988. From left to right: A. J. Gerrard, E. M. Harris, HIH Crown Princess Masako, S. A. McGuckian, R. Cipolla.

C28. C. R. Lucas, Master 1994–, in the 1995 Encaenia procession, walking with Sir Christopher Zeeman, Principal of Hertford College.

C27. B. S. Blumberg, Master 1989–94, by Paul Brason.

C29.   Dervorguilla of Galloway, from the mural by C. E. Fremantle (Balliol 1925)
in the author's room on Staircase II (see p. 268, n. 21).

C30.   The ruins of Buittle Castle, 1994.

29. HM King Olav V of Norway leaving the JCR Norway Room after inspecting it (he had performed the opening ceremony 15 years previously), followed by the Master, 14 November 1981. On the same visit he also unveiled his portrait in Hall.

in office. He announced that it would be his intention to resign after a shorter term than this, which overcame the reservations. When he was elected, it was put on record that he intended to resign not later than 30 September 1990.[49] A few cynics may have thought at the time that this was just his way of securing their votes, but later when the College resolved that he should not feel bound by his undertaking,[50] and some senior Fellows privately urged him to stay, they found him resolute; he stepped down in 1989 at the age of fifty-eight to become Warden of Rhodes House (with a Fellowship at St John's College), and shortly thereafter he was also elected President of the British Academy. Kenny was a philosopher with a most unusual background: he had been a Roman Catholic priest[51] before joining the College as Tutor in philosophy. He continued his academic work whilst Master, just as Hill had done, and indeed expanded his horizons, writing many books on remarkably diverse subjects.

In the later years of his long Chancellorship,[52] Harold Macmillan often joked that he would gladly step aside to make way for an older man. This was what Kenny did, for Baruch S. Blumberg was sixty-four when he took office in 1989. This time, the Fellows did not need to worry that they might be landing themselves with a long period of, on the one hand, stagnation or, on the other, uncheckable change. On the contrary, the Statutes had to be amended to allow Blumberg to stay beyond normal retirement age of sixty-seven by giving him a five-year term; it would otherwise have been necessary to begin the process of finding his successor almost as soon as he had been sworn in. Blumberg was the first scientist (Nobel Laureate 1976,[53] for his work on hepatitis B) and the first non-Brit to be Master. He was tremendously popular, especially with students, and in many ways brought new ideas and a breath of fresh air into College affairs. Administrative detail, however, he preferred to delegate, and under him the office of Vice-Master held in turn by A. M. Howatson, O. Murray, A. W. M. Graham, and Howatson again, grew in stature.

Colin Lucas, a scholar of the French Revolution, was a Fellow from 1973 until 1990, when he left for a chair at the University of Chicago. In 1993 he became Dean of the Division of Social Sciences there, but he

[49] College Meeting Minute CM77/95.

[50] College Meeting Minutes CM85/50 and CM87/180, *nemine contradicente* both times; see also (i) The Master's Letter, *Balliol College Record*, 1988; (ii) D.3.206–8.

[51] A. [J. P.] Kenny, *A Path from Rome*, 1985.

[52] 1960–86. His successor was Lord Jenkins, the fifth Balliol man to be elected to the office since 1900: the others were Lords Curzon, Milner (who died before taking up office), and Grey.

[53] B. S. Blumberg, 'Australia Antigen and the Biology of Hepatitis B', pp. 133–58 in *Les Prix Nobel en 1976*, pub. The Nobel Foundation, 1977; this also includes an autobiographical summary.

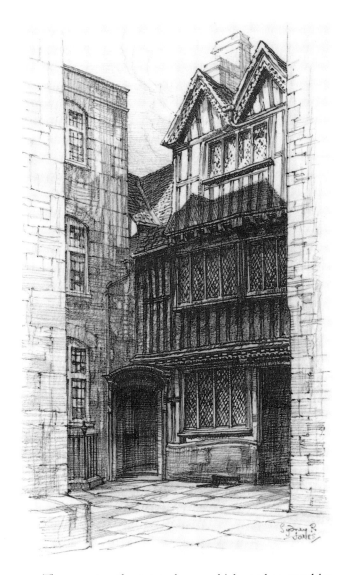

30. The seventeenth-century house which used to stand by
Staircase XXI. Drawn by Sydney R. Jones, 1942. Demolished
in 1966.

came home to Balliol as Master in 1994. Even before the end of his first year as Master, he was nominated Vice-Chancellor-elect (to serve 1997–2001). This appointment was important not only for the University, but also for the College, which had for many years been under-represented in the upper reaches of the University hierarchy.[54]

As in earlier times, the expansion of the student body (see Appendix E) since World War II has been coupled to the provision of more accommodation and the creation of more Fellowships. None of this would have been possible without the influx of new capital from appeals: the War Memorial Fund (closed in 1951—raised about £70,000), the Septcentenary Appeal (launched 1962—target £1m, achieved), the Dervorguilla Appeal (commemorating the 700th anniversary in 1982 of Dervorguilla's Statutes—target £2m, achieved), and the Jowett Appeal (marking the centenary of Benjamin Jowett's death, launched after an extended gestation in 1993–4, going well at the time of writing).

Although various grand schemes for the partial reconstruction of the Broad Street range were considered soon after the War, none was executed,[55] and the extra accommodation needed in the fifties was provided by internal rearrangement, so that by about 1960 almost all the student rooms in College and Holywell Manor were single bed-sitters. In the same period, the Library[56] and Master's Lodgings were transformed, again by internal reorganization, leaving the buildings externally unchanged. On the strength of the Septcentenary Appeal, the JCR was extended, and the Victorian Staircases XX and XXII were demolished and rebuilt (doubling the number of rooms in that part of the College). A quaint seventeenth-century house which used to stand in the corner by Staircase XXI was also destroyed—without adequate recording, to the College's shame. In the north-east corner of the Garden Quad a new Senior Common Room block, comprising also a Lecture Room and

---

[54] P. G. H. Sandars and W. H. Newton-Smith, however, had served as Proctors 1971–2 and 1984–5 respectively; and P. A. W. Bulloch was Assessor 1995–6.

[55] Building on the so-called 'Master's Garden', and along the boundary with Trinity, was also considered; these are ideas which have surfaced afresh at least three times this century. Other schemes which have been seriously debated several times have included radical features such as the bisection of the Garden Quad with a building extending from Staircase XV towards the Fellows' Garden, and the demolition of the Brackenbury Building. See, for example, MCOP 10a.

[56] A mezzanine floor was inserted (1959) into the Lower Library (the former Hall) to create the present reading room (thenceforth known as the New Library) on the same level as the Upper Library (since known as the Old Library). The device of inserting a mezzanine floor was also used (1966) to convert the Lecture Room between Staircases VI and VII into new offices for the Bursary (which was formerly housed on Staircase III, as the legend over the entrance, exposed by cleaning the stonework, reminds us still).

teaching rooms, was built.[57] Sir Edward Maufe was the principal architect on College commissions until the end of the fifties, when he was succeeded by G. J. Beard, who was responsible for many schemes great and small until well into the seventies. But the new residential block on the edge of the Master's Field opposite the Holywell church of St Cross, which was part of the development of Holywell Manor as a Graduate Institution, was designed by Sir Leslie Martin, hence its name—the Martin Building (1966). Until the sixties, the provision of new student rooms went hand in hand with rising numbers, so that the proportions living in College accommodation and in the City remained roughly the same. But whereas City rents were considerably less than College rents (despite subsidy) in the sixties, by the eighties the opposite was the case, and the Dellal Building (1986), partly funded by a major donor to the Dervorguilla Appeal[58]) was intended to enable a greater proportion of the College's students to avoid the crippling cost of increasingly seedy private-sector housing. In 1995–6, in anticipation of the Jowett Appeal, the first phase of an ambitious plan to develop along the edge of Jowett Walk was built, creating 65 rooms (and other facilities, including the Michael Pilch Room for theatricals), bringing to 90 per cent the proportion who can be housed throughout their student years—almost enough to satisfy the demand.

The impact of rising housing costs in the City on student finance was aggravated by Conservative Government policy on student grants, which were steadily eroded in real value terms, and began to be replaced by a student loans system. The College struggled to offset this drift by keeping its domestic charges down, but the JCR was rarely satisfied and the annual negotiations on the subject were sometimes tedious, with occasional rent strikes when payments were withheld. In 1995 the Governing Body, in step with other colleges, decided that it had to reduce what was in effect a subsidy to all, and raise accommodation charges by some 40 per cent over a period of three or four years. The plan was to set aside 20 per cent of the increased revenue which would be generated thereby and redistribute this to students in proven need, i.e. to replace a general subsidy by a targeted subsidy. This provoked strident protest from the undergraduates, although the graduates acquiesced—the first time the student body had not acted as one on a major issue, but consistent with other signs of divergence between graduates and undergraduates.

---

[57] The majority of the funds were provided by the Bernard Sunley Foundation, in recognition of which the block is called the Bernard Sunley Building.

[58] The Dellal Foundation contributed £100,000 of the £550,000 required to build and commission: the name was not officially attached to the building until after J. D. D. Dellal (Balliol 1986) had gone down.

The urban and agricultural properties with which the College was endowed by its early Benefactors were scattered all over England, and efficient management was never easy. Between the two World Wars, a policy of sale and reinvestment of the proceeds in other ways was applied, and continued later; the last vestige of our old estates was taken from us by compulsory purchase in 1980.[59] Of the lands held since antiquity, only that on which the present collegiate buildings stand remains in our possession. What then is there to link us with our distant past, other than mere tradition? Not much of the buildings, for sure. The Old Library, the New Library—which was the Hall until Jowett's time—and parts of the Master's Lodgings preserve some bits and pieces of very old stonework, but by and large what we see is the result of rebuilding and repair. For tangible reminders of our long history, we must look for things less obvious than land or masonry. Dervorguilla's Statutes and the seal matrix she gave in 1282 are the most evocative items to survive. Books come next to mind; the Library still possesses many manuscript books from its earliest days. We also think of administrative archives, 'evidences' or 'muniments' preserved from the very beginning out of prudence in case anyone should question the College's corporate status or good title to any of its property. Then perhaps we will remember our plate, and the portraits too, acquired over more recent centuries. All these treasures have been more actively appreciated since Hitler's War than ever before, and catalogues have been compiled—of manuscripts,[60] the Archives,[61] plate,[62] and portraits.[63] And at the time of writing the College has just decided to embark on a programme of restoring and conserving the ancient stained glass in the Old Library and Chapel. But there is another, less obvious, link with the College's earliest days in its ecclesiastical patronage. Balliol is still sole Patron, or Patron in turn, of a number of livings—at Long Benton, Abbotsley, and Fillingham—which were first put at its disposal in the fourteenth century, and it retains an interest in several others of more recent, but still very ancient, association. Some

[59] College Meeting Minute CM80/88 and Executive Committee Minute EC79/25B (see the related Report of the Estates Committee, 1a) record that Four Lane Ends, Benton (the sole remnant of Sir Philip Somervyle's lands) had, as a result of a compulsory purchase order, been conveyed to Tyne and Wear County Council.

[60] R. A. B. Mynors, *Catalogue of the Manuscripts of Balliol College Oxford*, 1963. This catalogue is a work of prodigious scholarship which took Mynors some 30 years to compile: it is generally recognized as a model of its kind.

[61] J. [H.] Jones, *The Archives of Balliol College Oxford*, 1984.

[62] Compiled by D. W. Jackson: an exhaustive set of photographs with commentary in six albums, mostly compiled 1974–85, but also updated by him thereafter: Plate Records 30.

[63] J. [H.] Jones, *The Portraits of Balliol College. A Catalogue*, 1990.

take the view that ecclesiastical patronage except by the episcopate is now an anachronism, and in 1988, when reforming legislation gave an opportunity for it to be shed, there was a discussion of the matter; in the end it was decided that the parishes concerned should be consulted. All but one of the twenty-odd then under the College's patronage asked for the relationship to be continued.[64]

The College has been governed since time immemorial by the Master and Fellows acting together, but since the last war the growth in the size of the Fellowship has made the delegation of much business inevitable. Until the sixties, there was a set of some eight or nine Committees, all reporting directly to the full Governing Body, by which all significant decisions were taken at formal College Meetings, of which a detailed record was kept. Matters of policy and controversy needing extended debate were usually discussed at informal meetings called Consilia; no minutes or attendance records were kept at these Consilia, but sometimes informal resolutions made thereat were submitted to the next formal College Meeting for ratification, which was usually automatic. In 1963, however, the College invoked an enabling Statute[65] which had long been available, and brought into being a Tutorial Board, which was given authority to deal with all tutorial and student matters.[66] Continuing discussions on the government of the College led to the appointment of a Committee, under the chairmanship of D. R. Harris, to deliberate on the subject. The Committee reported in 1968, and the essentials of the Harris Report,[67] as it became known, were adopted. The key novel feature was the creation of an Executive Committee, which was to meet frequently and deal with the great majority of non-academic business; it was to comprise all major office-holders and an equal number of ordinary Fellows chosen to represent different seniorities and subjects, and it was to be under the chairmanship of the Vice-Master. This Committee was to have authority to take binding decisions, but the rights of the rest of the Governing Body were protected by giving all Fellows the right to receive the agenda, papers, and minutes, and the right to attend meetings and be heard (but not vote), and also providing that a short delay was to be observed before decisions could become effective, allowing objectors—if there were enough of them—to force reconsideration at a College Meeting. This system has worked remarkably smoothly ever since, with very few instances of the Executive Committee's decisions being subjected to review. At the present time, the Executive Committee meets practically

---

[64] Additional Patronage Papers 12.
[65] Statute VII.4 (1949 edition).
[66] College Meeting Minute CM63/60.
[67] College Meeting Minute CM68/55. See also MBP 258.

every week in term-time, with student representatives present for all except financial and delicate matters; there are three College Meetings and three meetings of Tutorial Board a term; Consilia take place anything between four and seven times a term under the chairmanship of the Vice-Master, invariably before dinner on a Wednesday;[68] and there are also some twenty other standing Committees, many with student members, as well as *ad hoc* Committees set up *ad lib.*

At the first College Meeting of Michaelmas Term 1945, it was resolved that disciplinary normality should be reintroduced, in the following terms:[69]

That, from the beginning of Michaelmas Term, the College revert, with some modifications, to the disciplinary rules in force in Trinity Term 1939, viz.:

(*a*) Except with the special permission of the Dean, women shall not be allowed in College after the commencement of dinner in Hall, and shall not be allowed in the stores at any time.

(*b*) The College gate shall be closed at 9.15 p.m., but undergraduates may leave College at will between 9.15 p.m. and 12 o'clock midnight; no fines shall be payable for exits and entrances between 9.15 p.m. and 12 o'clock midnight, but the Porter shall keep a record of such exits and entrances; the regulations for entering College after 12 o'clock midnight shall be those in force in Trinity Term 1939.

(*c*) All undergraduates resident in College shall be required to appear at breakfast in Hall on five days a week.

Many of the undergraduates in the years immediately following this edict were men blooded in war, not schoolboys, but if there was resentment at this petty discipline it does not show in the Archives. The prospects for controlling men like W. F. Ash (with numerous escapes from POW camps on his record)[70] would seem to have been poor. Perhaps there was a judicious exercise of the decanal blind eye: the Dean, A. B. Rodger, had served in both World Wars and, remarkably, in all three services. There was an easing of the rule on lady guests in 1953[71]—the entertainment of ladies was to be allowed from 12 noon until 10.30 p.m. without special permission. By 1965 another half hour had been allowed, but there was by then much breach of the rule, with the connivance of cheerfully and

---

[68] The dinner on every Wednesday of full term is called Consilium Dinner, whether there is a debate beforehand or not. Only the Master and Fellows (including Emeritus and Honorary Fellows) may attend; members of the Governing Body are expected to be there, which is no penance because it is always an excellent dinner.

[69] College Meeting Minutes, 12 Oct. 1945. The rule about attending breakfast was abolished in 1946 (College Meeting Minutes, 11 Nov.).

[70] W. F. Ash, *A Red Square*, 1978. A copy of his POW *Personalkarte* detailing his escapes and punishments has been deposited in his College dossier.

[71] College Meeting Minutes, 22 June 1953.

cheaply corruptible domestic staff. So far as exits and entrances were concerned, the Porter was still keeping records in that period, but he too was corruptible, and in any case there were well-known routes for climbing in—as well-known to the Dean and Praefectus as to everyone else.

From the College Rules, 1965

Late leave: leave to return to College or Holywell Manor after midnight is given by the Dean or Praefectus. The form, obtained from the Dean or Praefectus, is handed in at the Lodge before leaving.

Exeat: leave of absence for the night is given by the Dean or Praefectus. An exeat form, procurable at the Lodge, is signed first by the Tutor and then by the Dean or Praefectus: it is handed in at the Lodge before leaving.

Lady Visitors

Ladies are forbidden to enter College or Holywell Manor after 11.0 p.m. without special leave of the Dean or Praefectus. Special leave, however, is not required for ladies entering the College only to attend lectures and tutorials.

Ladies leaving the College or Holywell Manor between 7.30 p.m. and 11.0 p.m. must be accompanied by the undergraduate who has entertained them, and he must sign his name in the book at the Lodge when they leave.

Ladies are not allowed in the Stores.

Until about 1966 or 1967, although there was occasional grumbling about such restrictions, nobody really cared enough for tempers to be raised. But by then the first rumbles of international student unrest and radicalism were being heard, with demands being made for student participation in all aspects of academic government, all mixed up with very confused idealism and extreme left-wing politics.[72] Emboldened perhaps by this, the JCR Committee pressed the Governing Body hard during the years 1968–72; petty discipline was swept away, and a degree of involvement of junior members in the government of the College was conceded. It was a difficult time, during which the patience of the representatives of the senior and junior parts of the College was often tested to its limits, but fragile civility was generally maintained. Complete breakdown of relations did, sadly, happen twice—when personal attacks were made on the Dean and Chaplain (F. L. M. Willis-Bund),[73] and when the College was mortified by the misbehaviour of its students on the occasion of a

[72] For background, see K. O. Morgan, *The Peoples' Peace*, 1990, pp. 292–8; N. Annan, *Our Age*, 1991, paperback edn., especially pp. 512–15; and *Report of the Committee on Relations with Junior Members*, Supplement* No. 7, *Oxford University Gazette*, xcix, May 1969 (the 'Hart Report').

[73] See papers of 1970 in MCOP 24ii.

visit by Sir Edward Heath, then Prime Minister.[74] From 1972 onwards, with a new disciplinary procedure agreed[75] and notionally in place, and with consultative machinery covering a wide range of College business beginning to work, confrontations and disagreements became more and more infrequent.[76] But Balliol students acquired a reputation for being rabble-rousers and remained prominent in agitation outside the College. A major issue between the University authorities and those *in statu pupillari* was a demand for central student union facilities. In a silly 1974 attempt to further this cause, activists, among whom Balliol men were leaders, staged a demo outside the Indian Institute (now the History Faculty building) which escalated into a riot and occupation of the building.[77] Three Balliol men were found guilty by the Magistrates of offences in the street, and another four were brought by the Proctors, together with a dozen or so members of other colleges, before the University Disciplinary Court. The case against another was dropped because he was taken ill, and there was at least one more Balliol occupier who was not caught. There were several days of hearings, often wonderfully farcical and occasionally enlivened by courtroom brawls. In the end the Balliol Four were rusticated for a year; no doubt if the University had not done them this service they would have soon been asking for leave of absence to catch up on their work.

The high-profile involvement of Balliol students in left-wing agitation, especially the frequent TV appearances of the JCR's red demo banner in the forefront of the mob, served to consolidate the public perception of the College as an institution given to trouble-making over left-wing issues.[78]

---

[74] Offensive slogans (a series of photographs has been preserved but is closed for the time being: see PHOT 8) were painted inside the SCR and elsewhere in College on the night of 21/22 June 1971; when the Prime Minister walked across the Garden Quad to dinner on the following evening, there was a noisy demonstration of his unpopularity from junior members. One man was rusticated for a year and another was effectively expelled from the College for the slogan-painting: College Meeting Minutes, 26 June 1971. See also *Oxford Mail* 23 June 1971.

[75] JCR General Meeting Minutes, 30 Nov. 1972; College Meeting Minutes, 11 Dec. 1972. References to the detailed rules and prescribed procedures has, however, rarely been made, and the College Court has yet to sit.

[76] There is a great deal of material in the Archives concerning relations between the Governing Body and the JCR 1960–89. See especially MCOP 24, 38, and 47.

[77] The Dean's detailed file on this bizarre affair survives (closed for the time being) in the Archives as Studies and Discipline 5*.

[78] This image also attracted left-wing activist students from home and abroad. Their admission sometimes generated internal controversy. In 1969, for example, the Senior Tutor (R. M. Ogilvie, who left shortly afterwards to become Headmaster of Tonbridge School) wrote to the Tutor for Admissions (W. L. Weinstein) 'I am deeply disturbed ... that you have admitted Magaziner. I heard a great deal about him in the States and I fear

'I've had more graduates of mine on the Cowley assembly line than you've had hot dinners!'

31. An *Evening Standard* cartoon by Jak, poking fun at the left-wing tendency of the College, 1983.

Some Fellows, especially Denis Noble, refreshed that interpretation by their prominence in the successful campaign to block the award of an honorary degree to Mrs Thatcher in 1985,[79] which alienated a number of crusty old members. As recently as 1993, John Patten, right-wing Minister of Education, his feathers ruffled by a noisy protest at his grant-cutting policy, made a fuss in the House of Commons. A constituency meeting he had held in a Botley church hall had been disturbed. Those responsible, he said, were led by 'yobs from Balliol College'. His melodramatic account of the affair was shown on Breakfast TV (possibly the worst start to the day the Dean has ever had), and he made himself appear very ridiculous, raising his voice and waving his arms about. In fact, as the police confirmed, the gathering which had given him such offence was well-behaved and attended by only about thirty people, of whom a mere handful were from Balliol.[80] Twenty years earlier, an unpopular Minister showing his face in Oxford could have expected an angry riot on ten times the scale of this non-event. The College's image took an unfair knock all the same.

Much of the tension between the Governing Body and the JCR in the later sixties was really to do with differential rates of change between the young and the old in attitudes to sex. The formal record rarely admits this, and is full of subtle euphemism, but it was so. The hours during which 'ladies' could legitimately be 'entertained' was not the only issue. Despite the fact that thieves could easily slip past the porters, there was reluctance on the part of the authorities to put locks on room doors, because (so students believed) that would facilitate—encourage, even—fornication. And, while the battle to preserve old values was being lost on both these fronts, the young attacked in strength on another, asserting their right to install a condom-vending machine in the JCR. This was controversial too, but, after some acrimony, a machine was permitted. How strange all this now seems, only a quarter of a century later. Had none of the dons ever enjoyed making love in the permissible afternoon hours? Now, if rooms had no locks on the doors and condoms were not freely available, the Dean would be agitating vigorously on both counts, because of the prevalence of theft and the threat of AIDS.

that his admission may irresponsibly lead us into a great deal of trouble.' Ira Magaziner's friend President Clinton became a member of University College, albeit one with numerous close Balliol contacts: see MISC 196. For most of October 1969 he actually lived in Holywell Manor, sharing No. 37 (South Wing) with R. G. Stearns (another Rhodes Scholar, Balliol 1968).

[79] B. Harrison, 'Mrs Thatcher and the Intellectuals', *Twentieth Century British History*, v (1994), 206.

[80] The Dean was asked to make a detailed investigation. His report, with newspaper cuttings etc., is in the Archives: MISC 194.

Drugs were rarely the subject of open debate in the Balliol of thirty years ago, but there was a small circle within the community,[81] of which the majority of senior and junior members were only vaguely aware, within which marijuana was used regularly. The discerning nose has sometimes been aware of the stuff since, but not often, and ethanol is now, as ever, by far the greater problem.

Hardly noticed at the time in the tumult over rules, regulations and representation, Balliol student life changed a lot during the flower-power years.[82] The wearing of gowns (except for the matriculation ceremony and University examinations) by junior members was abolished. Under Keir and before, a gown had been obligatory for dinner, Chapel (but Scholars wore surplices, like Fellows), tutorials, and interviews with the Master or Dean. Dinner in Hall on ordinary nights became just a meal, no longer much of an occasion. The Commemoration Ball of 1969 was the last extravagance of its kind. Male staircase 'scouts', and with them the Jeeves–Wooster relationships which many struck up with their men, began to be replaced by staircase ladies who were very often rather like Mum, but more tolerant. By the end of the seventies, nearly all the old-style scouts had gone, and although meals were still available in Hall, Hall provided for students only a cafeteria service. There was now competition from the JCR kitchen, because the JCR had changed from being a sort of club-room for tea and coffee after meals to being a place where plain food could be obtained three times a day, with snacks between. By the eighties, indeed, there was competition from self-catering, as little kitchens were put on many staircases. Meanwhile, the life of the Senior Common Room remained, and lingers still, in an agreeable time warp, with gowns for College Meetings and also for dinner, which is conducted with enough formality to make it an event but not—as in some other colleges—enough to make it stuffy.

Many of the creeping changes in College life which have taken place in the last quarter-century were taking place simultaneously in other colleges and in society at large. But in one respect at least Balliol has bucked the trends: the profiles of the Chapel and Chaplain have risen while the Church of England generally has been diminishing in size and influence. Canon P. B. Hinchliff (Chaplain 1972–86) revitalized the Chapel,

---

[81] In his time, Howard Marks (Balliol 1964) was at the hub of this circle. He was sentenced to 25 years imprisonment by a US Court in 1990 (paroled and deported 1995) for large-scale trafficking in marijuana; a great deal has been written about him, not all of it reliable. See, e.g., D. Leigh, *High Time*, 1984, and P. Eddy and S. Walden, *Hunting for Marco Polo*, 1991. For his own account, see his autobiography: [D.] H. Marks, *Mr Nice*, 1996.

[82] For a perceptive account of college life in the University generally (but with many Balliol allusions) 1945–70, see K. [V.] Thomas, chapter 8 in *The History of the University of Oxford*, viii (ed. B. Harrison), 1994.

especially by establishing a choir (which had female voices from other colleges initially), and his successor Douglas Dupree has maintained its momentum. Extrapolation from the decline of the sixties would have the Chapel utterly defunct by now, perhaps converted to some secular use. In fact it is often filled on Sunday evenings—visiting preachers have, most remarkably, included two Speakers of the House of Commons in recent years; and the annual Carol Service packs it tight. Members have been baptized, confirmed, married, and ordained in it; a few great men like Jack de Wet have had their funeral formalities conducted in it. In all sorts of ways it has become a focal point for communal life, which would have seemed natural at any point in the history of the College up to, say, 1939, but which seems a little surprising in 1995, at least to one of those who attended it (erratically) 1961–6. The tradition that the Chaplain should be pastorally concerned for the welfare of all members, whether Chapel-goers or not, was established by F.L.M. Willis-Bund (Chaplain 1945–72), who included the discreet administration of financial hardship funds among his many responsibilities. Hinchliff and Dupree followed him in these things, and like him, got to know well, and earn the affection of, more junior members than other dons.

The Governing Body and JCR Committees of the sixties were all inconsistent in their approaches on issues relating to women. The former began to think about co-residence, and in Holywell Manor actually introduced it for graduates (in co-operation with St Anne's) while still resisting pressure to remove all restrictions on the hours for the entertainment of female guests in College; and the latter kept up that pressure while still maintaining the JCR itself as a no-go area for women most of the time.[83]

The politics behind the debates which led to the admission of women to membership of Balliol were complex. It was not just a matter of the necessary majority for reform building itself up through turnover and conversion, although it might have been if Balliol had been a lone pioneer. In fact, New College had taken the lead in 1964, resolving by more than the necessary two-thirds majority to declare its wish to change its Statutes to permit the admission of women.[84] By 1970, many other colleges[85] were

[83] A motion 'That the JCR be open to ladies between 3.30 and 5.30 p.m. each day' was proposed by A. N. Ridley and E. J. Mortimer on 18 Oct. 1964, and carried by 80:27, after a lively debate. Against, it was asserted that 'Members wanted a place they could slum around in, and they could not do that with women about' (JCR General Meeting Minutes).

[84] G. E. M. de Ste Croix, 'The Admission of Women to New College', *The Oxford Magazine*, 15 Oct. 1964.

[85] Including at least one women's college: St Anne's approached Balliol (in view of the 'special relationship' between the two colleges) on the subject in confidence in January 1970 (see MCOP 17, which is the Master's file on the admission of women 1970–7).

seriously considering taking both sexes as members. The womens' colleges were apprehensive, thinking that the traditional and vastly richer mens' colleges would deprive them of talent. Even the most eager coeducationalists did not want the womens' colleges to suffer as a result of the opening of other doors all over Oxford. In any case, the concerns of the womens' colleges were well appreciated by the University, which was also uneasy because a rush of colleges simultaneously admitting women for the first time might have precipitated chaos. And the University had control, since colleges need its permission before petitioning the Privy Council for any change of Statute which affects it.[86] A Consilium resolved on 2 June 1971,[87] by 26 votes to 2,

that the College should announce its intention to remove statutory barriers to the entry of women, with a view to admitting women at a later stage, if the Governing Body after consultation with old members so decided,[88] and provided that the interests of the existing womens' Colleges were protected.

On the 10th of November following, Balliol resolved to submit to the University and to the Privy Council that the words 'no woman may be admitted a member of the College' should be deleted from the Statutes,[89] but this was immediately followed by a resolution that the actual admission of women should only take place if there was a two-thirds majority in favour. An Emergency College Meeting was convened a week later, and the motion was put that the College should seek to join a group of colleges which was expected to admit women students very soon. Voting was 20 : 17 in favour, so the motion was lost because of the decision previously taken to act only on a two-thirds majority.[90] It was agreed at the same time, however, that there should be discussion at the next College Meeting of 'steps which might be taken towards the eventual admission of women, in particular whether the College should now open its Fellowships to women'. And in the minutes of that College Meeting it is recorded as follows:[91]

[86] Universities of Oxford and Cambridge Act, 1923, Section 7(2)(*b*).

[87] College Meeting Minute CM71/103 confirmed this informal resolution; for the voting figures, see the paper dated 4 June 1971 which was circulated to all Fellows, a copy of which survives in MCOP 17.

[88] The Master invited old members to write to him on the subject (*Balliol College Record*, 1971, p. 9). Some 50 responded (*Balliol College Record*, 1972, p. 7), most of them in favour: the letters survive in MCOP 18.

[89] College Meeting Minute CM71/203 (resolved by a vote of 29:7). The Statute containing the prohibition was Statute VII.6(*c*).

[90] College Meeting Minute CM71/227. Some of the votes against were cast by Fellows who supported the admission of women in principle, but who wanted to slow things down in order to ensure an orderly transition.

[91] College Meeting Minute CM71/236.

32. Elena Ceva-Valla at the College gates. She was the first woman student to arrive, 16 September 1979.

From College Meeting Minutes 6 Dec. 1971

Admission of Women. It was resolved by 30 votes to 8,

That the College should open its Fellowship to women as soon as the change in its Statutes permitting this was approved by the Privy Council,

and, by 31 votes to 8,

That the College declares its intention now of admitting women undergraduates at a future date.

Balliol was thus not in the first wave of mens' colleges to go mixed,[92] and indeed the University's consent to the necessary change in Statutes was conditional upon the College giving an undertaking that women students would not be admitted without the approval of the University.[93] Very soon after the formalities for changing the Statutes had been attended to, the College elected its first woman Fellow, Carol Clark.[94] Three years later, with an increasing feeling of urgency, and concern that the College might be left behind, it was resolved at a Consilium by 29 : 5 to 'admit graduate and undergraduate students of both sexes as soon as possible after the College's undertaking to the University has ceased to be operative', subject to 'full consideration of the interests of the womens' colleges' and acceptable admissions procedures.[95]

The College was released from its undertaking to the University as one of the consequences of a debate in Congregation on 8 March 1977.[96] The first women students (31 undergraduates and 9 graduates)[97] were admitted in Michaelmas Term 1979; the first woman undergraduate to come into residence was Elena Ceva-Valla, who crossed the threshold on 16 September 1979.

In the two years immediately before this historic change, there was much discussion of domestic detail which was thought to be relevant.

---

[92] Brasenose, Hertford, Jesus, St Catherine's, and Wadham were the first of the former mens' colleges permitted to admit women undergraduates (on a regulated basis), in 1974.

[93] College Meeting Minute CM72/129. The undertaking was given reluctantly, and not without talk of rebellion. New College was similarly constrained by the University.

[94] She was the first woman to be elected a Fellow of any of the former mens' colleges (1973).

[95] The paper setting out the Consilium resolution and voting survives in MCOP 17; the resolution was confirmed at the next College Meeting (CM76/108) by a vote of 36 : 3.

[96] *Oxford University Gazette*, Supplement (2) to No. 3691, 16 March 1977. In effect, the University abandoned its attempt to control the admission of women, partly because a review of the situation seemed to show that the interests of the womens' colleges had not in fact been damaged by the admission of women to the former mens' colleges (*Oxford University Gazette*, Supplement (1) to No. 3686, 3 Feb. 1977), and partly because of the passing of the Sex Discrimination Act 1975.

[97] Cf. 87 and 29 men respectively (*Balliol College Record*, 1979, p. 10); but no quota was imposed—this would have been illegal, as the Sex Discrimination Act 1975 was in force.

33. The Master with some Boat Club people at the Eights Week Dinner 1992 (*from left to right*: S. J. Garner, Women's Captain D. J. Savin, L. E. Cameron, C. M. Denny, C. J. Dykers, K. A. Lythgoe, Coach C. H. Nicholls of Christ Church, S. E. Joyner, and C. M. Brune); and, above, the Womens' 1st VIII on the river, Trinity Term 1992.

Should women be segregated within the College? Would they demand full-length mirrors in their rooms? And what about bathrooms? In the event, there was only one practical problem of any significance associated with the admission of women, and nobody had thought of it: a high proportion of them took to rowing with enthusiasm (there were two Balliol womens' eights on the river in the first year), so there was a need for light-weight equipment. Socially, there was no detectable discontinuity, as everyone was already accustomed to seeing young women about the place. Within a very short time, the feeling of novelty had worn off. Practically all the men welcomed the women without undue fuss, and nearly all the women settled in without being over-assertive. The process of integration was complete by 1981, when for the first time the JCR elected a woman to be President[98]—but not because she was a woman, she was just effortlessly superior.

Holywell Manor served simply as a College annexe until the early sixties, when some fifty or so graduates and senior undergraduates were housed in it, with Russell Meiggs as resident Praefectus. It had some social life of its own, but only breakfast was served there. Residents were expected to go to the Broad Street site for other meals, and for most social activity. But by about 1963, with the number of graduates rising, and an increasingly sympathetic attitude to their special needs, the policy of integrating the graduate and undergraduate membership was called into question. On 16 March 1964, the College agreed 'in principle to the creation, if practicable, of a separate graduate institution either of its own or in conjunction with another college'.[99] Only two months later, a Committee was authorized to make approaches to a 'Ladies College' with a view to setting up a joint Graduate Institution.[100] The first detailed report of the Committee was submitted to a Consilium on 3 June 1964;[101] it was resolved to set up a Graduate Institution in Holywell Manor, and to have plans for conversion and additional building made 'as soon as possible'; and a formal approach to St Anne's with a view to establishing a mixed community was approved. It was envisaged that members of the Graduate Institution would remain members of their respective colleges, but dinner was to be served at the Institution; discipline was to be largely

---

[98] Catherine Roe, President of the JCR 1981–2.
[99] College Meeting Minute CM64/36(3); see also Appendix C to the College Meeting Minutes of 16 March 1964.
[100] College Meeting Minute CM64/64(4).
[101] See MBP 252, which is the Domestic Bursar's file on the Graduate Institution Committee 1964–6. The file kept 1964–7 by M. L. H. Green, a Committee member, also survives, as HM.3.Misc.ii. The informal resolutions made were confirmed on 22 June; CM64/80.

a matter of self-regulation, and the members were to be consulted about domestic matters; Fellows were to be encouraged to associate themselves with the Institution; and it was hoped that seminars etc. would take place there. The formal approach to St Anne's, however, was to be made by the Senior Fellow—an unusual step, no doubt taken because the Master was firmly against the scheme.[102] The JCR was also uneasy, thinking that it might lose its graduates (and with them their subscriptions); and it protested because it had not been consulted in advance.[103]

But the Committee was unstoppable by this stage,[104] and in 1967 the joint Balliol–St Anne's Graduate Institution came fully into being at Holywell Manor, which, with the completion of the Martin Building, became an expanded complex straddling the road. The accommodation capacity of the whole complex was about 80, of which 25 places were initially allocated to St Anne's. Russell Meiggs was Praefectus at the very beginning, and then A. M. Howatson for a few years, so that the whole enterprise was a going concern when Denis Noble was appointed in 1971. By that time, the Graduate Institution had acquired an identity and momentum of its own: under Noble the Graduate Institution was even more successful than its progenitors had hoped.[105] But in 1977 St Anne's decided to admit men, and as the numbers of Balliol graduates of both sexes had grown there was pressure on accommodation for them, so the Balliol–St Anne's liaison was gently phased out and gracefully terminated in 1984. A reception was held to mark the ending of the arrangement: the Praefectus described it as 'a celebration of the fact that the two colleges pioneered co-residence a decade or so before the wave of admission of men and women to each other's colleges became an avalanche'.[106] And the letter of the Principal of St Anne's to the Master is worth quoting in full:[107]

Dear Master,

The Governing Body has asked me to convey to yours the College's deep gratitude to Balliol for the joint Graduate Centre, shortly to cease its existence.

[102] As well as declaring this publicly (see n. 45 above), he circulated two long papers (dated 9 Oct. 1964 and 10 Mar. 1965; copies survive in MBP 252) arguing against the scheme.

[103] See the paper by the President (J. R. C. Guy) for College Meeting 22 June 1964 (a copy survives in MBP 252), and JCR General Meeting Minutes, 14 June 1964.

[104] The original Committee—a forceful group, who, if Holywell Manor ever becomes an independent institution, will all deserve the title *Founder*—comprised R. P. Bell, R. M. Ogilvie, P. G. Bennett, L. M. Fox, and M. L. H. Green: College Meeting Minute CM64/36.3(*d*).

[105] See, for example, the programmes of Praefectus's Seminars: HM.3.Misc.viii contains some from 1972–86.

[106] The Praefectus to the Principal of St Anne's, 17 May 1984 (copy in HM.4.Misc.i).

[107] The Principal of St Anne's to the Master, 28 June 1984 (HM.4.Misc.i).

The initiative came from Balliol in 1964 and the Centre was formally opened in Michaelmas Term 1967, originally at Holywell Manor to which the Martin building was subsequently added.[108] Before mixed colleges became the general rule our two Colleges wished to provide such an environment for as many as possible of our graduate students. We believe that the venture has been a conspicuous success and of great benefit to members of St Anne's.

It was also an act of conspicuous generosity to a poor College. Throughout our dealings over the last seventeen years Balliol have always been generous and considerate to St Anne's and we should like you to know how greatly we have appreciated that. We are much obliged to the three Balliol men who have held the office of Praefectus, Mr. Meiggs, Dr. Howatson (assisted, of course, by *our* Dr. Howatson) and Dr. Noble.

Yours sincerely,

Nancy Trenaman

Not long after the withdrawal of St Anne's, Balliol added the Dellal building to the complex, and in 1993 the James Fairfax Yard development increased its capacity again. At the time of writing, the student population of Holywell Manor numbers 145 souls, 107 graduates and 38 final-year undergraduates, making together a lively body. It shows few signs of any wish to be independent, and that has never been anyone's intention, but it is of a viable size and has the spirit and sense of corporate identity to be so; it will be no surprise if that is the eventual outcome.

Finally, let all Balliol people be mindful that nothing chronicled in this book would have happened without the faith of our predecessors and the generosity of our Benefactors, to whom this our ancient house is a living memorial.

THE BIDDING PRAYER [109]

We render most humble and hearty thanks unto Thee, O Eternal and Heavenly Father, for all Thy gifts and graces most bountifully and mercifully bestowed upon us; and namely, for Thy benefits, our Exhibitions and maintenance here at the study of virtue and good learning, by the liberality of John Balliol and

---

[108] The Principal was mistaken here. The Martin Building was not completely finished until November 1967 (it was officially opened by Lady Ogilvie on 2 Nov.), but it was occupied from the beginning of Michaelmas Term by both Balliol and St Anne's graduates: information from W. H. Newton-Smith (appointed Praefectus 1989), who was a fresher graduate student resident in the Martin Building in that first term.

[109] Revised to September 1995. This prayer seems to derive from a long Latin grace which was written down (F.12.22') by John Davey about 1770; it has been updated and corrected as appropriate since then, but it was already inadequate in its recognition of pre-Reformation Benefactors (in 1568 the *Rotulus Benefactorum* comprised 152 names: see p. 75). The 'others our pious Benefactors' must by now number several thousand.

Dervorguilla his wife, Founders of this College; Hugh de Vienne, William Burnel, Sir Philip Somervyle, Sir William Felton, Thomas Chace Master of this College, William Gray Bishop of Ely, Dr John Bell Bishop of Worcester, William Hammond, Peter Blundell, the Lady Elizabeth Periam, Dr John Warner Bishop of Rochester, Sir Thomas Wendy, Dr Richard Busby, John Snell Esquire, Dr Henry Compton and Dr John Robinson, successive Bishops of London, the Reverend Henry Fisher, the Reverend Thomas Williams and Jane his wife, Dr Richard Prosser, Dr Richard Jenkyns Master of this College, Miss Hannah Brackenbury, Francis Charles Hastings Duke of Bedford, the Reverend Benjamin Jowett Master of this College, Sir John Conroy, James Leigh Strachan Davidson Master of this College, Thomas Allnutt Earl Brassey, Eustace John Jervis-Smith, William Lambert Newman, Kenneth Edelman Chalmers, James Hozier Baron Newlands, Gerard Henry Craig-Sellar, Mrs Charlotte Byron Green, Francis Fortescue Urquhart, Andrew Cecil Bradley, Percy Hide and Anne his wife, Oliver Gatty, Sir Walter Nicholson, Sir George Leveson Gower, Bernard Sunley, Vincent Massey Governor-General of Canada, Vivian Bulkeley-Johnson, Sir Theodore Tylor, the Reverend Dr John Stewart MacArthur, Mrs Annie Billmeir, James Westlake Platt, Harold Greville Smith, Roy Herbert Thomson Baron Thomson of Fleet, William Alexander Waters, Ian Robert Maxwell, Sir William Younger, William Appleton Coolidge, and others our pious Benefactors: most humbly beseeching Thee to give us grace so to use them, as may make most for our furtherance in virtue, and increase in learning, for the comfort and salvation of our own souls, and the benefit and edification of the human race, and, above all, for the glory of Thy Holy Name, through Jesus Christ our Lord and Saviour. *Amen.*

34. The gnarled mulberry tree in the Garden Quad—photographed here in August 1995 by Norman McBeath—symbolizes the history of the College. A hundred years ago, already very ancient, it was split asunder in a cataclysmic storm, but it still flourishes and produces excellent fruit.

APPENDIX A

Dervorguilla's Statutes[1]

DERVORGUILLA of Galloway, Lady of Balliol,[2] to her beloved in Christ, Brother Hugh of Hartlepool,[3] and Master William de Menyl,[4] eternal salvation in the Lord.

Desiring, with maternal affection, to provide for the well-being of our sons and Scholars dwelling in Oxford, we direct, ordain, and prescribe that they observe punctiliously all that is hereinafter written. Therefore, to the honour of Our Lord Jesus Christ, His Glorious Mother Mary, and all the Saints:

Firstly, we direct and ordain that our Scholars, each and every one, unless prevented by urgent necessity or good reason, be bound to be present at the Divine Office on Sundays and the chief festivals, and also at the sermons or discourses held on those days and festivals; but that on other days they should diligently attend the Schools and concentrate on their studies, according to the Statutes of the University of Oxford, and to the rules herein laid down.

Also, we ordain that our Scholars should obey our Procurators in all matters concerning their government and well-being which are covered in our ordinance, grant, and commission.

Also, we desire that our Scholars elect from among themselves a Principal

---

[1] The Latin text is printed in H. E. Salter, *Oxford Balliol Deeds*, 1913, p. 277, with a large pull-out photograph of the manuscript and seal.

[2] 'Deruorgulla de Galwedia, domina de Balliolo.' The name Dervorguilla, to give it its usual modern spelling, was spelt very variably even in this, its Latinized form, which is derived from the Gaelic Derbforgaill. It means 'true oath' according to E. G. Withycombe, *The Oxford Dictionary of English Christian Names*, 3rd edn, 1977, p. 83, but it is translated 'daughter of Forgall [a god]' by D. Ó Corráin and F. Maguire, *Gaelic Personal Names*, Dublin, 1981, p. 72. It is a rare but not unique name (see A. B. Scott and F. X. Martin, *Expugnatio Hibernica ...*, Dublin, 1978, p. 286, nn. 5 and 6; G. Stell, in K. J. Stringer (ed.), *Essays on the Nobility of Medieval Scotland*, 1985, p. 163, n. 34). It has been noted (Withycombe, op. cit.) that the name has occasionally been given 'to the daughters of patriotic Balliol men'. J. M. L. Dervorguilla Ogston (daughter of A. G. Ogston, Fellow of Balliol 1937–60, President of Trinity 1970–8), who was born at Oxford on 25 June 1942, is an example. A prominent crater on the planet Venus (3.99E, 15.33N) was officially designated Dervorguilla, following intercession by members of the College, in 1992.

[3] A Franciscan; Provincial Minister of the order in England; he died and was buried at Assisi, 1302. His massive marble grave-slab, with an inscription and full-length effigy, survives on the floor of the middle church of St Francis, under the archway between the chapels of St Anthony and St Mary Magdalene. See Fig. 2.

[4] Rector of Normanton-on-Soar, Notts., but licensed to study at the University.

whom all the rest shall humbly obey in those matters which, according to the Statutes and customs approved and followed among them, are his concern. And when the aforesaid Principal has been lawfully chosen, he shall be presented to our Procurators: he shall not exercise any of his functions until he has been installed by them, acting with our authority, in the aforesaid office.

Also, we decree that our Scholars shall have three masses solemnly celebrated every year for the soul of our beloved husband, the Lord John de Balliol, and for the souls of our predecessors, and for all the faithful departed, and for our own salvation here and hereafter. Of these the first mass shall be celebrated in the first week of the Advent of our Lord, and the second in the week of Septuagesima, and the third in the first week after the octave of Easter; and the aforesaid masses shall be of the Holy Ghost, or of the Blessed Virgin, or for the Dead, as the Procurators shall decide.

And every day, both at dinner and at supper, they shall say a benediction before they eat, and after the meal they shall give thanks. And they shall pray in particular for the soul of our beloved husband aforesaid, and for the souls of all our predecessors, and likewise for the souls of our children that are dead; and for our own salvation, and for that of our children, and of all our friends yet living; and also for our Procurators, according to the traditional forms.

And in order that better provision be made for the support of the poor, for whose benefit our Foundation is intended, we desire that the richer members in the society of our Scholars be careful to live temperately so that the poorer are not burdened by heavy expenses. And if it happens that the communal expenses of our Scholars exceed our allowance in any week, we desire and prescribe strictly that for the payment of the excess expenses not more than a penny a week be required from those who, in the judgement of our Procurators, have no means, or means which would be insufficient for them to pay, if the excess were equally apportioned among all the members. However, we do not intend this to apply in the long vacation, which lasts from the Translation of Blessed Thomas the Martyr [7 July], till the Feast of St Luke [18 October]; nor in those weeks which include the Feast of the Nativity or of the Circumcision of our Lord, or of the Epiphany, or of Easter or of Pentecost; nor when our Procurators think it desirable to dispense with the rule. We wish our Procurators to make diligent examination concerning cases of inability to pay, and the Scholars themselves may apply to our Procurators, and inform them of their needs with every confidence. And if any of our Scholars complain about this rule, or, on any occasion of it being enforced, taunt the poorer Scholars by word or sign, we desire that our Scholars be bound to reveal to the Procurators, under oath sworn to us, the names of those guilty of such conduct. And the Procurators, if they have sufficient proof of the matter, shall by the authority of these presents expel any such person or persons forthwith, without hope of return.

We also appoint that our Scholars shall commonly speak Latin, and he who habitually does otherwise shall be admonished by the Principal. And if, having been admonished twice or thrice, he does not mend his ways, he shall be banned from the common table, and eat alone, being served last of all. And if he remains incorrigible throughout a week, he shall be expelled by our Procurators.

We desire also that in every other week a sophism[5] shall be disputed and determined[6] among our Scholars in their own house, and this shall be done in rotation, so that the Sophisters[7] shall introduce and reply, and those who have determined in the Schools shall determine. But if any Sophister is so advanced that he is almost ready to determine in the Schools, then the Principal shall bid him determine at home among his colleagues first. And at the end of each disputation, the Principal shall fix the day of the next. He shall regulate the disputations and restrain the loquacious. He shall decide the sophisms to be discussed on the next occasion, and shall appoint those who are to introduce, reply, and determine in advance, so that they can prepare themselves. A question[8] shall be treated similarly in alternate weeks.

We also ordain and strictly enjoin upon our Scholars to keep diligently the prayer-book[9] which we have given them in memory of our beloved husband, and not to permit it to be pledged, or in any other way alienated.

Also, our Scholars shall support a poor Scholar, who shall be appointed by our Procurators: they shall be bound to save the remnants from their table for him every day unless our Procurators rule otherwise.

In order that each and every one of the above ordinances be strictly observed by our Scholars, whoever the Procurators may be at any time, we have validated this writing with the authority of our seal.

Given at Buittle[10] in the octave of the Assumption of the Glorious Virgin Mary, in the year of Grace one thousand two hundred and eighty-two.

---

[5] *Sophisma*. A specious but fallacious argument—i.e. a problem in formal logic.

[6] The determination of a disputation was the summing-up, the assessment of the arguments, and the judgement of the determiner or moderator. Determination in the Schools was part of the graduation process.

[7] Advanced undergraduates.

[8] *Questio*. This could be a problem of any kind.

[9] *Portitorium*, probably the scribe's error for *portiforium*, which is usually translated as 'portable breviary'. It is not heard of again.

[10] The site, and vestigial remains, of Dervorguilla's castle at Buittle, in the Stewartry of Kirkcudbright (OS map reference NX 819616), were conveyed to the College through the kindness of Lord Maxwell, in 1984. See A. M. T. Maxwell-Irving, 'The Castles of Buittle', *Trans. Dumfriesshire and Galloway Natural History and Antiquarian Society*, lxvi (3rd ser.), 1991, 59; R. D. Oram, 'Bruce, Balliol and the Lordship of Galloway: South-West Scotland and the Wars of Independence' and 'A Note on the Ownership of the Barony of Buittle,' ibid. lxvii (3rd ser.), 1992, 29, 80. For general background, see D. Brooke, *Wild Men and Holy Places. St Ninian, Whithorn and the Medieval Realm of Galloway*, 1994.

APPENDIX B
Visitors

THE medieval visitatorial arrangements were complex, and the names of the individuals who had supreme authority in College affairs are known in only a few instances. The office of Visitor in its modern form was first defined by Richard Fox, Bishop of Winchester (who himself acted as Visitor initially), in his Statutes of 1507. Although the College was given by these Statutes the unique privilege of electing its own Visitor, it became customary for the Bishop of Lincoln to have authority *ex officio*. This was no doubt because Oxford was originally in the diocese of Lincoln, but the convention survived the creation of the diocese of Oxford in 1542, and continued until the late seventeenth century. Laurence Stubbs, President of Magdalen 1525–7, who was Visitor in 1531, is an exception who was presumably elected (he was the brother of Richard Stubbs, Master 1518–25). William Laud, Archbishop of Canterbury, appears in the role in 1637, probably intruding by virtue of being Chancellor of the University and Archbishop, during the rightful Visitor's imprisonment. Other authorities exercised power over and above that of the Visitor at various times—John Allen for Cardinal Wolsey in 1525; Thomas Cromwell in 1539; Royal Visitors on several occasions in the sixteenth century; and Parliamentary Visitors during the Commonwealth. The semi-automatic link with the See of Lincoln was broken with the election of Richard Busby in 1691. The list of his successors is probably complete: when the date of election is not known, the years given are those of first appearance as Visitor.

    1691   Richard Busby, Headmaster of Westminster School
    1695   Henry Compton, Bishop of London
    1713   John Robinson, Bishop of London
    1723   The Hon. and Revd Henry Brydges
    1728   The Revd Sir John Dolben, Bt.
    1755   The Revd Sir William Bunbury, Bt.
    1764   Robert Hay Drummond, Archbishop of York
    1777   Frederick Cornwallis, Archbishop of Canterbury
    1783   John Moore, Archbishop of Canterbury
    1805   Shute Barrington, Bishop of Durham
    1826   William Howley, Bishop of London and Archbishop of Canterbury
    1848   John Kaye, Bishop of Lincoln
    1853   John Jackson, Bishop of Lincoln and of London
    1885   Charles Synge Christopher Bowen, Baron Bowen of Colwood

1894   Arthur Wellesley Peel, 1st Viscount Peel
1912   Robert Threshie Reed, 1st Earl Loreburn
1923   Edward Grey, 1st Viscount Grey of Falloden
1933   Robert Younger, 1st Baron Blanesburgh of Alloa

Younger, a Law Lord, was followed by the Liberal statesman Lord Samuel in 1946, but the College has chosen an eminent Balliol lawyer for every subsequent vacancy: Lord Monckton, 1957; Lord Pearson, 1965; Lord Kilbrandon, 1974; and Lord Bingham, 1986.

APPENDIX C
Masters

THE succession of Heads of House (the title varied initially) can be given with certainty of completeness only from the admission of Thomas Cisson in 1511. A precise contemporary record of his admission, and of most of his successors, exists. His predecessors, on the other hand, are mostly known to us only by their chance appearances in deeds and in the records of other bodies. The list which follows is more nearly complete than any previously printed, but may still lack a few names. Down to 1511, the dates are dates of appearance in the record; thereafter the duration of each term of office is given.

1283	Robert of Abberwick	1481, 1483	Robert Abdy
1284, 1292	Walter of Fotheringhay	1484, 1495	William Bell
1295	Hugh de Warkenby	1496, 1511	Richard Barnyngham
1307	Stephen of Cornwall	1511–18	Thomas Cisson
1321	Thomas de Waldeby	1518–25	Richard Stubbs
1324	Henry de Seton	1525–39	William Whyte
1328	Nicholas de Luceby	1539–45	George Cotes
1329	Richard de Chikwelle	1545–7 and 1555–9	William Wright
1332, 1337	John of Pocklington		
1340, 1345	Hugh of Corbridge	1547–55	James Brookes
1349	William de Kyrneshale	1559–60	Francis Babington
		1560–3	Anthony Garnet
1356	Robert of Derby	1563–70	Robert Hooper
1360, 1361	John Wyclif	1570–1	John Piers
1366	John Hugate	1571–80	Adam Squire
1379, 1395	Thomas Tyrwhit	1580–1610	Edmund Lilly
1397	Hamond Askham	1610–16	Robert Abbot
1407	William Lambert	1617–37	John Parkhurst
1411, 1416	Thomas Chace	1637–48	Thomas Laurence
1420, 1422	Richard Rotherham	1648–51	George Bradshaw
1423, 1427	Robert Burley	1651–72	Henry Savage
1428, 1429	Richard Stapilton	1672–8	Thomas Good
1440, 1441	William Brandon	1678–87	John Venn
1450, 1456	Robert Thwaytes	1687–1704	Roger Mander
1458, 1465	William Lambton	1705–22	John Baron
1469, 1475	John Segden	1722–6	Joseph Hunt

1726–85	Theophilus Leigh	1893–1907	Edward Caird
1785–98	John Davey	1907–16	James Leigh Strachan
1798–1819	John Parsons		Davidson
1819–54	Richard Jenkyns	1916–24	Arthur Lionel Smith
1854–70	Robert Scott	1924–49	Alexander Dunlop
1870–93	Benjamin Jowett		Lindsay

Lord Lindsay was followed by Sir David Lindsay Keir, 1949; J. E. C. Hill, 1965; A. J. P. Kenny, 1978; B. S. Blumberg, 1989; and C. R. Lucas, 1994. In 1996 A. W. M. Graham was appointed to be Acting Master during the tenure of the Vice-Chancellorship by C. R. Lucas, 1997–2001.

APPENDIX D

Fellows Elected 1500–1939

THE dates given in the following roll are dates of first election, or first definite appearance in the record. The list is clearly deficient to begin with, but is probably complete from the late sixteenth century. An asterisk indicates Blundell Fellows. Some uncertain names are omitted. Dates of tenure are not given, because they can be very misleading. W. L. Newman is an extreme example. He held his Fellowship from 1854 until his death in 1923. This was the longest tenure in the history of the College, but he only resided until 1870, when he left Oxford on grounds of ill health.

1505	Lionel Jackson	1529	Thomas Parke
1507	Peter Wade		Leonard Robinson
1510	Richard Currowe	1531	John Elyngworth
	John Robinson		John Smythe
1511	Richard Caley	1535	John Hanson
1518	Thomas Nelson		Robert Cosyn
1520	Thomas Appleby		John Thomson
	Richard Blunston	1537	William Francis
	Peter Hoghton		John Nowell
	Edmund Burton	1539	Robert Stopys
	Henry Scott	1540	William Brogden
1521	Thomas Kendall		Robert Knight
1522	Thomas Austen	1541	Michael Simpson
	Walter Brown	1542	Roger Browne
	George Cotes	1543	Philip Crome
1523	Thomas Alen		William Byrkby
1526	John Bradley	1544	Robert Stockes
	William Baker	1546	William Taler
	Thomas Brodley	1548	Anthony Garnet
	John Kitson		William Oliver
	William Wright	1551	Brian Nedham
1527	Henry Markham	1553	Bartholomew Green
	Christopher Worsley		Alan Higginson
1528	John Foster	1556	Richard Shaghnes
1529	John Michell		Robert Wood

1557	Arthur Gracewith	1585	Henry Bright
	Edmund Ratcliff	1588	William Bradshawe
1559	Roger Barker		Nicholas Higgs
	John Atkinson		Thomas Wenman
	Adam Squire	1589	George Holland
1560	Ralph Latham	1592	Lionel Daye
1562	William Bell		Champion Gyttyns
	Robert Hammond		Eustace Moore
1563	George Godsalf	1596	Nicholas Bradshaw
	John Lee		Robert Wakeman
1564	Thomas Coventry		Thomas Munday
	John Tunckis		Richard Smith
1566	Robert Benson	1597	John Abbot
	John Wilson	1598	Timothy Gates
1567	Richard Garnet	1601	Thomas Blanchard
1568	Adam Hill	1602	John Berry*
	Robert Persons	1604	Thomas Hollaway
1570	Thomas Hyde		William Boswell
	James Stancliffe	1605	John Barfote
1572	Peter Bingley	1608	Christopher West*
	Christopher Bagshaw		Thomas Wilkinson
	Robert Crane	1609	Caleb Morley
	Hugh Thornley	1610	John Chenell
	George Turner		Jonathan Radcliffe
1573	Thomas Holland		Edward Wilson
1575	Robert Knight	1612	Matthew Williams
	Robert Pistor	1613	Thomas Abbot
1576	James Hawley		Robert Chapman
	Martin Hill		John English
	Thomas Pylcher		Robert Godfrey
	Matthew Pinder	1614	William Armstone
	William Staverton		John Churchar
	Francis Whitmore	1615	John Wood*
1581	William Hill	1617	Thomas Chambers
	Robert Abbot		Thomas Crane
1582	John Bayly		Giles Thorne
	Laurence Keymis	1618	John Pitts
	Thomas Rastoll	1619	Richard Kerry
	Thomas Sanderson		Richard Trimnell
	Edward Wickham	1620	Robert Parry
1583	George Abbot	1621	Thomas White*
	Richard Phynes	1623	Peter Wentworth

1626	Edmund Ellis	1667	George Burton*
	Edward Cooper	1668	John Venn
1628	Henry Bayliffe	1669	William Oldisworth
	Thomas Merest	1671	Henry Hibbins
	Henry Savage		John Hughes
1629	Thomas Good		Roger Mander
	Edward Prowse*		Walter Sloper
1630	Jeremy Oakeley	1672	Francis White
1631	John Harris	1675	Richard Greaves
1633	Herbert Boughton	1676	Thomas Norwood
	George Bradshaw		William Jackson
1637	John Michael		John Newte*
1640	James Thickens	1679	John Haycroft*
	Nicholas Crouch	1680	William Abell*
	Anthony Palmer	1681	James Gwillym
1642	Richard Spurway*	1682	Robert Crosse
1643	Robert Feilden	1683	Peter Lancaster
1645	John Good	1685	William Chilcot*
1648	Richard Bennett*		Thomas Shewring
	John Friend	1686	Adam Lugg*
	Matthew Poore	1687	Theophilus Downes
1649	William Dickins		William Hockin
	Edward Newton		Sampson Potter
	George Swinnock	1689	William Bishop
1650	Jonas Holmes	1690	Ralph Newham
	Thomas Careless	1691	John Baron
1651	Robert Hawkins		William Foster
1652	Ambrose Atfield		John Pain*
1653	Thomas Allam	1692	Sheldon Cole
1654	Hugh Standon*		Walter Elford*
1655	Edmund Ellis	1693	Lewis Lawley
1656	Thomas Price	1695	Edward Strong
1657	George Hemming	1697	Jeremiah Milles
	Simon Venn		Richard Monox
1658	Thomas Swift	1698	John Wills
1659	John English	1699	Abraham Pain*
1662	Roger Tozer*	1700	John Bradford*
1663	Richard Kyrton*		Joseph Hunt
1664	Thomas Hodges	1702	Reginald Jones
1665	Edward Price	1705	Samuel Reynolds
1666	William Good		James Chetham
1667	William Beach	1707	Henry Fisher*

1707	Samuel Newte	1755	Theophilus Blackall*
1713	Benjamin Kennet		John Hippisley
	Henry Muxloe	1758	John Bree
	Bartholomew Richards*	1760	John Cooke
1714	Joseph Sanford	1762	Samuel Cooke*
1716	William Best	1764	John Coles*
	William Bree	1766	George White
	William Lux	1768	Samuel Love
1717	John Jones*		Thomas Williams
	Robert Layng	1770	Richard Heighway
	Thomas Rich		Henry Hutton*
1720	Thomas Loveday		James Sanford
	John Spurway*	1771	William Brudenell Barter*
	Brydges Thomas		John Wood
	Thomas Wilson	1773	Richard Prosser
1721	Thomas Coxe	1774	Harry Farr Yeatman
1722	Charles Godwyn		Thomas Tanner*
1723	Thomas Walker	1775	John Barnes*
1724	Humphrey Quick*	1779	Philip Fernyhaugh
1728	John Land*	1780	Henry Edwards Davis
1729	Robert Dagge*		John Squary Clapp*
1730	William Fernyhaugh	1782	John Matthew
1733	John Walker*	1783	Peter Wright
1734	William Burchinsaw	1784	Thomas How
1735	George Sanford*	1785	John Parsons
1736	John Hunsdon		Thomas Sweet*
	George Drake		Charles Wood
1737	Gerard Andrewes	1786	George Powell
	William Parker	1792	Richard Hoblyn*
1738	William Daddo	1793	Peregrine Ilbert
	Arthur Culme*	1796	William Marshall
1740	John Abbot	1797	George Scobell*
1744	John Foot*	1798	Matthew Hodge
1745	John Darch		Thomas Cooke Rogers
1747	George Wilmot	1800	William Cowlard*
1749	John Vivian		William Warrington
1751	John Wickham	1803	Richard Jenkyns
1752	John Coxe	1804	John Mousley
	John Davey*	1805	Thomas Moore*
	Bartholomew Davey*	1806	Charles Barter*
1754	Nathaniel Forster		William Vaux
	Roger Watkins	1809	Carrington Ley*

1810	Benjamin Cheese	1845	James Riddell
1816	Noel Thomas Ellison	1848	William Charles Salter*
	Charles Trelawney Collins*	1850	Henry John Stephen Smith
	William David Longlands		Theodore Walrond
	Charles Atmore Ogilvie	1852	Donald Millman Owen*
1817	William Marwood Tucker*	1854	William Lambert Newman
1818	Charles Girdlestone	1857	Charles Synge Christopher
	William Greswell		Bowen
	Thomas Parry	1861	Thomas Hill Green
1819	John Carr	1862	Edward Lyulph Stanley
1820	James Thomas Round	1864	Courtenay Peregrine Ilbert
1823	John Besly*	1866	James Leigh Strachan
	Archer John Langley		Davidson
1825	John Mitchel Chapman		John Purves
1826	Edward Kitson*	1868	Thomas Kelly Cheyne
	George Moberly	1869	Richard Lewis Nettleship
	Francis William Newman	1872	Robert Grey Tatton
1827	Frederick Oakeley		Alfred Goodwin
1828	Herman Merivale	1873	William Henry Forbes
1830	Edward Turner Boyd	1874	Evelyn Abbott
	Twisleton		Andrew Cecil Bradley
1831	Peter Samuel Henry Payne		Herbert Henry Asquith
	Samuel Henry Walker*	1878	Francis de Paravicini
1834	Archibald Campbell Tait	1882	Monier Williams
	William George Ward		Arthur Lionel Smith
1835	Edward Cardwell		John William Mackail
	Robert Scott		William Henry Fremantle
1836	Lewis Welsh Owen*	1883	William Markby
1837	Richard Hill*		Alfred Marshall
1838	William Charles Lake	1884	William Ross Hardie
	James Gylby Lonsdale	1886	Albert Venn Dicey
	Benjamin Jowett		Harold Bailey Dixon
	Edward Cooper	1890	John Conroy
	Woollcombe		William Hudson Shaw
1839	Henry Wall	1891	Edwin James Palmer
1840	William James Jenkins*		James Alexander Smith
1841	Edward Kent Karslake	1896	Francis Fortescue Urquhart
	Ralph Robert Wheeler	1898	Arthur Wallace Pickard-
	Lingen		Cambridge
1842	Constantine Estlin Prichard	1900	Arthur Anthony Macdonell
	Frederick Temple*	1901	Harold Brewer Hartley
1845	Edwin Palmer	1902	Cyril Bailey

1902	Henry William Carless Davis	1931	Oliver Gatty
1905	Edward Hilliard		Donald James Allan
1906	Alexander Dunlop Lindsay		William Maurice Allen
1908	Hugh McKinnon Wood		Wesley Clair Mitchell
1909	Neville Stuart Talbot	1932	Thomas Wentworth Pym
1911	Robert Gibson	1933	Ronald Percy Bell
1912	Arnold Joseph Toynbee		Felix Frankfurter
1913	Henry Hensman Gibbon		John Henry Constantine
1914	Charles Graham Stone		Whitehead
1918	Richard Henry Tawney	1934	John St Leger Philpot
1919	Thomas Ralph Merton		Arthur Holly Compton
	Kenneth Norman Bell		Albrecht Mendelssohn
	Duncan Campbell		Bartholdy
	Macgregor	1935	Herbert Spencer Jennings
1920	Maurice Roy Ridley	1936	David Daiches
	Cyril Norman Hinshelwood	1937	Hugh William Bell Cairns
1921	John William Nicholson		Edward Hamilton Johnston
1922	John Macmurray		Joshua Harold Burn
	Charles Richard Morris		Richard William Southern
	Charles Stewart Orwin		Simon Flexner
1924	Alexander Bankier Rodger		Allen Spencer Hoey
1925	Benedict Humphrey Sumner		Alexander George Ogston
1926	James Andrew Gunn	1938	Herbert Morgan Keyes
	Roger Aubrey Baskerville		Thomas Malcolm Layng
	Mynors		John Edward Christopher
1927	Frederick William Thomas		Hill
1928	Francis Russell Barry		William Smith Watt
	Vivian Hunter Galbraith		Tenney Frank
	Colin Graham Hardie	1939	Russell Meiggs
	John Scott Fulton		John Wilfred Linnett
1929	Augustus Cecil Hare Duke		Joseph Perkins Chamberlain
1930	Theodore Henry Tylor		
	John Livingston Lowes		

For continuations of this list, see *Balliol College Register*, 5th edn., ed. J. [H.] Jones and S. Viney, 1983, p. 556, and 6th edn., ed. J. [H.] Jones and C. Willbery, 1993, p. 567.

APPENDIX E

Student Numbers

T H E total numbers of students in residence, at various times between 1550 and 1939, are given below. No data are available any earlier than 1550, but it is likely that for most of the medieval period there were in the region of a dozen. The numbers represented are approximate. Numbers fell to below 100 during the Second World War, rose swiftly during 1945–6 to 400, and then after a 2-year bulge at that level fell to 330 in 1950, rising slowly to about 420 in 1960 (with a late fifties bulge caused by the abolition of National Service), around 460 in the seventies and about 525 by 1995. The proportion of students doing research or advanced degrees was around 15% in 1950, 25–30% in the nineties. The number of Fellows was between 10 and 13 for the whole period 1550–1900, rising to 29 by 1939; there were 58 in 1995.

1550	10–20	1775	27
1576	42	1800	19
1600	45	1825	76
1625	59	1850	87
1645	7	1885	165
1650	49	1910	183
1675	93	1915	41
1700	83	1917	39
1725	100	1920	275
1750	54	1938	264

The figures to 1850 are taken from the analyses of the Bursars' Books by Andrew Clark (A. Clark's Tables, ii). Clark's results show erratic variations from year to year, but the underlying trends are clear. From 1885 the figures are derived from the printed College lists.

APPENDIX F

Regional Bias 1600–1900

APPROXIMATE averaged percentage figures for the distribution of members' origins are as follows:

	1600	1700	1800	1900
Scotland	0	4	11	12
Gloucestershire, Herefordshire, Shropshire, Worcestershire, Warwickshire, and Staffordshire	34	33	16	1
Cornwall, Devon, Dorset, and Somerset	14	34	40	4
Elsewhere	52	29	33	83

For comparison, the approximate figures for 1985 were: Scotland 2%, Gloucestershire etc. 4%, Cornwall etc. 2%, elsewhere 92%. Presenting the figures in this simplified manner conceals some extremes (Cornwall etc. was over 50%, and Devon alone more than 30%, at some points in the late eighteenth century) and takes no account of shifts within the groups (e.g. there was a shift from Warwickshire and Staffordshire to Herefordshire and Worcestershire during the seventeenth century). 'Elsewhere' was almost entirely within Great Britain south of a line from Liverpool to London until 1850. Before 1500, the Statutes prescribed, and fragmentary data indicate, a bias to counties in the North of England—these counties are only represented very rarely 1600–1800. From the Reformation to 1600, sparse data suggest an even more marked bias to the midland counties than was the case later; until *c.*1600, very few members came from the West Country.

APPENDIX G
Sources for the History of the College

THE principal sources are as follows.

PRINTED

Previous histories

H. Savage, *Balliofergus*, 1668. The earliest history of any college based on the study of original documents.

A. Wood, 'Balliol College', in J. Gutch (ed.), *The History and Antiquities of the Colleges and Halls in the University of Oxford*, 1786.

R. L. Poole, 'Balliol College', in A. Clark (ed.), *The Colleges of Oxford*, 1891. Cites some interesting sources.

F. de Paravicini, *Early History of Balliol College*, 1891. Includes some transcripts and translations of early documents.

H. W. C. Davis, *Balliol College*, 1899. A list of sources is given; this was not repeated in the revised and extended edition of 1963.

'Balliol College', in *VCH*, Oxfordshire, iii, 1954 (R. W. Hunt, 'History of the College', pp. 82–9; R. H. C. Davis, 'Buildings', pp. 90–5). Sources are cited precisely.

H. W. C. Davis, *A History of Balliol College*, revised by R. H. C. Davis and R. [W.] Hunt, 1963.

Other works about the College

W. I. Addison, *The Snell Exhibitions from the University of Glasgow to Balliol College, Oxford*, 1901.

H. E. Salter, *Oxford Balliol Deeds*, printed for private circulation, 1913. Full transcripts are given of the College's Foundation Deeds and Statutes, and the topography of the College site is fully discussed. It should be noted, however, that this work does not contain all the early deeds in the Archives—only those touching the College's Foundation and property in Oxford are included.

Balliol College War Memorial Book 1914–1919, two volumes, printed for private circulation, 1924.

R. A. B. Mynors, *Catalogue of the Manuscripts of Balliol College Oxford*, 1963. The introduction is practically a history of the College Library.

J. [M.] Prest (ed.), *Balliol Studies*, 1982.

Balliol College Registers

Six College Registers have been printed for private circulation:

E. Hilliard (ed.), *Balliol College Register 1832–1914*, 1914.

I. Elliott (ed.), *Balliol College Register 1833–1933*, 1934.

I. Elliott (ed.), *Balliol College Register 1900–1950*, 1953.

E. Lemon (ed.), *Balliol College Register 1916–1967*, 1969.

J. [H.] Jones and S. Viney (eds.), *Balliol College Register 1930–1980*, 1983.

J. [H.] Jones and C. [E.] Willbery (eds.), *Balliol College Register 1940–1990*, 1993.

Sources of information about earlier members are surveyed in J. [H.] Jones, *The Archives of Balliol College, Oxford. A guide*, 1984, p. 8.

Royal Commissions

Publications resulting from Royal and other Commissions are a valuable source of information, especially:

Oxford University Commission, Report and Evidence, 1852. Several Fellows and former Fellows gave evidence.

Statutes of the Colleges of Oxford. Balliol College, 1853. The Statutes of Dervorguilla and all modifications down to 1838 are given in full, together with the texts of deeds establishing the Blundell, Periam, Busby, and Dunch Foundations, and also an Act of Parliament (1778) concerning Huntspill Rectory.

Books about prominent Balliol men

E. Abbott and L. Campbell, *The Life and Letters of Benjamin Jowett MA*, two volumes, 1897; and the subsequent Supplement, *Letters of Benjamin Jowett MA*, 1899.

G. Faber, *Jowett, a Portrait with Background*, 1957.

Dear Miss Nightingale. A selection of Benjamin Jowett's letters to Florence Nightingale 1860–1893, eds. [E.] V. Quinn and J. [M.] Prest, 1987.

P. [B.] Hinchliff, *Benjamin Jowett and the Christian Religion*, 1987.

H. Jones and J. H. Muirhead, *The Life and Philosophy of Edward Caird*, 1921.

J. W. Mackail, *James Leigh Strachan-Davidson, Master of Balliol, a Memoir*, 1925.

[M. F. Smith], *Arthur Lionel Smith, Master of Balliol (1916–1924), a Biography and Some Reminiscences by His Wife*, 1928.

C. Bailey, *Francis Fortescue Urquhart, a Memoir*, 1936.

D. Scott, *A. D. Lindsay, a Biography*, 1971.

The College Library has an extensive collection of biographies of other Balliol men, shelved together and arranged by year of Balliol admission. Many have chapters, letters, etc. concerning Balliol.

The Balliol College [Annual] Record

Published annually (with wartime gaps) in various formats since before the First

World War, this periodical contains a substantial amount of information about College affairs and alumni, with occasional articles on aspects of College history.

MANUSCRIPT

Unpublished previous work on the history of the College

The Revd Andrew Clark's collections and manuscripts (*c*.1900–10) for the history of the College. Bodleian Library.

Mr L. K. Hindmarsh's collections and manuscripts (*c*.1945) on Balliol heraldry and Balliol benefactors. The College Library.

Mrs Gwen Beachcroft's collections (*c*.1960–75) on Theophilus Leigh and Balliol in the eighteenth century. Bodleian Library.

H. P. Smith's notes (*c*.1967) on Balliol and extramural education. The College Library.

The College Archives

The College's Archives obviously provide the principal original sources for its history: see J. [H.] Jones, *The Archives of Balliol College Oxford. A guide*, 1984, for an introduction. A copy of the complete Archives List as at April 1992 was published in microfiche form in 1992: *Archives of Balliol College*, Unit 61, NIDS UK & Ireland, Chadwyck-Healey Ltd., Cambridge, UK.

Special collections and manuscripts in the College Library

The most important manuscript sources in the College Library are listed in Jones, op. cit. Separate guides have been published for three collections of particular importance: *The Conroy Papers* (K. Hudson and J. [H.] Jones, 1987), *The Jenkyns Papers* (J. [H.] Jones, 1988), and *The Jowett Papers* (R. Darwall-Smith, 1993).

Other manuscript material

Further relevant documents are found in many record repositories, most notably as follows:

The Bodleian Library. Diverse material.

The British Library. Diverse material.

Churchill College Cambridge. Hartley Papers.

Devon Record Office. Acland family papers.

Hereford Record Office. Especially the Belmont Papers and the Brydges of Tibberton Papers.

The Huntington Library, San Marino, California. Stowe Collection, especially the Letter Books of James Brydges, 1st Duke of Chandos.

Keele University Library. Lindsay Papers.

Lambeth Palace Library. Especially the Tait Papers.

Lincolnshire Archives Office. Papers of Bishops of Lincoln as Visitors.

Northamptonshire Record Office. Dolben and Isham collections.

Oxford University Archives. Especially probate material.

The Public Record Office. PCC wills and State Papers.

Pusey House, Oxford. Scott letters.

The Library of the Royal College of Surgeons of England. Matthew Baillie material.

Shakespeare's Birthplace Trust Record Office, Stratford-upon-Avon. Leigh and Mills of Pillerton Hersey collections.

The Temple Reading Room, Rugby. Letters by A. P. Stanley.

Plans of the College Sites and Buildings

THE development of the College main site over the last seven centuries is roughly outlined in Plans I–IV. Plan V shows Balliol in Holywell since 1890.

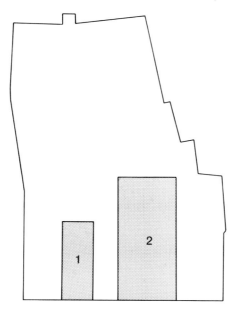

Plan I. The College site in the thirteenth century.
1. The site of Old Balliol Hall, *c.*1260.
2. The site of New Balliol Hall, 1284.

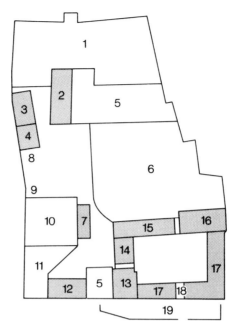

Plan II.   The College site about 1695.
1. This area was not yet owned or occupied by the College.
2. Ellis's Lodgings, alias Pompey.
3. Caesar's Lodgings.
4. Brewhouse.
5. The Master's Garden.
6. The Fellows' Garden.
7. Trencher House, alias The Barn.
8. Ball Court.
9. Back gate.
10. The 'Catherine Wheel', leased out.
11. Tenements, leased out.
12. Hammond's Lodgings.
13. The Master's Lodgings.
14. Hall.
15. Common Room; Library above.
16. Chapel.
17. Residential.
18. Front gate.
19. Enclosed forecourt, lost in 1772.

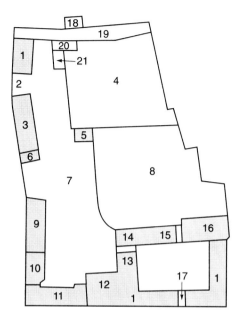

Plan III.   The College site in 1848.
1. Residential.
2. Back gate.
3. Stables
4. The Master's Garden.
5. Coach-house.
6. Latrines (Lady Periam).
7. The Grove.
8. The Fellows' Garden.
9. Basevi Building, 1826.
10. Bristol Building, c.1720.
11. Fisher Building, 1759.
12. The Master's Lodgings.
13. Hall.
14. Kitchen.
15. Common Room, Library above.
16. Chapel.
17. Front gate.
18. Not acquired until 1906.
19. Not acquired until 1873.
20. Leased out until 1852.
21. Ashpits.

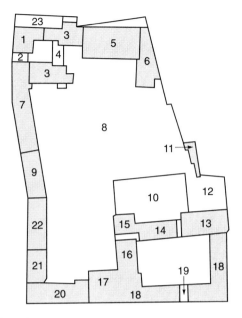

Plan IV.   The College site in 1996.
1. Warren Building (Staircase XXI), 1906.
2. Back gate.
3. Staircase XXII; Beard, 1968.
4. The Snell Bridge, 1968.
5. Hall; A. Waterhouse, 1877.
6. The Senior Common Room Staircase (XXIII), alias The Bernard Sunley Building; Beard, 1966.
7. Salvin Building (Staircases XVI–XIX), 1853.
8. The Garden Quadrangle.
9. The Junior Common Room Staircase (XV); Warren, 1912.
10. The Fellows' Garden.
11. Gardeners' outhouse, formerly latrines (Lady Periam).
12. The Master's Garden.
13. Chapel, 1857.
14. Old Common Room, Library above.
15. Salvin Tower, alias Library Tower, 1853.
16. Library.
17. The Master's Lodgings.
18. Brackenbury Building (Staircases I–VII); A. Waterhouse, 1869.
19. Front gate.
20. Fisher Building (Staircases X and XI).
21. Bristol Building (Staircase XII, Dicey above).
22. Basevi Building (Staircases VIII and XIV, Dicey above).
23. 1 St Giles. Acquired in 1989 with a 25-year leaseback agreement in favour of the occupants, Morrell, Peel, and Gamlen, Solicitors. See J. [H.] Jones, *Balliol College Record*, 1990, p. 78.

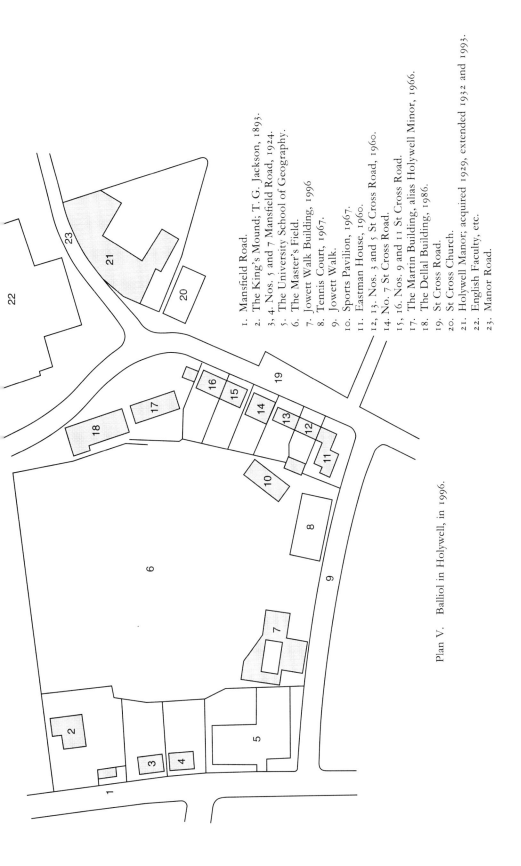

1. Mansfield Road.
2. The King's Mound; T. G. Jackson, 1893.
3, 4. Nos. 5 and 7 Mansfield Road, 1924.
5. The University School of Geography.
6. The Master's Field.
7. Jowett Walk Building, 1996
8. Tennis Court, 1967.
9. Jowett Walk.
10. Sports Pavilion, 1967.
11. Eastman House, 1960.
12, 13. Nos. 3 and 5 St Cross Road, 1960.
14. No. 7 St Cross Road.
15, 16. Nos. 9 and 11 St Cross Road.
17. The Martin Building, alias Holywell Minor, 1966.
18. The Dellal Building, 1986.
19. St Cross Road.
20. St Cross Church.
21. Holywell Manor; acquired 1929, extended 1932 and 1993.
22. English Faculty, etc.
23. Manor Road.

Plan V. Balliol in Holywell, in 1996.

INDEX